# Collins Junior Illustrated Dictionary

Collins

Published by Collins
An imprint of HarperCollins*Publishers*
77-85 Fulham Palace Road, Hammersmith, London W6 8JB

**Browse the complete Collins catalogue at
www.collinseducation.com**

First published 2000
This edition published 2010
© HarperCollins*Publishers* Ltd 2010

10 9 8 7 6 5 4 3 2 1

ISBN-13   978-0-00-735390-3

British Library Cataloguing in Publication Data
A catalogue record for this publication is available from the British Library.

Defined words that we have reason to believe constitute trademarks have been designated as such. However, neither the presence nor absence of such labels should be regarded as affecting the legal status of any trademark.

**Compiler:** Evelyn Goldsmith
**Literacy consultants:** Kay Hiatt, Rosemary Boys
**Numeracy consultant:** Jan Henley
**Science consultant:** Rona Wyn Davies
**Cover design:** LCD (lcd.uk.com)
**Cover illustration:** Kevin Windsor
**Design:** Neil Adams, Grasshopper Design Co.
**Illustrators:** Tim Archbold, Tamsin Cook, Felicity House, Pat Murray, Sarah Wimperis, Sue Woollatt (all of Graham-Cameron Illustration)
**Photos:** All commissioned photos by Steve Lumb.

The publishers wish to thank the following for permission to use photographs:
**Andes Press:** p. 61 Diwali; **Art Directors & Trip:** p. 7 acorn, p. 8 aeroplane, p. 12 antelope, p. 9 bridge, p. 31 butterfly, p. 32 cactus, p. 34 carnival, p. 48 coral, p. 62 dragonfly, p. 64 duck, p. 65 Earth, p. 65 eclipse, p. 68 erupt, p. 69 evergreen, p. 86 giraffe, p. 95 harvest, p. 101 horse, p. 102 hurricane, p. 103 illuminations, p. 107 ivy, p. 113 ladybird, p. 115 leaves, p. 128 mill, p. 147 pagoda, p. 172 ray, p. 174 reflection, p. 178 rhinoceros, p. 180 rose, p. 209 statue, p. 223 thatched, p. 230 tractor; **BBC:** p. 213 studio; **Biofotos/Heather Angel:** p. 18 badger, p. 57 desert, p. 81 fox, p. 158 polar bear; **Oxford Scientific Films:** p. 13 ape, p. 14 aquarium, p. 32 camel, p. 38 cheetah, p. 52 crystal, p. 85 gerbil, p. 88 gorilla, p. 103 iceberg, p. 108 jellyfish, p. 148 panda, p. 157 plough, p. 171 rainbow, p. 191 shark, p. 206 springbok, p. 218 swan, p. 226 tiger, p. 253 x-ray; **Papilio:** p. 25 bluebells, p. 56 deer, p. 117 lighthouse.

All other photos and illustrations © HarperCollins*Publishers* Ltd 2005.

**Acknowledgements**
The publishers would like to thank all the teachers, staff and pupils who contributed to this book:

*Models*
Lauren Carroll, Elizabeth Fison, Petra Pavlovic, Stacey Cleary, Jesse Johnson, Milo Petrie-Foxell, Tom Crane, Ismael KhaN, Dexter Sampson, Katherine Davis, Margaret Omoboade,  Mauri-Joy Smith, William Davis, Zina Patel, Tom Symonds, Ruby Feroze, Dunia Pavlovic, Rosie Ward

*Schools*
Aberhill Primary, Fife; ASDAC, Fife; Canning St Primary, Newcastle upon Tyne; Cowgate Primary, Newcastle upon Tyne; Crombie Primary, Fife; the Literacy Team at Dryden Professional Development Centre, Gateshead; Dunshalt Primary, Fife; Ecton Brook Lower, Northampton; English Martyrs RC Primary, Newcastle upon Tyne; Hotspur Primary, Newcastle upon Tyne; John Betts Primary, London; Lemington First, Newcastle upon Tyne; LMTC Education Development Centre, Northumberland; Melcombe Primary, London; Methilhill Primary, Fife; Newcastle Literacy Centre, Newcastle upon Tyne; Northampton High, Northampton; Pitcoudie Primary, Fife; Pitreavie Primary, Fife; Ravenswood Primary, Newcastle upon Tyne; St Andrew's CE Primary, London; Simon de Senlis Lower, Northampton; Sinclairtown Primary, Fife; Standens Barn Lower, Northampton; Touch Primary, Fife; Towcester Infants, Northampton; Wooton Primary, Northampton.

Printed and bound by Printing Express, Hong Kong

# Contents

## ★ ★ Collins Word Wizard

# Using this dictionary

A dictionary tells you what a word means and how to spell it. The words in a dictionary are listed in alphabetical order.

## How to find a word

Look up the word **fossil**. What letter does it begin with? Use the alphabet line at the side of the page. The green box tells you that the words on this page start with **f**.

Think about the second letter of the word. You are looking for a word beginning with **fo**. Use the guide word at the top of the page. A guide word at the top left tells you the *first word* on that page. A guide word at the top right tells you the *last word* on that page. The guide word for this page is **frequent** – it starts with **fr**. Does **fo** come before **fr**?

When you think you have the right page, look at the blue words. These are called headwords. The headwords are in alphabetical order. If you run your finger down the headwords on this page, you will see more than one that begins with **fo**. Think about the next letter or letters in your word and look for a headword that begins with **fos**.

Keep looking until you find the word **fossil**.

frequent ⤑ **guide word**

① **headword**

⑦ **phrase**

③ **part of speech**

④ **definition**

⑨ **irregular form**

⑥ **photo**

⑩ **more information**

forward
  ADVERB If you move **forward** or **forwards**, you move the way you are facing.
  look forward PHRASE If you **look forward** to something, you want it to happen.
fossil **fossils**
  NOUN A **fossil** is the hardened remains of a prehistoric animal or plant that are found inside a rock.
fought
  VERB **Fought** is the past tense of **fight**.
foul **fouler, foulest**
  ADJECTIVE If something is **foul**, it is extremely unpleasant.
found
  VERB **Found** is the past tense of **find**.
foundation **foundations**
  NOUN The **foundations** of a building are the solid layers of material put below the ground to support it.
fountain **fountains**
  NOUN A **fountain** is a jet or spray of water forced up into the air by a pump.
fox **foxes**
  NOUN A **fox** is a wild animal like a dog, with reddish-brown fur and a thick tail.

fraction **fractions**
  NOUN **1** In maths, a **fraction** is a part of a whole number, for example $\frac{1}{4}$.
  See *Fractions* on page 272.
  NOUN **2** A **fraction** is also a tiny part of something.

fracture **fractures**
  NOUN A **fracture** is a crack or break in something, especially a bone.
fragile
  ADJECTIVE Something that is **fragile** is easily broken or damaged.
fragment **fragments**
  NOUN A **fragment** of something is a small piece or part of it.
frame **frames**
  NOUN A **frame** is the part surrounding something like a window or picture, or the lenses of a pair of glasses.

freckle **freckles**
  NOUN **Freckles** are small, light brown spots on someone's skin.
free
  ADJECTIVE **1** If a person or animal is **free**, they can go where they want. *Tom opened the cage and set the bird free.*
  ADJECTIVE **2** If something is **free**, it does not cost anything.
  freedom NOUN
freeze **freezes, freezing, froze, frozen**
  VERB **1** If a liquid **freezes**, it becomes solid because the temperature is low.
  VERB **2** If you **freeze** something, you store it at a very low temperature.
freezer **freezers**
  NOUN A **freezer** is a refrigerator for freezing and storing food.
frequent
  ADJECTIVE If something is **frequent**, it happens often.
  frequency NOUN   frequently ADVERB

**Ff** ⤑ **alphabet line**

⑥ **illustration**

⑤ **example sentence**

② **other forms**

⑧ **related words**

a b c d e Ff g h i j k l m n o p q r s t u v w x y z

## Finding out about a word

① The headword is the word you are looking up.

② On the same line as the headword, you will see how to spell other forms of the word, such as plural nouns, verb tenses or other adjective forms, called comparatives and superlatives.

③ Next you will see the part of speech. This tells you what type of word the headword is, such as a noun, verb, adjective, adverb or pronoun.

④ After the part of speech, you will find the definition. The definition tells you what the word means. The definitions are numbered if there is more than one. Each definition has its own part of speech.

⑤ Some words have an example sentence in *italics*. This shows you how the word might be used in speech or writing.

⑥ Some words have a photo or other illustration to help you read the word and understand its meaning.

⑦ A phrase may also be included. For example, under the word **forward**, you will also find the definition of the phrase **look forward**.

⑧ Sometimes, other related words are given at the end, with their parts of speech. These tell you, for example, the noun or adverb form of the word.

⑨ An irregular form of a word is a plural noun or verb tense which does not follow the usual spelling rules. You can find many irregular forms in this dictionary.

⑩ Some definitions tell you where to look for more information, such as another headword, or the pages at the back of the dictionary.

## Other features of this dictionary

● Pronunciation is how you say a word. Some words can be spelled the same, but sound different and mean different things – these words are called homographs. This dictionary gives you pronunciation help for some words, including homographs. For example:

tear **tears, tearing, tore, torn**
(*rhymes with* **fear**) NOUN **1** Tears are the drops of liquid that come out of your eyes when you cry.
(*rhymes with* **fair**) VERB **2** If you **tear** something, such as paper or fabric, you pull it apart.

● Some definitions include a label, such as FORMAL, INFORMAL or TRADEMARK. This tells you a little more about the word or how it is used. For example:

Rollerblade **Rollerblades**
NOUN; TRADEMARK **Rollerblades** are roller skates which have the wheels set in one straight line on the bottom of the boot.

## ✭ ✭ Collins Word Wizard

The **Collins Word Wizard** section at the back of the dictionary gives you extra help with grammar, writing and using the Internet.

It has pages to help you understand parts of speech, punctuation and prefixes and suffixes as well as handy hints for learning tricky spellings and cool new words.

Look out for the themed picture pages, web links and games to play with the dictionary.

# Aa

**abacus**  **abacuses**
NOUN An **abacus** is a frame with beads that slide along rods. It is used for counting.

**abandon**  **abandons, abandoning, abandoned**
VERB **1** If you **abandon** something, you leave it and do not return. *The cub had been abandoned by its mother.*
VERB **2** If you **abandon** a piece of work, you stop doing it before it is finished.

**abbreviation**  **abbreviations**
NOUN An **abbreviation** is a short form of a word or phrase. *The abbreviation for compact disc is CD.*
See *Abbreviations* on page 270.

**ability**  **abilities**
NOUN If you have the **ability** to do something, you are able to do it.

**able**  **abler, ablest**
ADJECTIVE If you are **able** to do something, you can do it.

**aboard**
PREPOSITION If you are **aboard** a ship or plane, you are on or in it.

**about**
ADVERB **1** You say **about** in front of a number to show it is not exact. *I'll be home at about five o'clock.*
PREPOSITION **2** If you talk or write **about** something, you say things to do with that subject. *He is talking about boats.*

**above**
PREPOSITION If something is **above** something else, it is over it, or higher up.

**abroad**
ADVERB When you go **abroad**, you go to a different country.

**absent**
ADJECTIVE If someone is **absent**, they are not here.

**absolutely**
ADVERB You can use **absolutely** to make what you are saying sound stronger. *You must stay absolutely still.*

**absorb**  **absorbs, absorbing, absorbed**
VERB If something **absorbs** a liquid, it soaks it up or takes it in.

**absurd**
ADJECTIVE Something that is **absurd** seems silly, because it is quite different from what you would expect. *It's absurd to wear your jumper in this heat.*

**abuse**
NOUN **Abuse** is cruel treatment of someone.

**accelerate**  **accelerates, accelerating, accelerated**
VERB When someone **accelerates**, they speed up.

**accept**  **accepts, accepting, accepted**
VERB If you **accept** something you have been offered, you say yes to it.

**accident**  **accidents**
NOUN An **accident** is something nasty that happens by chance. *He broke his leg in a climbing accident.*
**accidentally** ADVERB

**account** accounts

NOUN **1** An **account** is something written or spoken that tells you what has happened.

NOUN **2** An **account** is also money that you keep at a bank.

**accurate**

ADJECTIVE An **accurate** measurement or description is exactly right.

**ache** aches

NOUN An **ache** is a dull, lasting pain.

**achieve** achieves, achieving, achieved

VERB If you **achieve** something, you usually get it by hard work.

**achievement** NOUN

**acid** acids

NOUN Some **acids** give food a sharp, sour taste. Lemons and vinegar contain acid. Strong acid can burn your skin.

**acid rain**

NOUN **Acid rain** is rain that is mixed with dirty gases in the air. It can damage buildings, trees and fish.

**acorn** acorns

NOUN An **acorn** is a nut. Acorns grow on oak trees.

**acrobat** acrobats

NOUN An **acrobat** is someone who does difficult and exciting tricks, like balancing on a high wire.

**across**

PREPOSITION If you go **across** something, you go from one side to the other.

**act** acts, acting, acted

VERB **1** When you **act**, you do something. *He had to **act** quickly to put out the fire.*

VERB **2** If you **act** in a play or film, you have a part in it.

NOUN **3** An **act** is something that you do.

**action** actions

NOUN An **action** is a movement of part of your body.

**active**

ADJECTIVE **1** Someone who is **active** moves about a lot, or is very busy.

ADJECTIVE **2** In grammar, a verb in the **active** voice is one where the subject does the action, rather than having it done to them. See **voice**.

**activity** activities

NOUN **Activity** is when there are a lot of things happening.

**actor** actors

NOUN An **actor** is a man or woman whose job is to act in plays or films.

**actress** actresses

NOUN A female actor is sometimes called an **actress**. See **actor**.

**actual**

ADJECTIVE You describe something as **actual** when you mean it is real. *The shop said the paint was red, but the actual colour was pink.*

**actually** ADVERB

**adapt** adapts, adapting, adapted

VERB **1** If you **adapt** to something new, you change in some way that helps you.

VERB **2** If you **adapt** something, you change it to suit your needs. *The book was adapted to make a film.*

**adaptable**

ADJECTIVE Someone who is **adaptable** can change to deal with new situations.

**add** adds, adding, added

VERB **1** If you **add** something, you put it with whatever you have already. *Put flour in the bowl and add an egg.*

VERB **2** If you **add** numbers of things together, you find out how many you have. The sign + means add. *I have two marbles in the bag. If I add these three, it makes five altogether.* 2 + 3 = 5

**addition**

NOUN **Addition** is adding numbers or things together.

# address

**address** **addresses**

NOUN Your **address** is the name or number of your house, and the street and town where you live.

**adjective** **adjectives**

NOUN An **adjective** is a word that describes someone or something. "Beautiful" and "green" are adjectives. See *Adjective* on page 263.

**admire** **admires, admiring, admired**

VERB **1** When you **admire** someone, you think very highly of them.

VERB **2** When you **admire** something, you enjoy looking at it. *They stopped the car to admire the view.*

**admit** **admits, admitting, admitted**

VERB **1** If you **admit** something, you agree that it is true.

VERB **2** If people are **admitted** to a place, they are allowed to go in.

**adopt** **adopts, adopting, adopted**

VERB If a person **adopts** a child, they make the child their own by law.

**adore** **adores, adoring, adored**

VERB If you **adore** someone, you love them very much.

**adult** **adults**

NOUN An **adult** is a grown-up person or animal.

**advance** **advances, advancing, advanced**

VERB If someone **advances**, they move forward. *The army advanced nine miles in one day.*

**advantage** **advantages**

NOUN An **advantage** is something that helps you do better than other people. *His long legs gave him an advantage in the race.*

**adventure** **adventures**

NOUN If you are having an **adventure**, you are doing something exciting.

**adverb** **adverbs**

NOUN An **adverb** is a word that answers questions like how, when, where and why. In the sentence "The girl came quietly into the room", the word "quietly" is an adverb telling you how the girl came in. See *Adverb* on page 263.

**advertise** **advertises, advertising, advertised**

VERB If you **advertise** something, you tell people about it through newspapers, posters or TV.

**advertisement** **advertisements**

NOUN An **advertisement** is a notice in the paper, or on a poster or TV, about a job or things for sale.

**advice**

NOUN If you give someone **advice**, you say what you think they should do.

**advise** **advises, advising, advised**

VERB When you **advise** someone, you tell them what you think they should do.

**aerial** **aerials**

NOUN An **aerial** is a wire that sends or receives radio or television signals.

**aeroplane** **aeroplanes**

NOUN An **aeroplane** is a flying vehicle with wings and one or more engines.

**affect** **affects, affecting, affected**
VERB When something **affects** someone or something else, it changes them in some way.

**affection**
NOUN **Affection** is a feeling of caring for someone.

**afford** **affords, affording, afforded**
VERB If you can **afford** something, you have enough money to buy it or do it.

**afraid**
ADJECTIVE Someone who is **afraid** thinks that something nasty might happen.

**after**
PREPOSITION If something happens **after** something else, it happens at a later time. *We'll watch television **after** supper.*

**afternoon** **afternoons**
NOUN The **afternoon** is the time of day between 12 o'clock (noon) and about six o'clock in the evening.

**again**
ADVERB If you do something **again**, you do it once more.

**against**
PREPOSITION **1** If you play **against** someone, you are not on their side.
PREPOSITION **2** If you are **against** something, you are touching it and leaning on it. *She felt tired and leaned **against** the tree.*

**age** **ages**
NOUN **1** Your **age** is how old you are.
NOUN **2** An **age** is a special period in history, like the Stone Age.

**ago**
ADVERB If something happened four days **ago**, it is four days since it happened.

**agree** **agrees, agreeing, agreed**
VERB **1** If you **agree** with someone, you think the same about something.
VERB **2** If you **agree** to do something, you say you will do it.
**agreement** NOUN

**ahead**
ADVERB Something or someone who is **ahead** of you is in front of you. *She walked fast and went on **ahead** of me.*

**aim** **aims, aiming, aimed**
VERB **1** If you **aim** at something, you point a weapon at it.
VERB **2** If you **aim** to do something, you plan to do it.

**air**
NOUN **Air** is the mixture of gases that we breathe.

**aircraft**
NOUN An **aircraft** is a vehicle that flies. Helicopters and aeroplanes are aircraft.

**air force** **air forces**
NOUN An **air force** is a force that a country uses for fighting in the air.

**airport** **airports**
NOUN An **airport** is a place where aircraft land and take off.

**alarm** **alarms**
NOUN **1** An **alarm** is something like a bell or flashing light that warns you of something.
NOUN **2** **Alarm** is a feeling of fear. *He looked at the hungry bear in **alarm**.*

**album** **albums**
NOUN An **album** is a book that you put things like stamps or photographs in.

**alien** **aliens**
NOUN In science fiction, an **alien** is a creature from outer space.

# alight

**alight**
ADJECTIVE If something is **alight**, it is burning.

**alike**
ADJECTIVE If two or more things are **alike**, they are the same in some way.

**alive**
ADJECTIVE If a person, animal or plant is **alive**, they are living now.

**all**
ADJECTIVE You say **all** when you mean the whole of a particular group or thing. *Put **all** your toys away.*

**allergy** **allergies**
NOUN If you have an **allergy** to something, it makes you ill. *Tom has an **allergy** to nuts, so he must not eat them.*

**alley** **alleys**
NOUN An **alley** is a narrow path with buildings or walls on both sides.

**alligator** **alligators**
NOUN An **alligator** is a reptile. It is of the same family as a crocodile, but smaller. *See Reptiles on page 259.*

**alliteration**
NOUN **Alliteration** is the use of words close together which begin with the same sound, for example "hundreds of huge hairy horses".

**allow** **allows, allowing, allowed**
VERB If someone **allows** you to do something, they let you do it.

**all right**
ADJECTIVE **1** If someone is **all right**, they are well or safe. *See if the baby's **all right**.*
INTERJECTION **2** You say **all right** if you agree to something.

**almost**
ADVERB **Almost** means very nearly, but not quite. *He tripped and **almost** fell.*

**alone**
ADJECTIVE If you are **alone**, there is nobody with you.

**along**
PREPOSITION If you go **along** something, you move towards the end of it.

**aloud**
ADVERB If you read something **aloud**, you read it so that people can hear you.

**alphabet** **alphabets**
NOUN An **alphabet** is all the letters used to write words, written in a special order.

**alphabetical**
ADJECTIVE **Alphabetical** means arranged in the order of the letters of the alphabet. *She read out the names on the register in **alphabetical** order.*

**already**
ADVERB If you have done something **already**, you did it earlier.

**also**
ADVERB You say **also** when you want to add to something you have just said.

**alter** **alters, altering, altered**
VERB When you **alter** something, you change it in some way.

**alternate** **alternates, alternating, alternated**
VERB When two things **alternate**, they regularly happen one after the other. *He **alternates** between being friendly and completely ignoring me.*

**although**
CONJUNCTION You say **although** when you expected something different. ***Although** my dad was cross, he still gave me my pocket money.*

**altogether**

ADVERB If you say there are a number of things **altogether**, you are counting all of them. *I've picked four apples and you've picked two, so that's six **altogether**.*

**aluminium**

NOUN **Aluminium** is a light, silver-coloured metal. It is used for making rolls of foil and containers like cans and pie dishes.

**always**

ADVERB **1** If you **always** do something, you do it every time. *He **always** puts his things away when he has used them.*
ADVERB **2** If something has **always** been so, it has been that way at all times. *They have **always** been good friends.*

**a.m.**

ADVERB **a.m.** is the time between midnight and noon. *I get up at 7 **a.m.*** See **p.m.**

**amaze** amazes, amazing, amazed

VERB If something **amazes** you, it surprises you very much.
**amazement** NOUN

**amazing**

ADJECTIVE Something that is **amazing** is very surprising or wonderful.

**ambition** ambitions

NOUN If you have an **ambition** to do something, you want to do it very much.

**ambulance** ambulances

NOUN An **ambulance** is a vehicle that is used to take people to hospital.

**among**

PREPOSITION **1** If something is **among** a number of things, it is surrounded by them. *He sat **among** piles of books.*
PREPOSITION **2** If something is divided **among** several people, they all have a share.

**amount** amounts

NOUN An **amount** of something is how much there is of it.

**amphibian** amphibians

NOUN An **amphibian** is an animal that is able to live on land and in water.
**amphibious** ADJECTIVE

See *Amphibians* on page 259.

**amuse** amuses, amusing, amused

VERB If you **amuse** somebody, you make them smile or stop them feeling bored.

**analogue**

ADJECTIVE An **analogue** watch or clock shows the time with hands that move round a dial. See **digital**.

**anchor** anchors

NOUN An **anchor** is a heavy metal hook on a long chain. It is dropped over the side of a boat to stop it moving.

**ancient**

ADJECTIVE If something is **ancient**, it is very old.

**and**

CONJUNCTION You use **and** to join two or more words or phrases together. *I like chocolate, **and** my brother does too.*

**angel** angels

NOUN **Angels** are beings some people believe act as messengers for God.

**anger**

NOUN **Anger** is the strong feeling you have about something that is unfair.

**angle** angles

NOUN An **angle** is the shape that is made when two lines or surfaces join. The size of an angle is measured in degrees.

**Aa**
b
c
d
e
f
g
h
i
j
k
l
m
n
o
p
q
r
s
t
u
v
w
x
y
z

**angry** **angrier, angriest**
ADJECTIVE If you feel **angry**, you are very cross.
**angrily** ADVERB

**animal** **animals**
NOUN **Animals** are living things which are not plants. Humans, dogs, birds, fish, reptiles and insects are all animals.

**ankle** **ankles**
NOUN Your **ankle** is the joint between your foot and your leg.

**anniversary** **anniversaries**
NOUN An **anniversary** is a day when you remember something special which happened on that date in an earlier year.

**announce** **announces, announcing, announced**
VERB If you **announce** something important, you tell people about it publicly. *My sister's engagement was **announced** last week.*

**annoy** **annoys, annoying, annoyed**
VERB If you do something which **annoys** someone, you make them cross.

**annual** **annuals**
ADJECTIVE **1** Something that is **annual** happens once a year, like a birthday.
NOUN **2** An **annual** is a book that comes out once a year.

**another**
ADJECTIVE **Another** means one more. *Amy finished her chocolate and took **another** one immediately.*

**answer** **answers, answering, answered**
VERB **1** When you **answer**, you say or write something to someone who has asked you a question.
NOUN **2** Your **answer** is what you say or write to a question.

**ant** **ants**
NOUN **Ants** are small insects which live in large groups called colonies.
See *Insects* on page 259.

**antelope** **antelopes**
NOUN **Antelopes** are animals that look like deer, but their horns are not branch-shaped. They live in Africa and Asia.

**antenna** **antennae or antennas**
NOUN The **antennae** of an insect are the two long, thin parts on its head that it uses to feel with.

**anthology** **anthologies**
NOUN An **anthology** is a book of writings by different authors.

**anti-**
PREFIX **Anti-** is put in front of a word to mean against or opposite to that word. *See Prefixes on page 264.*

**anticlockwise**
ADVERB If something goes **anticlockwise**, it moves in the opposite direction to the hands of a clock.

**antique** **antiques**
NOUN An **antique** is an old object which is valuable because it is beautiful or rare.

**antiseptic** **antiseptics**
NOUN An **antiseptic** is a substance that prevents infection by killing germs.

**antonym** **antonyms**
NOUN An **antonym** is a word that means the opposite of another word. *See Antonyms on page 267.*

**anxious**
ADJECTIVE Someone who is **anxious** is nervous or worried about something.

**any**
ADJECTIVE **1 Any** means one, some, or several. *Do you have **any** milk?*
ADJECTIVE **2 Any** can also mean even the smallest amount. *I mustn't eat **any** nuts.*

**anybody**

PRONOUN **Anybody** is any person.

**anyone**

PRONOUN **Anyone** is any person.

**anything**

PRONOUN **Anything** means any object, event, situation or action.

**anywhere**

ADVERB **Anywhere** means in, at or to any place. *Just put it down* **anywhere**.

**apart**

ADJECTIVE If something is **apart** from something else, there is a space between them. *He stood with his feet* **apart**.

**ape** **apes**

NOUN **Apes** are like monkeys but are larger and have no tails. Chimpanzees and gorillas are apes. The ape in the photo is an orang-utan.

**apex** **apexes**

NOUN The **apex** is the highest point of something.

**apologize** **apologizes, apologizing, apologized**; also spelt **apologise**

VERB When you **apologize**, you say you are sorry for something you have done.

**apology** **apologies**

NOUN An **apology** is something you say or write to tell someone you are sorry.

**apostrophe** **apostrophes**

NOUN An **apostrophe** is a punctuation mark (') used in contractions and to show belonging.
See *Punctuation* on page 264.

**apparatus**

NOUN The **apparatus** for a particular task is the equipment you use for it.

**appear** **appears, appearing, appeared**

VERB **1** When something **appears**, it moves into a place where you can see it.
VERB **2** If something **appears** to be a certain way, that is how it seems.

**appearance** **appearances**

NOUN **1** Someone's **appearance** in a place is their sudden arrival there.
NOUN **2** Your **appearance** is the way you look to other people.

**appetite** **appetites**

NOUN If you have an **appetite**, you are looking forward to eating something.

**applause**

NOUN **Applause** is clapping your hands to show that you liked something.

**apple** **apples**

NOUN An **apple** is a round crisp fruit which grows on a tree.
See *Fruit* on page 257.

**apply** **applies, applying, applied**

VERB If you **apply** for something, like a job, you usually ask for it in writing.

**appreciate** **appreciates, appreciating, appreciated**

VERB If you **appreciate** something, you feel grateful for it.

**approach** **approaches, approaching, approached**

VERB When someone **approaches** you, they get nearer to you.

**approve** **approves, approving, approved**

VERB If you **approve** of something, you think it is good.
**approval** NOUN

**approximate**

ADJECTIVE An **approximate** answer may not be exactly right. *What is the* **approximate** *distance between those trees?*

**Aa**

### approximately
ADVERB If you say **approximately**, you mean about. *It is **approximately** 5 metres long.*

### apricot  apricots
NOUN An **apricot** is a small, round yellow-orange fruit with a large stone in the centre.

### April
NOUN **April** is the fourth month of the year. It has 30 days.

### apron  aprons
NOUN An **apron** is a piece of material that you wear to keep your clothes clean when you are cooking.

### aquarium  aquaria or aquariums
NOUN An **aquarium** is a glass tank for fish and other underwater animals.

### arch  arches
NOUN An **arch** is a curved part of a bridge, wall or building.

### archery
NOUN **Archery** is a sport in which people shoot at a target with a bow and arrow.

### architect  architects
NOUN An **architect** is a person who designs buildings.

### area  areas
NOUN **1** The **area** of something is the size of its surface. To find the area of a rectangle, you multiply the length by the breadth. The area of this rectangle is 12 square centimetres.

2 cm

6 cm

NOUN **2** You use the word **area** to mean in or around a place. *There are lots of shops in this **area**.*

### argue  argues, arguing, argued
VERB If you **argue** with someone, you say that you do not agree with them, and give your reasons.

### argument  arguments
NOUN An **argument** is a talk between people who do not agree. In some arguments, people shout angrily.

### arithmetic
NOUN **Arithmetic** is about adding, subtracting, multiplying and dividing numbers.

### arm  arms
NOUN Your **arm** is the part of your body between the shoulder and the hand.

### armchair  armchairs
NOUN An **armchair** is a chair with a support on each side for your arms.

### armour
NOUN **Armour** is metal clothing that soldiers used to wear in battle.

### army  armies
NOUN An **army** is a large organized group of people who are trained to fight in case of war.

### around
PREPOSITION **1** You say **around** when things are in various places. *There are lots of cupboards **around** the house.*
PREPOSITION **2** You can use **around** when something is on all sides of something else. *The Earth's atmosphere is the air **around** it.*

**arrange** **arranges, arranging, arranged**
VERB **1** If you **arrange** something like a party, you make plans and organize it.
VERB **2** If you **arrange** things like flowers, you group them in a special way.

**array** **arrays**
NOUN **1** An **array** is a group of things set out neatly in columns and rows.
NOUN **2** An **array** is also a large number of things displayed together. *Ben's mouth watered at the array of cakes.*

**arrest** **arrests, arresting, arrested**
VERB If the police **arrest** someone, they take them to the police station.

**arrive** **arrives, arriving, arrived**
VERB When you **arrive** at a place, you reach it at the end of your journey.
**arrival** NOUN

**arrow** **arrows**
NOUN **1** An **arrow** is a thin stick with a pointed end, which is shot from a bow.
NOUN **2** An **arrow** can also be a sign which shows people which way to go.

**art**
NOUN **Art** is something like painting or sculpture, which is beautiful or has a special meaning.

**artery** **arteries**
NOUN An **artery** is a tube which carries blood from your heart to the rest of your body.

**article** **articles**
NOUN **1** An **article** is a piece of writing in a magazine or newspaper.
NOUN **2** An **article** can also be an object. *What is this strange article?*

**artificial**
ADJECTIVE **Artificial** things are made by people. They do not occur naturally.

**artist** **artists**
NOUN An **artist** is a person who does things like painting or sculpture.

**ascend** **ascends, ascending, ascended**
VERB When you **ascend**, you move upwards. *He ascended the stairs to his room.*

**ascending**
ADJECTIVE When things are arranged in **ascending** order, each thing is higher than the one before it. *The numbers 21, 37 and 49 are in ascending order.*

**ash** **ashes**
NOUN **1** **Ash** is the dust left after a fire.
NOUN **2** An **ash** is a large tree.

**ashamed**
ADJECTIVE If you are **ashamed**, you feel sorry about something you have done.

**ask** **asks, asking, asked**
VERB **1** If you **ask** someone a question, you are trying to find something out.
VERB **2** If you **ask** someone for something, you want them to give it to you.

**asleep**
ADJECTIVE If you are **asleep**, your eyes are closed and your body is resting.

**aspirin** **aspirins**
NOUN **Aspirin** is a drug which you take to help you if you have a pain, fever or cold. An **aspirin** is a tablet of this drug.

**ass** **asses**
NOUN An **ass** is like a horse but smaller and with longer ears.

**assemble** **assembles, assembling, assembled**
VERB **1** If you **assemble** something, you fit the parts of it together.
VERB **2** When people **assemble**, they come together in a group.

**Aa**

**assembly** **assemblies**

NOUN **Assembly** is a gathering of all the teachers and pupils in a school.

**assistant** **assistants**

NOUN **1** A person's **assistant** is someone whose job is to help them.

NOUN **2** A shop **assistant** is a person who works in a shop selling things.

**asthma**

NOUN **Asthma** is a disease of the chest. It causes wheezing and makes it difficult for you to breathe properly.

**astonish** **astonishes, astonishing, astonished**

VERB If you are **astonished** by something or someone, you are very surprised.

**astronaut** **astronauts**

NOUN An **astronaut** is a person who travels in space.

**astronomer** **astronomers**

NOUN An **astronomer** is a scientist who studies the stars and planets.

**ate**

VERB **Ate** is the past tense of **eat**.

**atlas** **atlases**

NOUN An **atlas** is a book of maps.

**atmosphere** **atmospheres**

NOUN **1** A planet's **atmosphere** is the layer of air or other gas around it.

NOUN **2** You can use **atmosphere** to talk about the general mood of a place. *In the classroom the **atmosphere** was relaxed.*

**atom** **atoms**

NOUN An **atom** is the smallest part of any substance.

**attach** **attaches, attaching, attached**

VERB When you **attach** something to an object, you join the two things together.

**attack** **attacks, attacking, attacked**

VERB If a person **attacks** somebody, they try to hurt them.

**attempt** **attempts, attempting, attempted**

VERB If you **attempt** something difficult, you try to do it.

**attend** **attends, attending, attended**

VERB If someone **attends** something like a meeting, they are present at it.

**attention**

NOUN **1** If something attracts your **attention**, you notice it suddenly.

NOUN **2** If you pay **attention** to someone, you listen carefully to them.

**attic** **attics**

NOUN An **attic** is a room at the top of a house, just under the roof.

**attract** **attracts, attracting, attracted**

VERB **1** If something or somebody **attracts** you, you find them interesting. *Joe was **attracted** to the fair by the lights.*

VERB **2** If something like a magnet **attracts** an object, it makes it move towards it.

**attractive**

ADJECTIVE If something is **attractive**, it is nice to look at.

**audience** **audiences**

NOUN An **audience** is a group of people watching or listening to something like a play, film, talk or piece of music.

**August**

NOUN **August** is the eighth month of the year. It has 31 days.

**aunt** **aunts**

NOUN Your **aunt** is the sister of one of your parents, or the wife of your uncle.

**author** **authors**

NOUN The **author** of a book is the person who wrote it.

**authority** **authorities**

NOUN **1** **Authority** is a quality that someone has that makes people take notice of what they say.

NOUN **2** The **authorities** are people like the police who have a lot of power.

**autograph** **autographs**

NOUN An **autograph** is the signature of a famous person.

**automatic**

ADJECTIVE An **automatic** machine is one that can do things on its own.

**automatically** ADVERB

**autumn** **autumns**

NOUN **Autumn** is the season between summer and winter. The weather cools and many trees lose their leaves.

**available**

ADJECTIVE If something is **available**, you can get it. *Tickets are* **available** *now.*

**avalanche** **avalanches**

NOUN An **avalanche** is a huge mass of snow and ice that falls down a mountain.

**avenue** **avenues**

NOUN An **avenue** is a wide road with trees on either side.

**avocado** **avocados**

NOUN An **avocado** is a fruit with dark green skin and a large stone.
See *Fruit* on page 257.

**avoid** **avoids, avoiding, avoided**

VERB If you **avoid** someone or something, you keep away from them.

**awake**

ADJECTIVE If you are **awake**, you are not sleeping.

**award** **awards**

NOUN An **award** is a prize that you are given for doing something well.

**aware**

ADJECTIVE If you are **aware** of something, you know about it.

**away**

ADVERB **1** If you move **away** from somewhere, you move so that you are further from that place.

ADVERB **2** If you are **away** from somewhere, you are not in that place. *Katherine is* **away** *from school today.*

**awful**

ADJECTIVE Something **awful** is very unpleasant or bad.

**awkward**

ADJECTIVE **1** If something is **awkward**, it is difficult to do or use.

ADJECTIVE **2** If people are **awkward**, they move in a clumsy way.

**axe** **axes**

NOUN An **axe** is a tool with a long handle and a heavy sharp blade at one end. It is used for chopping wood.

**axis** **axes**

NOUN **1** An **axis** is an imaginary line through the centre of something, around which it moves.

NOUN **2** An **axis** is also one of the two sides of a graph. A graph has a horizontal axis and a vertical axis.

a
**Bb**
c
d
e
f
g
h
i
j
k
l
m
n
o
p
q
r
s
t
u
v
w
x
y
z

# Bb

**baby** babies
NOUN A **baby** is a very young child.

**back** backs
NOUN **1** The **back** of something is the part opposite the front.
ADVERB **2** If you go **back** to a place, you go somewhere you have been before.
NOUN **3** Your **back** is the part of your body which is behind you, from your neck to the top of your legs.
NOUN **4** The **back** of an animal is the part on top, between its neck and the beginning of its tail.
**back to front** PHRASE If you have something on **back to front**, you are wearing it the wrong way round.

**background** backgrounds
NOUN The **background** of a picture is everything behind the main part.

**backwards**
ADVERB **1** If you move **backwards**, you move with your back facing in the direction you are going.
ADVERB **2** If you do something **backwards**, you do it in the opposite of the usual way. *Let's try counting backwards from one hundred.*

**bacon**
NOUN **Bacon** is salted meat from a pig.

**bacteria**
PLURAL NOUN **Bacteria** are very tiny living things which break down waste. They can cause diseases.

**bad** worse, worst
ADJECTIVE **1** You say somebody is **bad** if they are naughty or wicked.
ADJECTIVE **2** If something is **bad**, it can hurt or upset you in some way.

**badge** badges
NOUN A **badge** is a sign people wear to show they belong to a school or club.

**badger** badgers
NOUN A **badger** is a strongly built animal with short legs and neck. It has long grey fur and a striped head.

**badminton**
NOUN **Badminton** is a game in which players use rackets to hit a small feathered object called a shuttlecock across a net.

**bag** bags
NOUN A **bag** is a soft container for carrying or holding things.

**bait**
NOUN **Bait** is food used to trap animals.

**bake** bakes, baking, baked
VERB When you **bake** food, you cook it in an oven.

**baker** bakers
NOUN A **baker** makes and sells bread, cakes and pies.

**balance** balances, balancing, balanced
VERB When you **balance**, you keep steady. *She tried to balance on one leg.*

**balcony** balconies
NOUN A **balcony** is a platform on the outside of a building. Balconies have a railing or wall around them.

**bald** balder, baldest
ADJECTIVE People who are **bald** have no hair on the top of their head.

**ball** balls
NOUN Anything round can be called a **ball**. You need a ball for lots of games, like tennis and football.

## ballet  **ballets**

NOUN A **ballet** is a sort of play where the story is told with dancing and music.

## balloon  **balloons**

NOUN A **balloon** is a small rubber bag. If you blow hard into it, it gets bigger and makes a very light toy or decoration.

## bamboo

NOUN **Bamboo** is a kind of grass with strong hollow stems which are useful as garden canes or for making furniture.

## ban  **bans, banning, banned**

VERB If someone is **banned** from doing something, they are told by people in charge that they must not do it.

## banana  **bananas**

NOUN A **banana** is a long yellow fruit which grows on trees in hot countries. See *Fruit* on page 257.

## band  **bands**

NOUN **1** A **band** is a small number of people, like a gang of robbers or a group of musicians.

NOUN **2** A **band** can also be a strip of material such as iron, cloth or rubber.

## bandage  **bandages**

NOUN A **bandage** is a strip of cloth used to cover a wound.

## bang  **bangs, banging, banged**

NOUN **1** A **bang** is a sudden loud noise.

VERB **2** If something **bangs**, or you bang it, it makes a loud noise.

## bank  **banks**

NOUN **1** A **bank** is a business that looks after people's money.

NOUN **2** The **bank** of a river is the ground either side of the water.

## banner  **banners**

NOUN A **banner** is a long strip of cloth or paper with a message written on it.

## bar  **bars**

NOUN **1** A **bar** is a long piece of something hard, like metal or wood.

NOUN **2** A **bar** can also be a counter where people can buy drink.

## barbecue  **barbecues**

NOUN A **barbecue** is a grill on which food is cooked outdoors over hot charcoal.

## barber  **barbers**

NOUN A **barber** is someone who cuts men's hair.

## bar chart  **bar charts**

NOUN A **bar chart** is a graph where information is shown in bars.

Hair Colour in Our Class

## bar code  **bar codes**

NOUN A **bar code** is a pattern of numbers and lines printed on something that is for sale, so that the price can be read by a machine.

## bare  **barer, barest**

ADJECTIVE **1** If part of your body is **bare**, it is not covered by clothes.

ADJECTIVE **2** If something is **bare**, it has nothing in it or on it. *It was winter and the trees were* **bare**.

## bargain  **bargains**

NOUN A **bargain** is something which is sold at a low price, and which you think is good value.

## bark  **barks, barking, barked**

VERB **1** When a dog **barks**, it makes a sudden rough, loud noise.

NOUN **2** **Bark** is the outside covering of a tree.

## barley

NOUN **Barley** is a cereal that is grown for food and drink.

a
**Bb**
c
d
e
f
g
h
i
j
k
l
m
n
o
p
q
r
s
t
u
v
w
x
y
z

**barn** **barns**

NOUN A **barn** is a large building where a farmer stores hay and other crops.

**barrel** **barrels**

NOUN A **barrel** is a large wooden, metal or plastic container for holding liquids.

**barrier** **barriers**

NOUN A **barrier** is something like a fence or wall, that stops people getting past.

**base** **bases**

NOUN **1** The **base** is the bottom of something.

NOUN **2** Number **bases** are a whole pattern of counting. A base ten counting system uses units, tens and hundreds.

**basement** **basements**

NOUN The **basement** of a building is a floor below ground level.

**basic**

ADJECTIVE **1** Basic is used to describe things like the food and equipment that people really need in their lives.

ADJECTIVE **2** Basic also means the simplest things you need to know about a subject. *I'm not good at this yet, but I've got the **basic** idea.*

**basically** ADVERB

**basin** **basins**

NOUN A **basin** is a wide round container which is open at the top.

**basket** **baskets**

NOUN A **basket** is used for holding or carrying things. It is usually made from strips of thin wood or cane.

**bat** **bats, batting, batted**

NOUN **1** In some games, like table tennis, you use a wooden **bat** to hit the ball.

NOUN **2** A **bat** is also a small animal like a mouse with leathery wings. Bats fly at night, and sleep hanging upside down.

VERB **3** If you are **batting**, you are having a turn at hitting the ball with a bat in cricket, baseball or rounders.

**bath** **baths**

NOUN A **bath** is a container for water. It is big enough to sit or lie in, so that you can wash yourself all over.

**bathroom** **bathrooms**

NOUN The **bathroom** is the room where the bath or shower is.

**battery** **batteries**

NOUN A **battery** is an object which stores electric power. There are tiny batteries for things like watches, and larger batteries for torches.

**battle** **battles**

NOUN A **battle** is a fight between enemy forces, on land, at sea or in the air.

**bawl** **bawls, bawling, bawled**

VERB If a child is **bawling**, it is crying very loudly and angrily.

**bay** **bays**

NOUN A **bay** is a deep curve in a coastline.

**beach** **beaches**

NOUN The **beach** is the land covered with sand or pebbles that is next to the sea.

**bead** **beads**

NOUN A **bead** is a small piece of glass or plastic with a hole through it. Beads can be threaded together to make a necklace or bracelet.

**beak** **beaks**

NOUN A **beak** is the hard outside part of a bird's mouth.

**beam** **beams, beaming, beamed**

NOUN **1** A **beam** is a long thick bar of wood, metal or concrete, used to support part of a building.

NOUN **2** A **beam** is also a line of light from an object such as a torch or the sun.

VERB **3** If you **beam**, you give a big smile.

**bean** **beans**

NOUN A **bean** is a vegetable. Its outer covering is called a pod, and inside it has large seeds, also called beans.

See *Vegetables* on page 256.

**bear** **bears, bearing, bore**

NOUN **1** A **bear** is a large, strong animal with thick fur and sharp claws.

VERB **2** If you **bear** something, you put up with it. *I can't bear all this homework.*

**beard** **beards**

NOUN A **beard** is the hair which grows on the lower part of a man's face.

**beat** **beats, beating, beat, beaten**

VERB **1** If you **beat** someone in a race or competition, you do better than they do.

VERB **2** If someone **beats** another person or an animal, they hit them hard.

VERB **3** If you **beat** eggs, you stir them very fast.

VERB **4** Your heart **beats** with a regular rhythm all the time.

**beautiful**

ADJECTIVE **1** You say something is **beautiful** if it gives you great pleasure to look at it or listen to it.

ADJECTIVE **2** You say someone is **beautiful** if they are lovely to look at.

**beaver** **beavers**

NOUN A **beaver** is a furry animal which lives in or near water.

**because**

CONJUNCTION You say **because** when you are going to give a reason for something. *I left the party because they were playing silly games.*

**become** **becomes, becoming, became, become**

VERB To **become** means to start being different in some way. *The smell became stronger.*

**bed** **beds**

NOUN **1** A **bed** is a piece of furniture to lie down on when you rest or sleep.

NOUN **2** The **bed** of the sea or of a river is the ground beneath it.

**bedroom** **bedrooms**

NOUN Your **bedroom** is the room where you sleep.

**bedtime**

NOUN Your **bedtime** is the time when you usually go to bed.

**bee** **bees**

NOUN A **bee** is a flying insect. People keep bees for the honey that they make. See **beehive**.

See also *Insects* on page 259.

**beech** **beeches**

NOUN A **beech** is a large tree.

**beef**

NOUN **Beef** is the meat from a cow.

**beehive** **beehives**

NOUN A **beehive** is a house for bees, where a beekeeper collects the honey.

**beer** **beers**

NOUN **Beer** is a drink made from grain.

**beetle** **beetles**
NOUN A **beetle** is an insect with four wings. The front two act as hard covers to the body when the beetle is not flying. *See Insects on page 259.*

**beetroot** **beetroots**
NOUN **Beetroot** is a dark red root vegetable. *See Vegetables on page 256.*

**before**
PREPOSITION **1** If something happens **before** something else, it happens earlier. *Can I see you **before** lunch?*
ADVERB **2** If you have done something **before**, it is not the first time.

**beg** **begs, begging, begged**
VERB If you **beg** someone to do something, you ask them very anxiously to do it. *Tom **begged** his dad to take him to the football match.*

**begin** **begins, beginning, began, begun**
VERB When you **begin**, you start. *I **began** school on Thursday.*

**beginner** **beginners**
NOUN A **beginner** is someone who has just started to learn something.

**beginning** **beginnings**
NOUN The **beginning** of something is the first part of it.

**begun**
VERB **Begun** is the past participle of **begin**.

**behave** **behaves, behaving, behaved**
VERB The way you **behave** is the way you act.
**behaviour** NOUN

**behind**
PREPOSITION **1 Behind** means on the other side of something. *She was **behind** the counter.*
PREPOSITION **2** If you are **behind** someone, you are at the back of them.

**beige**
ADJECTIVE Something that is **beige** is a pale creamy-brown colour. *See Colours on page 271.*

**believe** **believes, believing, believed**
VERB If you **believe** something or someone, you think what is said is true.

**bell** **bells**
NOUN A **bell** is a piece of metal shaped like a cup, which rings when something hits it.

**belong** **belongs, belonging, belonged**
VERB **1** If something **belongs** to you, it is your own.
VERB **2** If you **belong** to something, like a club, you are a member of it.

**below**
PREPOSITION If something is **below** something else, it is underneath it.

**belt** **belts**
NOUN A **belt** is a strip of leather or other material that you put round your waist.

**bench** **benches**
NOUN A **bench** is a long seat, usually made of wood.

**bend** **bends, bending, bent**
VERB When something **bends**, it becomes curved or crooked.

**beneath**
PREPOSITION If something is **beneath** something else, it is below it.

**bent**

ADJECTIVE If something is **bent**, it has become curved or crooked. See **bend**.

**berry** **berries**

NOUN A **berry** is a small round soft fruit that grows on a bush or a tree.

**beside**

PREPOSITION If something is **beside** something else, it is at the side of it.

**best**

ADJECTIVE **Best** means the "most good", or better than anything else. *That's the best programme I've seen.*

**better**

ADJECTIVE **1** Something that is **better** than something else is of a higher standard or quality. *Your bicycle is better than mine.*

ADJECTIVE **2 Better** can also mean more sensible. *It would be better to go home.*

ADJECTIVE **3** If you are feeling **better** after an illness, you are not feeling so ill.

**between**

PREPOSITION If something is **between** two other things, it is in the space or time that separates them. *The toyshop is between the bank and the library.*

**beware**

VERB You tell people to **beware** if there is danger of some kind. *Beware of the bull.*

**bicycle** **bicycles**

NOUN A **bicycle** is a vehicle with two wheels. You sit on it and turn pedals with your feet to make it go.

**big** **bigger, biggest**

ADJECTIVE Something or somebody **big** is large in size or importance.

**bike** **bikes**

NOUN **Bike** is an abbreviation of **bicycle**.

**bill** **bills**

NOUN **1** A **bill** is a piece of paper saying how much money you owe. *Mum's just had the electricity bill.*

NOUN **2** A bird's **bill** is its beak.

**bin** **bins**

NOUN A **bin** is a container, usually with a lid, for putting rubbish in.

**bind** **binds, binding, bound**

VERB If you **bind** something, you tie something like string or cloth tightly round it so that it is held in place.

**biology**

NOUN **Biology** is the study of living things.

**birch** **birches**

NOUN A **birch** is a tall tree that has thin peeling bark.

**bird** **birds**

NOUN A **bird** is an animal with two legs, two wings and feathers.

handlebars · saddle · brake lever · reflector · light · brake · wheel · tyre · spoke · pedal · chain

**birth** **births**

NOUN The **birth** of a baby is when it comes out of its mother's body.

**birthday** **birthdays**

NOUN Your **birthday** is a special date that is remembered every year, because it was the day you were born.

**biscuit** **biscuits**

NOUN A **biscuit** is a small, flat, crisp kind of cake.

**bit** **bits**

NOUN **1** A **bit** of something is a small piece of it.

NOUN **2** A **bit** is a piece of metal that goes in a horse's mouth.

VERB **3** Bit is also the past tense of **bite**.

**bite** **bites, biting, bit, bitten**

VERB If you **bite** something, you use your teeth to hold, cut or tear it.

**bitter**

ADJECTIVE **1** If something has a **bitter** taste, it tastes sharp and unpleasant.

ADJECTIVE **2** Someone who is **bitter** feels angry and disappointed.

**black** **blacker, blackest**

ADJECTIVE If the colour of something is **black**, it is the colour of these letters. See *Colours* on page 271.

**blackberry** **blackberries**

NOUN **Blackberries** are small, soft, dark purple fruits that grow on brambles.

**blackbird** **blackbirds**

NOUN A **blackbird** is a European songbird.

**blackboard** **blackboards**

NOUN A **blackboard** is a dark board that people can write on in chalk.

**blackcurrant** **blackcurrants**

NOUN **Blackcurrants** are very small, dark purple fruits.

**blade** **blades**

NOUN **1** A **blade** is the sharp edge of a knife or sword.

NOUN **2** A single piece of grass is a **blade**.

**blame** **blames, blaming, blamed**

VERB If somebody **blames** a person for something bad that happened, they say that person made it happen.

**blank** **blanker, blankest**

ADJECTIVE If something is **blank**, it has nothing written or drawn on it.

**blanket** **blankets**

NOUN A **blanket** is a large warm cloth, often used to cover people in bed.

**blaze** **blazes**

NOUN A **blaze** is a strong bright fire.

**blazer** **blazers**

NOUN A **blazer** is a kind of jacket, often in the colours of a school or sports team.

**bleed** **bleeds, bleeding, bled**

VERB If part of your body **bleeds**, blood comes out of it.

**blend** **blends, blending, blended**

VERB When you **blend** two or more things together, they become a smooth mixture.

**blew**

VERB **Blew** is the past tense of **blow**.

**blind** **blinds**

NOUN **1** A **blind** is rolled material that you pull down to cover a window.

ADJECTIVE **2** Someone who is **blind** cannot see.

**blindness** NOUN

**blindfold** **blindfolds**

NOUN A **blindfold** is a strip of cloth tied over someone's eyes so that they cannot see.

**blink** **blinks, blinking, blinked**

VERB When you **blink**, you shut your eyes and open them again quickly.

**blister** **blisters**

NOUN A **blister** is a small bubble on your skin, containing watery liquid. Blisters are caused by a burn or rubbing.

**blizzard** **blizzards**

NOUN A **blizzard** is a bad snowstorm with strong winds.

**block** **blocks, blocking, blocked**

NOUN 1 A **block** of flats or offices is a large tall building.

NOUN 2 A **block** of something like stone or wood is a large rectangular piece of it.

VERB 3 To **block** means to get in the way.

**block graph** **block graphs**

NOUN A **block graph** is used to show information clearly, by using blocks to make columns.

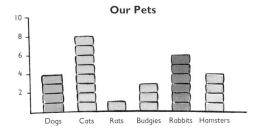

**blood**

NOUN **Blood** is the red liquid that your heart pumps round inside your body.

**bloom** **blooms, blooming, bloomed**

VERB When a plant **blooms**, its flowers open.

**blossom**

NOUN **Blossom** is the flowers that appear on a tree before the fruit.

**blot** **blots**

NOUN A **blot** is a mark made by a drop of liquid, especially ink.

**blouse** **blouses**

NOUN A **blouse** is a kind of shirt worn by a girl or a woman.

**blow** **blows, blowing, blew, blown**

VERB 1 When the wind **blows**, the air moves faster.

VERB 2 If you **blow**, you send out a stream of air from your mouth.

NOUN 3 A **blow** is a hard hit.

**blue** **bluer, bluest**

ADJECTIVE Something that is **blue** is the colour of the sky on a sunny day. See *Colours* on page 271.

**bluebell** **bluebells**

NOUN A **bluebell** is a flower that often grows wild in woods in Europe.

**blunt** **blunter, bluntest**

ADJECTIVE 1 A **blunt** knife is not sharp.

ADJECTIVE 2 Something that is **blunt** has a rounded, rather than pointed, end. *My pencil's **blunt**.*

**blur** **blurs**

NOUN A **blur** is a shape that you cannot see clearly. *The car went past so fast it was just a **blur**.*

**blurred** ADJECTIVE    **blurry** ADJECTIVE

**blurb** **blurbs**

NOUN A **blurb** is a short piece written to attract people's interest. There is usually a blurb on the back of a book. *The **blurb** says this book is exciting.*

a
**Bb**
c
d
e
f
g
h
i
j
k
l
m
n
o
p
q
r
s
t
u
v
w
x
y
z

# blush

**blush**  blushes, blushing, blushed
VERB When you **blush** you become red in the face, usually because you are embarrassed.

**boar**  boars
NOUN A **boar** is a male pig.

**board**  boards
NOUN A **board** is a flat, thin piece of wood.

**boast**  boasts, boasting, boasted
VERB If you **boast**, you talk too proudly about something.

**boat**  boats
NOUN A **boat** is a small vessel for travelling on water. See **ship**.

**body**  bodies
NOUN **1** Your **body** is every part of you. Some animals, like elephants, have very large bodies.
See *Your body* on page 258.
NOUN **2** You can say **body** when you mean just the main part of a person, not counting head, arms and legs.
NOUN **3** A **body** is a dead person.

**bog**  bogs
NOUN A **bog** is an area of land that is always wet and spongy.

**boil**  boils, boiling, boiled
VERB **1** When liquid **boils** it gets very hot. It bubbles and steam rises from it.
VERB **2** If you **boil** food, you cook it in boiling water.
NOUN **3** A **boil** is a painful red swelling on the skin.

**bold**  bolder, boldest
ADJECTIVE **1** Someone who is **bold** is not afraid of risk or danger.
ADJECTIVE **2** Letters that are in **bold** type are thicker than ordinary printed letters.

**bolt**  bolts, bolting, bolted
NOUN **1** A **bolt** is a long round metal pin with a flat end. It screws into a nut to fasten things.

NOUN **2** A **bolt** is a metal bar that you can slide across to keep a door shut.
VERB **3** If you **bolt** a door or window, you lock it with a bolt.
VERB **4** When a person or animal **bolts**, they suddenly run very fast.

**bomb**  bombs
NOUN A **bomb** is a weapon which explodes and damages a large area.

**bone**  bones
NOUN Your **bones** are the hard parts inside your body which make up your skeleton.

**bonfire**  bonfires
NOUN A **bonfire** is a fire lit outdoors, usually to burn garden rubbish.

**bonnet**  bonnets
NOUN **1** A **bonnet** is the metal cover over a car's engine.
NOUN **2** A **bonnet** is also a baby's or woman's hat tied under the chin.

**book**  books, booking, booked
NOUN **1** A **book** is a number of pages held together inside a cover.
VERB **2** If you **book** something, you ask someone to keep it for you. *We **booked** seats at the cinema.*

**boot**  boots
NOUN **1** **Boots** are strong shoes that cover your ankle and sometimes your calf.
NOUN **2** The **boot** of a car is a space for luggage.

**border**  borders
NOUN **1** A **border** is the line dividing two countries.
NOUN **2** A **border** is a strip along the edge of something, usually as a decoration.

**bore**  bores, boring, bored
VERB **1** If somebody **bores** you, you do not find them interesting.
VERB **2** If you **bore** a hole in something, you make a hole with a drill.
VERB **3** **Bore** is the past tense of **bear**.

**bored**

ADJECTIVE When you are **bored**, you feel tired and impatient because you have nothing interesting to do.
**boredom** NOUN

**boring**

ADJECTIVE Something **boring** is so dull that you have no interest in it.

**born**

VERB When a baby is **born**, it comes out of its mother's body.

**borrow** **borrows, borrowing, borrowed**

VERB When you **borrow** something, someone lets you have it for a while but they expect you to give it back later.

**boss** **bosses**

NOUN Someone's **boss** is the head of the place where they work.

**bossy**

ADJECTIVE A **bossy** person likes to tell others what to do.

**both**

ADJECTIVE OR PRONOUN You use **both** when you are talking about two things or people. *She wanted **both** pairs of jeans.*

**bother** **bothers, bothering, bothered**

VERB **1** If something **bothers** you, it annoys you or makes you feel worried.
VERB **2** If you **bother** about something, you care about it and take trouble over it.

**bottle** **bottles**

NOUN A **bottle** is a container for keeping liquids in. Bottles are usually made of glass or plastic.

**bottom** **bottoms**

NOUN **1** The **bottom** of something is the lowest part of it.
NOUN **2** Your **bottom** is the part of your body that you sit on.

**bought**

VERB **Bought** is the past tense of **buy**.

**boulder** **boulders**

NOUN A **boulder** is a big rounded rock.

**bounce** **bounces, bouncing, bounced**

VERB When something **bounces**, it springs back in the opposite direction as soon as it hits something hard.

**bound** **bounds, bounding, bounded**

VERB **1** When animals or people **bound**, they move quickly with large leaps.
ADJECTIVE **2** If something is **bound to** happen, it is sure to happen.

**boundary** **boundaries**

NOUN The **boundary** of an area of land is its outer limit.

**bow** **bows, bowing, bowed**
(*rhymes with* **low**)

NOUN **1** A **bow** is a kind of knot with two loops used to tie laces and ribbons.
NOUN **2** A **bow** is also a weapon used for shooting arrows.
NOUN **3** The **bow** for a stringed musical instrument is a long piece of wood with horsehair stretched along it.
(*rhymes with* **now**) VERB **4** When you **bow**, you bend your body forward.

**bowl** **bowls**

NOUN A **bowl** is an open container used for holding liquid or serving food.

**box** **boxes**

NOUN A **box** is a container with straight sides, made from something stiff, like cardboard, wood or plastic.

**boy** **boys**

NOUN A **boy** is a male child.

**bracelet** **bracelets**

NOUN A **bracelet** is a band or chain which is worn round the wrist or arm as an ornament.

# bracket

**bracket** **brackets**
NOUN **Brackets** are a pair of written marks ( ) placed round words that are not part of the main text.
See *Punctuation* on page 264.

**Braille**
NOUN **Braille** is a form of writing using raised dots that blind people can read by touching the dots with their fingers.

**brain** **brains**
NOUN Your **brain** is inside your head and controls your whole body. It lets you think, feel and remember.

**brainstorm** **brainstorms, brainstorming, brainstormed**
VERB When people **brainstorm**, they get together to develop ideas. *This morning we are **brainstorming** words about dogs.*

**brake** **brakes**
NOUN The **brake** is the part of a vehicle that slows it down or stops it.

**bramble** **brambles**
NOUN A **bramble** is a wild bush with thorns. The fruit are called blackberries.

**branch** **branches**
NOUN A **branch** is part of a tree that grows out from the trunk.

**brass**
NOUN **Brass** is a yellow metal made from copper and zinc. It is used for making things like ornaments and some musical instruments.

**brave** **braver, bravest**
ADJECTIVE If you are **brave**, you show you can do something even if it is frightening.
**bravely** ADVERB    **bravery** NOUN

**bread**
NOUN **Bread** is a very common food, made with flour and baked in an oven.

**breadth**
NOUN The **breadth** of something is the distance that it measures from one side to the other.

**break** **breaks, breaking, broke, broken**
VERB **1** If you **break** something, it splits into pieces or stops working.
VERB **2** If you **break** a rule or a promise, you fail to keep it.

**breakdown** **breakdowns**
NOUN If someone's car has a **breakdown**, it stops working during a journey.

**breakfast** **breakfasts**
NOUN **Breakfast** is the first meal of the day.

**breast** **breasts**
NOUN **Breasts** are the two round parts on the front of a woman's body, which can produce milk to feed a baby.

**breath**
NOUN Your **breath** is the air that you take into and let out of your lungs.

**breathe** **breathes, breathing, breathed**
VERB When you **breathe**, you take air into your lungs through your nose or mouth, and then let it out again.

**breed** **breeds**
NOUN A **breed** of an animal is a particular kind. For example, a labrador is a breed of dog.

**breeze** **breezes**
NOUN A **breeze** is a gentle wind.

**brick** **bricks**
NOUN A **brick** is a block used for building. It is made of baked clay.

**bride** **brides**
NOUN A **bride** is a woman on or near her wedding day.

**bridegroom** **bridegrooms**
NOUN A **bridegroom** is a man on or near his wedding day.

**bridesmaid** **bridesmaids**
NOUN A **bridesmaid** is a woman or girl who helps a bride on her wedding day.

**bridge** **bridges**
NOUN A **bridge** is something built over things like rivers, railways or roads, so that people or vehicles can get across.

**brief** **briefer, briefest**
ADJECTIVE Something that is **brief** lasts only a short time.
**briefly** ADVERB

**briefcase** **briefcases**
NOUN A **briefcase** is a flat case used for carrying papers.

**bright** **brighter, brightest**
ADJECTIVE **1 Bright** colours are clear and easy to see.
ADJECTIVE **2** A light that is **bright** shines strongly.
ADJECTIVE **3** Someone who is **bright** is quick at learning or noticing things.

**brilliant**
ADJECTIVE **1** A **brilliant** colour or light is extremely bright.
ADJECTIVE **2** Someone who is **brilliant** is extremely clever or skilful.

**brim** **brims**
NOUN **1** If you fill a cup to the **brim**, you fill it right up to the top.
NOUN **2** The **brim** of a hat is the part that sticks outwards from the head.

**bring** **brings, bringing, brought**
VERB **1** If you **bring** someone on a visit, they come with you.
VERB **2** If you **bring** something, you have it with you when you arrive.

**bristle** **bristles**
NOUN The **bristles** of a brush are the thick hairs or thin pieces of plastic which are fixed to the main part of it.

**brittle**
ADJECTIVE If something is **brittle**, it is hard but easily broken.

**broad** **broader, broadest**
ADJECTIVE Something such as a road or river that is **broad** is very wide.

**broadcast** **broadcasts**
NOUN A **broadcast** is a programme or announcement on radio or television.

**broke**
VERB **Broke** is the past tense of **break**.

**broken**
VERB **Broken** is the past participle of **break**.

**brooch** **brooches**
NOUN A **brooch** is a small piece of jewellery which is worn pinned to a dress, blouse or coat.

**broom** **brooms**
NOUN A **broom** is a kind of brush with a long handle.

**brother** **brothers**
NOUN Someone's **brother** is a boy or man who has the same parents as they have.

**brought**
VERB **Brought** is the past tense of **bring**.

**brown** **browner, brownest**
ADJECTIVE Something that is **brown** is the colour of earth or of wood.
See *Colours* on page 271.

**bruise** **bruises**
NOUN A **bruise** is a purple mark on your skin where something has hit it.

a
**Bb**
c
d
e
f
g
h
i
j
k
l
m
n
o
p
q
r
s
t
u
v
w
x
y
z

# brush

**brush** **brushes**

NOUN A **brush** is a lot of bristles fixed to a handle. Different brushes are used for jobs like cleaning your teeth or painting.

**bubble** **bubbles**

NOUN A **bubble** is a ball of air or gas. You can make bubbles with soapy water. Fizzy lemonade has bubbles, too.

**bucket** **buckets**

NOUN A **bucket** is a container with a handle, often used for carrying water.

**buckle** **buckles**

NOUN A **buckle** is a fastening on the end of a belt or strap.

**bud** **buds**

NOUN A **bud** is a small lump on a plant which will open into a leaf or flower.

**Buddhist** **Buddhists**

NOUN A **Buddhist** is someone who follows the teachings of Buddha.

**budgerigar** **budgerigars**

NOUN Budgerigars are small brightly-coloured birds, often kept as pets.

**buffalo** **buffaloes**

NOUN A **buffalo** is an animal like a large cow with long curved horns.

**bug** **bugs**

NOUN 1 A **bug** is an insect.

NOUN 2 A **bug** is also an illness, such as a flu bug or a stomach bug.

**build** **builds, building, built**

VERB If you **build** something, you make it by joining things together.

**builder** **builders**

NOUN A **builder** is a person whose job is to build houses and other buildings.

**building** **buildings**

NOUN A **building** is a place like a house that has walls and a roof.

**bulb** **bulbs**

NOUN 1 A **bulb** is the glass part of a lamp that gives out light.

NOUN 2 A **bulb** is also a root shaped like an onion. Many spring flowers such as daffodils and tulips grow from bulbs.

**bulge** **bulges, bulging, bulged**

VERB If something **bulges**, it sticks out in a lump. *His pockets **bulged** with conkers.*

**bull** **bulls**

NOUN A **bull** is a male cow, elephant or whale.

**bulldozer** **bulldozers**

NOUN A **bulldozer** is a tractor with a steel blade on the front. It is used for moving large amounts of earth or stone.

**bullet** **bullets**

NOUN 1 A **bullet** is a small piece of metal fired from a gun.

NOUN 2 A **bullet point** is a heavy dot used to draw attention to a piece of text.

**bully** **bullies**

NOUN A **bully** is someone who hurts or frightens other people.

**bump** **bumps, bumping, bumped**

VERB 1 If you **bump** into something, you hit it while you are moving.

NOUN 2 If you hear a **bump**, it sounds like something falling to the ground.

NOUN 3 A **bump** is a raised uneven part on a surface such as a road.

**bumper** **bumpers**

NOUN Bumpers are bars on the front and back of a vehicle that protect it if there is an accident.

**bun** **buns**

NOUN A **bun** is a small round cake.

**bunch** **bunches**

NOUN A **bunch** is a group of things together, like flowers or grapes. *See Collective nouns on page 262.*

**bundle** **bundles**

NOUN A **bundle** is a number of small things that have been tied together.

**bungalow** **bungalows**

NOUN A **bungalow** is a house with all its rooms on one floor.

**bunk beds**

NOUN **Bunk beds** are two single beds fixed one above the other.

**burger** **burgers**

NOUN A **burger** is a flat piece of minced meat. It is often eaten in a bread roll.

**burglar** **burglars**

NOUN A **burglar** is someone who breaks into buildings to steal things.

**burn** **burns, burning, burned** or **burnt**

VERB **1** If something is **burning**, it is being spoiled or destroyed by fire.

VERB **2** People often **burn** fuel, such as coal, to keep warm.

NOUN **3** A **burn** is an injury caused by heat or fire.

**burrow** **burrows**

NOUN A **burrow** is a hole in the ground that an animal lives in.

**burst** **bursts, bursting, burst**

VERB When something like a balloon or tyre **bursts**, it splits open suddenly.

**bury** **buries, burying, buried**

VERB If you **bury** something, you put it in a hole in the ground and cover it.

**bus** **buses**

NOUN A **bus** is a large motor vehicle. People pay to go on buses.

**bush** **bushes**

NOUN A **bush** is a large woody plant with lots of branches. It is smaller than a tree.

**business** **businesses**

NOUN **1** **Business** is the work of making, buying and selling things or services.

NOUN **2** A **business** is a group of people who make and sell things.

**bus stop** **bus stops**

NOUN A **bus stop** is a place where people can get on or off buses.

**busy** **busier, busiest**

ADJECTIVE **1** When you are **busy**, you are working hard on something.

ADJECTIVE **2** A place that is **busy** is full of people doing things or moving about.

**but**

CONJUNCTION You use **but** to join two parts of a sentence when the second part is unexpected. *Megan likes most green vegetables,* **but** *she won't eat broccoli.*

**butcher** **butchers**

NOUN A **butcher** is a shopkeeper who cuts up meat and sells it.

**butter**

NOUN **Butter** is a yellow fat made from cream. You spread it on bread or use it for cooking.

**butterfly** **butterflies**

NOUN A **butterfly** is an insect with four large wings which flies during the day. *See Insects on page 259.*

**button** **buttons**

NOUN **1** A **button** is a small disc used to fasten clothes.

NOUN **2** A **button** is also a part of a machine that you press to make it work.

**buy** **buys, buying, bought**

VERB When you **buy** something, you get it by paying money for it.

**buzz** **buzzes, buzzing, buzzed**

VERB If something **buzzes**, it makes a "zzz" sound like a bee.

# Cc

**cab** cabs

NOUN **1** The **cab** is the place where the driver sits in a bus, truck or train.

NOUN **2** A **cab** is another word for a taxi.

**cabbage** cabbages

NOUN A **cabbage** is a vegetable that looks like a large ball of leaves.

See *Vegetables* on page 256.

**cabin** cabins

NOUN **1** A **cabin** is a room in a ship, boat or aeroplane for passengers or crew.

NOUN **2** A **cabin** is also a small house in a wild place such as a forest.

**cable** cables

NOUN **1** A **cable** is a thick rope or chain.

NOUN **2** A **cable** is also a bundle of wires with a rubber covering, which carries electricity.

NOUN **3** Cable television is a system in which the signals are sent along wires.

**cactus** cactuses

or **cacti**

NOUN A **cactus** is a plant with spines. It can grow in hot, dry places like deserts.

**café** cafés

NOUN A **café** is a place with tables and chairs where you buy drinks and snacks.

**cage** cages

NOUN A **cage** is a box or room with bars in which birds or animals are kept.

**cake** cakes

NOUN A **cake** is a sweet food made with flour, sugar, fat and eggs, and baked in an oven.

**calculate** calculates, calculating, calculated

VERB If you **calculate** something in maths, you work it out.

**calculation** calculations

NOUN A **calculation** is something you work out in maths.

**calculator** calculators

NOUN A **calculator** is a small electronic machine which you can use to give you the answer to different calculations.

**calendar** calendars

NOUN A **calendar** is a list of the months, weeks and days in a year.

**calf** calves

NOUN **1** Calves are young cows, elephants and whales.

See *Young animals* on page 260.

NOUN **2** Your **calf** is the part at the back of your leg between the knee and ankle.

**call** calls, calling, called

VERB **1** If you **call** someone, you shout for them, or telephone them.

VERB **2** If you **call** someone something, you give them a name.

VERB **3** If an animal or thing is **called** something, that is their name.

**calm** calmer, calmest

ADJECTIVE **1** If you are **calm**, you do not seem worried or excited.

ADJECTIVE **2** If the sea is **calm**, it is smooth and still because there is no wind.

**came**

VERB Came is the past tense of **come**.

**camel** camels

NOUN A **camel** is a large animal which carries people and things in the desert.

**camera** cameras

NOUN A **camera** is a piece of equipment you use to take pictures.

**camouflage** **camouflages, camouflaging, camouflaged**
VERB To **camouflage** something is to hide it by giving it the same colour or appearance as its surroundings.

**camp** **camps**
NOUN A **camp** is a place where people stay in tents.

**can** **could; cans**
VERB **1** If you **can** do something, you are able to do it. *I can swim.*
NOUN **2** A **can** is a metal container for something like food, drink or paint.

**canal** **canals**
NOUN A **canal** is a narrow stretch of water made for boats to travel along.

**cancel** **cancels, cancelling, cancelled**
VERB If you **cancel** something that has been planned, you stop it from happening.

**candle** **candles**
NOUN A **candle** is a wax stick with a string called a wick inside. You light the wick and it burns to give light.

**cane** **canes**
NOUN **1** A **cane** is the long hollow stem of a plant such as bamboo.
NOUN **2** A **cane** is a tall narrow stick used to support things.

**cannot**
VERB **Cannot** is the same as **can not**.

**canoe** **canoes**
NOUN A **canoe** is a small light boat, moved with a paddle.

**can't**
VERB **Can't** is a contraction of **cannot**.

**canvas**
NOUN **Canvas** is strong cloth, used for making things like tents and sails.

**canyon** **canyons**
NOUN A **canyon** is a narrow valley with very steep sides, often with a river.

**cap** **caps**
NOUN **1** A **cap** is a soft flat hat with a peak at the front.
NOUN **2** A **cap** is also a small flat lid on a bottle or container.

**capable**
ADJECTIVE If a person is **capable** of doing something, they are able to do it. *He's capable of doing better.*

**capacity** **capacities**
NOUN The **capacity** of something is the largest amount it can hold, produce or carry. *The capacity of this jug is one litre.*

**capital** **capitals**
NOUN **1** The **capital** is the main city in a country. *Paris is the capital of France.*
NOUN **2** A **capital** is a big letter of the alphabet, such as A, B and C. Capital letters are also called upper-case letters. See **lower-case**.
See *Punctuation* on page 264.

**captain** **captains**
NOUN **1** A **captain** is the person in charge of a ship or an aeroplane.
NOUN **2** A **captain** is the person who leads a team in sports like football.

**caption** **captions**
NOUN A **caption** is the words printed underneath a picture which explain what the picture is about.

**capture** **captures, capturing, captured**
VERB If you **capture** somebody, you take them prisoner.

**car** **cars**
NOUN A **car** is a road vehicle with wheels and an engine. It needs a driver and has room for passengers.

a b **Cc** d e f g h i j k l m n o p q r s t u v w x y z

**caravan** **caravans**

NOUN A **caravan** is a vehicle pulled by a car in which people live or spend their holidays.

**card** **cards**

NOUN **1** Card is strong, stiff paper.

NOUN **2** A greetings **card** usually has a picture on the front and is sent to people on special days such as birthdays.

NOUN **3** Playing **cards** are small pieces of card with numbers or pictures on them. They are used for card games.

**cardboard**

NOUN **Cardboard** is thick, stiff paper.

**cardigan** **cardigans**

NOUN A **cardigan** is a knitted jacket. You fasten it at the front with buttons.

**care** **cares, caring, cared**

VERB **1** If you **care** about something or someone, you think they are important.

VERB **2** If you **care** for a person or animal, you look after them.

NOUN **3** If you do something with **care**, you take trouble over it.

**career** **careers**

NOUN Someone's **career** is the work they do, which they hope to do for a long time. *John wants a **career** in teaching.*

**careful**

ADJECTIVE If someone is **careful**, they try to do things safely and well.

**careless**

ADJECTIVE If you are **careless**, you do not pay attention to what you are doing.

**caretaker** **caretakers**

NOUN A **caretaker** is a person who looks after a large building such as a school.

**cargo** **cargoes**

NOUN **Cargo** is the goods carried on a ship or plane.

**carnival** **carnivals**

NOUN A **carnival** is a sort of party in the streets. There is usually music and dancing, and people dress up and decorate cars and trucks.

**carpenter** **carpenters**

NOUN A **carpenter** is a person who works with wood, usually for furniture.

**carpet** **carpets**

NOUN A **carpet** is a thick covering for a floor, often made of wool.

**carriage** **carriages**

NOUN **1** A **carriage** is one of the vehicles that make up a passenger train.

NOUN **2** A **carriage** is also a vehicle with wheels, pulled by horses.

**carrot** **carrots**

NOUN A **carrot** is a long thin orange vegetable that grows under the ground. *See Vegetables on page 256.*

**carry** **carries, carrying, carried**

VERB When you **carry** something, you pick it up and take it with you.

**cart** **carts**

NOUN A **cart** is a heavy wooden vehicle pulled by horses or cattle on farms.

**carton** **cartons**

NOUN A **carton** is a strong cardboard or plastic box for holding food or drink.

**cartoon** **cartoons**

NOUN **1** A **cartoon** is a film where the characters are drawn instead of being real people.

NOUN **2** A **cartoon** is also a funny drawing in a magazine, newspaper or book.

**cartwheel** **cartwheels**

NOUN A **cartwheel** is a movement. You put your hands on the floor and move your legs round in a circle until you land on your feet again.

**carve** **carves, carving, carved**

VERB 1 If you **carve** an object, you cut it out of something like stone or wood.

VERB 2 If someone **carves** a piece of meat, they cut slices from it.

**case** **cases**

NOUN A **case** is a box for keeping or carrying things in.

**cash**

NOUN **Cash** is coins and paper money.

**cassette** **cassettes**

NOUN A **cassette** is a small flat container with magnetic tape inside, which is used for recording and playing back sounds.

**cast** **casts, casting, cast**

NOUN 1 The **cast** of a play or film is all the people who act in it.

NOUN 2 A **cast** is an object made by pouring liquid plaster or metal into a container and leaving it to harden.

VERB 3 If something **casts** a shadow onto a place, it makes a shadow fall there.

VERB 4 If someone like a witch **casts** a spell on someone or something, they do magic that affects that person or thing.

**castle** **castles**

NOUN A **castle** is a large building with walls or ditches round it to protect it from attack.

**cat** **cats**

NOUN A **cat** is a small furry animal, often kept as a pet. There are also larger, wild cats, such as lions and tigers.

**catalogue** **catalogues**

NOUN A **catalogue** is a list of things for sale or for looking at.

**catch** **catches, catching, caught**

VERB 1 If you **catch** something, you take hold of it while it is moving.

VERB 2 If you **catch** a bus or train, you get on it to go somewhere.

VERB 3 If you **catch** something like measles, you get that illness.

**catching**

ADJECTIVE An illness that is **catching** can spread very quickly.

**category** **categories**

NOUN A **category** is a set of things with a particular feature or quality in common.

**caterpillar** **caterpillars**

NOUN A **caterpillar** is a very small animal like a worm with legs, that will change into a butterfly or moth.

**cathedral** **cathedrals**

NOUN A **cathedral** is a large, important church.

**cattle**

NOUN Bulls and cows are called **cattle**.

**caught**

VERB **Caught** is the past tense of **catch**.

**cauliflower** **cauliflowers**

NOUN A **cauliflower** is a round white vegetable with green leaves on the outside.

See *Vegetables* on page 256.

**cause** **causes, causing, caused**

VERB To **cause** something means to make it happen.

**cautious**

ADJECTIVE Someone who is **cautious** acts carefully to avoid possible danger.

a
b
**Cc**
d
e
f
g
h
i
j
k
l
m
n
o
p
q
r
s
t
u
v
w
x
y
z

## cave caves

NOUN A **cave** is a large hole in the side of a hill or cliff, or under the ground.

## CD CDs

NOUN CD is an abbreviation of **compact disc**.

## CD-ROM CD-ROMs

NOUN CD-ROM is an abbreviation of **compact disc read-only memory**. It is a disc which can be played on a computer to show sounds and pictures.

## ceiling ceilings

NOUN The **ceiling** is the inside roof of a room.

## celebrate celebrates, celebrating, celebrated

VERB If you **celebrate** something, you do something enjoyable like having a party, to show it is a special occasion.

## celery

NOUN **Celery** is a vegetable with long, pale green stalks.
See *Vegetables* on page 256.

## cell cells

NOUN 1 Animals and plants are made from tiny parts called **cells**.
NOUN 2 A **cell** is also a small room where a prisoner lives.

## cellar cellars

NOUN A **cellar** is a room under a house where you can store things.

## Celsius

ADJECTIVE You use degrees **Celsius** to measure temperature. In the Celsius scale, 0 degrees (0°C) is the freezing point of water and 100 degrees (100°C) is its boiling point.

## cement

NOUN **Cement** is a grey powder which is mixed with sand and water and used to make bricks stick together.

## cemetery cemeteries

NOUN A **cemetery** is a place where dead people are buried.

## centigrade

ADJECTIVE **Centigrade** means the same as **Celsius**.

## centimetre centimetres

NOUN A **centimetre** (cm) is a measure of length. It is the same as 10 millimetres.

## centipede centipedes

NOUN A **centipede** is a tiny animal like a worm, but with lots of legs.

## central

ADJECTIVE Something that is **central** is in the middle of an object or an area.

## centre centres

NOUN 1 The **centre** of anything is the middle of it.
NOUN 2 A **centre** is a place where people can go for a particular purpose, for example sports.

## century centuries

NOUN A **century** is a period of 100 years. The 21st century is the time between 2000 and 2099.

## cereal cereals

NOUN 1 **Cereal** is a plant which has seeds called grain that can be used for food.
NOUN 2 **Cereal** is also a food made from grain that is often eaten for breakfast.

## ceremony ceremonies

NOUN A **ceremony** is a set of formal actions performed at a special occasion such as a wedding.

**certain**

ADJECTIVE If you are **certain** of something, you are sure it is true.

**certificate** **certificates**

NOUN A **certificate** is a piece of paper which says that something important like a birth or marriage took place.

**chain** **chains**

NOUN A **chain** is made from rings of metal joined together in a line.

**chair** **chairs**

NOUN A **chair** is a seat with a back, for one person.

**chalk**

NOUN **Chalk** is a soft white rock. It can be made into sticks for writing on blackboards.

**champion** **champions**

NOUN A **champion** is a person who has beaten everyone else in a contest.

**chance** **chances**

NOUN **1** If there is a **chance** that something will happen, it might happen.

NOUN **2** If you are given a **chance** to do something, you are allowed to do it if you want to.

by chance PHRASE If something happens **by chance**, it has not been planned.

**change** **changes, changing, changed**

VERB **1** When something **changes**, it becomes different.

VERB **2** When you **change** your clothes, you put on different ones.

NOUN **3** If there is a **change** in something, it is different in some way.

NOUN **4** **Change** is the money you are given when you pay more than the right amount for something.

**channel** **channels**

NOUN **1** A **channel** is a passage for water or other liquid.

NOUN **2** Television companies use **channels** to broadcast programmes.

**chaos**

NOUN **Chaos** is a state of complete confusion, where nothing is organized.

**chapter** **chapters**

NOUN A **chapter** is a part of a book.

**character** **characters**

NOUN **1** The **characters** of a book, film or play are the people it is about.

NOUN **2** Someone's **character** is the sort of person they are. *She has a kind character*.

**charge** **charges, charging, charged**

VERB **1** If someone **charges** you money, they ask you to pay for something.

VERB **2** If something or someone **charges** towards you, they rush forward.

in charge PHRASE If you are **in charge** of something, you are the person looking after it.

**charity** **charities**

NOUN A **charity** is an organization which raises money for a particular cause, such as people in need.

**charm** **charms**

NOUN **1** A **charm** is a small ornament that is fixed to a bracelet or necklace.

NOUN **2** A **charm** is also a magical spell or an object that is supposed to bring good luck.

**chart** **charts**

NOUN **1** A **chart** is a sheet of paper that shows things like dates or numbers.

NOUN **2** A **chart** can also be a map of the sea or of the stars.

**chase** **chases, chasing, chased**

VERB If you **chase** someone, you run after them to try and catch them.

**chat** **chats**

NOUN A **chat** is a friendly talk about things that are not very important.

a b **Cc** d e f g h i j k l m n o p q r s t u v w x y z

a
b
**Cc**
d
e
f
g
h
i
j
k
l
m
n
o
p
q
r
s
t
u
v
w
x
y
z

**cheap** cheaper, cheapest
ADJECTIVE Something **cheap** costs very little, or less than you might expect.

**cheat** cheats, cheating, cheated
VERB When someone **cheats**, they lie or do unfair things to get what they want.

**check** checks, checking, checked
VERB 1 If you **check** something, you make sure it is correct or safe.
NOUN 2 A **check** is a pattern of squares.

**checkout** checkouts
NOUN A **checkout** is the place in a supermarket where you pay.

**cheek** cheeks
NOUN Your **cheeks** are the sides of your face below your eyes.

**cheer** cheers, cheering, cheered
VERB When you **cheer**, you shout to show you are pleased about something or to encourage a person or team.

**cheerful**
ADJECTIVE Someone who is **cheerful** shows they are feeling happy.

**cheese** cheeses
NOUN **Cheese** is a food made from milk. Some cheeses have a strong flavour.

**cheetah** cheetahs
NOUN A **cheetah** is a large wild animal of the cat family, with black spots.

**chemist** chemists
NOUN 1 A **chemist** is a person who makes up medicine.
NOUN 2 The **chemist** is a shop where you can buy medicine and things like soap and toothpaste.

NOUN 3 A **chemist** can be a scientist trained in chemistry.

**chemistry**
NOUN **Chemistry** is the scientific study of how substances are made up and how they work together.

**cheque** cheques
NOUN A **cheque** is a piece of paper that people use to pay for things.

**cherry** cherries
NOUN A **cherry** is a small round red or black fruit with a hard seed called a stone in the middle.
See *Fruit* on page 257.

**chess**
NOUN **Chess** is a game for two people. It is played on a board marked in black and white squares.

**chest** chests
NOUN 1 Your **chest** is the top part of the front of your body, between your neck and your waist.
NOUN 2 A **chest** is a large heavy box, usually made of wood.

**chestnut** chestnuts
NOUN 1 A **chestnut** is a large tree.
NOUN 2 A **chestnut** is also a shiny brown nut that grows on a chestnut tree.

**chew** chews, chewing, chewed
VERB When you **chew** food, you bite it several times.

**chick** chicks
NOUN A **chick** is a baby bird.
See *Young animals* on page 260.

**chicken** chickens
NOUN A **chicken** is a bird kept on a farm for its eggs and meat.

**chickenpox**
NOUN **Chickenpox** is an illness that gives you itchy spots.

**chief** **chiefs**

NOUN A **chief** is a person in charge of other people.

**child** **children**

NOUN A **child** is a young boy or girl.

**childhood**

NOUN A person's **childhood** is the time of life when they are a child.

**childish**

ADJECTIVE You call a person **childish** if they are not acting in an adult way.

**children**

PLURAL NOUN **Children** is the plural of **child**.

**chilly** **chillier, chilliest**

ADJECTIVE If you feel **chilly**, you are not quite warm enough to be comfortable.

**chime** **chimes**

NOUN A **chime** is the musical sound made by a bell or a clock.

**chimney** **chimneys**

NOUN A **chimney** is a pipe which takes smoke from a fire up into the air.

**chimpanzee** **chimpanzees**

NOUN A **chimpanzee** is a small ape with dark fur that lives in forests in Africa.

**chin** **chins**

NOUN Your **chin** is the part of your face below your mouth.

**chip** **chips, chipping, chipped**

NOUN **1** A **chip** is a long thin fried piece of potato.

NOUN **2** A silicon **chip** is a tiny piece of special material used in computers.

VERB **3** When you **chip** something, you break a small piece off it.

**chisel** **chisels**

NOUN A **chisel** is a tool with a long thin blade and a sharp end, which is used for cutting wood or stone.

**chocolate** **chocolates**

NOUN **1** **Chocolate** is a brown sweet or drink made from cocoa.

NOUN **2** A **chocolate** is a sweet covered with a layer of chocolate.

**choice** **choices**

NOUN **1** A **choice** is the different things that you can choose from.

NOUN **2** A **choice** can also be someone or something that you choose. *If you need a captain, Jessica would be a good **choice**.*

**choir** **choirs**

NOUN A **choir** is a group of people who sing together.

**choke** **chokes, choking, choked**

VERB If you **choke**, you cannot breathe because not enough air can get to your lungs. *He **choked** on a chicken bone.*

**choose** **chooses, choosing, chose, chosen**

VERB To **choose** something is to decide which thing you want to have or do.

**chop** **chops, chopping, chopped**

VERB **1** When someone **chops** something like wood, they cut it with an axe.

NOUN **2** A **chop** is a slice of meat on a bone.

**chorus** **choruses**

NOUN A **chorus** is a part of a song which is repeated after each verse.

a
b
Cc
d
e
f
g
h
i
j
k
l
m
n
o
p
q
r
s
t
u
v
w
x
y
z

**chose**

VERB **Chose** is the past tense of **choose**.

**chosen**

VERB **Chosen** is the past participle of **choose**.

**Christian** **Christians**

NOUN A **Christian** is someone who follows the teachings of Jesus Christ.

**Christmas** **Christmases**

NOUN **Christmas** is a Christian festival held on December 25, when the birth of Jesus Christ is celebrated.

**chrysalis** **chrysalises**

NOUN A **chrysalis** is a butterfly or moth when it is developing from a caterpillar to a fully grown adult.

**chuckle** **chuckles, chuckling, chuckled**

VERB When you **chuckle**, you laugh quietly.

**church** **churches**

NOUN A **church** is a building where Christians worship.

**cigarette** **cigarettes**

NOUN A **cigarette** is a thin roll of paper with tobacco in, which people smoke.

**cinema** **cinemas**

NOUN A **cinema** is a place where people watch films.

**circle** **circles**

NOUN A **circle** is a perfect round shape.
**circular** ADJECTIVE
See *Colours and flat shapes* on page 271.

**circuit** **circuits**

NOUN A **circuit** is the complete path that an electric current flows through. You can make a simple circuit with a battery, a bulb and wires.

**circumference** **circumferences**

NOUN The **circumference** of a circle is the distance around its edge.

**circus** **circuses**

NOUN A **circus** is a travelling group of people such as clowns and acrobats.

**city** **cities**

NOUN A **city** is a large busy town.

**claim** **claims, claiming, claimed**

VERB **1** If someone **claims** something, they ask for it because it is theirs.
VERB **2** If you **claim** something is the case, you say it is the case. *Amy **claims** she was the first to finish.*

**clap** **claps, clapping, clapped**

VERB When you **clap**, you make a noise by hitting your hands together.

**class** **classes**

NOUN **1** A **class** is a group of people who are taught together.
NOUN **2** A **class** is also a group of people or things that are alike in some way.

**classify** **classifies, classifying, classified**

VERB To **classify** things is to arrange them in groups with similar features. *These books are **classified** as non-fiction.*

**classroom** **classrooms**

NOUN A **classroom** is a room in a school where children have lessons.

**clause** **clauses**

NOUN In grammar, a **clause** is a group of words with a subject and a verb. It may be a complete sentence or one part of a sentence. For example, "the girl laughed" is a clause because it has a subject (the girl) and a verb (laughed).

**claw** **claws**

NOUN The **claws** of a bird or animal are the hard curved nails at the end of its feet.

**clay**

NOUN **Clay** is a type of sticky earth that goes hard when it is dry. It is used to make bricks and pots.

**clean** **cleaner, cleanest**

ADJECTIVE If something is **clean**, it is free from dirt.

**clear** **clearer, clearest; clears, clearing, cleared**

ADJECTIVE **1** If a thing is **clear**, you can see through it.

ADJECTIVE **2** If something you say or write is **clear**, it is easy to understand.

VERB **3** If you **clear** an area, you move things that are not wanted out of the way.

**clench** **clenches, clenching, clenched**

VERB When you **clench** your fist or teeth, you close them tightly.

**clever** **cleverer, cleverest**

ADJECTIVE Someone who is **clever** is able to learn and understand things easily.

**click** **clicks, clicking, clicked**

VERB When you **click** something, it makes a short snapping sound.

**cliff** **cliffs**

NOUN A **cliff** is a steep hill by the sea.

**climate** **climates**

NOUN The **climate** of a place is the sort of weather it usually has.

**climb** **climbs, climbing, climbed**

VERB When you **climb** something, you move upwards using your hands and feet.

**cling** **clings, clinging, clung**

VERB If you **cling** to someone or something, you hold onto them tightly.

**clinic** **clinics**

NOUN A **clinic** is where people go to get help from a doctor or nurse.

**clip** **clips, clipping, clipped**

NOUN **1** A **clip** is something small and springy which holds things in place.

VERB **2** If you **clip** something like a hedge, you cut small pieces off it.

**cloak** **cloaks**

NOUN A **cloak** is a loose coat without sleeves that fastens at the neck.

**cloakroom** **cloakrooms**

NOUN A **cloakroom** is a room where coats can be left.

**clock** **clocks**

NOUN A **clock** is an instrument that measures and shows the time.

**clockwise**

ADVERB If something goes **clockwise**, it moves in the same direction as the hands on a clock.

**clockwork**

ADJECTIVE **Clockwork** toys move when they are wound up with a key.

**close** **closer, closest; closes, closing, closed**

(*rhymes with* **dose**) ADJECTIVE **1** If something is **close**, it is very near.

(*rhymes with* **doze**) VERB **2** When you **close** something like a door, you shut it.

**closed**

ADJECTIVE If something is **closed**, it is not open.

**cloth** **cloths**

NOUN **1** Cloth is material made from something like cotton or wool.

NOUN **2** A **cloth** is a piece of cloth used for cleaning.

**clothes**

PLURAL NOUN **Clothes** are the things people wear, such as shirts, trousers and dresses.

**cloud** **clouds**

NOUN **1** A **cloud** is a patch of white or grey mist that floats in the sky.

NOUN **2** You can use **cloud** to describe a lot of smoke, steam or dust.

**cloudy** ADJECTIVE

**clover**

NOUN **Clover** is a small wild plant. It has white or purple flowers, and leaves divided into three parts.

**clown** **clowns**

NOUN A **clown** is someone in a circus who wears funny clothes and does silly things to make people laugh.

**club** **clubs**

NOUN A **club** is an organization joined by people who are interested in the same thing, such as chess or riding.

**clue** **clues**

NOUN A **clue** is something that helps to solve a problem or mystery.

**clump** **clumps**

NOUN A **clump** is a small group of plants growing together.

**clumsy** **clumsier, clumsiest**

ADJECTIVE Someone who is **clumsy** moves awkwardly and carelessly.

**clumsily** ADVERB

**clung**

VERB **Clung** is the past tense of **cling**.

**cluster** **clusters**

NOUN A **cluster** is a number of things close together in a small group.

**clutch** **clutches, clutching, clutched**

VERB **1** If you **clutch** something, you hold it tightly with your hand.

NOUN **2** A **clutch** is a group of eggs laid by a bird.

See *Collective nouns* on page 262.

**clutter**

NOUN **Clutter** is an untidy mess.

**co-**

PREFIX Co- means together. For example, "coeducation" is boys and girls being taught together.

See *Prefixes* on page 264.

**coach** **coaches**

NOUN **1** A **coach** is a long motor vehicle used for taking passengers on long journeys.

NOUN **2** A **coach** is also a section of a train that carries passengers.

NOUN **3** A **coach** is someone who trains you for a sport or gives you extra lessons.

**coal**

NOUN **Coal** is a hard black rock which is dug out of the ground and burned to give heat.

**coarse** **coarser, coarsest**

ADJECTIVE Anything that is **coarse** looks and feels rough.

**coast** **coasts**

NOUN The **coast** is the place where the land meets the sea.

**coat** **coats**

NOUN **1** A **coat** is a piece of clothing with long sleeves, that you wear over other clothes when you go out.

NOUN **2** An animal's **coat** is its fur.

NOUN **3** A layer of paint is called a **coat**.

**cobweb** **cobwebs**

NOUN A **cobweb** is a net made by a spider to trap insects.

**cock** **cocks**
NOUN A **cock** is any male bird.

**cocoa**
NOUN **Cocoa** is a brown powder made from the seeds of the cacao tree, and also a hot drink made from this powder.

**coconut** **coconuts**
NOUN A **coconut** is a large nut with white flesh, milky juice, and a hard hairy shell.

**cocoon** **cocoons**
NOUN A **cocoon** is a covering of silky threads that some young insects make for themselves before they grow into adults.

**cod**
NOUN A **cod** is a large sea fish which is caught for food.

**code** **codes**
NOUN **1** A **code** is a system of changing letters in a message for other letters or symbols, so that only people who know the code can read it.
NOUN **2** A **code** is also a group of letters and numbers that identify something. *Do you know the telephone* **code** *for York?*
NOUN **3** A **code** is also a set of rules.

**coffee**
NOUN **Coffee** is a coarse powder made by grinding roasted coffee beans, and also a hot drink made from this powder.

**cog** **cogs**
NOUN A **cog** is a wheel with teeth which turns another part of a machine.

**coil** **coils**
NOUN A **coil** is a series of loops into which something has been wound.

**coin** **coins**
NOUN A **coin** is a small piece of metal used as money.

**cold** **colder, coldest; colds**
ADJECTIVE **1** If the weather is **cold**, the temperature outside is low.
NOUN **2** A **cold** is a common illness. You sneeze and your nose feels blocked.

**collage** **collages**
NOUN A **collage** is a picture made by sticking pieces of paper or cloth onto a surface.

**collapse** **collapses, collapsing, collapsed**
VERB If someone or something **collapses**, they suddenly fall down.

**collar** **collars**
NOUN **1** The **collar** of a shirt or jacket is the part that fits round your neck.
NOUN **2** A **collar** is also a leather band round the neck of a dog or cat.

**collect** **collects, collecting, collected**
VERB **1** If you **collect** a number of things, you bring them together for a special reason. *She* **collected** *sticks for firewood.*
VERB **2** If you **collect** someone or something from a place, you call there and take them away. *We had to* **collect** *her from school.*

**collection** **collections**
NOUN A **collection** is a group of things brought together over a period of time. *My dad's got a huge stamp* **collection**.

**collective noun** **collective nouns**
NOUN In grammar, a **collective noun** refers to a group of things. For example, a group of sheep is called a "flock". See *Collective nouns* on page 262.

**college** **colleges**
NOUN A **college** is where people go to study after they have left school.

**collide** **collides, colliding, collided**
VERB If a moving object **collides** with something, it hits it.
**collision** NOUN

**colon** **colons**
NOUN The punctuation mark : is a **colon**. You can use it in several ways, for example in front of a list of things.
See *Punctuation* on page 264.

**colour** **colours**
NOUN The **colour** of something is the way it looks in daylight. *The colour of grass is green.*
See *Colours* on page 271.

**colt** **colts**
NOUN A **colt** is a young male horse.

**column** **columns**
NOUN **1** A **column** is a tall stone post which supports part of a building.

NOUN **2** A **column** is also a vertical strip of print in a newspaper or magazine.
NOUN **3** If numbers are arranged in vertical lists, these are called **columns**.

**comb** **combs**
NOUN A **comb** is a flat piece of plastic or metal with narrow teeth on one edge. You use it to tidy your hair.

**come** **comes, coming, came, come**
VERB **1** To **come** to a place is to move there or arrive there.
VERB **2** If you **come** from a place, you were born there, or it is your home.

**comedy** **comedies**
NOUN A **comedy** is a play or film that makes people laugh.

**comet** **comets**
NOUN A **comet** is an object which travels around the sun, leaving a long bright trail behind it.

**comfort** **comforts, comforting, comforted**
VERB If you **comfort** someone, you make them feel less worried or unhappy.

**comfortable**
ADJECTIVE If something is **comfortable**, it is easy to wear or use.

**comic** **comics**
NOUN A **comic** is a magazine that tells stories in pictures.

**comma** **commas**
NOUN A **comma** is a punctuation mark (,) which is used to separate parts of a sentence or items on a list.
See *Punctuation* on page 264.

**command** **commands, commanding, commanded**
VERB If you **command** someone to do something, you order them to do it.

**commercial** **commercials**
NOUN A **commercial** is an advertisement on television or radio.

**common**
ADJECTIVE If something is **common**, you often see it or it often happens.

**common noun** **common nouns**
NOUN **Common nouns** name things in general. For example, "boy", "dog" and "computer" are all common nouns.
See *Noun* on page 262.

**common sense**
NOUN If you have **common sense**, you usually act sensibly and do the right thing.

**commotion**

NOUN A **commotion** is a lot of noise, confusion and excitement.

**communicate** **communicates, communicating, communicated**

VERB If you **communicate** with someone, you give them information by talking or writing to them.

**compact disc** **compact discs**

NOUN A **compact disc** is a round flat silver-coloured object which can store information. It is called a **CD** for short.

**company** **companies**

NOUN **1 Company** is being with others so you are not lonely.

NOUN **2** A **company** is a group of people who work together to make or sell things.

**comparative** **comparatives**

NOUN In grammar, the **comparative** is the form of an adjective which has "more" of that adjective. For example, "happier" is the comparative of "happy".

See *Adjective* on page 263.

**compare** **compares, comparing, compared**

VERB When you **compare** two or more things, you look at them to see in what ways they are the same or different.

**compass** **compasses**

NOUN **1** A **compass** is an instrument with a needle that always points to north.

NOUN **2** A **pair of compasses** is an instrument used for drawing circles.

**compass point** **compass points**

NOUN The main **compass points** are north, south, east and west.

**competition** **competitions**

NOUN A **competition** is an event to find out who is best at doing something.

**complain** **complains, complaining, complained**

VERB If you **complain**, you say that you are not happy about something.

**complete**

ADJECTIVE **1** If something is **complete**, it has been finished.

ADJECTIVE **2** If you talk about a **complete** thing, you mean all of it. *I need a complete change of clothes.*

**complicated**

ADJECTIVE Something **complicated** is made up of so many parts that it is difficult to understand or deal with.

**compose** **composes, composing, composed**

VERB If you **compose** something, like a poem or a piece of music, you write it.

**compound** **compounds**

NOUN In language, a **compound** is a word that is made up of two or more words. "Playground", "armchair" and "toothache" are all compounds.

**computer** **computers**

NOUN A **computer** is a machine that stores information and works things out according to instructions in a program.

**concave**

ADJECTIVE A **concave** surface curves inwards.

**conceal** **conceals, concealing, concealed**

VERB If you **conceal** something, you hide it carefully.

**concentrate** **concentrates, concentrating, concentrated**

VERB If you **concentrate** on something, you give it all your attention.

**concerned**

ADJECTIVE If you are **concerned** about something, it worries you.

**concert** concerts

NOUN A **concert** is a performance by musicians, usually in a big hall.

**conclusion** conclusions

NOUN **1** A **conclusion** is something you decide is true after you have thought carefully.

NOUN **2** The **conclusion** of something is its ending.

**concrete**

NOUN **Concrete** is a building material made of cement, sand and water, which goes hard when it is set.

**condition** conditions

NOUN **1** The **condition** of something is the state it is in.

NOUN **2** A **condition** is a rule you must agree to before you are allowed to do something. *You can go out on one condition – you must be home by five.*

**conductor** conductors

NOUN A **conductor** is someone who controls the way musicians play together.

**cone** cones

NOUN A **cone** is a solid curved shape with a flat circular base and a pointed top.

See *Solid shapes* on page 271.

**confess** confesses, confessing, confessed

VERB If you **confess**, you say that you have done something wrong.

**confident**

ADJECTIVE **1** If you are **confident** about something, you are sure about it.

ADJECTIVE **2** People who are **confident** know that they can do something well.

**confuse** confuses, confusing, confused

VERB **1** To **confuse** someone means to make them unsure what to do. *The new road layout confused everyone.*

VERB **2** If you **confuse** two things, you mix them up by mistake. *I always confuse the twins because they are so alike.*

**congratulate** congratulates, congratulating, congratulated

VERB If you **congratulate** someone, you say you are pleased that something special has happened to them.

**conjunction** conjunctions

NOUN In grammar, a **conjunction** is a word that joins two other words or parts of a sentence. "And", "but", "while" and "although" are all conjunctions.

**conker** conkers

NOUN **Conkers** are hard brown nuts from a horse chestnut tree.

**connect** connects, connecting, connected

VERB If you **connect** two things, you join them together.

**connective** connectives

NOUN In grammar, a **connective** is a word or phrase that joins parts of a text. For example, "and", "at last" and "because" are connectives.

**conquer** conquers, conquering, conquered

VERB To **conquer** people is to take control of their country by force.

**conscious**

ADJECTIVE If you are **conscious**, you are awake and know what is happening.

**consecutive**

ADJECTIVE If things are **consecutive**, they happen one after the other. *October, November and December are consecutive months.*

**consider** considers, considering, considered

VERB If you **consider** something, you think about it carefully.

**consist** consists, consisting, consisted

VERB Something that **consists** of particular things is made up of them.

**consonant** consonants

NOUN A **consonant** is any letter of the alphabet except a, e, i, o and u. See **vowel**.

**constant**

ADJECTIVE Something that is **constant** happens all the time. *She complained of a constant headache.*

**construct** constructs, constructing, constructed

VERB If you **construct** something, you build it or make it.

**consume** consumes, consuming, consumed

VERB If you **consume** something, you eat or drink it, or use it up.

**contain** contains, containing, contained

VERB The things that something **contains** are the things in it.

**container** containers

NOUN A **container** is something you put things in.

**content**

ADJECTIVE If you are **content**, you are happy and satisfied with your life.

**contents**

PLURAL NOUN The **contents** of something like a box or cake are the things in it. The **contents page** of a book tells you what is in it.

**contest** contests

NOUN A **contest** is a competition or game which you try to win.

**continent** continents

NOUN A **continent** is a very large area of land, such as Africa or Asia.

**continue** continues, continuing, continued

VERB If you **continue** to do something, you go on doing it.

**continuous**

ADJECTIVE Something that is **continuous** goes on without stopping.

**contraction** contractions

NOUN A **contraction** is a shortened form of word or words. For example, "I'm" is a contraction of "I am".

**contradict** contradicts, contradicting, contradicted

VERB If you **contradict** someone, you say the opposite of what they have just said.

**control** controls, controlling, controlled

VERB **1** If you **control** something, you make it behave exactly as you want it to. NOUN **2** The **controls** on a machine are knobs or other things used to work it.

**convenient**

ADJECTIVE If something is **convenient**, it is easy to use or do.

**conversation** conversations

NOUN If you have a **conversation** with someone, you talk to each other.

**convex**

ADJECTIVE A **convex** surface curves outwards.

# convince

**convince** convinces, convincing, convinced
VERB If someone or something **convinces** you, they make you believe that something is true.

**cook** cooks, cooking, cooked
VERB When you **cook** food, you prepare it for eating by heating it.

**cooker** cookers
NOUN A **cooker** is a piece of equipment for cooking food.

**cool** cooler, coolest
ADJECTIVE If something is **cool**, its temperature is low but it is not cold.

**coordinates**
NOUN **Coordinates** are two numbers or letters which help you find the exact position of something. They are often used on maps, graphs and charts.

**cope** copes, coping, coped
VERB If you **cope** with a task or problem, you deal with it successfully.

**copper**
NOUN **Copper** is a reddish-brown metal.

**copy** copies, copying, copied
NOUN **1** A **copy** is something made to look exactly like something else.
VERB **2** If you **copy** something, you make a copy of it.
VERB **3** If you **copy** what someone does, you do the same thing.

**coral** corals
NOUN **Coral** is a hard substance that forms in the sea from the skeletons of tiny animals called corals.

**cord** cords
NOUN **Cord** is thick, strong string.

**core** cores
NOUN The **core** of a fruit is the hard part in the middle that contains seeds.

**cork** corks
NOUN **1** **Cork** is the light bark of the cork oak tree.
NOUN **2** A **cork** is a piece of cork used to block the open end of a bottle.

**corn**
NOUN **Corn** is a cereal crop, such as wheat or sweet corn.

**corner** corners
NOUN A **corner** is the place where two edges or roads join.

**correct** corrects, correcting, corrected
ADJECTIVE **1** Something that is **correct** is true and has no mistakes.
VERB **2** If you **correct** your work, you put right any mistakes you made.

**corridor** corridors
NOUN A **corridor** is a long passage in a building or train.

**cost** costs, costing, cost
VERB If something **costs** an amount of money, you can buy it for that amount.

**costume** costumes
NOUN A **costume** is the clothes worn by an actor, or that people wear for special events.

**cosy** cosier, cosiest
ADJECTIVE A house or room that is **cosy** is comfortable and warm, and not too big.

**cot** cots
NOUN A **cot** is a bed with high sides for a baby or a young child.

**cottage** cottages

NOUN A **cottage** is a small house, usually in the country.

**cotton**

NOUN **1 Cotton** is cloth made from the soft fibres of the cotton plant.

NOUN **2 Cotton** is also a thread used for sewing.

NOUN **3 Cotton wool** is soft fluffy cotton, often used for cleaning the skin.

**cough** coughs

NOUN A **cough** is a noise made by someone forcing air out of their throat.

**could**

VERB **1 Could** is part of the verb **can**. You use **could** to say that something might happen. *It could rain tomorrow.*

VERB **2** You also say **could** when you are asking for something politely. *Could you please tell me the way to the station?*

**council** councils

NOUN The **council** is a group of people who look after the affairs of a town, district or county.

**count** counts, counting, counted

VERB **1** When you **count**, you say numbers in order. *Count up to a hundred.*

VERB **2** If you **count** a number of things, you are finding out how many there are.

**counter** counters

NOUN **1** A **counter** is a long narrow table in a shop, where things are sold.

NOUN **2** A **counter** is also a small round flat object, usually made of plastic, that is used in board games.

**country** countries

NOUN **1** A **country** is a land that has its own government and language.

NOUN **2** The **country** is land away from towns and cities.

**couple** couples

NOUN **1** A **couple** of things or people means two of them. *It should only take a couple of days.*

NOUN **2** Two people are sometimes called a **couple**, especially if they are married or having a relationship.

**coupon** coupons

NOUN A **coupon** is a piece of printed paper that allows you to pay less than usual for something.

**courage**

NOUN **Courage** is not showing that you are afraid of something.

**course** courses

NOUN **1** A **course** is a series of lessons.

NOUN **2** A **course** can also be one part of a meal.

**of course** PHRASE You use **of course** to make something you are saying stronger. *Of course I still want to go.*

**court** courts

NOUN **1** A **court** is an area marked out for a game like tennis or badminton.

NOUN **2** A **court** is also a place where things to do with the law are decided.

NOUN **3** The **court** of a king or queen is where they live with their family.

**courtyard** courtyards

NOUN A **courtyard** is an open flat area of ground with walls all round it.

**cousin** cousins

NOUN Your **cousin** is a child of your uncle or aunt.

**cover** covers, covering, covered

VERB **1** If you **cover** something, you put something over it to protect or hide it.

NOUN **2** The **covers** on a bed are the blankets or duvet that you have over you to keep you warm.

NOUN **3** The **cover** of a book or magazine is the outside of it.

a
b
Cc
d
e
f
g
h
i
j
k
l
m
n
o
p
q
r
s
t
u
v
w
x
y
z

**cow** **cows**

NOUN A **cow** is a large farm animal that gives milk.

**coward** **cowards**

NOUN A **coward** is someone who avoids anything dangerous, painful or difficult.

**cowboy** **cowboys**

NOUN A **cowboy** is a man whose job is to look after cattle.

**crab** **crabs**

NOUN A **crab** is a sea animal. It has four pairs of legs, two pincers, and a flat round body covered by a shell.

**crack** **cracks, cracking, cracked**

VERB **1** If you **crack** something, or it cracks, it has a small split in it but does not quite break.

NOUN **2** A **crack** is the line on something that shows it is nearly broken.

NOUN **3** A **crack** is also a sudden loud noise.

**cracker** **crackers**

NOUN **1** A **cracker** is a thin crisp biscuit, often slightly salty.

NOUN **2** A **cracker** can be a cardboard tube covered in coloured paper, that people have at parties. It makes a sharp sound when you pull the ends apart.

**cradle** **cradles**

NOUN A **cradle** is a small box-shaped bed for a baby.

**crane** **cranes**

NOUN **1** A **crane** is a machine that moves heavy things by lifting them.

**crane**

NOUN **2** A **crane** is also a large water bird with long legs and a long neck.

**crash** **crashes, crashing, crashed**

NOUN **1** A **crash** is a traffic accident.

NOUN **2** A **crash** is also a sudden loud noise like something breaking.

VERB **3** If something **crashes**, it hits something else and makes a loud noise.

**crate** **crates**

NOUN A **crate** is a large box used for transporting or storing things.

**crawl** **crawls, crawling, crawled**

VERB When you **crawl**, you move forward on your hands and knees.

**crayon** **crayons**

NOUN A **crayon** is a coloured pencil.

**craze** **crazes**

NOUN A **craze** is something that is very popular for a short time.

**crazy** **crazier, craziest**

ADJECTIVE **1** Someone or something **crazy** is very strange or foolish.

ADJECTIVE **2** If you are **crazy** about something, you are very keen on it.

**creak** **creaks, creaking, creaked**

VERB If something **creaks**, it makes an odd squeaking sound.

**cream**

ADJECTIVE **1** Something that is **cream** in colour is yellowish-white.

NOUN **2** Cream is the pale yellow liquid taken from the top of milk.

**crease** **creases, creasing, creased**

NOUN **1** A **crease** is a line made by folding or wrinkling something.

VERB **2** If you **crease** something, you make lines appear on it.

**create** **creates, creating, created**

VERB To **create** something means to cause it to happen, or exist.

**creature** **creatures**

NOUN A **creature** is any animal, such as a bird, fish or insect.

**creep** creeps, creeping, crept
VERB If you **creep** somewhere, you move quietly and slowly.

**crescent** crescents
NOUN A **crescent** is a curved shape that is wider in the middle than at the ends, like a new moon.

**crew** crews
NOUN A **crew** is the people who work on a ship, aircraft or spaceship.

**cricket** crickets
NOUN **1** Cricket is an outdoor game between two teams of eleven players.
NOUN **2** A **cricket** is a small jumping insect that makes a chirping sound by rubbing its wings together.

**cried**
VERB **Cried** is the past tense of **cry**.

**cries**
VERB **Cries** is a present tense form of **cry**.

**crime** crimes
NOUN A **crime** is something which is against the law.

**criminal** criminals
NOUN A **criminal** is someone who has done something that is against the law.

**crimson**
ADJECTIVE **Crimson** is dark red.

**crinkle** crinkles, crinkling, crinkled
VERB When something **crinkles**, it becomes slightly creased.

**crisp** crisper, crispest; crisps
ADJECTIVE **1** Things like fruit and biscuits that are **crisp** are fresh and firm.
NOUN **2** A **crisp** is a crunchy, thinly sliced piece of fried potato.

**criticize** criticizes, criticizing, criticized;
also spelt criticise
VERB If you **criticize** someone, you say what you think is wrong with them.

**crocodile** crocodiles
NOUN A **crocodile** is a large reptile, about five metres long.
See *Reptiles* on page 259.

**crocus** crocuses
NOUN **Crocuses** are small yellow, purple or white spring flowers.

**crooked**
ADJECTIVE Something that is **crooked** is bent or twisted.

**crop** crops
NOUN A **crop** is plants grown for food.

**cross** crosser, crossest; crosses, crossing, crossed
ADJECTIVE **1** Someone who is **cross** is angry about something.
NOUN **2** A **cross** is a mark like + or ×.
VERB **3** If you **cross** something like a road, you go from one side to the other.

**crossing** crossings
NOUN A **crossing** is a place where you can cross the road safely.

**crouch** crouches, crouching, crouched
VERB If you **crouch** down, you bend your legs under you so that you are close to the ground.

a
b
**Cc**
d
e
f
g
h
i
j
k
l
m
n
o
p
q
r
s
t
u
v
w
x
y
z

**crow** **crows**

NOUN A **crow** is a large black bird.

**crowd** **crowds**

NOUN A **crowd** is a large number of people together in one place.

**crowded**

ADJECTIVE A place that is **crowded** is full of people.

**crown** **crowns**

NOUN A **crown** is an ornament that kings and queens sometimes wear on their heads.

**cruel** **crueller, cruellest**

ADJECTIVE Someone who is **cruel** hurts people or animals without caring.

**cruise** **cruises**

NOUN A **cruise** is a holiday on a ship that travels to different places.

**crumb** **crumbs**

NOUN A **crumb** is a very small piece of dry food such as bread or biscuit.

**crumble** **crumbles, crumbling, crumbled**

VERB If you **crumble** something that is soft, it breaks into lots of little pieces.

**crumple** **crumples, crumpling, crumpled**

VERB If you **crumple** paper or cloth, you squash it so that it is full of creases.

**crunch** **crunches, crunching, crunched**

VERB If you **crunch** something, you crush it noisily, for example between your teeth or under your feet.

**crush** **crushes, crushing, crushed**

VERB To **crush** something is to destroy its shape by squeezing it.

**crust** **crusts**

NOUN The **crust** is a hard layer on the outside of something such as bread.

**cry** **cries, crying, cried**

VERB **1** When you **cry**, tears come from your eyes.

NOUN **2** A **cry** is a sudden sound that you make when you are surprised or hurt.

**crystal** **crystals**

NOUN A **crystal** is a mineral that has formed into a regular shape.

**cub** **cubs**

NOUN A **cub** is a young wild animal such as a lion, fox or bear.
See *Young animals* on page 260.

**cube** **cubes**

NOUN A **cube** is a solid shape with six square faces all the same size.
See *Solid shapes* on page 271.

**cuboid** **cuboids**

NOUN A **cuboid** is a rectangular box shape with six faces. All the faces are rectangles.
See *Solid shapes* on page 271.

**cuckoo** **cuckoos**

NOUN A **cuckoo** is a grey bird. Cuckoos lay their eggs in other birds' nests.

**cucumber** **cucumbers**

NOUN A **cucumber** is a long, thin, dark green vegetable, eaten raw.
See *Vegetables* on page 256.

**cuddle** **cuddles, cuddling, cuddled**

VERB When you **cuddle** someone, you put your arms round them.

**culprit** **culprits**

NOUN A **culprit** is someone who has done something harmful or wrong.

**cunning**

ADJECTIVE Someone who is **cunning** plans to get what they want, often by tricking other people.

**cup** **cups**

NOUN **1** A **cup** is a small container with a handle, which you drink out of.

NOUN **2** A **cup** is also a prize for the winner of a game or competition.

**cupboard cupboards**
NOUN A **cupboard** is a piece of furniture with doors and shelves.

**cure cures, curing, cured**
NOUN **1** A **cure** is something that makes people better when they have been ill.
VERB **2** If someone or something **cures** a person, they make them well again.

**curiosity**
NOUN **Curiosity** is wanting to know about things.

**curious**
ADJECTIVE **1** Someone who is **curious** wants to know more about something.
ADJECTIVE **2** Something that is **curious** is unusual and hard to explain.

**curl curls, curling, curled**
VERB **1** If an animal **curls** up, it makes itself into a rounded shape.
NOUN **2** **Curls** are pieces of hair shaped in curves and circles.
**curly** ADJECTIVE

**currant currants**
NOUN **Currants** are small dried grapes.

**current currents**
NOUN **1** A **current** is a steady movement of water or air.
NOUN **2** A **current** is also the movement of electricity through a wire.

**curriculum curriculums or curricula**
NOUN A **curriculum** is the different courses taught at a school or college.

**curry curries**
NOUN **Curry** is an Indian dish made with spices.

**cursor cursors**
NOUN A **cursor** is a small sign on a computer screen that shows where the next letter or number will appear.

**curtain curtains**
NOUN A **curtain** is a large piece of material that you pull across a window to cover it.

**curve curves**
NOUN A **curve** is a smooth, gradually bending line.
**curved** ADJECTIVE

**cushion cushions**
NOUN A **cushion** is a soft object put on a seat to make it more comfortable.

**custom customs**
NOUN A **custom** is something that people usually do. *It's his custom to take the dog for a walk after supper.*

**customer customers**
NOUN A **customer** is a person who buys something, especially from a shop.

**cut cuts, cutting, cut**
VERB **1** If you **cut** yourself, you hurt yourself by accident on something sharp.
VERB **2** If you **cut** something, you use a knife or scissors to remove parts of it.

**cutlery**
NOUN **Cutlery** is the knives, forks and spoons that you eat your food with.

**cycle cycles, cycling, cycled**
NOUN **1** A **cycle** is a bicycle.
VERB **2** If you **cycle**, you ride a bicycle.
**cyclist** NOUN

**cygnet cygnets**
NOUN A **cygnet** is a young swan.
See *Young animals* on page 260.

**cylinder cylinders**
NOUN A **cylinder** is a three-dimensional shape like a tube with flat circular ends.
**cylindrical** ADJECTIVE
See *Solid shapes* on page 271.

# Dd

**dad** **dads**
NOUN Your **dad** is your father.

**daffodil** **daffodils**
NOUN A **daffodil** is a yellow trumpet-shaped flower that blooms in the spring.

**dagger** **daggers**
NOUN A **dagger** is a weapon like a knife.

**daily**
ADJECTIVE Something that is **daily** happens every day.

**dairy** **dairies**
NOUN A **dairy** is a shop or company that sells milk and food made from milk, such as butter and cheese.

**daisy** **daisies**
NOUN A **daisy** is a small wild flower with white petals and a yellow centre.

**dam** **dams**
NOUN A **dam** is a wall built across a river or stream to hold back water.

**damage** **damages, damaging, damaged**
VERB To **damage** something means to harm or spoil it.

**damp** **damper, dampest**
ADJECTIVE Something that is **damp** is slightly wet.

**dance** **dances, dancing, danced**
VERB When you **dance**, you move your body in time to music.

**dandelion** **dandelions**
NOUN A **dandelion** is a wild plant with bright yellow flowers.

**danger** **dangers**
NOUN A **danger** is something that could harm you.

**dangerous**
ADJECTIVE If something is **dangerous**, it is likely to harm you.

**dare** **dares, daring, dared**
VERB If you **dare** to do something, you are brave enough to do it.

**dark** **darker, darkest**
ADJECTIVE When it is **dark**, there is not enough light to see properly.
**darkness** NOUN

**dart** **darts, darting, darted**
VERB **1** If a person or animal **darts**, they move suddenly and quickly.
NOUN **2** A **dart** is a short arrow that you throw in the game of darts.

**dash** **dashes, dashing, dashed**
VERB **1** If you **dash** somewhere, you run or go there quickly.
NOUN **2** A **dash** is the punctuation mark (–) which shows a change of subject, or which may be used instead of brackets. See *Punctuation* on page 264.

**data**
NOUN **Data** is information, usually in the form of facts or figures.

**database** **databases**
NOUN A **database** is a collection of information, often stored in a computer.

**date** **dates**
NOUN **1** If someone asks you the **date**, you tell them the day and the month.
NOUN **2** A **date** is a small brown sticky fruit which grows on palm trees.

**daughter** **daughters**
NOUN A girl is the **daughter** of her parents.

**dawdle** **dawdles, dawdling, dawdled**
VERB If you **dawdle**, you walk slowly, taking more time than you should.

**dawn**

NOUN **Dawn** is the time of day when it first begins to get light.

**day** **days**

NOUN A **day** is the 24 hours between one midnight and the next.

**daylight**

NOUN **Daylight** is the light that there is during the day before it gets dark.

**dazzle** **dazzles, dazzling, dazzled**

VERB If a light **dazzles** you, it is so bright that you cannot really see for a while.

**de-**

PREFIX When **de-** is added to a noun or verb, it means to remove. For example, "deforest" means to take away the forest.
See *Prefixes* on page 264.

**dead**

ADJECTIVE A person, animal or plant that is **dead** is no longer living.

**deaf** **deafer, deafest**

ADJECTIVE Someone who is **deaf** cannot hear very well, or cannot hear at all.

**deal** **deals, dealing, dealt**

VERB **1** When you **deal** in a card game, you give cards to the players.

VERB **2** If you **deal** with something, you do what needs to be done with it.

**dear** **dearer, dearest**

ADJECTIVE **1** You use **Dear** at the beginning of a letter before the name of the person you are writing to.

ADJECTIVE **2** If something is **dear**, it costs a lot of money.

**death**

NOUN **Death** is the end of life, when an animal or person dies.

**decade** **decades**

NOUN A **decade** is a period of ten years.

**decay** **decays, decaying, decayed**

VERB When something like a plant or piece of meat **decays**, it becomes rotten.

**deceive** **deceives, deceiving, deceived**

VERB If someone **deceives** you, they make you believe something untrue.

**December**

NOUN **December** is the 12th month of the year. It has 31 days.

**decide** **decides, deciding, decided**

VERB If you **decide** to do something, you make up your mind to do it.

**decimal** **decimals**

ADJECTIVE **1** A **decimal** system involves counting in units of ten.
NOUN **2** A **decimal** or **decimal fraction** is written with a dot followed by numbers, such as 0·2, 8·35. The numbers after the dot represent tenths, hundredths and so on.
NOUN **3** A **decimal point** is the dot that comes between whole numbers and fractions.
NOUN **4** A **decimal place** is the position of a number after a decimal point.

**decision** **decisions**

NOUN A **decision** is a choice you make about what you think should be done.

**deck** **decks**

NOUN A **deck** is a floor on a ship or bus.

**decorate** **decorates, decorating, decorated**

VERB **1** If you **decorate** something, you add things to make it more attractive.
VERB **2** If someone **decorates** a room, they paper it or paint it.
**decorations** PLURAL NOUN

# decrease

**decrease** **decreases, decreasing, decreased**
VERB If something **decreases**, or if you decrease it, it becomes less.

**deep** **deeper, deepest**
ADJECTIVE If something is **deep**, it goes a long way down. *The river is very deep.*

**deer**
NOUN A **deer** is a large hoofed animal. Male deer have horns called antlers.

**defeat** **defeats, defeating, defeated**
VERB If you **defeat** someone, you beat them in a game or battle.

**defend** **defends, defending, defended**
VERB If you **defend** someone or something, you do something to protect them against danger.
**defence** NOUN

**define** **defines, defining, defined**
VERB If you **define** something, you say what it is or what it means.

**definite**
ADJECTIVE **1** Something that is **definite** is unlikely to be changed. *We have a definite date for the outing.*
ADJECTIVE **2** Definite can also mean certain or true. *Lots of stories were going round, but they heard nothing definite.*
**definitely** ADVERB

**definition** **definitions**
NOUN A **definition** explains the meaning of a word.

**degree** **degrees**
NOUN **1** A **degree** is a unit of measurement of temperature, for example, 20°C.
NOUN **2** In maths, a **degree** is a unit of measurement of angles. For example, a right angle is 90°.

**delay** **delays, delaying, delayed**
VERB If something **delays** you, it causes you to slow down or be late.

**delete** **deletes, deleting, deleted**
VERB If you **delete** some writing, you cross it out or remove it.

**deliberate**
ADJECTIVE If you do something that is **deliberate**, you do it on purpose.
**deliberately** ADVERB

**delicate**
ADJECTIVE **1** Something that is **delicate** is small and graceful.
ADJECTIVE **2** Someone who is **delicate** becomes ill easily.

**delicious**
ADJECTIVE Food that is **delicious** tastes or smells very nice.

**delight** **delights, delighting, delighted**
VERB If something **delights** you, it gives you a lot of pleasure.
**delighted** ADJECTIVE

**deliver** **delivers, delivering, delivered**
VERB If you **deliver** something, you take it to someone and hand it to them.

**demand** **demands, demanding, demanded**
VERB If you **demand** something, you say strongly that is what you want.

**demonstrate** **demonstrates, demonstrating, demonstrated**
VERB **1** If someone **demonstrates** something, they show you how to do it.
VERB **2** If people **demonstrate**, they hold a public meeting or march to show they are strongly for or against something.
**demonstration** NOUN

**den** **dens**
NOUN A **den** is the home of some wild animals such as lions or foxes.

**dense** **denser, densest**
ADJECTIVE Something **dense** is hard to see through. *They were in a **dense** forest.*

**dent** **dents, denting, dented**
VERB If somebody **dents** something, they make a dip in it by hitting it.

**dentist** **dentists**
NOUN A **dentist** is someone who looks after people's teeth.

**deny** **denies, denying, denied**
VERB If you **deny** something, you say that it is untrue.

**depart** **departs, departing, departed**
VERB When someone or something **departs** from a place, they leave it.
**departure** NOUN

**depend** **depends, depending, depended**
VERB **1** If you **depend** on someone, you need them.
VERB **2** If you can **depend** on someone, you know you can trust them.

**depth**
NOUN The **depth** of something is how deep it is.

**descend** **descends, descending, descended**
VERB To **descend** means to go down.

**descending**
ADJECTIVE When things are in **descending** order, each thing is lower than the one before it. *The numbers 10, 9, 8 and 7 are in **descending** order.*

**describe** **describes, describing, described**
VERB If you **describe** a person or thing, you say what they are like.
**description** NOUN

**desert** **deserts**
NOUN A **desert** is very dry land with very little plant life.

**deserted**
ADJECTIVE If a place is **deserted**, there are no people there.

**deserve** **deserves, deserving, deserved**
VERB If you **deserve** something, you have earned it by what you have done.

**design** **designs, designing, designed**
NOUN **1** A **design** is a pattern that is used to decorate something.
VERB **2** If you **design** something, you plan it and make a drawing of it.

**desk** **desks**
NOUN A **desk** is a special table that you use for writing or reading.

**dessert** **desserts**
NOUN A **dessert** is a sweet food served after the main course of a meal.

**destroy** **destroys, destroying, destroyed**
VERB To **destroy** something means to damage it so much it cannot be mended.

**detail** **details**
NOUN A **detail** is a small part or thing that you notice when you look at something carefully.

a
b
c
**Dd**
e
f
g
h
i
j
k
l
m
n
o
p
q
r
s
t
u
v
w
x
y
z

**detective** **detectives**

NOUN A **detective** is a person whose job is to find out who did a crime.

**determined**

ADJECTIVE If you are **determined** to do something, nothing will stop you.

**develop** **develops, developing, developed**

VERB When something **develops**, it grows or becomes more advanced.

**dew**

NOUN **Dew** is the small drops of water that form on surfaces outdoors at night.

**diagonal**

ADJECTIVE A **diagonal** line slants from one corner of something to the opposite corner.

**diagram** **diagrams**

NOUN A **diagram** is a drawing that explains something.

**dial** **dials**

NOUN A **dial** is a numbered disc on an instrument like a clock.

**dialogue** **dialogues**

NOUN In a story, play or film, **dialogue** is conversation.

**diameter** **diameters**

NOUN A **diameter** is a straight line drawn right through the centre of a circle.

**diamond** **diamonds**

NOUN **1** A **diamond** is a very hard, clear jewel which sparkles.

NOUN **2** A **diamond** is also a shape with four straight sides, like a square but slightly flattened.

See *Colours and flat shapes* on page 271.

**diary** **diaries**

NOUN A **diary** is a book in which to write about what you have done.

**dice**

NOUN **Dice** are small cubes with spots on each of their six sides.

**dictionary** **dictionaries**

NOUN A **dictionary** is a book in which words are listed alphabetically and explained.

**did**

VERB **Did** is the past tense of **do**.

**didn't**

VERB **Didn't** is a contraction of **did not**.

**die** **dies, dying, died**

VERB When a person, animal or plant **dies**, they stop living.

**diesel** **diesels**

NOUN A **diesel** is a kind of engine that burns a special oil instead of petrol.

**diet** **diets**

NOUN **1** A **diet** is the food that a person or animal normally eats.

NOUN **2** A **diet** is also a special range of foods that a doctor tells someone to eat if they have a health or weight problem.

**difference** **differences**

NOUN **1** The **difference** between two things is the way in which they are unlike each other.

NOUN **2** In maths, you can work out the **difference** between two numbers by taking the smaller number away from the larger number.

**different**

ADJECTIVE Something that is **different** from something else is not like it in one or more ways.

**difficult**

ADJECTIVE Something that is **difficult** is not easy to do or understand.

**difficulty** NOUN

**dig** digs, digging, dug

VERB When people **dig**, they break up soil or sand with a spade or garden fork.

**digest** digests, digesting, digested

VERB When you **digest** food, your body breaks it down so that it can be used. **digestion** NOUN

**digit** digits

NOUN A **digit** is a written symbol for any of the numbers from 0 to 9. For example, 384 is a three-digit number.

**digital**

ADJECTIVE **1 Digital** instruments such as watches have changing numbers instead of a dial with hands. See **analogue**.

NOUN **2 Digital television** is television in which the picture is sent in digital form.

**dim** dimmer, dimmest

ADJECTIVE If the light is **dim**, it is rather dark and it is hard to see things.

**din**

NOUN A **din** is a loud, annoying noise.

**dinghy** dinghies

NOUN A **dinghy** is a small open boat that you sail or row.

**dining room** dining rooms

NOUN A **dining room** is the room where people have their meals.

**dinner** dinners

NOUN **Dinner** is the main meal of the day.

**dinosaur** dinosaurs

NOUN A **dinosaur** was a large reptile which lived and became extinct in prehistoric times.

Triceratops

Stegosaurus

**dip** dips, dipping, dipped

VERB If you **dip** something into a liquid, you put it in quickly.

**direct** directs, directing, directed

VERB **1** If you **direct** someone, you show them the way to go.

VERB **2** A person who **directs** something, like a film, is in charge of it.

ADJECTIVE **3 Direct** means in a straight line without stopping, for example on a journey. *Is there a **direct** flight to Paris?*

**direction** directions

NOUN **1** A **direction** is the way in which someone or something is moving or pointing.

NOUN **2 Directions** are instructions that tell you what to do or which way to go.

**dirt**

NOUN **Dirt** is dust, mud or stains on a surface or fabric.

**dirty** dirtier, dirtiest

ADJECTIVE Something that is **dirty** is marked or covered with mud or stains.

**dis-**

PREFIX **Dis-** is added to the beginning of words to form a word that means the opposite, for example "agree" → "disagree".

See *Prefixes* on page 264.

**disabled**

ADJECTIVE A **disabled** person has a condition or injury that makes it hard or impossible to do some things. **disability** NOUN

**disagree** disagrees, disagreeing, disagreed

VERB If you **disagree** with someone, you think what they are saying is wrong.

**disappear** disappears, disappearing, disappeared

VERB If someone **disappears**, they go out of sight.

**disappoint** disappoints, disappointing, disappointed

VERB If something **disappoints** you, it is not as good as you thought it would be. **disappointment** NOUN

a
b
c
**Dd**
e
f
g
h
i
j
k
l
m
n
o
p
q
r
s
t
u
v
w
x
y
z

# disapprove

**disapprove**
VERB If you **disapprove** of something, you think it is wrong or bad.

**disaster** disasters
NOUN A **disaster** is something very bad that happens, such as an air crash.
**disastrous** ADJECTIVE

**disc** discs
NOUN A **disc** is a flat round object.

**disco** discos
NOUN A **disco** is a place where people go to dance to pop music.

**discover** discovers, discovering, discovered
VERB When you **discover** something, you find it or find out about it.
**discovery** NOUN

**discuss** discusses, discussing, discussed
VERB When you **discuss** something, you talk about it with someone else.
**discussion** NOUN

**disease** diseases
NOUN A **disease** is an illness in people, animals or plants.

**disguise** disguises
NOUN A **disguise** is something that changes the way you look, so that people do not recognize you.

**disgust**
NOUN **Disgust** is a feeling of strong dislike for someone or something.

**dish** dishes
NOUN A **dish** is a shallow container for cooking or serving meals in.

**dishonest**
ADJECTIVE If someone is **dishonest**, they are not to be trusted.

**dishwasher** dishwashers
NOUN A **dishwasher** is a machine that washes things like plates.

**disk** disks
NOUN A **disk** is used for storing information in a computer.

**dislike** dislikes, disliking, disliked
VERB If you **dislike** someone or something, you do not like them.

**dismiss** dismisses, dismissing, dismissed
VERB When someone in authority **dismisses** you, they tell you to leave.

**display** displays
NOUN A **display** is an arrangement of things which is done to show to people.

**dissolve** dissolves, dissolving, dissolved
VERB If something **dissolves** in a liquid, it becomes mixed in with it. See **solution**.

**distance** distances
NOUN The **distance** between two things is the amount of space between them.

**distant**
ADJECTIVE **Distant** means far away.

**distinct**
ADJECTIVE If something is **distinct**, you can hear or see it clearly.

**distribute** distributes, distributing, distributed
VERB If you **distribute** things like leaflets, you hand them out to several people.

**district** districts
NOUN A **district** is the area around a place. *He's the only doctor in this **district**.*

**disturb** disturbs, disturbing, disturbed
VERB If you **disturb** someone, you interrupt them or spoil their peace and quiet.

**disturbance**  **disturbances**

NOUN A **disturbance** is something that spoils people's peace and quiet.

**ditch**  **ditches**

NOUN A **ditch** is a channel dug at the side of a road or field, to drain water.

**dive**  **dives, diving, dived**

VERB To **dive** is to jump head first into water with your arms above your head.
**diver** NOUN

**divide**  **divides, dividing, divided**

VERB **1** When something is **divided**, it is separated into smaller parts.
VERB **2** When you **divide** numbers, you share them into equal groups. For example, 15 can be divided into 3 groups of 5, or 5 groups of 3.
$15 \div 3 = 5$  or  $15 \div 5 = 3$

**divisible**

ADJECTIVE A number that is **divisible** can be divided by another number without leaving a remainder. 27 is divisible by 3.

**division**  **divisions**

NOUN **1** Division is separating something into two or more parts.
NOUN **2** In maths, **division** is the process of dividing one number by another. The sign $\div$ is used for division.

**divorce**  **divorces**

NOUN A **divorce** is the legal ending of a marriage.

**Diwali**

NOUN **Diwali** is a Hindu festival of light that is celebrated in the autumn.

**dizzy**  **dizzier, dizziest**

ADJECTIVE If you feel **dizzy**, your head feels funny, as if you are going to fall over.

**do**  **does, doing, did, done**

VERB **1** If you **do** something, you get on and finish it. *Have you **done** your work?*
VERB **2** Do can be used with other verbs. *Do you want some more?*

**doctor**  **doctors**

NOUN A **doctor** is a person who treats people when they are ill.

**document**  **documents**

NOUN **1** A **document** is a piece of paper which is an official record of something.
NOUN **2** A **document** is also a piece of text stored as a file in a computer.

**dodge**  **dodges, dodging, dodged**

VERB If you **dodge**, you move suddenly out of the way.

**does**

VERB **Does** is a present tense form of **do**.

**doesn't**

VERB **Doesn't** is a contraction of **does not**.

**dog**  **dogs**

NOUN A **dog** is an animal. Dogs bark and are often kept as pets, or used to guard things.

**doll**  **dolls**

NOUN A **doll** is a child's toy that looks like a baby or a small person.

**dollar**  **dollars**

NOUN A **dollar** is a unit of money in countries such as the USA and Australia.

**dolphin**  **dolphins**

NOUN A **dolphin** is a mammal which lives in the sea.

**dome** domes

NOUN A **dome** is a round roof.

**domino** dominoes

NOUN A **domino** is a small black rectangular block, marked with spots. Dominoes are used for playing games.

**done**

VERB **Done** is the past participle of **do**.

**donkey** donkeys

NOUN A **donkey** is an animal like a small horse, with longer ears.

**don't**

VERB **Don't** is a contraction of **do not**.

**door** doors

NOUN A **door** swings or slides to open and close the entrance to something.

**dose** doses

NOUN A **dose** is the amount of a medicine that you have to take.

**dot** dots

NOUN A **dot** is a small round mark.

**double**

ADJECTIVE If something is **double** the size or amount of something else, it is twice as big.

**doubt** doubts

NOUN If you have a **doubt** about something, you are not sure about it.

**doubtful**

ADJECTIVE **1** If you are **doubtful** about something, you are not sure about it.
ADJECTIVE **2** Something that is **doubtful** seems unlikely or uncertain.

**dough**

NOUN **Dough** is the floury mixture used to make things like pastry or bread.

**doughnut** doughnuts

NOUN A **doughnut** is a ring of sweet dough cooked in hot fat.

**dove** doves

NOUN A **dove** is a bird like a small pigeon.

**down**

PREPOSITION **1** If you go **down** a hill, you go to a lower level.
ADVERB **2** If you put something **down**, you put it on a surface.
ADVERB **3** If an amount of something goes **down**, it gets less. *My pocket money's gone down.*
NOUN **4 Down** is soft feathers.

**downstairs**

ADVERB If you go **downstairs**, you go towards the ground floor.

**doze** dozes, dozing, dozed

VERB When you **doze**, you sleep lightly.

**dozen** dozens

NOUN If you have a **dozen** things, you have 12 of them.

**draft** drafts

NOUN A **draft** is an early rough version of something you are writing.

**drag** drags, dragging, dragged

VERB If you **drag** a heavy object, you pull it along the ground.

**dragon** dragons

NOUN In stories, a **dragon** is a fierce animal like a big lizard. It has wings and claws and breathes fire.

**dragonfly** dragonflies

NOUN A **dragonfly** is a brightly-coloured insect, usually found near water.

See *Insects* on page 259.

**drain** drains, draining, drained

NOUN **1** A **drain** is a pipe that carries water away.
VERB **2** If a liquid **drains** away, it flows slowly to somewhere else.

**drake** **drakes**

NOUN A **drake** is a male duck.

**drama** **dramas**

NOUN **1** A **drama** is a serious play for the theatre, television or radio.
NOUN **2 Drama** is exciting and interesting things that happen.

**dramatic**

ADJECTIVE Something **dramatic** is very exciting and interesting.
**dramatically** ADVERB

**drank**

VERB **Drank** is the past tense of **drink**.

**draught** **draughts**

NOUN **1** A **draught** is a current of cold air coming into a room or vehicle.
PLURAL NOUN **2 Draughts** is a game played with round pieces on a board.

**draw** **draws, drawing, drew, drawn**

VERB **1** When you **draw**, you use something like a pencil or crayon to make a picture or a pattern.
VERB **2** When you **draw** the curtains, you pull them across a window.
NOUN **3** A **draw** is the result in a game or competition in which nobody wins.

**drawbridge** **drawbridges**

NOUN A **drawbridge** is a bridge that can be pulled up to stop people getting into a castle.

**drawer** **drawers**

NOUN A **drawer** is a box that slides in and out of a piece of furniture.

**drawing** **drawings**

NOUN A **drawing** is a picture made with a pencil, pen or crayon.

**dread** **dreads, dreading, dreaded**

VERB If you **dread** something, you feel worried and frightened about it.

**dreadful**

ADJECTIVE Something that is **dreadful** is very bad or unpleasant.

**dream** **dreams, dreaming, dreamed** or **dreamt**

VERB **1** When you **dream**, you see events in your mind while you are asleep.

VERB **2** If you **dream** while you are awake, you think about things you would like to happen.
**dream** NOUN

**dress** **dresses, dressing, dressed**

VERB **1** When you **dress**, you put on your clothes.
NOUN **2** A **dress** is a piece of clothing for women or girls made up of a skirt and top joined together.

**drew**

VERB **Drew** is the past tense of **draw**.

**dribble** **dribbles, dribbling, dribbled**

VERB **1** When babies **dribble**, water trickles from their mouth.
VERB **2** When players **dribble** the ball in a game like football, they kick it several times quickly to keep it moving.

**drift** **drifts, drifting, drifted**

VERB **1** When something **drifts**, it is carried along slowly by wind or water.
NOUN **2** A **drift** is a pile of snow heaped up by the wind.

**drill** **drills**

NOUN A **drill** is a tool for making holes.

**drink** **drinks, drinking, drank, drunk**

VERB **1** When you **drink**, you take liquid into your mouth and swallow it.
NOUN **2** A **drink** is a liquid which you swallow to stop you being thirsty.

a
b
c
**Dd**
e
f
g
h
i
j
k
l
m
n
o
p
q
r
s
t
u
v
w
x
y
z

# drip

**drip** drips, dripping, dripped
VERB When something **drips**, drops of liquid fall from it one after the other.

**drive** drives, driving, drove, driven
VERB If someone **drives** a vehicle, they make it move and control it.

**drizzle**
NOUN **Drizzle** is light rain.

**drop** drops, dropping, dropped
VERB 1 If you **drop** something, you let it fall.
NOUN 2 A **drop** is a tiny amount of liquid.

**drought** droughts
NOUN A **drought** is a long period of time when no rain falls.

**drove**
VERB **Drove** is the past tense of **drive**.

**drown** drowns, drowning, drowned
VERB If someone **drowns**, they die because they have gone under water and cannot breathe.

**drug** drugs
NOUN A **drug** is a substance that is used to treat or prevent disease, or stop pain. Some drugs can be dangerous.

**drum** drums
NOUN A **drum** is a musical instrument which you hit to make a noise. It has skin stretched tightly over the end.

**drunk**
VERB **Drunk** is the past participle of **drink**.

**dry** drier or dryer, driest
ADJECTIVE Something that is **dry** has no water in it at all.
**dry** VERB

**duck** ducks
NOUN A **duck** is a common water bird with short legs and webbed feet.

**due**
ADJECTIVE If something is **due** at a particular time, it should happen then.

**dug**
VERB **Dug** is the past tense of **dig**.

**dull** duller, dullest
ADJECTIVE 1 Something that is **dull** is not interesting.
ADJECTIVE 2 **Dull** means not bright.
ADJECTIVE 3 A **dull** pain is not sharp.

**dumb**
ADJECTIVE Someone who is **dumb** is unable to speak.

**dungeon** dungeons
NOUN A **dungeon** is a dark underground prison in a castle.

**during**
PREPOSITION Something that happens **during** a period of time happens in that period. *I worked **during** the holidays.*

**dusk**
NOUN **Dusk** is the part of the day when it is beginning to get dark.

**dust**
NOUN **Dust** is dry fine powdery material such as particles of earth, dirt or pollen.
**dusty** ADJECTIVE

**dustbin** dustbins
NOUN A **dustbin** is a large container with a lid, for rubbish.

**duty** duties
NOUN A **duty** is something you feel you should do. *He only went to see his aunt because he felt it was his **duty**.*

**duvet** duvets
NOUN A **duvet** is a bed cover filled with feathers or other light material.

**dye** dyes, dyeing, dyed
VERB If you **dye** something such as hair or cloth, you change its colour by soaking it in a special liquid.

**dying**
VERB See **die**.

# Ee

## each

ADJECTIVE **Each** means every one taken separately. *She gave **each** child a pencil.*

## eager

ADJECTIVE If you are **eager**, you very much want to do or have something.

## eagle  eagles

NOUN An **eagle** is a large strong bird with a sharp curved beak and claws.

## ear  ears

NOUN Your **ears** are the parts of your body that you use for hearing.

## early  earlier, earliest

ADJECTIVE OR ADVERB **1 Early** means near the beginning of a period of time. *We took the **early** train to school.*

ADJECTIVE OR ADVERB **2** You also use **early** to mean sooner than expected. *I arrived at the party **early**.*

## earn  earns, earning, earned

VERB If you **earn** something, such as money, you get it by working for it.

## earring  earrings

NOUN An **earring** is a piece of jewellery that is fixed to the ear for decoration.

## earth

NOUN **1** The **Earth** is the planet we live on.

NOUN **2** The soil that plants grow in is also called **earth**.

## earthquake  earthquakes

NOUN An **earthquake** is when the ground shakes because of movement beneath the surface.

## east

NOUN **East** is one of the four main points of the compass. It is the direction in which the sun rises. See **compass point**.

**eastern** ADJECTIVE

## Easter

NOUN **Easter** is a Christian festival that celebrates Christ's return to life.

## easy  easier, easiest

ADJECTIVE Something that is **easy** can be done without difficulty.

**easily** ADVERB

## eat  eats, eating, ate, eaten

VERB When you **eat**, you chew and swallow food.

## echo  echoes

NOUN An **echo** is a sound that bounces back from something like the walls of a cave or building.

## eclipse  eclipses

NOUN An **eclipse** of the Sun is when the Moon comes in front of the Sun and hides it for a short time.

## edge  edges

NOUN **1** An **edge** is the end or side of something.

NOUN **2** An **edge** is where two faces of a three-dimensional shape meet. For example, a cuboid has 12 edges.

## edible

ADJECTIVE Something that is **edible** is safe to eat.

## edit  edits, editing, edited

VERB **1** If you **edit** a piece of writing, you correct it so that it is ready for printing.

VERB **2** When someone **edits** a film or television programme, they select different parts and arrange them in a particular order.

## educate  educates, educating, educated

VERB To **educate** someone means to teach them over a long period, so that they learn about many different things.

## education

NOUN **Education** is the teaching you receive at school, college or university.

## eel **eels**

NOUN An **eel** is a long thin fish that looks like a snake.

## effect **effects**

NOUN An **effect** is a change made by something. *I'm still suffering from the effects of my cold.*

## effort **efforts**

NOUN **Effort** is the physical or mental energy needed to do something.

## egg **eggs**

NOUN **1** An **egg** is an oval object laid by female birds. Reptiles, fish and insects also lay eggs. A baby animal develops inside the egg until it is ready to be born.

NOUN **2** In a female mammal, an **egg** is a cell produced in its body which can develop into a baby.

## elastic

ADJECTIVE **1** Something **elastic** is able to stretch easily.

NOUN **2** **Elastic** is a material, like rubber, which stretches and can then return to its original size.

## elbow **elbows**

NOUN Your **elbow** is the joint in the middle of your arm where it bends.

## electric

ADJECTIVE A machine or other object that is **electric** works by using electricity.
**electrical** ADJECTIVE

## electricity

NOUN **Electricity** is a form of energy that is used for heating and lighting, and to work machines. It comes along wires.

## electronic

ADJECTIVE Something **electronic** has transistors or silicon chips which control an electric current.
**electronically** ADVERB

## elephant **elephants**

NOUN An **elephant** is a large four-legged mammal with a long trunk, large ears, and ivory tusks.

## elf **elves**

NOUN In fairy stories, an **elf** is a tiny boy who can do magic things.

## else

ADVERB You can use **else** to mean other than this or more than this. *Can you think of anything else?*

## e-mail or email

NOUN **E-mail** is the sending of messages from one computer to another.

## embarrass **embarrasses, embarrassing, embarrassed**

VERB To **embarrass** someone means to make them feel shy, ashamed or guilty about something.

## embryo **embryos**

NOUN An **embryo** is a human being or animal which has just begun to develop inside its mother's body.

## emerald **emeralds**

NOUN An **emerald** is a bright green precious stone.

## emerge **emerges, emerging, emerged**

VERB If someone **emerges** from a place, they come out so that they can be seen.

## emergency **emergencies**

NOUN An **emergency** is an unexpected and serious event which needs immediate action to deal with it.

## emotion **emotions**

NOUN **Emotion** is a strong feeling, such a love or fear.

**employ** employs, employing, employed
VERB If someone **employs** you, they pay you to work for them.

**employer** employers
NOUN **Employers** are people who pay other people to work for them.

**empty** emptier, emptiest; empties, emptying, emptied
ADJECTIVE **1** Something that is **empty** has no people or things in it.
VERB **2** If you **empty** a container, you pour or take everything out of it.

**enchanted**
ADJECTIVE In stories, something that is **enchanted** is under a magic spell.

**encourage** encourages, encouraging, encouraged
VERB If you **encourage** someone, you tell them that what they are doing is good and they should go on doing it.

**encyclopedia** encyclopedias
NOUN An **encyclopedia** is a book or set of books giving information about many different subjects.

**end** ends, ending, ended
NOUN **1** The **end** of a period of time or an event is the last part.
NOUN **2** The **end** of something is the farthest point of it. *The bathroom is at the end of the passage.*
VERB **3** If something **ends**, it finishes.

**ending** endings
NOUN An **ending** is the last part of a word, story, play or film.

**enemy** enemies
NOUN Your **enemy** is someone who fights or works against you.

**energetic**
ADJECTIVE Someone who is **energetic** is active and lively.
**energetically** ADVERB

**energy**
NOUN **1** **Energy** is the strength you need to do things. You get energy from food.
NOUN **2** **Energy** is also the power that makes things heat up, make a sound, give light or move. Electricity is one kind of energy.

**engine** engines
NOUN **1** An **engine** is a machine that makes things move.
NOUN **2** An **engine** is also a large vehicle that pulls a railway train.

**engineer** engineers
NOUN An **engineer** is a person who designs or builds things such as machinery, instruments or bridges.

**enjoy** enjoys, enjoying, enjoyed
VERB If you **enjoy** doing something, you like doing it very much.
**enjoyable** ADJECTIVE   **enjoyment** NOUN

**enormous**
ADJECTIVE Something that is **enormous** is extremely large.

**enough**
ADJECTIVE **Enough** means as much as you need. *Have you had **enough** to eat?*

**enter** enters, entering, entered
VERB **1** If you **enter** a place, you go into it.
VERB **2** If you **enter** a competition or examination, you take part in it.

**entertain** entertains, entertaining, entertained
VERB If you **entertain** somebody, you do something that they enjoy and find amusing.

a b c d **Ee** f g h i j k l m n o p q r s t u v w x y z

**entertainment**

NOUN **Entertainment** is things that people watch for pleasure, such as shows and films.

**enthusiastic**

ADJECTIVE If you are **enthusiastic** about something, you are very interested in it, or excited about it.

**entire**

ADJECTIVE **Entire** means the whole of something. *The entire class came to my party.*

**entrance** **entrances**

NOUN An **entrance** is the way into a place.

**envelope** **envelopes**

NOUN An **envelope** is a folded paper cover for a letter or card.

**envious**

ADJECTIVE If you are **envious** of somebody, you wish you could have the same things that they have.

**environment** **environments**

NOUN The **environment** is the natural world around us.

**envy** **envies, envying, envied**

VERB If you **envy** somebody, you wish you could have the same things that they have.

**episode** **episodes**

NOUN An **episode** is one of several parts of a story or drama.

**equal**

ADJECTIVE If two things are **equal**, they are the same as each other in size, number or amount.

**equals**

VERB In maths, the symbol = stands for **equals**. The numbers on each side of it have the same value: $2 + 2 = 4$

**equation** **equations**

NOUN **Equations** are sometimes called number sentences. The numbers on the left equal the numbers on the right. For example, $3 + 3 = 2 \times 3$ is an equation.

**equator**

NOUN The **equator** is an imaginary line drawn round the centre of the earth, lying halfway between the North and South Poles.

**equipment**

NOUN **Equipment** is the things that you need to do something. *We need some new kitchen equipment – especially a fridge.*

**erupt** **erupts, erupting, erupted**

VERB When a volcano **erupts**, it throws out hot molten lava, ash and steam.

**escape** **escapes, escaping, escaped**

VERB If a person or animal **escapes**, they get away from somebody or something.

**especially**

ADVERB You say **especially** to mean most of all. *I like cats, especially black ones.*

**essay** **essays**

NOUN An **essay** is a short piece of writing on a particular subject.

**essential**

ADJECTIVE Something that is **essential** is absolutely necessary.

**estate** **estates**

NOUN **1** An **estate** is a large area of land in the country, belonging to one person or group.

NOUN **2** An **estate** is also an area of land with lots of houses on it.

**estimate** estimates, estimating, estimated

VERB If you **estimate** something, you guess the size or amount of it.

**evaporate** evaporates, evaporating, evaporated

VERB When a liquid **evaporates**, it becomes less because it is changing from a liquid into a gas.
evaporation NOUN

**even**

ADVERB **1** You say **even** when something is rather surprising. *I like to play outside* **even** *when it is raining.*
ADJECTIVE **2** If something like a path is **even**, it is smooth and flat.
ADJECTIVE **3** An **even** number can be divided by two, with no remainder. *2, 18 and 36 are all* **even** *numbers.*

**evening** evenings

NOUN The **evening** is the part of the day between late afternoon and the time you usually go to bed.

**event** events

NOUN An **event** is something important that happens.

**eventually**

ADVERB **Eventually** means in the end, after a lot of delays or problems.

**ever**

ADVERB **Ever** means at any time in the past or future. *Have you* **ever** *seen such a big dog?*

**evergreen** evergreens

NOUN An **evergreen** is a tree or other plant which keeps its leaves all year round.

**every**

ADJECTIVE **Every** means each one. *I spoke to* **every** *child in that class.*

**every other** PHRASE **Every other** means one in every two. *I see my friend* **every other** *week.*

**everybody**

PRONOUN **Everybody** means every person. *Everybody has to eat.*

**everyone**

PRONOUN You can use **everyone** instead of **everybody**.

**everything**

PRONOUN **Everything** means all of something.

**everywhere**

ADVERB **Everywhere** means in all places. *Children* **everywhere** *love stories.*

**evidence**

NOUN **Evidence** is anything you see, read or are told which gives you reason to believe something.

**evil**

ADJECTIVE An **evil** person is extremely wicked.

**ewe** ewes

NOUN A **ewe** is a female sheep.

**ex-**

PREFIX **Ex-** means former, for example "husband" → "ex-husband".
See *Prefixes* on page 264.

**exact**

ADJECTIVE Something that is **exact** is accurate in every detail.

**exactly**

ADVERB You say **exactly** when you mean no more and no less. *My father is* **exactly** *two metres tall.*

**exaggerate** exaggerates, exaggerating, exaggerated

VERB If you **exaggerate**, you say something is better or worse than it really is.

**examination** examinations

NOUN **1** An **examination**, called an **exam** for short, is a test people take to find out how much they have learned.

NOUN **2** A doctor makes a medical **examination** to find out how healthy you are.

**examine** examines, examining, examined

VERB If you **examine** something, you look at it carefully or closely.

**example** examples

NOUN An **example** is one thing which shows what the rest of a set is like. *This is an example of my work.*

**excellent**

ADJECTIVE Something that is **excellent** is extremely good.

**except**

PREPOSITION **Except** means apart from. *Everyone went outside except David.*

**exception** exceptions

NOUN An **exception** is something that does not fit in with a general rule. *With the exception of bats, mammals cannot fly.*

**exchange** exchanges, exchanging, exchanged

VERB If you **exchange** something, you change it for something else.

**excite** excites, exciting, excited

VERB If something **excites** you, it makes you feel happy and interested.

**exciting** ADJECTIVE    **excitement** NOUN

**excited**

ADJECTIVE If you feel **excited**, you feel happy and unable to rest.

**exclaim** exclaims, exclaiming, exclaimed

VERB When you **exclaim**, you speak suddenly or loudly, because you are excited or angry.

**exclamation** NOUN

**exclamation mark** exclamation marks

NOUN An **exclamation mark** is a punctuation mark (!) used in writing to express a strong feeling.

See *Punctuation* on page 264.

**excuse** excuses

NOUN An **excuse** is a reason you give for doing something, or not doing it.

**exercise** exercises

NOUN **1** **Exercise** is regular movements you make to keep fit.

NOUN **2** An **exercise** is a piece of work that you do to help you learn something.

**exhausted**

ADJECTIVE When you are **exhausted**, you are so tired you have no energy left.

**exhibition** exhibitions

NOUN An **exhibition** is a collection of pictures or other things in a public place where people can come to see them.

**exist** exists, existing, existed

VERB Things that **exist** are present in the world or universe now.

**existence** NOUN

**exit** exits

NOUN An **exit** is the way out of a place.

**expand** expands, expanding, expanded

VERB When something **expands**, it gets bigger.

**expect** expects, expecting, expected

VERB If you **expect** something, you think it will happen.

**expedition** expeditions

NOUN An **expedition** is a journey made for a special reason.

**expel** **expels, expelling, expelled**
VERB If someone is **expelled** from school, they are told not to come back because their behaviour has been so bad.

**expensive**
ADJECTIVE Something that is **expensive** costs a lot of money.

**experience** **experiences**
NOUN **1** An **experience** is something that happens to you.
NOUN **2** Experience is knowing about something because you have been doing it for a long time.

**experiment** **experiments**
NOUN An **experiment** is the testing of something, either to find out its effect or to prove something.

**expert** **experts**
NOUN An **expert** is someone who is very skilled at doing something or who knows a lot about something.

**explain** **explains, explaining, explained**
VERB **1** To **explain** means to say things to help people understand.
VERB **2** When you **explain**, you give reasons for something that happened.

**explanation** **explanations**
NOUN **1** An **explanation** is something that helps people understand something. *She gave us a clear explanation of the way the machine works.*
NOUN **2** An **explanation** is something that tells you why something happened.

**explode** **explodes, exploding, exploded**
VERB If something such as a firework **explodes**, it bursts with a loud bang.
**explosion** NOUN

**explore** **explores, exploring, explored**
VERB If you **explore** a place, you travel in it to find out what it is like.
**exploration** NOUN **explorer** NOUN

**explosive** **explosives**
NOUN An **explosive** is a substance that can explode.

**express** **expresses, expressing, expressed**
VERB If you **express** an idea or feeling, you put it into words or show it by the way you act. *He could only express the way he felt by bursting into tears.*

**expression** **expressions**
NOUN Your **expression** is the look on your face that lets people know what you are thinking or feeling.

**extinct**
ADJECTIVE If an animal or plant family is **extinct**, it no longer has any living members. *The dodo has been extinct for more than 300 years.*

**extra**
ADJECTIVE You use **extra** to mean more than usual. *You'd better take an extra jumper – it's going to be cold.*

**extraordinary**
ADJECTIVE Someone or something that is **extraordinary** is very special or unusual.

**extreme**
ADJECTIVE **Extreme** means very great. *Extreme cold can cause many problems.*
**extremely** ADVERB

**eye** **eyes**
NOUN **1** Your **eyes** are the part of your body that you use for seeing.

NOUN **2** The **eye** of a needle is the small hole at one end.

**eyesight**
NOUN **Eyesight** is the ability to see.

# Ff

**fable** **fables**

NOUN A **fable** is a story that is meant to teach you something. Fables often have animals as the main characters.

**fabric** **fabrics**

NOUN **Fabric** is material made in some way such as by weaving or knitting.

**face** **faces, facing, faced**

NOUN **1** Your **face** is the front part of your head from your chin to your forehead. See *Your face* on page 258.

VERB **2** If you **face** something, you have your face towards it.

NOUN **3** The **face** of a clock or watch is the part with the numbers on it that show the time.

NOUN **4** A **face** is a surface of a three-dimensional shape.

**fact** **facts**

NOUN A **fact** is something that is true.

**factual** ADJECTIVE

**factor** **factors**

NOUN A **factor** is a whole number which will divide exactly into another whole number. For example, 3 is a factor of 12.

**factory** **factories**

NOUN A **factory** is a large building where a lot of things are made.

**fade** **fades, fading, faded**

VERB **1** If a colour **fades**, it gets paler.

VERB **2** If the light **fades**, it gets darker.

**fail** **fails, failing, failed**

VERB **1** If someone **fails** when they try to do something, they cannot do it.

VERB **2** If something **fails**, it stops working. *The brakes **failed**, and the car hit a wall.*

**failure** **failures**

NOUN If something is a **failure**, it does not work as planned. *The picnic was a **failure** because it rained all day.*

**faint** **faints, fainting, fainted; fainter, faintest**

VERB **1** If someone **faints**, they become unconscious for a short time.

ADJECTIVE **2** Something like a sound or mark that is **faint** is not easy to hear or see.

**fair** **fairer, fairest; fairs**

ADJECTIVE **1** Something that is **fair** seems reasonable to most people.

ADJECTIVE **2** People who are **fair** have light-coloured hair.

NOUN **3** A **fair** is a form of entertainment that takes place outside with stalls, sideshows, and machines to ride on.

**fairly**

ADVERB **Fairly** means quite or rather.

**fairy** **fairies**

NOUN In stories, **fairies** are tiny people with wings, who have magical powers.

**fairy tale** **fairy tales**

NOUN A **fairy tale** is a story in which magical things happen.

**faithful**

ADJECTIVE If you are **faithful** to someone, you can be trusted and relied on.

**fake** **fakes**

NOUN A **fake** is a copy of something made to trick people into thinking that it is genuine.

**fall** falls, falling, fell, fallen

VERB **1** When someone or something **falls**, they drop towards the ground.
VERB **2** If someone's face **falls**, they suddenly look upset or disappointed.

**false**

ADJECTIVE **1** If something is **false**, it is not the real thing. *My uncle has a false tooth.*
ADJECTIVE **2** If something you say is **false**, it is not true.

**familiar**

ADJECTIVE Something **familiar** is well-known or easy to recognize. *It was good to see a familiar face.*

**family** families

NOUN **1** A **family** is a group of people made up of parents and their children.
NOUN **2** A **family** is also a group of animals or plants of the same kind. *Lions and tigers belong to the cat family.*

**famine** famines

NOUN A **famine** is a shortage of food which may cause many people to die.

**famous**

ADJECTIVE Someone or something **famous** is very well known.

**fan** fans

NOUN **1** A **fan** is an object which creates a draught of cool air when it moves.

NOUN **2** If you are a **fan** of something or of someone famous, you are very interested in them.

**fantastic**

ADJECTIVE Something **fantastic** is wonderful and very pleasing.

**fantasy** fantasies

NOUN **1** A **fantasy** is a story about things that do not exist in the real world.
NOUN **2** **Fantasy** is imagining things.

**far** farther or further; farthest or furthest

ADVERB **1** **Far** means a long way away. *Are you going far?*
ADVERB **2** You use **far** to ask questions about distance. *How far is the town?*

**fare** fares

NOUN A **fare** is the money that you pay to go on something like a plane or a bus.

**farm** farms

NOUN A **farm** is a large area of land together with buildings, used for growing crops or keeping animals.

**farmer** farmers

NOUN A **farmer** is a person who owns or manages a farm.

**fascinate** fascinates, fascinating, fascinated

VERB If something **fascinates** you, it interests you very much.

**fashion** fashions

NOUN A **fashion** is the style of things like clothes that are popular for a time.
**fashionable** ADJECTIVE

**fast** faster, fastest; fasts, fasting, fasted

ADJECTIVE **1** Someone or something that is **fast** can move very quickly.
ADJECTIVE **2** If a clock is **fast**, it shows a time that is later than the real time.
VERB **3** If someone **fasts**, they eat no food for a period of time.

**fasten** fastens, fastening, fastened

VERB When you **fasten** something, you close it or do it up. *Remember to fasten your seat belt.*

**fat** fatter, fattest; fats

ADJECTIVE **1** A **fat** person or animal has a heavy body.
NOUN **2** **Fat** is a solid or liquid substance used in cooking. It comes from animals or vegetables.

# father

**father** **fathers**
NOUN Your **father** is your male parent.

**fault** **faults**
NOUN **1** If people say something is your **fault**, they are blaming you for something bad that has happened.
NOUN **2** A **fault** is something wrong with the way something was made.
**faulty** ADJECTIVE

**favour** **favours**
NOUN A **favour** is something helpful you do for someone.

**favourite** **favourites**
NOUN Your **favourite** person or thing is the one you like better than all the others. *This teddy is my favourite toy.*

**fax** **faxes**
NOUN A **fax** is a copy of a document that can be sent along a telephone line.

**fear** **fears, fearing, feared**
NOUN **1** Fear is the nasty feeling you have when you think you are in danger.
VERB **2** If you **fear** someone or something, you are frightened of them.

**feast** **feasts**
NOUN A **feast** is a large and special meal for many people.

**feat** **feats**
NOUN A **feat** is a brave or impressive act.

**feather** **feathers**
NOUN A **feather** is one of the very light pieces that make up a bird's coat.

**February**
NOUN **February** is the second month of the year. It has 28 days except in a leap year, when it has 29.

**fed**
VERB **Fed** is the past tense of **feed**.

**feed** **feeds, feeding, fed**
VERB If you **feed** a person or animal, you give them food.

**feel** **feels, feeling, felt**
VERB **1** If you **feel** something, like happy or sad, that is how you are at that time.
VERB **2** If you **feel** an object, you touch it to find out what it is like.

**feeling** **feelings**
NOUN A **feeling** is something you feel, like anger or happiness.

**feet**
PLURAL NOUN **Feet** is the plural of **foot**.

**felt**
VERB **1** Felt is the past tense of **feel**.
NOUN **2** Felt is a thick cloth made by pressing short threads together.

**female** **females**
NOUN A **female** is a person or animal that belongs to the sex that can have babies or young.
**female** ADJECTIVE

**feminine**
ADJECTIVE Someone who is **feminine** has the qualities generally expected of a woman, such as gentleness.

**fence** **fences**
NOUN A **fence** is a wooden or wire barrier between two areas of land.

**ferocious**
ADJECTIVE A **ferocious** animal or person is violent and fierce.

**ferry** **ferries**
NOUN A **ferry** is a boat that takes passengers and sometimes vehicles across a short stretch of water.

**festival** **festivals**
NOUN **1** A **festival** is an organized series of events and performances.
NOUN **2** A **festival** can also be a special day or period of religious celebration.

**fetch** fetches, fetching, fetched

VERB If you **fetch** something, you go and get it and bring it back.

**fete** fetes

NOUN A **fete** is an outdoor event with competitions and stalls which sell things.

**fever** fevers

NOUN If you have a **fever** when you are ill, you have a high temperature.

**few** fewer, fewest

ADJECTIVE **Few** means a small number of things. *I saw him a few minutes ago.*

**fibre** fibres

NOUN A **fibre** is a thin thread of something such as wool or cotton.

**fiction**

NOUN **Fiction** is books or stories about people and events which are made up by the author. See **non-fiction**.

**fidget** fidgets, fidgeting, fidgeted

VERB If you **fidget**, you keep moving about because you are nervous or bored.

**field** fields

NOUN A **field** is a piece of land with a fence around, used to grow crops or keep animals in.

**fierce** fiercer, fiercest

ADJECTIVE An animal that is **fierce** is dangerous.

**fight** fights, fighting, fought

VERB If you **fight** someone, you try to hurt them.

**figure** figures

NOUN **1** A **figure** is any of the numbers from 0 to 9. See **digit**.

NOUN **2** A **figure** is also the shape of a person. *It was just getting dark when I saw a small figure coming towards me.*

**file** files

NOUN **1** A **file** is a box or folded piece of card that you keep papers in.

NOUN **2** A **file** is also a set of data in a computer, which is stored under a name.

NOUN **3** A **file** is also a metal tool with rough surfaces which is used to smooth things like wood or metal.

**fill** fills, filling, filled

VERB If you **fill** something, you put so much into it there is no room for any more.

**film** films

NOUN **1** A **film** is moving pictures shown on a screen.

NOUN **2** **Film** is a long narrow piece of plastic that is used in a camera to take photographs.

**filthy** filthier, filthiest

ADJECTIVE Something **filthy** is very dirty.

**fin** fins

NOUN A fish's **fins** are like small wings that stick out of its body. They help the fish to swim and to keep its balance.

**final**

ADJECTIVE In a series of any kind, the **final** one is the last one.

**finally** ADVERB

**find** finds, finding, found

VERB When you **find** someone or something, you see the person or thing you have been looking for.

# fine

**fine** finer, finest; fines
ADJECTIVE **1** Something that is **fine** is extremely good.
ADJECTIVE **2** Something like a thread or nib that is **fine** is very thin.
ADJECTIVE **3** If you say you are **fine**, you mean you are well and happy.
ADJECTIVE **4** When the weather is **fine**, it is dry and sunny.
NOUN **5** A **fine** is money that is paid as a punishment.

**finger** fingers
NOUN Your **fingers** are the four long jointed parts at the end of your hand.

**fingernail** fingernails
NOUN Your **fingernails** are the thin hard areas that cover the ends of your fingers.

**fingerprint** fingerprints
NOUN A **fingerprint** is a mark that shows the skin pattern at the tip of a finger.

**finish** finishes, finishing, finished
VERB When you **finish** something, like a meal or a book, you reach the end of it.

**fir** firs
NOUN A **fir** is a tall pointed evergreen tree with cones, and leaves like needles.

**fire** fires, firing, fired
NOUN **1** Fire is the flames produced when something burns.
NOUN **2** A **fire** is also something powered by coal, gas or electricity that gives out heat.
VERB **3** If someone **fires** a gun, a bullet is sent from the gun they are using.

**fire engine** fire engines
NOUN A **fire engine** is a large vehicle that carries firefighters and equipment for putting out fires.

**firefighter** firefighters
NOUN A **firefighter** is a person whose job is to put out fires and rescue trapped people and animals.

**fireplace** fireplaces
NOUN A **fireplace** is the opening beneath a chimney where a fire can be lit.

**firework** fireworks
NOUN A **firework** is a thing that burns with coloured sparks when you light it. Some fireworks make a loud noise.

**firm** firmer, firmest
ADJECTIVE **1** Something that is **firm** does not move easily when you press or push it. *This pear isn't ripe – it is too **firm**!*
ADJECTIVE **2** If someone is **firm** with you about something, you know they will not change their mind.

**first**
ADJECTIVE OR ADVERB If something is **first** or happens first, it is number one and comes before anything else.

**first aid**
NOUN **First aid** is simple treatment given as soon as possible to a person who is injured or who suddenly becomes ill.

**first person**
NOUN The **first person** refers to yourself when you are speaking or writing. It is expressed as "I" or "we".

**fish** fishes, fishing, fished
NOUN **1** A **fish** is an animal that lives in water. It has gills, fins and a scaly skin.
VERB **2** To **fish** is to try and catch fish for food or sport.

**fisherman** fishermen
NOUN A **fisherman** is a person who catches fish as a job or for sport.

**fist** fists

NOUN You make a **fist** by tucking your fingers into the palm of your hand.

**fit** fitter, fittest; fits, fitting, fitted

ADJECTIVE **1** Someone who is **fit** is healthy.
VERB **2** If something such as clothing **fits** you, it is the right size for you.
VERB **3** If something **fits** something else, it is the right size to go with it. *This is the lid that **fits** that box.*

**fix** fixes, fixing, fixed

VERB **1** If you **fix** something that has broken, you make it work again.
VERB **2** If you **fix** something somewhere, you put it there firmly so that it cannot be moved. *She **fixed** a lamp to the wall.*

**fizzy** fizzier, fizziest

ADJECTIVE A **fizzy** drink is full of little bubbles of gas.

**flag** flags

NOUN A **flag** is a piece of cloth that can be fixed to a pole as a symbol of a nation, or as a signal.

**flake** flakes

NOUN A **flake** is a small thin piece of something.

**flame** flames

NOUN A **flame** is a flickering tongue or blaze of fire.

**flamingo** flamingos

NOUN A **flamingo** is a long-legged wading bird with pink feathers.

**flannel** flannels

NOUN A **flannel** is a small square of towelling, used for washing yourself.

**flap** flaps, flapping, flapped

NOUN **1** A **flap** is something flat that is fixed along one edge so that the rest of it can move freely.
VERB **2** When a bird **flaps** its wings, it moves them up and down quickly.

**flash** flashes, flashing, flashed

NOUN **1** A **flash** is a bright light which comes suddenly and only lasts a moment, like lightning in a storm.
VERB **2** If something **flashes** past, it moves so fast that you cannot see it properly.

**flask** flasks

NOUN A **flask** is a bottle for carrying drinks. It keeps hot drinks hot and cold drinks cold.

**flat** flats; flatter, flattest

NOUN **1** A **flat** is a set of rooms, usually on one level, for living in.
ADJECTIVE **2** Something that is **flat** is level and smooth.
ADJECTIVE **3** A battery that is **flat** has lost its electrical power.
ADJECTIVE **4** A **flat** shape is one like a circle, that is two-dimensional.
See *Colours and flat shapes* on page 271.

**flavour** flavours

NOUN The **flavour** of food is its taste.

**flea** fleas

NOUN A **flea** is a small jumping insect that feeds on blood.

**fleece** fleeces

NOUN **1** A sheep's **fleece** is its woollen coat.
NOUN **2** A **fleece** is a kind of warm jacket or pullover.

**flesh**

NOUN **1** Flesh is the soft part of your body.
NOUN **2** The **flesh** of a fruit or vegetable is the soft inner part that you eat.

**flew**

VERB **Flew** is the past tense of **fly**.

**flick** flicks, flicking, flicked

VERB If you **flick** something, you move it sharply with your finger.

a
b
c
d
e
**Ff**
g
h
i
j
k
l
m
n
o
p
q
r
s
t
u
v
w
x
y
z

**flies**

VERB **Flies** is a present tense form of **fly**.

NOUN **Flies** is also the plural of **fly**.

**flight** **flights**

NOUN **1** A **flight** is a journey through the air by a bird or an aircraft.

NOUN **2** A **flight** of stairs is a set that leads from one level to another without changing direction.

**flimsy** **flimsier, flimsiest**

ADJECTIVE Something that is **flimsy** is made of something very thin or weak.

**flip** **flips, flipping, flipped**

VERB If you **flip** something, you turn or move it quickly. *He **flipped** a coin.*

**flipper** **flippers**

NOUN **1** A **flipper** is one of the broad flat limbs of sea animals, for example seals, that are used for swimming.

NOUN **2** **Flippers** are broad flat pieces of rubber that you can wear on your feet to help you swim.

**float** **floats, floating, floated**

VERB **1** Something that **floats** is supported by water and does not sink.

VERB **2** Something that **floats** through the air moves along gently, supported by the air.

**flock** **flocks**

NOUN A **flock** is a group of birds, sheep or goats.

*See Collective nouns on page 262.*

**flood** **floods**

NOUN A **flood** is a large amount of water covering an area that is usually dry.

**floor** **floors**

NOUN **1** The **floor** of a room is the flat part that you walk on.

NOUN **2** A **floor** of a building is all the rooms on that level. *Our flat is on the third **floor**.*

**flop** **flops, flopping, flopped**

VERB If someone or something **flops**, they fall loosely and rather heavily.

**floppy disk** **floppy disks**

NOUN A **floppy disk** is a small magnetic disk on which computer data is stored.

**flour**

NOUN **Flour** is a powder made by grinding grain such as wheat. It is used to make things like bread and cakes.

**flow** **flows, flowing, flowed**

VERB If liquid **flows** in a certain direction, it moves there steadily.

**flow chart** **flow charts**

NOUN A **flow chart** is a diagram which shows how one action follows on from another. This flow chart shows how to make a cup of tea.

**flower** **flowers**

NOUN A **flower** is the part of a plant that has coloured petals. When the petals fade, fruit or seeds develop.

**flown**

VERB **Flown** is the past participle of **fly**.

**flu**

NOUN **Flu** is an illness that gives you a fever and makes you ache all over. Flu is an abbreviation of **influenza**.

**fluffy** **fluffier, fluffiest**

ADJECTIVE Something that is **fluffy** is very soft and light.

**fluid** **fluids**
NOUN **Fluid** is another word for liquid.

**flute** **flutes**
NOUN A **flute** is a musical wind instrument consisting of a long tube with holes and keys.

**flutter** **flutters, fluttering, fluttered**
VERB If something **flutters**, it flaps or waves with small quick movements.

**fly** **flies, flying, flew, flown**
NOUN **1** A **fly** is a small insect with two wings.
See *Insects* on page 259.
VERB **2** When a bird, insect or aircraft **flies**, it moves through the air.

**foal** **foals**
NOUN A **foal** is a young horse.
See *Young animals* on page 260.

**foam**
NOUN **Foam** is a mass of tiny bubbles.

**focus** **focuses, focusing, focused**
VERB If you **focus** something like a camera or a telescope, you adjust it so that you can see through it clearly.

**fog** **fogs**
NOUN **Fog** is a thick mist of water droplets in the air.
**foggy** ADJECTIVE

**fold** **folds, folding, folded**
NOUN **1** **Folds** in material are the curves in it when it does not hang flat. *The curtains hung in soft folds.*
VERB **2** If you **fold** something, you bend it so that one part lies over another.

**folder** **folders**
NOUN A **folder** is a piece of folded cardboard for keeping papers in.

**folk** **folks**
NOUN **Folk** or folks are people.

**follow** **follows, following, followed**
VERB **1** If you **follow** someone who is moving, you move along behind them.
VERB **2** If one thing **follows** another, it happens after it.
VERB **3** If you **follow** instructions or advice, you do what you are told.

**fond** **fonder, fondest**
ADJECTIVE If you are **fond** of someone, you like them very much.

**font** **fonts**
NOUN In printing, a **font** is a complete set of type of one style and size.

**food**
NOUN **Food** is what people and animals eat to stay alive.

**food chain** **food chains**
NOUN A **food chain** is a series of living things that are linked because each one feeds on the next. For example, a plant may be eaten by a rabbit that may be eaten by a fox.

grass → rabbit → fox

**foolish**
ADJECTIVE Something or somebody **foolish** is silly or unwise.

**foot** **feet**
NOUN **1** Your **feet** are the parts of your body that touch the ground when you stand or walk.
NOUN **2** A **foot** is a measure of length, equal to about 30 centimetres.

**football** **footballs**
NOUN **1** **Football** is a game between two teams who try to kick a ball into each other's goal.
NOUN **2** A **football** is a large ball used in games of football.

**footprint** footprints

NOUN A **footprint** is a mark in the shape of a foot that a person or animal leaves on a surface.

**footstep** footsteps

NOUN A **footstep** is the sound made by someone walking.

**forbid** forbids, forbidding, forbade, forbidden

VERB If someone **forbids** you to do something, they order you not to do it.

**force** forces, forcing, forced

VERB 1 If you **force** someone or something, you use your power or strength to make them do what you want. *Dad forced me to save half my pocket money.*

NOUN 2 A **force** is a push or a pull.

NOUN 3 The **force** of something is also the powerful effect it has. *The force of the storm damaged many trees.*

**forecast** forecasts, forecasting, forecast

VERB 1 If someone **forecasts** something, they say what they think is going to happen in the future.

NOUN 2 A weather **forecast** tells you what sort of weather to expect.

**forehead** foreheads

NOUN Your **forehead** is the front of your head, between your hair and eyebrows.

**foreign**

ADJECTIVE Something that is **foreign** is to do with a country that is not your own.

**forest** forests

NOUN A **forest** is a large area where trees grow close together.

**forgave**

VERB **Forgave** is the past tense of **forgive**.

**forget** forgets, forgetting, forgot, forgotten

VERB If you **forget** something, you do not remember or think about it.

**forgive** forgives, forgiving, forgave, forgiven

VERB If you **forgive** someone who has done something bad, you stop being cross with them.

**fork** forks

NOUN 1 A **fork** is a tool with three or four prongs on the end of a handle. You use a small fork for eating and a large fork for digging in the garden.

NOUN 2 A **fork** in a road or tree is the point where it divides into two.

**form** forms, forming, formed

NOUN 1 A **form** is a piece of paper with questions on it and spaces where you should write the answers.

NOUN 2 A **form** is also a class in school.

VERB 3 When something **forms**, it takes shape.

**formal**

ADJECTIVE Something **formal** is correct and serious.

**fortnight** fortnights

NOUN A **fortnight** is two weeks.

**fortress** fortresses

NOUN A **fortress** is a castle or other strong place that is built with defences to keep enemies out.

**fortunate**

ADJECTIVE 1 Someone who is **fortunate** has good luck.

ADJECTIVE 2 Something that is **fortunate** brings you success or gives you an advantage.

**fortune** fortunes

NOUN 1 **Fortune** is good or bad luck.

NOUN 2 A **fortune** is a lot of money.

## forward

ADVERB If you move **forward** or **forwards**, you move the way you are facing.

**look forward** PHRASE If you **look forward** to something, you want it to happen.

## fossil   fossils

NOUN A **fossil** is the hardened remains of a prehistoric animal or plant that are found inside a rock.

## fought

VERB **Fought** is the past tense of **fight**.

## foul   fouler, foulest

ADJECTIVE If something is **foul**, it is extremely unpleasant.

## found

VERB **Found** is the past tense of **find**.

## foundation   foundations

NOUN The **foundations** of a building are the solid layers of material put below the ground to support it.

## fountain   fountains

NOUN A **fountain** is a jet or spray of water forced up into the air by a pump.

## fox   foxes

NOUN A **fox** is a wild animal like a dog, with reddish-brown fur and a thick tail.

## fraction   fractions

NOUN **1** In maths, a **fraction** is a part of a whole number, for example $\frac{1}{4}$.
*See Fractions on page 272.*
NOUN **2** A **fraction** is also a tiny part of something.

## fracture   fractures

NOUN A **fracture** is a crack or break in something, especially a bone.

## fragile

ADJECTIVE Something that is **fragile** is easily broken or damaged.

## fragment   fragments

NOUN A **fragment** of something is a small piece or part of it.

## frame   frames

NOUN A **frame** is the part surrounding something like a window or picture, or the lenses of a pair of glasses.

## freckle   freckles

NOUN **Freckles** are small, light brown spots on someone's skin.

## free

ADJECTIVE **1** If a person or animal is **free**, they can go where they want.
*Tom opened the cage and set the bird free.*
ADJECTIVE **2** If something is **free**, it does not cost anything.
**freedom** NOUN

## freeze   freezes, freezing, froze, frozen

VERB **1** If a liquid **freezes**, it becomes solid because the temperature is low.
VERB **2** If you **freeze** something, you store it at a very low temperature.

## freezer   freezers

NOUN A **freezer** is a refrigerator for freezing and storing food.

## frequent

ADJECTIVE If something is **frequent**, it happens often.
**frequency** NOUN   **frequently** ADVERB

a
b
c
d
e
**Ff**
g
h
i
j
k
l
m
n
o
p
q
r
s
t
u
v
w
x
y
z

# fresh

**fresh** **fresher, freshest**
ADJECTIVE **1** If food is **fresh**, it has been picked or made recently.
ADJECTIVE **2** **Fresh** water is water that is not salty.
ADJECTIVE **3** If you feel **fresh**, you feel rested and full of energy.
ADJECTIVE **4** **Fresh** air is the air outside.

**friction**
NOUN **Friction** is the force which is produced when two surfaces rub against each other.

**Friday** **Fridays**
NOUN **Friday** is the day between Thursday and Saturday.

**fridge** **fridges**
NOUN A **fridge** is a large metal container. It is kept cool so that the food in it stays fresh longer. Fridge is an abbreviation of **refrigerator**.

**friend** **friends**
NOUN A **friend** is someone you know well and like very much.

**friendly** **friendlier, friendliest**
ADJECTIVE If you are **friendly** to someone, you behave in a kind and pleasant way to them.

**fright**
NOUN **Fright** is a sudden feeling of fear.

**frighten** **frightens, frightening, frightened**
VERB If something **frightens** you, it makes you afraid.

**frightening**
ADJECTIVE Something that is **frightening** makes you feel afraid.

**frog** **frogs**
NOUN A **frog** is a small amphibious animal with smooth skin, big eyes, and long back legs which it uses for jumping. See *Amphibians* on page 259.

**front** **fronts**
NOUN **1** The **front** of something is the part that faces forward.
ADJECTIVE **2** A **front** room or garden is on the side of a building that faces the street.
in front PHRASE **In front** means ahead or further forward.
in front of PHRASE If you do something **in front of** someone, you do it while they are there.

**frost** **frosts**
NOUN When there is a **frost**, the weather is very cold and the ground becomes covered with tiny ice crystals.

**frown** **frowns, frowning, frowned**
VERB If you **frown**, your eyebrows are drawn together. People frown when they are angry, worried, or thinking hard.

**froze**
VERB **Froze** is the past tense of **freeze**.

**frozen**
VERB **1** **Frozen** is the past participle of **freeze**.
ADJECTIVE **2** If something like a lake or river is **frozen**, its surface has turned to ice.
ADJECTIVE **3** If you say you are **frozen**, you mean you are very cold.

**fruit** **fruits**
NOUN A **fruit** is the part of a plant that develops from the flower and contains the seeds. Many fruits are good to eat. See *Fruit* on page 257.

**fry** **fries, frying, fried**
VERB When you **fry** food, you cook it in a pan that contains hot fat or oil.

**fuel** **fuels**

NOUN **Fuel** is something like petrol or coal, that is burned to provide heat or power.

**full** **fuller, fullest**

ADJECTIVE If something is **full**, there is no room for anything more.

**full stop** **full stops**

NOUN A **full stop** is the punctuation mark (.) which you use at the end of a sentence.

See *Punctuation* on page 264.

**fun**

NOUN **Fun** is something enjoyable that makes you feel happy.

**funeral** **funerals**

NOUN A **funeral** is a ceremony held when a person has died. The body is buried or burned.

**fungus** **fungi** or **funguses**

NOUN A **fungus** is a plant such as a mushroom or mould that does not have flowers or leaves.

**funnel** **funnels**

NOUN **1** A **funnel** is an open cone which narrows to a tube. You use a funnel to pour liquid into containers.

NOUN **2** A **funnel** is also a metal chimney on a ship or steam engine.

**funny** **funnier, funniest**

ADJECTIVE **1** **Funny** people or things make you laugh.

ADJECTIVE **2** Something that is **funny** is rather strange or surprising.

**funnily** ADVERB

**fur**

NOUN **Fur** is the soft thick body hair of many animals.

**furry** ADJECTIVE

**furious**

ADJECTIVE Someone who is **furious** is extremely angry.

**furniture**

NOUN **Furniture** is large objects such as tables, beds and chairs, that people have in rooms.

**further** **furthest**

ADJECTIVE **1** **Further** is a comparative form of **far**.

ADJECTIVE **2** **Further** can mean more. *Write for **further** details.*

ADVERB **3** If someone goes **further** than someone else, they travel a longer way.

**fury**

NOUN **Fury** is violent or extreme anger.

**fuss** **fusses, fussing, fussed**

NOUN **1** A **fuss** is worried or anxious behaviour that is unnecessary and often not welcome. *I don't know why you're making such a **fuss** about it.*

VERB **2** If someone **fusses**, they worry about unimportant things.

**future** **futures**

NOUN **1** The **future** is the time that is to come.

ADJECTIVE **2** **Future** is to do with time that is to come. *We need to look after the environment for **future** generations.*

NOUN **3** The **future tense** of a verb is the form used to talk about something that will happen in the future. For example, the sentence "Ben will be at school tomorrow" is in the future tense.

a
b
c
d
e
f
**Gg**
h
i
j
k
l
m
n
o
p
q
r
s
t
u
v
w
x
y
z

# Gg

**gain**  **gains, gaining, gained**
NOUN **1** A **gain** is an increase in the amount of something.
VERB **2** If you **gain** from something, you get something good out of it.
VERB **3** If a clock or watch **gains**, it moves too fast.

**galaxy**  **galaxies**
NOUN **1** A **galaxy** is a large group of stars and planets in space.
NOUN **2** The **galaxy** is the group of stars and planets that the earth belongs to.
**galactic** ADJECTIVE

**gale**  **gales**
NOUN A **gale** is a strong wind.

**galleon**  **galleons**
NOUN A **galleon** is a large sailing ship used hundreds of years ago.

**gallery**  **galleries**
NOUN **1** A **gallery** is a place that shows paintings or sculptures.
NOUN **2** In a hall or theatre, a **gallery** is a raised area at the back where people can sit and get a good view of what is happening.

**gallon**  **gallons**
NOUN A **gallon** is a measure of volume equal to about four and a half litres.

**gallop**  **gallops, galloping, galloped**
VERB When a horse **gallops**, it runs fast.

**game**  **games**
NOUN A **game** is a something you play for sport or fun. Most games have rules.

**gander**  **ganders**
NOUN A **gander** is a male goose.

**gang**  **gangs**
NOUN A **gang** is a group of people who do things together.

**gaol**  **gaols**
**Gaol** is another spelling of **jail**.

**gap**  **gaps**
NOUN A **gap** is a space between two things, or a hole in something solid.

**garage**  **garages**
NOUN **1** A **garage** is a building in which someone can keep a car.
NOUN **2** A **garage** is also a place that sells petrol or repairs cars.

**garden**  **gardens**
NOUN A **garden** is land next to a house where people can grow things like trees, flowers or grass.

**garlic**
NOUN **Garlic** is the small white bulb of an onion-like plant which has a strong taste and smell. It is used in cooking.

**garment**  **garments**
NOUN A **garment** is a piece of clothing.

**gas**  **gases**
NOUN **Gas** is a substance that is not liquid or solid. Air is a mixture of gases. Another type of gas is used as a fuel for cookers and central heating.

**gasp**  **gasps, gasping, gasped**
VERB When you **gasp**, you take a short quick breath through your mouth, especially when you are surprised or in pain.

**gate** gates

NOUN A **gate** is a type of door that is used at the entrance to a garden or field.

**gather** gathers, gathering, gathered

VERB **1** If people or animals **gather**, they come together in a group.

VERB **2** If you **gather** things, you collect them from different places. *Early people used to gather berries for food.*

**gave**

VERB **Gave** is the past tense of **give**.

**gaze** gazes, gazing, gazed

VERB If you **gaze** at something, you look steadily at it for a long time.

**general** generals

ADJECTIVE **1** You use **general** when you are talking about most of the people in a group. *There was a general rush for the door when the bell rang.*

NOUN **2** A **general** is an army officer of very high rank.

**generally** ADVERB

**generous**

ADJECTIVE Someone who is **generous** is kind and willing to help others by giving them money or time.

**gentle** gentler, gentlest

ADJECTIVE Someone who is **gentle** is kind, calm and sensitive.

**gently** ADVERB

**gentleman** gentlemen

NOUN A **gentleman** is a polite name for a man.

**genuine**

ADJECTIVE Something **genuine** is real and not false or pretend.

**geography**

NOUN **Geography** is the study of the countries of the world, and of things like their rivers, mountains and people.

**geographical** ADJECTIVE

**gerbil** gerbils

NOUN A **gerbil** is a small furry animal with long back legs, often kept as a pet.

**germ** germs

NOUN A **germ** is a tiny living thing that can make people ill. You cannot see germs without using a microscope.

**get** gets, getting, got

VERB **1** Get often means the same as become. *It gets dark earlier in winter.*

VERB **2** If you **get** into a particular situation, you put yourself in that situation. *We got into a muddle.*

VERB **3** If you **get** something done, you do it or you persuade someone to do it.

VERB **4** If you **get** something, you fetch it or are given it. *I'll get us all a cup of tea.*

VERB **5** If you **get** a train, bus or plane, you travel on it.

**ghost** ghosts

NOUN A **ghost** is a shadowy figure of someone no longer living that some people believe they see.

**giant** giants

NOUN **1** In fairy stories, a **giant** is someone who is huge and strong.

ADJECTIVE **2** Anything that is much larger than usual can be called **giant**. *A giant wave was coming towards us.*

**giddy** giddier, giddiest

ADJECTIVE If you feel **giddy**, you feel dizzy.

**gift** **gifts**

NOUN A **gift** is a present.

**gigantic**

ADJECTIVE Something **gigantic** is extremely large.

**giggle** **giggles, giggling, giggled**

VERB If you **giggle**, you make quiet little laughing noises.

**gill** **gills**

NOUN The **gills** of a fish are the organs on its sides which it uses for breathing.

**ginger**

NOUN **Ginger** is a plant root with a hot spicy flavour, used in cooking.

**giraffe** **giraffes**

NOUN A **giraffe** is a large African mammal with a very long neck.

**girl** **girls**

NOUN A **girl** is a female child.

**give** **gives, giving, gave, given**

VERB If you **give** someone something, you hand it to them or provide it for them. *Dad **gave** me a job cleaning the car.*

**give way** PHRASE If something **gives way**, it collapses.

**glacier** **glaciers**

NOUN A **glacier** is a huge frozen river of slow-moving ice.

**glad** **gladder, gladdest**

ADJECTIVE If you are **glad**, you are happy and pleased.

**glance** **glances, glancing, glanced**

VERB **1** If you **glance** at something, you look at it quickly.

NOUN **2** A **glance** is a quick look.

**glare** **glares, glaring, glared**

VERB **1** If you **glare** at someone, you look at them angrily.

VERB **2** If the sun or a light **glares**, it shines with a very bright light.

**glass** **glasses**

NOUN **1** Glass is a hard transparent material that is easily broken. It is used to make windows and bottles.

NOUN **2** A **glass** is a container that you can drink from, made of glass.

**glasses**

PLURAL NOUN **Glasses** are two lenses in a frame, which some people wear over their eyes to help them see better.

**gleam** **gleams, gleaming, gleamed**

VERB If something **gleams**, it shines and reflects light.

**glide** **glides, gliding, glided**

VERB When something **glides**, it moves silently and smoothly.

**glider** **gliders**

NOUN A **glider** is an aircraft that does not have an engine, but flies by floating on air currents.

**glimpse** **glimpses, glimpsing, glimpsed**

VERB If you **glimpse** something, you see it very briefly.

**glisten** **glistens, glistening, glistened**

VERB If something **glistens**, it shines or sparkles. *Her eyes **glistened** with tears.*

**glitter** **glitters, glittering, glittered**

VERB If something **glitters**, it shines in a sparkling way. *Her diamond necklace **glittered** under the lights.*

a b c d e f **Gg** h i j k l m n o p q r s t u v w x y z

**gloat** gloats, gloating, gloated
VERB If you **gloat**, you show great pleasure in your own success or in other people's failure.

**globe** globes
NOUN A **globe** is a round model of the Earth with a map of the world drawn on it.

**gloomy** gloomier, gloomiest
ADJECTIVE **1** If a place is **gloomy**, it is dark and dull.
ADJECTIVE **2** If people are **gloomy**, they are unhappy and not at all hopeful.
**gloomily** ADVERB

**glossary** glossaries
NOUN A **glossary** is a list of explanations of special words, usually found at the back of a book.

**glossy** glossier, glossiest
ADJECTIVE Something that is **glossy** is smooth and shiny.

**glove** gloves
NOUN A **glove** is a piece of clothing which covers your hand, with separate places for each finger.

**glow** glows, glowing, glowed
VERB If something **glows**, it shines with a steady dull light.

**glue**
NOUN **Glue** is a thick sticky liquid used for joining things together.

**gnarled**
ADJECTIVE Something that is **gnarled** is old, twisted and rough. *The old gardener's hands were gnarled.*

**gnat** gnats
NOUN A **gnat** is a very small flying insect that bites people.

**gnaw** gnaws, gnawing, gnawed
VERB If people or animals **gnaw** something hard, they keep biting on it.

**gnome** gnomes
NOUN In fairy stories, a **gnome** is a tiny old man.

**go** goes, going, went, gone
VERB **1** If you **go** somewhere, you move or travel there.
VERB **2** If something **goes** well, it is successful.
VERB **3** If you are **going** to do something, you will do it.
VERB **4** If a clock or watch **goes**, it works.

**goal** goals
NOUN **1** A **goal** in games such as football or hockey is the space into which players try to get the ball so that they can score.
NOUN **2** It is also called a **goal** when a player gets the ball into the goal.
NOUN **3** If something is your **goal**, you hope to succeed in doing it one day.

**goat** goats
NOUN A **goat** is an animal with short coarse hair, horns, and a short tail.

**goblin** goblins
NOUN In fairy stories, a **goblin** is a small ugly creature who likes to make trouble.

**god** gods
NOUN **1** A **god** is a person or thing that people worship.
NOUN **2** The name **God** is given to the god who is worshipped by some people, such as Christians or Jews.

**goddess** goddesses
NOUN A **goddess** is a female god.

a
b
c
d
e
f
**Gg**
h
i
j
k
l
m
n
o
p
q
r
s
t
u
v
w
x
y
z

## goggles

PLURAL NOUN **Goggles** are special glasses that fit closely round your eyes to protect them.

## go-kart  go-karts

A **go-kart** is a very small motor vehicle with four wheels, used for racing.

## gold

NOUN **1 Gold** is a valuable, yellow-coloured metal that is used for making things like jewellery.

ADJECTIVE **2** Something that is **gold** in colour is warm yellow.

## golden

ADJECTIVE Something that is **golden** is made of gold or is a gold colour.

## goldfish

NOUN A **goldfish** is a gold or orange-coloured fish which is often kept as a pet.

## golf

NOUN **Golf** is a game in which players use long sticks called clubs to hit a small ball into special holes.

## gone

VERB **Gone** is the past participle of **go**.

## good  better, best

ADJECTIVE **1** Someone who is **good** is kind and caring, and can be trusted.

ADJECTIVE **2** A child or animal that is **good** is well-behaved and obedient.

ADJECTIVE **3** If something like a film or book is **good**, people like it.

ADJECTIVE **4** Someone who is **good** at something is skilful and successful at it.

## goodbye

You say **goodbye** to someone when you or they are leaving.

## good night

You say **good night** to someone when you or they are going to bed.

## goods

PLURAL NOUN **Goods** are things that can be bought or sold.

## goose  geese

NOUN A **goose** is a large bird with a long neck and webbed feet. Its cry is a loud honking noise.

## gorilla  gorillas

NOUN The **gorilla** is the largest of the apes. It lives in African forests.

## got

VERB **1 Got** is the past tense of **get**.

VERB **2** You can use **have got** instead of **have**. *We **have got** a map.*

VERB **3** You can use **have got to** instead of **have to**, when talking about something you must do. *We **have got to** win.*

## government  governments

NOUN A **government** is the group of people who run a country and decide about important things such as medical care and old age pensions.

## grab  grabs, grabbing, grabbed

VERB If you **grab** something, you take hold of it suddenly and roughly.

## graceful

ADJECTIVE Someone or something that is **graceful** moves in a smooth way which is pleasant to watch.

## gradual

ADJECTIVE Something that is **gradual** happens slowly.

**gradually** ADVERB

## graffiti

NOUN **Graffiti** is words or pictures that are scribbled on walls in public places.

**grain** **grains**

NOUN **1 Grain** is the seeds of plants like wheat or corn, that we use for food.

NOUN **2** A **grain** of something such as sand or salt is a tiny hard piece of it.

**gram** **grams**

NOUN A **gram** (g) is a small unit of mass and weight. One sheet of paper weighs about four grams. There are 1000 grams in a kilogram.

**grammar**

NOUN **Grammar** is the rules of a language.

**grand** **grander, grandest**

ADJECTIVE Buildings that are **grand** are large and look important.

**grandad** **grandads**

NOUN Your **grandad** is your grandfather.

**grandchild** **grandchildren**

NOUN Someone's **grandchild** is the child of their son or daughter.

**grandfather** **grandfathers**

NOUN Your **grandfather** is the father of one of your parents.

**grandmother** **grandmothers**

NOUN Your **grandmother** is the mother of one of your parents.

**grandparent** **grandparents**

NOUN Your **grandparents** are your parents' parents.

**granny** **grannies**

NOUN; INFORMAL Your **granny** is your grandmother.

**grape** **grapes**

NOUN A **grape** is a small green or purple fruit. Grapes grow in bunches on vines. They can be eaten raw, used for making wine, or dried to make raisins, sultanas or currants.

See *Fruit* on page 257.

**grapefruit** **grapefruits**

NOUN A **grapefruit** is a large round fruit. It is like an orange but it is larger and has a pale yellow skin.

See *Fruit* on page 257.

**graph** **graphs**

NOUN A **graph** is a diagram which shows how two sets of information are related.

**grasp** **grasps, grasping, grasped**

VERB **1** If you **grasp** something, you hold it firmly.

VERB **2** If you **grasp** an idea, you understand it.

**grass** **grasses**

NOUN **Grass** is a common green plant with long thin leaves. It grows on lawns and in parks.

**grasshopper** **grasshoppers**

NOUN A **grasshopper** is an insect. It has long back legs and can jump well. The male makes a chirping sound by rubbing its back legs against its wings.

See *Insects* on page 259.

**grate** **grates, grating, grated**

NOUN **1** A **grate** is a framework of metal bars in a fireplace.

VERB **2** If you **grate** food, you shred it into small pieces.

**grateful**

ADJECTIVE If you are **grateful** for something nice that someone has done, you have warm feelings towards them and want to thank them.

**grave** **graver, gravest; graves**

ADJECTIVE **1** Something that is **grave** is important, serious and worrying.

NOUN **2** A **grave** is a place where a dead person is buried.

**gravel**

NOUN **Gravel** is small stones used for making roads and paths.

**gravity**

NOUN **Gravity** is the force that makes things fall when you drop them.

**gravy**

NOUN **Gravy** is a brown sauce made from meat juices.

**graze** **grazes, grazing, grazed**

VERB **1** When animals **graze**, they eat grass.

VERB **2** If you **graze** your skin, you scrape it against something and hurt yourself.

**grease**

NOUN **1** **Grease** is a thick oil which is put on the moving parts of cars and other machines to make them work smoothly.

NOUN **2** **Grease** is also an oily substance produced by your skin and found in your hair.

**greasy** ADJECTIVE

**great** **greater, greatest**

ADJECTIVE **1** You say something is **great** when it is large in size, number or amount. *The waves threw a **great** shower of pebbles onto the seafront.*

ADJECTIVE **2** **Great** also means important. *I like to hear about **great** scientists.*

ADJECTIVE **3** INFORMAL **Great** can mean wonderful. *Paul had a **great** time.*

**greedy** **greedier, greediest**

ADJECTIVE Someone who is **greedy** wants more than they need of something.

**greedily** ADVERB

**green** **greener, greenest**

ADJECTIVE **1** Something that is **green** is the colour of grass.

See *Colours* on page 271.

ADJECTIVE **2** **Green** is used to describe people who are interested in protecting the environment.

**greengrocer** **greengrocers**

NOUN A **greengrocer** is a shopkeeper who sells fruit and vegetables.

**greenhouse** **greenhouses**

NOUN A **greenhouse** is a building which has glass walls and a glass roof. It is used to grow plants in.

**greet** **greets, greeting, greeted**

VERB When you **greet** someone, you look pleased to see them, and say something friendly.

**greeting** **greetings**

NOUN A **greeting** is something friendly that you say or do when you meet someone.

**grew**

VERB **Grew** is the past tense of **grow**.

**grey** **greyer, greyest**

ADJECTIVE Something that is **grey** is the colour of clouds on a rainy day. See *Colours* on page 271.

**grid** **grids**

NOUN A **grid** is a pattern of lines crossing each other to form squares.

**grief**

NOUN Someone who feels **grief** is very sad, often because a person or animal they love has died.

**grill** **grills, grilling, grilled**

VERB If you **grill** food, you cook it on metal bars under or over heat.

**grim** **grimmer, grimmest**

ADJECTIVE **1** If a situation or piece of news is **grim**, it is unpleasant and worrying.

ADJECTIVE **2** If someone looks **grim**, they are serious because they are worried or angry about something.

**grin** grins, grinning, grinned
VERB If you **grin**, you give a broad smile.

**grind** grinds, grinding, ground
VERB **1** If you **grind** something, such as pepper, you crush it into a fine powder.
VERB **2** If you **grind** your teeth, you rub your upper and lower teeth together.

**grip** grips, gripping, gripped
VERB **1** If you **grip** something, you take hold of it firmly.
VERB **2** If something **grips** you, you find it very interesting.

**groan** groans, groaning, groaned
VERB If you **groan**, you make a long low sound of pain or unhappiness.

**groceries**
PLURAL NOUN **Groceries** are foods such as flour, sugar and tinned foods.

**groove** grooves
NOUN A **groove** is a deep line cut into a surface.

**ground** grounds
NOUN **1** The **ground** is the surface of the earth or the floor of a room.
NOUN **2** A **ground** is an area of land where people play sports such as football or cricket.
PLURAL NOUN **3** The **grounds** of a large house are the land around it which belongs to it.
VERB **4 Ground** is the past tense of **grind**.

**group** groups
NOUN **1** A **group** of things or people is a number of them that are linked together in some way.
NOUN **2** A **group** is also a number of musicians who perform music together.

**grow** grows, growing, grew, grown
VERB **1** When a person **grows**, they get bigger. All living things can grow.
VERB **2** If you **grow** plants, you put seeds or young plants in the ground and look after them.
VERB **3** When someone **grows up**, they gradually change from being a child into being an adult.

**growl** growls, growling, growled
VERB When an animal **growls**, it makes a low rumbling sound, usually because it is angry.

**grown**
VERB **Grown** is the past participle of **grow**.

**grown-up** grown-ups
NOUN; INFORMAL A **grown-up** is an adult.

**growth**
NOUN **Growth** means getting bigger.

**grub** grubs
NOUN A **grub** is a wormlike insect that has just hatched from its egg.

**grumble** grumbles, grumbling, grumbled
VERB If you **grumble**, you complain in a bad-tempered way.

**grunt** grunts, grunting, grunted
VERB When a pig **grunts**, it makes a low rough noise.

**guarantee** guarantees, guaranteeing, guaranteed
VERB **1** If someone or something **guarantees** something, they make certain that it will happen.
NOUN **2** A **guarantee** is a written promise that if something you have bought goes wrong it will be replaced or mended free.

a
b
c
d
e
f
Gg
h
i
j
k
l
m
n
o
p
q
r
s
t
u
v
w
x
y
z

**guard** guards, guarding, guarded
VERB **1** If you **guard** a person or object, you stay near to them to keep them safe or to make sure they do not escape.
NOUN **2** A **guard** is a person who guards something or somewhere.

**guess** guesses, guessing, guessed
VERB If you **guess** something, you give an answer without knowing if it is right.

**guest** guests
NOUN A **guest** is someone who stays at your home or who goes to an event because they have been invited.

**guide** guides, guiding, guided
VERB **1** If you **guide** someone, you show them where to go or what to do.
NOUN **2** A **guide** is someone who shows you round places.

**guidebook** guidebooks
NOUN A **guidebook** is a book that gives information about a place.

**guilty** guiltier, guiltiest
ADJECTIVE **1** If you are **guilty** of doing something wrong, you did it.
ADJECTIVE **2** If you feel **guilty**, you are unhappy because you have done something wrong.

**guinea pig** guinea pigs
NOUN A **guinea pig** is a small furry animal without a tail, often kept as a pet.

**guitar** guitars
NOUN A **guitar** is a musical instrument with strings that you play with your fingers.

**gulf** gulfs
NOUN A **gulf** is a large area of sea which stretches a long way into the land.

**gulp** gulps, gulping, gulped
VERB **1** If you **gulp** food or drink, you swallow large amounts of it.
VERB **2** If you **gulp**, you swallow air because you are nervous.

**gum** gums
NOUN **1** Your **gums** are the firm flesh your teeth are set in.
NOUN **2** Gum is a soft sweet that people chew but do not swallow.
NOUN **3** Gum is also glue for sticking paper.

**gumboot** gumboots
NOUN Gumboots are long rubber boots that you wear to keep your feet dry.

**gun** guns
NOUN A **gun** is a weapon which fires bullets or shells.

**gunpowder**
NOUN Gunpowder is a powder that explodes when it is lit. It is used for making things such as fireworks.

**gust** gusts
NOUN A **gust** is a sudden rush of wind.

**gutter** gutters
NOUN **1** A **gutter** is the edge of a road next to the pavement, where rain collects and flows away.
NOUN **2** A **gutter** is also an open pipe at the edge of a roof, where rain collects and flows away.

**gym** gyms
NOUN **1** Gym is physical exercises, especially ones using equipment such as bars and ropes. Gym is an abbreviation of **gymnastics**.

NOUN **2** A **gym** is a room with special equipment for physical exercises. Gym here is an abbreviation of **gymnasium**.

# Hh

**habit** **habits**
NOUN A **habit** is something that you do often or regularly, sometimes without thinking about it.

**habitat** **habitats**
NOUN The **habitat** of an animal or plant is its natural home.

**had**
VERB **Had** is the past tense of **have**.

**haddock**
NOUN A **haddock** is an edible sea fish.

**haiku**
NOUN **Haiku** is a Japanese poem of 17 syllables in three lines.

**hail** **hails, hailing, hailed**
NOUN **1** Hail is frozen rain. It falls in small balls of ice called hailstones.
VERB **2** When it is **hailing**, frozen rain is falling.

**hair** **hairs**
NOUN Your **hair** is made up of a large number of fine threads that grow on your head. Hair also grows on other parts of the body and on the bodies of some other animals.

**hairdresser** **hairdressers**
NOUN A **hairdresser** is trained to cut and style people's hair.

**hairy** **hairier, hairiest**
ADJECTIVE Someone or something that is **hairy** is covered with hair.

**hajj**
NOUN The **hajj** is the journey to Mecca that every Muslim must make at least once in their life if they are healthy and wealthy enough to do so.

**half** **halves**
NOUN **1** A **half** is one of two equal parts of something.
See *Fractions* on page 272.

ADVERB **2** When you are talking about time, you can use **half** to mean 30 minutes after a particular hour. *She was home by **half** past three.*

**halfway**
ADVERB **Halfway** is the middle of the distance between two points. *He stopped **halfway** down the stairs.*

**hall** **halls**
NOUN **1** A **hall** is the room just inside the front door of a home which leads into other rooms.
NOUN **2** A **hall** is also a large room or building used for public events.

**Halloween**
NOUN **Halloween** is October 31. Children celebrate it by dressing up, often as ghosts and witches.

**halve** **halves, halving, halved**
VERB If you **halve** something, you divide it into two equal parts.

**ham**
NOUN **Ham** is meat from the back leg of a pig. It is specially treated so that it can be kept for a long time.

**hamburger** **hamburgers**
NOUN A **hamburger** is a piece of minced meat shaped into a flat disc. Hamburgers are often eaten in a bread roll.

**hammer**  **hammers**
NOUN A **hammer** is a tool that is used for hitting things, such as nails into wood.

**hammock**  **hammocks**
NOUN A **hammock** is a piece of strong cloth or netting which is hung between two supports and used as a bed.

**hamster**  **hamsters**
NOUN A **hamster** is a small furry rodent which is often kept as a pet. Hamsters have very short tails, and large cheek pouches for carrying food.

**hand**  **hands, handing, handed**
NOUN **1** Your **hand** is the part of your body which is at the end of your arm. It has four fingers and a thumb.
NOUN **2** The **hands** of a clock point to the numbers to tell you the time.
VERB **3** When you **hand** something to someone, you pass it to them.

**handbag**  **handbags**
NOUN A **handbag** is a small bag that women use to carry things such as money and keys.

**handkerchief**  **handkerchiefs**
NOUN A **handkerchief** is a small square of fabric that you use for wiping your nose.

**handle**  **handles, handling, handled**
NOUN **1** The **handle** of an object is the part you hold to pick it up and carry it.
NOUN **2** The **handle** of a door or window is the knob or lever that is used for opening or closing it.
VERB **3** If you **handle** something, you touch or feel it with your hands.

**handlebar**  **handlebars**
NOUN **Handlebars** are the bar and handles at the front of a bicycle, used for steering.

**handsome**
ADJECTIVE A **handsome** man has a very attractive face.

**handwriting**
NOUN Someone's **handwriting** is the way in which they write with a pen or pencil.

**handy**  **handier, handiest**
ADJECTIVE **1** If something is **handy**, it is near. *I like to keep my glasses **handy**.*
ADJECTIVE **2** If an object is **handy**, it is easy to handle or use.

**hang**  **hangs, hanging, hung**
VERB If you **hang** something up, you fix it there so that it does not touch the ground. ***Hang** your coat on the hook.*

**hangar**  **hangars**
NOUN A **hangar** is a large building where aircraft are kept.

**hanger**  **hangers**
NOUN A **hanger** is a curved piece of metal, wood or plastic that you hang clothes on.

**hang-glider**  **hang-gliders**
NOUN A **hang-glider** is an aircraft without an engine. The pilot hangs in a harness from the frame.

**Hanukkah** or **Chanukah**
NOUN **Hanukkah** is the eight-day Jewish festival of lights.

**happen**  **happens, happening, happened**
VERB **1** If something **happens**, it takes place. *What **happens** if I press this button?*
VERB **2** If you **happen** to do something, you do it by chance. *I **happened** to be near the phone when it rang.*

**happiness**
NOUN **Happiness** is a feeling of great pleasure.

**happy**  **happier, happiest**
ADJECTIVE If you are **happy**, you feel good because something nice has happened or because most things are the way you want.
**happily** ADVERB

**harbour**  **harbours**

NOUN A **harbour** is an area of deep water where boats can stay safely.

**hard**  **harder, hardest**

ADJECTIVE **1** An object that is **hard** is very firm and stiff.

ADJECTIVE **2** If something is **hard** to do, you can only do it with a lot of effort.

**hard disk**  **hard disks**

NOUN A **hard disk** is a permanent part of a computer. It is used to store large amounts of data.

**harden**  **hardens, hardening, hardened**

VERB If something **hardens**, it becomes hard or gets harder.

**hardly**

ADVERB If you can **hardly** do something, you can only just do it. *The box was so heavy I could **hardly** lift it.*

**hardware**

NOUN **1** Hardware is tools and equipment made of metal.

NOUN **2** Hardware is also computer machinery.

**hare**  **hares**

NOUN A **hare** is an animal like a large rabbit, but with longer ears and legs. It does not live in a burrow but rests in grass or in a ploughed field.

**harm**

NOUN **Harm** is injury to a person or animal.

**harmful** ADJECTIVE    **harmless** ADJECTIVE

**harness**  **harnesses**

NOUN **1** A **harness** is a set of straps which fit round a person's body to hold the person firmly in place.

NOUN **2** A horse's **harness** is a set of straps fastened round its head or body.

**harsh**  **harsher, harshest**

ADJECTIVE **1** A person who is **harsh** is unkind.

ADJECTIVE **2** Weather that is **harsh** is cold and unpleasant.

ADJECTIVE **3** A voice or other sound that is **harsh** sounds rough and unpleasant.

**harvest**  **harvests**

NOUN **Harvest** is the time when farmers cut and gather their ripe crop.

**has**

VERB **Has** is a present tense form of **have**.

**hat**  **hats**

NOUN A **hat** is a head covering for wearing outside.

**hatch**  **hatches, hatching, hatched**

VERB When a baby bird, insect or other animal **hatches**, it comes out of its egg by breaking the shell.

**hate**  **hates, hating, hated**

VERB If you **hate** something, you have a strong feeling of dislike for it.

**haul**  **hauls, hauling, hauled**

VERB To **haul** something means to move it with a long steady pull.

**haunted**

ADJECTIVE A place that is **haunted** is often visited by a ghost.

**have**  **has, having, had**

VERB **1** Have can be used with other verbs to form the past tense. *I **have** already seen that film.*

VERB **2** If you **have** something, you own or possess it. *We **have** two tickets for the football match.*

VERB **3** If you **have** to do something, you must do it.

a
b
c
d
e
f
g
**Hh**
i
j
k
l
m
n
o
p
q
r
s
t
u
v
w
x
y
z

# haven't

**haven't**

VERB **Haven't** is a contraction of **have not**.

**hawk**  **hawks**

NOUN A **hawk** is a large bird of prey that eats small animals.

**hay**

NOUN **Hay** is grass which has been cut and dried to feed animals.

**head**  **heads, heading, headed**

NOUN **1** Your **head** is the part of your body which has your brain, eyes and mouth in it.

NOUN **2** The **head** of something is the top, start or most important end. *Our teacher sat at the **head** of the table.*

NOUN **3** The **head** of a group or organization is the person in charge.

VERB **4** If you **head** in a particular direction, you move that way.

VERB **5** To **head** a ball means to hit it with your head.

**headache**  **headaches**

NOUN A **headache** is a pain in your head.

**heading**  **headings**

NOUN A **heading** is a title at the top of a piece of writing.

**headlight**  **headlights**

NOUN The **headlights** on a motor vehicle are the large powerful lights at the front.

**headline**  **headlines**

NOUN **1** A **headline** is the title of a newspaper article printed in large type.

NOUN **2** The **headlines** are the main points of the radio or television news.

**headphones**

PLURAL NOUN **Headphones** are a pair of small speakers that you wear over or in your ears to listen to a recording without other people hearing.

**headquarters**

NOUN The **headquarters** of an organization is the place where the leaders of the organization work.

**head teacher**  **head teachers**

NOUN The **head teacher** is the teacher who is in charge of a school.

**heal**  **heals, healing, healed**

VERB If something **heals**, it becomes healthy or normal again.

**health**

NOUN A person's **health** is how their body is, and whether they are well or ill.

**healthy**  **healthier, healthiest**

ADJECTIVE **1** Someone who is **healthy** is well and not suffering from any illness.

ADJECTIVE **2** Something that is **healthy** is good for your health.

**heap**  **heaps**

NOUN A **heap** is a lot of things piled up, usually rather untidily.

**hear**  **hears, hearing, heard**

VERB When you **hear** sounds, you notice them by using your ears.

**hearing**

NOUN **Hearing** is the sense which makes it possible for you to be aware of sounds.

**heart**  **hearts**

NOUN **1** Your **heart** is the organ that pumps the blood round inside your body.

NOUN **2** A **heart** is a shape like a heart, used especially as a symbol of love.

**heat**  **heats, heating, heated**

NOUN **1** Heat is warmth.

VERB **2** To **heat** something means to raise its temperature.

## heather

NOUN **Heather** is a plant with small purple or white flowers that grows wild on hills and moorland.

## heaven

NOUN **Heaven** is a place of happiness where God is believed to live.

## heavy   heavier, heaviest

ADJECTIVE Something that is **heavy** weighs a lot or weighs more than usual.

## Hebrew

NOUN **Hebrew** is an ancient language now spoken in Israel, where it is the official language.

## hedge   hedges

NOUN A **hedge** is a row of bushes growing close together.

## hedgehog   hedgehogs

NOUN A **hedgehog** is a small animal with sharp spikes all over its back. It defends itself by rolling up into a ball.

## heel   heels

NOUN **1** Your **heel** is the back part of your foot.
NOUN **2** The **heel** of a shoe is the raised part underneath, at the back.

## height   heights

NOUN **1** The **height** of a person is how tall they are.
NOUN **2** The **height** of an object is its measurement from bottom to top.

## held

VERB **Held** is the past tense of **hold**.

## helicopter   helicopters

NOUN A **helicopter** is an aircraft with large blades which turn very quickly. It can take off vertically, hover and fly.

## helmet   helmets

NOUN A **helmet** is a hard hat that you wear to protect your head.

## help   helps, helping, helped

VERB **1** To **help** someone means to make something better or easier for them.
VERB **2** If you **help yourself** to something, you take it. *Help yourself to sandwiches.*
VERB **3** If you can't **help** something, you cannot control it or change it. *I can't help feeling sorry for him.*
**helpful** ADJECTIVE

## helping   helpings

NOUN A **helping** of food is the amount of it that you get in a single serving.

## helpless

ADJECTIVE Someone who is **helpless** cannot cope on their own.

## hem   hems

NOUN The **hem** of a piece of material is the part that is folded over and sewn.

## hemisphere   hemispheres

NOUN A **hemisphere** is one half of a sphere. It can also be half of the Earth.
See *Solid shapes* on page 271.

## hen   hens

NOUN **1** A **hen** is a female chicken.
NOUN **2** A **hen** can also be any female bird.

## heptagon   heptagons

NOUN A **heptagon** is a flat shape with seven straight sides.
See *Colours and flat shapes* on page 271.

## her

PRONOUN **1** You use **her** to refer to a woman, girl or any female animal that has already been mentioned. *I like Katherine. I often play with her.*
ADJECTIVE **2** You also use **her** to show that something belongs to a particular female. *My dog Fluff won't eat her food.*

## herd   herds

NOUN A **herd** is a large group of animals of one kind that live together.
See *Collective nouns* on page 262.

# here

**here**

ADVERB You say **here** to mean the place where you are. *I'll stand **here** and wait.*

**here and there** PHRASE **Here and there** means in various places. *Bits of paper were lying **here and there** on the floor.*

**hero** **heroes**

NOUN **1** A **hero** is a man or boy who has done something brave and good.

NOUN **2** The **hero** of a story is the man or boy that the story is about. See **heroine**.

**heroine** **heroines**

NOUN **1** A **heroine** is a woman or girl who has done something brave and good.

NOUN **2** The **heroine** of a story is the woman or girl that the story is about. See **hero**.

**heron** **herons**

NOUN A **heron** is a bird that lives near water and eats fish.

**herring** **herrings**

NOUN A **herring** is a silvery fish that lives in large shoals in northern seas.

**herself**

PRONOUN If a girl or woman does something **herself**, no one else does it. *The baby pulled **herself** up.*

**hesitate** **hesitates, hesitating, hesitated**

VERB If you **hesitate**, you pause while you are doing something, or just before you do it.

**hexagon** **hexagons**

NOUN A **hexagon** is a flat shape with six straight sides.

**hexagonal** ADJECTIVE

See *Colours and flat shapes* on page 271.

**hibernate** **hibernates, hibernating, hibernated**

VERB When certain animals, such as bears, **hibernate**, they spend the winter in a sleep-like state.

**hide** **hides, hiding, hid, hidden**

VERB **1** If you **hide** somewhere, you go where you cannot be seen.

VERB **2** If you **hide** something, you put it in a place where it cannot be seen.

**hidden** ADJECTIVE

**high** **higher, highest**

ADJECTIVE **1** Something that is **high** is a long way from the bottom to the top. *The wall round the garden is quite **high**.*

ADJECTIVE or ADVERB **2** If something is **high**, it is a long way up. *There was an aeroplane **high** above her.*

**hill** **hills**

NOUN A **hill** is a rounded area of land which is higher than the land surrounding it.

**him**

PRONOUN You use **him** to refer to a man, boy or any male animal that has already been mentioned. *James asked me to ring **him** back.*

**himself**

PRONOUN If a boy or man does something **himself**, no one else does it. *Ben hurt **himself** quite badly.*

**Hindu**  **Hindus**

NOUN A **Hindu** is a person who believes in Hinduism, an Indian religion which has many gods. Hindus believe that people have another life on earth after death.

**hinge**  **hinges**

NOUN **Hinges** are pieces of metal, wood or plastic that are used to hold a door or lid so that it can swing freely.

**hint**  **hints, hinting, hinted**

NOUN **1** A **hint** is a suggestion, clue or helpful piece of advice.

VERB **2** If you **hint**, or **hint at** something, you suggest it in a way that is not obvious. *I **hinted** that I would like a bicycle for my birthday.*

**hip**  **hips**

NOUN Your **hips** are the two parts at the sides of your body between your waist and your upper legs.

**hippopotamus**  **hippopotamuses** or **hippopotami**

NOUN A **hippopotamus** is a large African animal with thick skin and short legs. It lives in herds on the banks of large rivers, and spends a lot of time in the water. It is often called a **hippo** for short.

**hire**  **hires, hiring, hired**

VERB If you **hire** something, you pay money so that you can use it for a time.

**his**

ADJECTIVE OR PRONOUN You use **his** to show that something belongs to a man, boy or any male animal. *Robert combed **his** hair.*

**hiss**  **hisses, hissing, hissed**

VERB To **hiss** means to make a long "sss" sound.

**historical**

ADJECTIVE **Historical** stories are stories about things that happened in the past.

**history**  **histories**

NOUN **History** is a study or record of the past.

**hit**  **hits, hitting, hit**

VERB If you **hit** something, you touch it quickly and hard.

**hive**  **hives**

NOUN A **hive** is a house for bees, made so that the beekeeper can collect the honey. See **beehive**.

**hoard**  **hoards, hoarding, hoarded**

VERB **1** If you **hoard** things, you save or store them even though they may no longer be useful.

NOUN **2** A **hoard** is a store of things that has been saved or hidden.

**hoarse**  **hoarser, hoarsest**

ADJECTIVE A **hoarse** voice sounds rough.

**hobby**  **hobbies**

NOUN A **hobby** is something you enjoy doing in your spare time, such as collecting stamps or bird-watching.

**hockey**

NOUN **Hockey** is a game in which two teams use long sticks with curved ends to try and hit a small ball into the other team's goal.

**hold**  **holds, holding, held**

VERB **1** When you **hold** something, you keep it in your hand or arms.

VERB **2** If something **holds** a particular amount of something, it can contain that amount. *This jug **holds** one litre.*

# hole

**hole** **holes**

NOUN A **hole** is an opening or space in something. *The dog buried his bone in a **hole** in the garden.*

**holiday** **holidays**

NOUN A **holiday** is time away from school or work.

**hollow**

ADJECTIVE Something that is **hollow** has a space inside it. *The owl lived in a **hollow** tree trunk.*

**holly**

NOUN **Holly** is an evergreen tree with prickly leaves. It often has bright red berries in winter.

**home** **homes**

NOUN Your **home** is the place where you live and feel you belong.

**homesick**

ADJECTIVE If you are **homesick**, you are sad because you are away from home.

**homework**

NOUN **Homework** is school work that children do at home.

**homograph** **homographs**

NOUN **Homographs** are words which are spelt the same but have different meanings, for example "calf" (part of your leg) and "calf" (a young cow).

**homonym** **homonyms**

NOUN **Homonyms** are words which are pronounced or spelt in the same way but which mean different things. Homographs and homophones are homonyms.

**homophone** **homophones**

NOUN **Homophones** are words which sound the same but have different meanings or spellings, for example "right" and "write".

**honest**

ADJECTIVE Someone who is **honest** tells the truth and can be trusted.

**honey**

NOUN **Honey** is a sweet sticky food that is made by bees.

**hood** **hoods**

NOUN A **hood** is a part of a coat or jacket that you can pull over your head.

**hoof** **hooves** or **hoofs**

NOUN The **hoof** of an animal such as a horse is the hard bony part of its foot.

**hook** **hooks**

NOUN A **hook** is a curved piece of metal or plastic that is used for catching, holding or hanging things, for example a picture hook.

**hoop** **hoops**

NOUN A **hoop** is a large ring, often used as a toy.

**hoot** **hoots, hooting, hooted**

VERB **1** To **hoot** means to make a long "oo" sound like an owl.

VERB **2** If a car horn **hoots**, it makes a loud honking noise.

**hop** **hops, hopping, hopped**

VERB **1** If you **hop**, you jump on one foot.

VERB **2** When animals or birds **hop**, they jump with two feet together.

**hope** **hopes, hoping, hoped**

VERB If you **hope** that something will happen, you want it to happen.

**hopeful**

ADJECTIVE If you are **hopeful**, you are fairly sure that something you want to happen will happen.

**hopeless**

ADJECTIVE **1** You say a situation is **hopeless** when it is very bad and you do not think it will get better.

ADJECTIVE **2** If somebody is **hopeless** at doing something, they cannot do it well. *I'm **hopeless** at arithmetic.*

**horizon  horizons**

NOUN The **horizon** is the line in the far distance where the sky seems to touch the land or the sea.

**horizontal**

ADJECTIVE Something that is **horizontal** is level, like the horizon. See **vertical**.

**horn  horns**

NOUN **1** Horns are the hard pointed growths on the heads of animals such as goats.

NOUN **2** A **horn** is a musical instrument made of brass.

NOUN **3** On vehicles, a **horn** makes a loud noise as a warning.

**horrible**

ADJECTIVE Someone or something that is **horrible** is awful or very unpleasant.

**horribly** ADVERB

**horror**

NOUN **Horror** is a strong feeling of fear or disgust.

**horse  horses**

NOUN A **horse** is a large animal which people can ride. Horses are also used for pulling things like carts.

**horseshoe  horseshoes**

NOUN A **horseshoe** is a piece of metal shaped like a U. It is fixed under a horse's hoof, to protect it.

**hose  hoses**

NOUN A **hose** is a long tube that sprays water.

**hospital  hospitals**

NOUN A **hospital** is a place where sick and injured people are cared for.

**hot  hotter, hottest**

ADJECTIVE **1** Something that is **hot** has a high temperature.

ADJECTIVE **2** If you feel **hot**, you feel too warm to be comfortable.

ADJECTIVE **3** You say food is **hot** if it has a strong taste caused by spices. *This curry is too **hot** for me.*

**hotel  hotels**

NOUN A **hotel** is a building where people pay to stay, usually for a few nights.

**hour  hours**

NOUN An **hour** is a period of 60 minutes. There are 24 hours in a day.

**house  houses**

NOUN A **house** is a building where people live.

**hover  hovers, hovering, hovered**

VERB When a bird or aircraft **hovers**, it stays in the same place in the air.

**hovercraft  hovercraft or hovercrafts**

NOUN A **hovercraft** is a vehicle that travels over water or land on a cushion of air.

**how**

ADVERB **1** You can use **how** in questions to ask about the way something is done or known. *How did you know that?*

ADVERB **2** How can also be used to ask about a measurement or quantity. *How much is the fare to Brighton?*

ADVERB **3** How is often used in greetings. *How are you?*

**however**

ADVERB You use **however** when you are adding a comment that is surprising after what you have just said. *I was sure I was going to win the race.* **However**, *a younger girl came first.*

**howl**   **howls, howling, howled**

VERB To **howl** means to make a long, loud cry. *The dog **howls** when I sing.*

**hug**   **hugs, hugging, hugged**

VERB If you **hug** someone, you put your arms round them and hold them close.

**huge**

ADJECTIVE Something that is **huge** is extremely big.

**hum**   **hums, humming, hummed**

VERB If you **hum**, you sing with your lips closed.

**human**   **humans**

NOUN A **human** is a person.

**hump**   **humps**

NOUN A **hump** is a large lump on the back of an animal such as a camel, which is used for storing fat and water.

**hundred**   **hundreds**

A **hundred** is the number 100.

**hung**

VERB **Hung** is the past tense of **hang**.

**hungry**   **hungrier, hungriest**

ADJECTIVE When you are **hungry**, you want to eat.

**hungrily** ADVERB

**hunt**   **hunts, hunting, hunted**

VERB **1** To **hunt** means to chase wild animals to kill them for food or sport.

VERB **2** If you **hunt** for something, you look for it.

**hurricane**   **hurricanes**

NOUN A **hurricane** is a storm with very high winds.

**hurry**   **hurries, hurrying, hurried**

VERB If you **hurry** somewhere, you go there as quickly as you can.

**hurt**   **hurts, hurting, hurt**

VERB **1** If part of your body **hurts**, you feel pain.

VERB **2** If you have been **hurt**, you have been injured.

ADJECTIVE **3** If someone feels **hurt**, they feel unhappy because someone has been unkind to them.

**husband**   **husbands**

NOUN A woman's **husband** is the man she is married to.

**hut**   **huts**

NOUN A **hut** is a small simple building with one or two rooms.

**hutch**   **hutches**

NOUN A **hutch** is a cage made of wood and wire netting. Pets such as rabbits are kept in hutches.

**hygiene**

NOUN **Hygiene** is keeping yourself and your surroundings clean, especially to stop the spread of disease.

**hymn**   **hymns**

NOUN A **hymn** is a Christian song in praise of God.

**hyphen**   **hyphens**

NOUN A **hyphen** is a punctuation mark (-) used to join together words or parts of words, for example "left-handed". See *Punctuation* on page 264.

# Ii

**ice** ices, icing, iced

NOUN **1** Ice is water that has frozen solid.
VERB **2** If you **ice** cakes, you cover them with icing.

**iceberg** icebergs

NOUN An **iceberg** is a large mass of ice floating in the sea.

**ice cream** ice creams

NOUN **Ice cream** is a very cold sweet-tasting creamy food.

**ice skate** ice skates

NOUN An **ice skate** is a boot with a metal blade fixed underneath. You wear it when you skate on ice.

**icicle** icicles

NOUN An **icicle** is a pointed piece of ice which hangs from roofs, or wherever water has been dripping and freezing.

**icing**

NOUN **Icing** is a mixture of powdered sugar and water or egg whites. It is used to cover cakes as a decoration.

**icy** icier, iciest

ADJECTIVE Something which is **icy** has ice on it, or is very cold. *This wind is icy.*

**idea** ideas

NOUN **1** If you have an **idea**, you suddenly think of a way of doing something.
NOUN **2** An **idea** is a picture in your mind.

**ideal**

ADJECTIVE The **ideal** person or thing is the best one possible for the situation.

**identical**

ADJECTIVE Things that are **identical** are exactly the same in every detail.

**idle** idler, idlest

ADJECTIVE An **idle** person is someone who does not do very much.

**igloo** igloos

NOUN An **igloo** is a dome-shaped house built out of blocks of snow.

**ignore** ignores, ignoring, ignored

VERB If you **ignore** someone, you deliberately take no notice of them.

**ill**

ADJECTIVE Someone who is **ill** has something wrong with their health.

**illness** illnesses

NOUN An **illness** is something like a cold or measles that people can suffer from.

**illuminations**

PLURAL NOUN **Illuminations** are coloured lights put up to decorate a town.

**illustrate** illustrates, illustrating, illustrated

VERB If you **illustrate** something, you add pictures to it.

**illustration** illustrations

NOUN An **illustration** is a picture or diagram in a book or magazine.

**illustrator** illustrators

NOUN An **illustrator** is an artist who draws pictures for books and magazines.

**I'm**

**I'm** is a contraction of **I am**.

**imaginary**

ADJECTIVE Something that is **imaginary** is not real. It is only in your mind. *She has imaginary talks with famous people.*

a b c d e f g h **Ii** j k l m n o p q r s t u v w x y z

# imagination

**imagination**

NOUN Your **imagination** is your ability to think of ideas, or to form pictures in your mind.

**imagine** imagines, imagining, imagined

VERB When you **imagine** something, you form a picture of it in your mind.

**imitate** imitates, imitating, imitated

VERB If you **imitate** someone, you copy the way they speak or behave.

**imitation** imitations

NOUN An **imitation** is a copy of something else.

**immediately**

ADVERB If something happens **immediately**, it happens right away.

**impatient**

ADJECTIVE Someone who is **impatient** does not like to be kept waiting.

**important**

ADJECTIVE **1** If someone says something is **important**, they mean it matters a lot.

ADJECTIVE **2** Someone who is **important** has a lot of power in a particular group.

**impossible**

ADJECTIVE Something that is **impossible** cannot be done.

**impressive**

ADJECTIVE If something is **impressive**, people admire it, usually because it is large or important.

**imprison** imprisons, imprisoning, imprisoned

VERB If someone is **imprisoned**, they are locked up, usually in a prison.

**improve** improves, improving, improved

VERB If something **improves**, it gets better.

**improvement** improvements

NOUN An **improvement** is a change in something that makes it better.

**in**

PREPOSITION **1** You use **in** to say where something is, or where it is going. *Put it in the box.*

PREPOSITION **2** You also use **in** to say when something should happen. *I'll be home in 20 minutes.*

ADVERB **3** You use **in** to mean at home. *Is anybody in?*

**inch** inches

NOUN An **inch** is a unit of length equal to about two and a half centimetres. There are 12 inches to a foot.

**include** includes, including, included

VERB If you **include** something in a whole thing, you make it part of the whole thing. *Batteries are included.*

**increase** increases, increasing, increased

VERB **1** If something **increases**, it becomes greater.

NOUN **2** An **increase** is a rise in the number, level or amount of something.

**index** indexes

NOUN An **index** is an alphabetical list at the back of a book that helps you find the things you want to read about.

**indignant**

ADJECTIVE If you are **indignant**, you feel angry about something that is unfair.

**individual**

ADJECTIVE **Individual** means to do with one particular person, rather than a whole group.

**infant** infants

NOUN An **infant** is a baby or young child.

**influence** influences

NOUN An **influence** is the effect that someone or something has on you, that can change the way you think or behave. *That boy is a bad influence on you.*

## informal

ADJECTIVE **1 Informal** means relaxed. You usually speak or behave in this way when you are with people you know well.

ADJECTIVE **2** In a dictionary, a word shown as **informal** is more suitable for everyday talk than it is for writing.

## information

NOUN If someone gives you **information** about something, they tell you about it.

## infuriate  infuriates, infuriating, infuriated

VERB If someone or something **infuriates** you, they make you extremely angry.

## ingredient  ingredients

NOUN **Ingredients** are the things that are used to make something, especially in cookery.

## inhabit  inhabits, inhabiting, inhabited

VERB If you **inhabit** a place, you live there.

## inhabitant  inhabitants

NOUN The **inhabitants** of a place are the people who live there.

## initial  initials

NOUN An **initial** is the first letter of a name. *David Hunt's* **initials** *are D.H.*

## injection  injections

NOUN If a doctor or nurse gives you an **injection**, they put medicine into your body with a special needle.

## injure  injures, injuring, injured

VERB If something **injures** a person or animal, it damages part of their body.
**injury** NOUN

## ink  inks

NOUN **Ink** is the coloured liquid that is used for writing and printing.

## inland

ADVERB If you go **inland**, you go away from the coast towards the middle of a country.

## inn  inns

NOUN An **inn** is a small hotel.

## innocent

ADJECTIVE Someone who is **innocent** has not done anything wrong.

## insect  insects

NOUN An **insect** is a small animal with six legs and usually wings. Ants, flies, butterflies and beetles are all insects.

See *Insects* on page 259.

## insert  inserts, inserting, inserted

VERB If you **insert** an object into something, you put it into it.
*She* **inserted** *the key in the lock.*

## inside

ADVERB, PREPOSITION OR ADJECTIVE **Inside** means in something. *It was raining so they had to play* **inside**... *It was very cold* **inside** *the church... He hid his money in an* **inside** *pocket.*

## insist  insists, insisting, insisted

VERB If you **insist** on doing something, you refuse to give in.

## inspect  inspects, inspecting, inspected

VERB If you **inspect** something, you look at every part of it carefully.

## inspire  inspires, inspiring, inspired

VERB If something **inspires** you, it gives you new ideas and enthusiasm.

## instant

ADJECTIVE Something **instant** happens immediately. *The new pop group were an* **instant** *success.*

a
b
c
d
e
f
g
h
Ii
j
k
l
m
n
o
p
q
r
s
t
u
v
w
x
y
z

**instead**

ADVERB **Instead** means in place of. *Take the stairs **instead** of the lift.*

**instruction** instructions

NOUN **1** An **instruction** is something that someone tells you to do.

PLURAL NOUN **2** **Instructions** are words that tell you how to do something.

**instrument** instruments

NOUN **1** An **instrument** is a tool that is used to do a particular job.

NOUN **2** An **instrument** is also an object such as a piano or guitar, that you play to make music.

**insult** insults, insulting, insulted

VERB If you **insult** someone, you offend them by being rude to them.

**integer** integers

NOUN An **integer** is any of the whole numbers used for counting.

**intelligent**

ADJECTIVE A person who is **intelligent** can understand, learn and think things out quickly and well.

**intend** intends, intending, intended

VERB If you **intend** to do something, you have decided to do it or plan to do it.

**interest** interests

NOUN If you have an **interest** in something, you want to learn or hear more about it.

**interesting**

ADJECTIVE If something is **interesting**, it attracts or keeps your attention.

**interfere** interferes, interfering, interfered

VERB If something **interferes** with something else, it gets in the way. *Don't let TV **interfere** with your homework.*

**interjection** interjections

NOUN An **interjection** is a word you say suddenly to show surprise, pain or anger, such as "Ouch!" or "Wow!".

**Internet**

NOUN The **Internet** is a worldwide communication system that people use through computers.

**interpret** interprets, interpreting, interpreted

VERB If you **interpret** what someone says or does, you say what it means.

**interrupt** interrupts, interrupting, interrupted

VERB **1** If you **interrupt** someone, you start talking before they have finished what they were saying.

VERB **2** If you **interrupt** what someone is doing, you make them stop doing it for a while.

**interval** intervals

NOUN An **interval** is a short break during a play or concert.

**interview** interviews, interviewing, interviewed

VERB If you **interview** someone, you ask them questions about themselves.

**introduction** introductions

NOUN An **introduction** is a piece of writing at the beginning of a book, which usually tells you what it is about.

**invent** invents, inventing, invented

VERB **1** If you **invent** a story or an excuse, you make it up.

VERB **2** If someone **invents** something, such as a machine or an instrument, they are the first person to think of it.

**invention** inventions

NOUN An **invention** is something that is a completely new idea. *She is working on an **invention** that will help people.*

a b c d e f g h **Ii** j k l m n o p q r s t u v w x y z

**inventor** inventors

NOUN An **inventor** is someone who thinks of new ideas and tries them out to see if they will work.

**inverse**

NOUN If you turn something upside down or back to front, you have its **inverse**. *Subtraction is the **inverse** of addition.*

**investigate** investigates, investigating, investigated

VERB If you **investigate** something, you try to find out all the facts about it.

**invisible**

ADJECTIVE If something is **invisible**, it cannot be seen. For example, germs are invisible unless you use a microscope.

**invitation** invitations

NOUN When you get an **invitation**, someone asks you to come to something such as a party.

**invite** invites, inviting, invited

VERB If you **invite** someone, you ask them to come to your home, or a party.

**involve** involves, involving, involved

VERB If a situation **involves** someone or something, it includes or concerns them. *This project will **involve** a lot of work.*

**iron** irons

NOUN **1** Iron is a hard metal used to make steel, and things like gates.
NOUN **2** An **iron** is an object with a handle and a flat base. You can heat it and use it to smooth clothes.

**irritable**

ADJECTIVE If you are feeling **irritable**, you could easily become annoyed.

**irritate** irritates, irritating, irritated

VERB **1** If something **irritates** you, it annoys you.
VERB **2** If something **irritates** part of your body, it makes it sore or itchy.

**Islam**

NOUN **Islam** is the Muslim religion, which teaches that there is only one God, Allah. Mohammed is his prophet.
**Islamic** ADJECTIVE

**island** islands

NOUN An **island** is a piece of land completely surrounded by water.

**IT**

**IT** is an abbreviation of **information technology**.

**italics**

PLURAL NOUN **Italics** are letters printed in a special sloping way. *This sentence is in italics.*

**itch** itches, itching, itched

VERB When your skin **itches**, it makes you feel that you want to scratch it.

**its**

ADJECTIVE You use **its** to show that something belongs to something that has already been mentioned. *The lion lifted **its** head.*

**it's**

**It's** is a contraction of **it is**.

**itself**

PRONOUN If an animal does something itself, no one else does it. *The cat washed itself.*

**ivory**

NOUN **Ivory** is the hard smooth creamy material that comes from the tusks of some animals, such as elephants.

**ivy**

NOUN **Ivy** is an evergreen plant which creeps along the ground and up walls.

a
b
c
d
e
f
g
h
Ii
j
k
l
m
n
o
p
q
r
s
t
u
v
w
x
y
z

a
b
c
d
e
f
g
h
i
Jj
k
l
m
n
o
p
q
r
s
t
u
v
w
x
y
z

# Jj

### jacket  jackets
NOUN A **jacket** is a short coat.

### jagged
ADJECTIVE Something **jagged** has an uneven edge with sharp points on it.

### jail  jails
NOUN A **jail** is a building where criminals are locked up.

### jam  jams, jamming, jammed
NOUN **1** Jam is a food that is made by cooking fruit with a lot of sugar. You usually spread jam on bread.
NOUN **2** A **jam** is when there are so many people or vehicles in a place it is impossible for them to move.
VERB **3** If something **jams**, it becomes fixed and will not move.

### January
NOUN **January** is the first month of the year. It has 31 days.

### jar  jars
NOUN A **jar** is a glass container with a wide top used for storing food.

### jaw  jaws
NOUN Your **jaw** is the bone in which your teeth are set. Some animals, like crocodiles, have very large jaws.

### jealous
ADJECTIVE Someone who is **jealous** feels upset because someone else has what they want.

### jeans
PLURAL NOUN **Jeans** are trousers that are usually made with a strong cotton cloth.

### jelly  jellies
NOUN **Jelly** is a clear sweet food that wobbles when you move it.

### jellyfish  jellyfishes
NOUN A **jellyfish** is a sea animal with a clear soft body and tentacles which may sting.

### jerk  jerks, jerking, jerked
VERB If something **jerks**, it moves suddenly and sharply.

### jersey  jerseys
NOUN A **jersey** is a knitted piece of clothing for the upper part of your body.

### jet  jets
NOUN **1** A **jet** is a stream of liquid, gas or flame forced out under pressure.
NOUN **2** A **jet** is also a plane that is able to fly very fast.

### Jew  Jews
NOUN A **Jew** is a person who follows the religion of Judaism.

### jewel  jewels
NOUN A **jewel** is a precious stone, such as a diamond or a ruby, used to make things like rings and necklaces.

### jewellery
NOUN **Jewellery** is the name for ornaments that people can wear, like rings and necklaces. It is often made of valuable metal such as gold or silver and may be decorated with precious stones.

**jigsaw** jigsaws

NOUN A **jigsaw** is a puzzle consisting of a picture on cardboard. The picture has been cut up into small pieces that have to be put together again.

**jingle** jingles

NOUN A **jingle** is a short catchy phrase or rhyme set to music and used to advertise something on radio or television.

**job** jobs

NOUN **1** A **job** is the work that someone does to earn money.

NOUN **2** A **job** can also be anything that has to be done. *There are always plenty of jobs to do when I get home.*

**joey**

NOUN A **joey** is a young kangaroo. See *Young animals* on page 260.

**jog** jogs, jogging, jogged

VERB **1** To **jog** means to run slowly, often as a form of exercise.

VERB **2** If you **jog** something, you knock it slightly so that it shakes or moves.

VERB **3** If someone or something **jogs** your memory, they remind you of something.

**join** joins, joining, joined

VERB **1** When two things **join**, they come together.

VERB **2** If you **join** a club or organization, you become a member of it.

NOUN **3** A **join** is a place where two things are fastened together. *Look! You can't see the join.*

**joint** joints

NOUN **1** A **joint** is a part of your body, such as your elbow or knee, where two bones meet and are able to move.

NOUN **2** A **joint** can also be any place where two things are fastened together.

NOUN **3** A **joint** is also a large piece of meat for roasting.

**joke** jokes

NOUN A **joke** is something that you say or do to make people laugh.

**jolt** jolts, jolting, jolted

VERB **1** To **jolt** something means to move or shake it roughly and violently.

NOUN **2** A **jolt** is a sudden jerky movement.

NOUN **3** A **jolt** is also an unpleasant shock or surprise.

**jot** jots, jotting, jotted

VERB If you **jot** something down, you write it quickly in the form of a short note.

**journal** journals

NOUN **1** A **journal** is a diary which someone keeps regularly.

NOUN **2** A **journal** is also a magazine that deals with a particular subject, for example a medical journal.

**journey** journeys

NOUN If you go on a **journey**, you travel from one place to another.

**joy**

NOUN **Joy** is a feeling of great happiness.
**joyful** ADJECTIVE

**joystick** joysticks

NOUN **1** On a computer, a **joystick** is a lever that controls movement of the cursor on the screen.

NOUN **2** A **joystick** is a lever in an aircraft which the pilot uses to control height and direction.

**Judaism**

NOUN **Judaism** is the religion of the Jewish people. It is based on the Old Testament of the Bible, and the Talmud or book of laws and traditions.

a
b
c
d
e
f
g
h
i
**Jj**
k
l
m
n
o
p
q
r
s
t
u
v
w
x
y
z

# judge

**judge** judges

NOUN **1** In law, a **judge** is a person who has the power to decide how the law should be used.

NOUN **2** The **judge** of a competition is a person who has been asked to choose the winner.

**jug** jugs

NOUN A **jug** is a container with a lip or spout used for holding or serving liquids.

**juggle** juggles, juggling, juggled

VERB If you **juggle** with objects, you keep throwing them into the air and catching them one at a time, so that there are several in the air at once.

**juggler** NOUN

**juice**

NOUN **Juice** is the liquid that comes from fruit such as oranges when you squeeze them.

**juicy** juicier, juiciest

ADJECTIVE **Juicy** food has a lot of juice in it.

**July**

NOUN **July** is the seventh month of the year. It has 31 days.

**jumble** jumbles, jumbling, jumbled

NOUN **1 Jumble** is an untidy muddle of things.

NOUN **2 Jumble** is also things like clothes and books that people no longer want.

VERB **3** If you **jumble** things, you mix them up untidily.

**jumble sale** NOUN

**jump** jumps, jumping, jumped

VERB **1** When you **jump**, you spring off the ground using your leg muscles.

VERB **2** If you **jump** something, you spring off the ground and move over or across it. *He jumped a low wall.*

VERB **3** If something or somebody makes you **jump**, you make a sudden sharp movement of surprise.

**jumper** jumpers

NOUN A **jumper** is a knitted piece of clothing for the top part of the body.

**junction** junctions

NOUN A **junction** is a place where roads or railway lines meet or cross.

**June**

NOUN **June** is the sixth month of the year. It has 30 days.

**jungle** jungles

NOUN A **jungle** is a dense tropical forest.

**junior**

ADJECTIVE **Junior** means younger, or less important.

**junk** junks

NOUN **1 Junk** is old or second-hand articles that are sold cheaply or thrown away.

NOUN **2** A **junk** is a Chinese sailing boat that has a flat bottom and square sails.

**just**

ADVERB **1** If you say that something has **just** happened, you mean it happened a short time ago.

ADVERB **2** If you say you are **just** going to do something, you mean you will do it very soon.

**justice**

NOUN **Justice** is fairness in the way that people are treated.

**justify** justifies, justifying, justified

VERB If you **justify** an action or idea, you explain why it is reasonable or necessary.

# Kk

**kangaroo** **kangaroos**
NOUN A **kangaroo** is a large Australian animal which moves forward by jumping on its back legs.

**keen** **keener, keenest**
ADJECTIVE Someone who is **keen** to do something wants to do it very much.

**keep** **keeps, keeping, kept**
VERB **1** If you **keep** something for somebody, you save it for them.
VERB **2** If you **keep** doing something, you do it over and over again.
VERB **3** If something **keeps** you a certain way, you stay that way because of it.
*That dog is **keeping** me awake.*

**kennel** **kennels**
NOUN A **kennel** is a small house for a dog.

**kept**
VERB **Kept** is the past tense of **keep**.

**kerb** **kerbs**
NOUN The **kerb** is the edge of the pavement.

**ketchup**
NOUN **Ketchup** is a cold tomato sauce.

**kettle** **kettles**
NOUN A **kettle** is a covered container used to boil water.

**key** **keys**
NOUN **1** A **key** is a specially shaped piece of metal that fits into a lock.
NOUN **2** The **keys** on something like a computer keyboard or a piano are the buttons that you press to use it.
ADJECTIVE **3 Key** words or sentences are an important part of a piece of text.

**keyboard** **keyboards**
NOUN A **keyboard** is a row of buttons called keys on a piano or computer.

**kick** **kicks, kicking, kicked**
VERB If you **kick** something, you hit it with your foot.

**kid** **kids**
NOUN **1** A **kid** is a young goat.
*See Young animals on page 260.*
NOUN **2** INFORMAL A **kid** is a child.

**kidnap** **kidnaps, kidnapping, kidnapped**
VERB If someone **kidnaps** another person, they take them away by force.

**kill** **kills, killing, killed**
VERB To **kill** someone or something means to cause them to die.

**kilogram** **kilograms**
NOUN A **kilogram** (kg) is a unit of mass and weight. One kilogram, or kilo, is equal to 1000 grams.

**kilometre** **kilometres**
NOUN A **kilometre** is a unit of distance equal to 1000 metres.

**kilt** **kilts**
NOUN A **kilt** is a pleated skirt worn by men as part of the national costume of Scotland.

**kind** **kinds; kinder, kindest**
NOUN **1** If you talk about a **kind** of object, you mean a sort of object.
ADJECTIVE **2** Someone who is **kind** behaves in a gentle, caring way.
**kindness** NOUN

**king** **kings**
NOUN A **king** is a man who rules a country. Kings are not chosen by the people, but are born into a royal family.

a
b
c
d
e
f
g
h
i
j
Kk
l
m
n
o
p
q
r
s
t
u
v
w
x
y
z

**kingdom** **kingdoms**

NOUN **1** A **kingdom** is a country or region that is ruled by a king or queen.

NOUN **2** The animal **kingdom** is all the animals in the world. *This creature is the largest in the animal* **kingdom**.

**kingfisher** **kingfishers**

NOUN A **kingfisher** is a brightly coloured bird that lives by rivers and eats fish.

**kiss** **kisses, kissing, kissed**

VERB If you **kiss** someone, you touch them with your lips.

**kit** **kits**

NOUN A **kit** is a set of things that are used for a particular purpose. *Have you seen my first aid* **kit**?

**kitchen** **kitchens**

NOUN A **kitchen** is a room that is used for cooking and washing-up.

**kite** **kites**

NOUN **1** A **kite** is a frame covered with paper or cloth which you fly in the sky at the end of a piece of string.

NOUN **2** In maths, a **kite** is a flat shape with four sides, with two pairs of the same length and none of the sides parallel to each other.

See *Colours and flat shapes* on page 271.

**kitten** **kittens**

NOUN A **kitten** is a young cat.

See *Young animals* on page 260.

**kiwi** **kiwis**

NOUN A **kiwi** is a type of bird found in New Zealand. Kiwis cannot fly.

**kiwi fruit** **kiwi fruits**

NOUN A **kiwi fruit** is a fruit with a brown hairy skin and green flesh.

See *Fruit* on page 257.

**knee** **knees**

NOUN Your **knee** is the joint where your leg bends.

**kneel** **kneels, kneeling, kneeled or knelt**

VERB When you **kneel**, you bend your legs until your knees are touching the ground.

**knew**

VERB **Knew** is the past tense of **know**.

**knickers**

PLURAL NOUN **Knickers** are pants worn by women and girls.

**knife** **knives**

NOUN A **knife** is a sharp metal tool that you use to cut things.

**knight** **knights**

NOUN Hundreds of years ago, a **knight** was a man in armour who rode into battle for his king or queen.

**knit** **knits, knitting, knitted**

VERB If you **knit**, you make something from wool using two long needles.

**knob** **knobs**

NOUN **1** A **knob** is a round handle on a door or a drawer.

NOUN **2** A **knob** is also a round button on a piece of equipment such as a radio.

**knock** **knocks, knocking, knocked**

VERB If you **knock** on something, you hit it hard.

**knot** **knots**

NOUN A **knot** is a tie in something such as string or cloth.

**know** **knows, knowing, knew**

VERB **1** If you **know** a fact, you have it in your mind and do not need to learn it.

VERB **2** If you **know** somebody, you have met them before.

**knowledge**

NOUN **Knowledge** is all the facts and information that you know.

**knuckle** **knuckles**

NOUN Your **knuckles** are the bony parts where your fingers join your hands and where your fingers bend.

**koala** **koalas**

NOUN A **koala** is an Australian animal that looks like a small bear with grey fur.

# Ll

**label** **labels**

NOUN A **label** is a small notice that tells you what something is or gives you information. *Read the **label** on the medicine bottle.*

**laboratory** **laboratories**

NOUN A **laboratory** is a place where scientists work, using special equipment.

**labour**

NOUN **Labour** is hard work.

**lace** **laces**

NOUN **1 Lace** is a very fine decorated cloth made with a lot of holes in it.
NOUN **2 Laces** are cords that you use to fasten your shoes.

**lack** **lacks, lacking, lacked**

VERB If you **lack** something, you do not have it when you need it.

**ladder** **ladders**

NOUN A **ladder** is a wooden or metal frame used for climbing up things like walls or trees.

**ladle** **ladles**

NOUN A **ladle** is a big deep spoon with a long handle, which is used to serve soup.
**ladle** VERB

**lady** **ladies**

NOUN **Lady** is a polite name for a woman. *I think this **lady** was in front of me.*

**ladybird** **ladybirds**

NOUN A **ladybird** is a small round flying beetle with spots on its wings.
See *Insects* on page 259.

**laid**

VERB **Laid** is the past tense of **lay**.

**lain**

VERB **Lain** is the past participle of **lie**.

**lake** **lakes**

NOUN A **lake** is a large area of fresh water with land all round it.

**lamb** **lambs**

NOUN A **lamb** is a young sheep.
See *Young animals* on page 260.

**lame**

ADJECTIVE An animal which is **lame** cannot walk properly.

**lamp** **lamps**

NOUN A **lamp** is an object that gives light.

**lamppost** **lampposts**

NOUN A **lamppost** is a tall column in the street, with a lamp at the top.

**land** **lands, landing, landed**

NOUN **1 Land** is the part of the world that is solid, dry ground.
VERB **2** When an aircraft **lands**, it comes down from the air on to land or water.

**landlady** **landladies**

NOUN A **landlady** is a woman who lets rooms to people.

**landlord** **landlords**

NOUN A **landlord** is a man who lets rooms to people.

**landmark** **landmarks**

NOUN A **landmark** is a building or a feature of the land that can be used to find out where you are.

**landscape** **landscapes**

NOUN A **landscape** is everything you can see when you look across an area of land.

**lane** **lanes**

NOUN **1** A **lane** is a narrow road, especially in the country.
NOUN **2** A **lane** is also part of a main road or motorway. It is marked with lines to guide drivers.

# language

**language** **languages**
NOUN A **language** is the words that are used by the people of a country when they speak or write to each other.

**lantern** **lanterns**
NOUN A **lantern** is a lamp in a container. It has sides which the light can shine through but which stop the wind from blowing out the light.

**lap** **laps, lapping, lapped**
NOUN **1** Your **lap** is the flat area formed by the tops of your legs when you are sitting down.
VERB **2** When an animal **laps** up liquid, it drinks using its tongue to get the liquid into its mouth.

**large** **larger, largest**
ADJECTIVE Something **large** is big.

**larva** **larvae**
NOUN A **larva** is an insect at an early stage of its life. It looks likes a short fat worm.

**laser** **lasers**
NOUN A **laser** is a machine which produces a narrow beam of light. Lasers are used for many different things, including medical operations.

**last** **lasts, lasting, lasted**
ADJECTIVE **1** The **last** thing or event is the most recent one. *I saw him **last** week.*
ADVERB **2** If something happens **last**, it happens after everything else. *I came **last** in the race.*
VERB **3** If something **lasts**, it continues to exist or happen. *Her speech **lasted** an hour.*
**at last** PHRASE If something happens **at last**, it happens after a long time.

**late** **later, latest**
ADJECTIVE OR ADVERB **1** If you are **late** arriving somewhere, you get there after the time you were supposed to.
ADJECTIVE OR ADVERB **2** Late means near the end of a period of time. *We had a picnic in the **late** afternoon.*

**lately**
ADVERB If something has happened **lately**, it happened not long ago. *Have you seen your cousin **lately**?*

**laugh** **laughs, laughing, laughed**
VERB When you **laugh**, you make the sound people make when they are happy or think something is funny.
**laughter** NOUN

**launch** **launches, launching, launched**
VERB **1** When a rocket or satellite is **launched**, it is sent into the sky.
VERB **2** To **launch** a ship means to send it into the water for the first time.

**launderette** **launderettes**
NOUN A **launderette** is a shop where people pay to use washing machines.

**lava**
NOUN **Lava** is a very hot, liquid rock which comes out of volcanoes.

**lavatory** **lavatories**
NOUN **1** A **lavatory** is a toilet.
NOUN **2** A **lavatory** is also the room where the lavatory is.

**law** **laws**
NOUN A **law** is a rule that is made by the government.

**lawn** **lawns**
NOUN A **lawn** is an area of short grass in a garden or park.

**lawnmower** **lawnmowers**
NOUN A **lawnmower** is a machine for cutting the grass on lawns.

**lawyer** **lawyers**

NOUN A **lawyer** is a person who understands the law and can advise people about it.

**lay** **lays, laying, laid**

VERB 1 If you **lay** something somewhere, you put it there carefully.

VERB 2 If you **lay** the table, you put things like knives and forks on the table ready for a meal.

VERB 3 When a bird **lays** an egg, it produces the egg out of its body.

**layer** **layers**

NOUN A **layer** is a single thickness of something that lies on top of or underneath something else.

**layout** **layouts**

NOUN The **layout** of something is the way it is arranged.

**lazy** **lazier, laziest**

ADJECTIVE Someone who is **lazy** does not want to work or do anything hard.

**lazily** ADVERB

**lead** **leads, leading, led**

(*rhymes with* **feed**)

VERB 1 If you **lead** someone to a particular place, you go with them to show them the way.

VERB 2 Someone who **leads** a group of people is in charge of them.

VERB 3 If you are **leading** in a race or game, you are winning at that point.

NOUN 4 A dog's **lead** is a long thin piece of leather or a chain. You fix one end to the collar and hold the other end.

(*rhymes with* **fed**) NOUN 5 **Lead** is a grey, heavy metal.

(*rhymes with* **fed**) NOUN 6 The **lead** in a pencil is the centre part of it that makes a mark on paper.

**leader** **leaders**

NOUN The **leader** of a group of people is the person who is in charge.

**leaf** **leaves**

NOUN A **leaf** is one of the flat green parts of a plant. Different sorts of plant have differently shaped leaves.

**leaflet** **leaflets**

NOUN A **leaflet** is a piece of paper with information or advertising printed on it.

**leak** **leaks, leaking, leaked**

VERB 1 If a pipe or container **leaks**, it has a hole which lets gas or liquid escape.

VERB 2 If liquid or gas **leaks**, it escapes from a pipe or container.

**lean** **leans, leaning, leant or leaned; leaner, leanest**

VERB 1 When you **lean** somewhere, you bend your body in that direction.

VERB 2 When you **lean** on something, you rest your body against it for support.

ADJECTIVE 3 **Lean** meat has little or no fat.

**leap** **leaps, leaping, leapt or leaped**

VERB If you **leap** somewhere, you jump over a long distance or high in the air.

**leap year** **leap years**

NOUN A **leap year** is a year with 366 days. There is a leap year every four years.

**learn** **learns, learning, learnt or learned**

VERB When you **learn** something, you get to know it or find out how to do it.

**least**

NOUN 1 The **least** is the smallest possible amount of something. *That is the **least** of my problems.*

ADJECTIVE OR ADVERB 2 **Least** is a superlative form of **little**, meaning very small in amount. *We bought the **least** expensive bike... She ate the **least** of all of them.*

## leather

NOUN **Leather** is the specially treated skin of animals. It is used for making things like shoes and furniture.

## leave  leaves, leaving, left

VERB **1** When you **leave** a place, you go away from it.

VERB **2** If you **leave** someone somewhere, they stay behind after you go away.

VERB **3** In maths, when you take one number from other, it **leaves** a third number.

## led

VERB **Led** is the past tense of **lead**.

## ledge  ledges

NOUN A **ledge** is a narrow shelf on the side of a cliff or rock face, or on the outside of a building.

## leek  leeks

NOUN A **leek** is a long white vegetable with green leaves.
*See Vegetables on page 256.*

## left

VERB **1** Left is the past tense of **leave**.

NOUN **2** The **left** is the side that you begin reading on in English.

ADJECTIVE OR ADVERB **3** Left means on or towards the left side of something.
*Turn **left** at the end of the road.*

## leg  legs

NOUN **1** Legs are the parts of your body which stretch from the hips to the feet.

NOUN **2** The **legs** of an object such as a table are the parts which rest on the floor and support the object's weight.

## legend  legends

NOUN A **legend** is an old and popular story which may or may not be true.

## lemon  lemons

NOUN A **lemon** is a yellow, oval fruit. Lemons are juicy but they taste sour.
*See Fruit on page 257.*

## lemonade

NOUN **Lemonade** is a drink made from lemons, sugar and water.

## lend  lends, lending, lent

VERB If you **lend** something to someone, you let them have it for a while.

## length  lengths

NOUN **1** The **length** of something is the distance that it measures from one end to the other.

NOUN **2** The **length** of something like a holiday is the period of time that it lasts.

## lens  lenses

NOUN A **lens** is a curved piece of glass that makes light go in a certain way. Lenses are used in things like cameras, telescopes and glasses.

## lent

VERB **Lent** is the past tense of **lend**.

## leopard  leopards

NOUN A **leopard** is a large wild cat that lives in the forests of Africa and Asia. It has yellow fur with black spots.

## less

ADJECTIVE OR ADVERB **Less** is a comparative form of **little**, meaning not as much.
*A shower uses **less** water than a bath.*

## lesson  lessons

NOUN A **lesson** is a short period of time when you are taught something.

## let  lets, letting, let

VERB **1** If you **let** someone do something, you allow them to do it.

VERB **2** If someone **lets** a house or flat that they own, they rent it out.

## letter  letters

NOUN **1** A **letter** is a written message to someone, usually sent through the post.

NOUN **2** Letters are written symbols which go together to make words.

**letter box** **letter boxes**

NOUN **1** A **letter box** is an oblong gap in the front door of a house or flat.

NOUN **2** A **letter box** is also a large metal container where you post letters.

**lettuce** **lettuces**

NOUN A **lettuce** is a plant with large green leaves that you eat raw in salads.

See *Vegetables* on page 256.

**level** **levels**

ADJECTIVE **1** A surface that is **level** is smooth, flat and parallel to the ground.

ADVERB **2** If you are **level** with someone, you are next to them.

NOUN **3** The **level** of a liquid is the height it comes up to. *After heavy rain the river rose to a dangerous level.*

**lever** **levers**

NOUN **1** A **lever** is a long bar that you put under a heavy object and press down on to make the object move.

NOUN **2** A **lever** is also a handle on a machine that you pull down to make the machine work.

**library** **libraries**

NOUN A **library** is a building where books are kept for people to come and read or borrow.

**lick** **licks, licking, licked**

VERB If you **lick** something, you move your tongue across it.

**lid** **lids**

NOUN A **lid** is a cover for a box or other container.

**lie** **lies, lying, lay, lain; lied**

VERB **1** To **lie** somewhere means to rest there horizontally.

VERB **2** To **lie** means to say something that is not true.

**life** **lives**

NOUN The **life** of a person or animal is the time between their birth and death.

**lifeboat** **lifeboats**

NOUN A **lifeboat** is a boat that is used to rescue people in danger at sea.

**lifetime**

NOUN Your **lifetime** is the period of time during which you are alive.

**lift** **lifts, lifting, lifted**

VERB **1** If you **lift** something, you move it to a higher position.

NOUN **2** A **lift** is a machine like a small room that carries passengers from one floor to another in a building.

**light** **lights; lighter, lightest; lights, lighting, lighted or lit**

NOUN **1** **Light** is the brightness from the sun, moon, fire or lamps, that lets you see things.

NOUN **2** A **light** is a lamp or other object that gives out brightness.

ADJECTIVE **3** A place that is **light** is bright because of the sun or the use of lamps.

ADJECTIVE **4** A **light** colour is pale.

ADJECTIVE **5** A **light** object does not weigh much.

VERB **6** To **light** something means to cause light to shine on it or in it.

VERB **7** To **light** a fire means to make it start burning.

**lighthouse** **lighthouses**

NOUN A **lighthouse** is a tower with a powerful flashing light at the top, which is used to guide ships or to warn them of danger.

**lightning**

NOUN **Lightning** is a bright flash of light in the sky produced by natural electricity during a thunderstorm.

a b c d e f g h i j k **Ll** m n o p q r s t u v w x y z

# like

**like** **likes, liking, liked**
PREPOSITION **1** If one thing is **like** another, it is similar to it.
VERB **2** If you **like** someone or something, you find them pleasant.

**likely** **likelier, likeliest**
ADJECTIVE Something that is **likely** will probably happen or is probably true.

**limb** **limbs**
NOUN A **limb** is an arm or leg.

**limerick** **limericks**
NOUN A **limerick** is a funny nonsense poem of five lines.

**limit** **limits**
NOUN A **limit** is a line or a point beyond which something cannot go. *There is a speed **limit** on this road.*

**limp** **limps, limping, limped; limper, limpest**
VERB **1** If you **limp**, you walk unevenly because you have hurt your leg or foot.
ADJECTIVE **2** Something that is **limp** is soft and floppy. *This lettuce is a bit **limp**.*

**line** **lines**
NOUN **1** A **line** is a long thin mark. Some writing paper has lines on it to show you where to write.
NOUN **2** A **line** of people or things is a number of them in a row.

NOUN **3** In a piece of writing, a **line** is a number of words together. *A limerick has five **lines**.*
NOUN **4** A railway **line** is one of the heavy metal rails that trains run on.

**linen**
NOUN **Linen** is a kind of cloth made from a plant called flax. It is used for things like sheets and tablecloths.

**liner** **liners**
NOUN A **liner** is a large passenger ship that makes long journeys.

**link** **links**
NOUN **1** A **link** is one of the rings in a chain.
NOUN **2** A **link** is also a connection between two things. *There's a high speed rail **link** between Brighton and London.*

**lion** **lions**
NOUN A **lion** is a large wild cat. Lions live in parts of Africa and Asia, in groups called prides.

**lioness** **lionesses**
NOUN A **lioness** is a female lion.

**lip** **lips**
NOUN Your **lips** are the top and bottom outer edges of your mouth.

**liquid** **liquids**
NOUN A **liquid** is anything which is not a solid or a gas, and which can be poured.

**list** **lists**
NOUN A **list** is a set of things that are written one below the other.

**listen** **listens, listening, listened**
VERB If you **listen** to a sound that you can hear, you pay attention to it.
**listener** NOUN

**lit**
VERB **Lit** is the past tense of **light**.

**literacy**
NOUN **Literacy** is the ability to read and write. See **numeracy**.

**litre** **litres**
NOUN A **litre** is a unit used to measure volume and capacity. A litre is equal to 1000 millilitres.

**litter** **litters**
NOUN **1** **Litter** is rubbish left lying untidily outside.
NOUN **2** A **litter** is a group of animals born to the same mother at the same time.
See *Collective nouns* on page 262.

**little** less, lesser, least
ADJECTIVE **1** Something or someone that is **little** is small in size.
ADVERB **2** Little can mean not much. *Our lazy cat does very **little**.*

**live¹** lives, living, lived
(*rhymes with **give***)
VERB **1** If you **live** in a place, that is where your home is.
VERB **2** To **live** means to be alive.

**live²**
(*rhymes with **hive***)
ADJECTIVE **1** A **live** animal is living.
ADJECTIVE **2** Live television or radio is broadcast as it happens.

**lively** livelier, liveliest
ADJECTIVE Someone who is **lively** is cheerful and full of energy.

**liver** livers
NOUN Your **liver** is a large organ in your body. Its job is to clean your blood.

**living**
ADJECTIVE **1** Living things are plants, animals and humans that are alive. All living things need food to grow.
NOUN **2** Someone who earns a **living** earns enough money to buy all the things they need. *She earns a **living** as an artist.*

**living room** living rooms
NOUN The **living room** in a house is the room where the family spend most of their time.

**lizard** lizards
NOUN A **lizard** is a small reptile with four short legs and a long tail. It has a rough dry skin. The babies hatch from eggs.
See  *Reptiles on page 259.*

**llama** llamas
NOUN A **llama** is a South American animal of the camel family, with long thick hair.

**load** loads, loading, loaded
NOUN **1** A **load** is things which are being carried somewhere.
VERB **2** When you **load** a camera, you put film into it so that it is ready to use.
VERB **3** When you **load** a computer, you put information or a program into it.

**loaf** loaves
NOUN A **loaf** is bread that has been baked into one shape. You cut a loaf into slices.

**lobster** lobsters
NOUN A **lobster** is a sea animal with a hard shell, two large claws and eight legs.

**local**
ADJECTIVE **Local** means belonging to the area where you live or work. *I read about it in the **local** paper.*

**locate** locates, locating, located
VERB To **locate** someone or something is to find out where they are.

**location** locations
NOUN A **location** is a place, or the position of something. *The school is being moved to a new **location**.*

**loch** lochs
NOUN **Loch** is a Scottish word for **lake**.

**lock** locks, locking, locked
VERB **1** If you **lock** something, you close it and fasten it with a key.

NOUN **2** A **lock** is used to keep something, such as a door or case, closed. You can only open a lock with the right key.

**locomotive** **locomotives**

NOUN A **locomotive** is the engine which pulls trains along railway tracks.

**loft** **lofts**

NOUN A **loft** is the space under the roof of a house, often used for storing things.

**log** **logs**

NOUN A **log** is a piece of a thick branch from a tree.

**lollipop** **lollipops**

NOUN A **lollipop** is a hard sweet on a stick.

**lolly** **lollies**

NOUN **Lolly** is an abbreviation of **lollipop**. A **lolly** is also a piece of flavoured ice or ice cream on a stick.

**lonely** **lonelier, loneliest**

ADJECTIVE Someone who is **lonely** is sad because they are on their own, or do not have any friends.

**long** **longer, longest; longs, longing, longed**

ADJECTIVE **1** Something **long** takes up more time than usual. *It was a long film.*
ADJECTIVE **2** Something that is **long** is far from one end to the other. *It's a long way from London to New York.*
VERB **3** If you **long** for something, you want it very much.

**look** **looks, looking, looked**

VERB **1** If you **look** in a particular direction, you turn your eyes that way.
VERB **2** If you say how someone **looks**, you tell them how they seem to you.
VERB **3** If you **look after** someone, you care for them.
VERB **4** If you **look for** someone or something, you try to find them.
VERB **5** If you are **looking forward** to something, you want it to happen because you think you will enjoy it.

**loop** **loops**

NOUN A **loop** is a circular shape in something long and thin. For example, when you tie shoelaces, the bow has two loops in it.

**loose** **looser, loosest**

ADJECTIVE **1** Something that is **loose** is not firmly fixed. *I've got a loose tooth.*
ADJECTIVE **2** Things that are **loose** are not fixed together. *She had four loose sheets of paper in her bag.*

**lord** **lords**

NOUN Hundreds of years ago, a **lord** was a man who had a lot of power. Now, **Lord** is a title in front of some men's names in Britain.

**lorry** **lorries**

NOUN A **lorry** is a large road vehicle that is used to carry loads.

**lose** **loses, losing, lost**

VERB **1** If you **lose** something, you cannot find it.
VERB **2** If someone **loses** weight, they become thinner.
VERB **3** If you **lose** something like a game or a race, someone does better than you.

**lost**

ADJECTIVE **1** If you are **lost**, you cannot find your way or do not know where you are.

VERB **2** **Lost** is the past tense of **lose**.

**lot** **lots**

NOUN A **lot** of something, or **lots** of something, is a large amount of it.

**lottery** **lotteries**

NOUN A **lottery** is a way of raising money by selling tickets. The winner is chosen by chance.

**loud** **louder, loudest**
ADJECTIVE A **loud** sound is one that makes a lot of noise. *The firework went off with a loud bang.*

**loudspeaker** **loudspeakers**
NOUN A **loudspeaker** is a piece of equipment that is used so that sounds can be heard. Microphones, radios and CD players all need loudspeakers.

**lounge** **lounges**
NOUN A **lounge** in a house or hotel is a room where people sit and relax.

**love** **loves, loving, loved**
VERB 1 If you **love** someone, you have strong feelings of affection for them.
VERB 2 If you **love** something, you like it very much. *I love pizza.*

**lovely** **lovelier, loveliest**
ADJECTIVE Something that is **lovely** is very pleasing to look at or listen to.

**low** **lower, lowest**
ADJECTIVE Something that is **low** measures only a short distance from the ground to the top. *He jumped over the low wall.*

**lower** **lowers, lowering, lowered**
VERB 1 If you **lower** something, you move it slowly downwards. *As it was getting dark, she lowered the blind.*
VERB 2 If you **lower** your voice, you speak more quietly.

**lower-case**
ADJECTIVE **Lower-case** letters are the small letters of the alphabet, such as a, b, c and d. *The letters down the side of this page are lower-case.* See **upper-case**.

**loyal**
ADJECTIVE If you are **loyal** to someone, you always support them.

**luck**
NOUN **Luck** is something that seems to happen without any reason. Luck can be good or bad.

**lucky** **luckier, luckiest**
ADJECTIVE Someone who is **lucky** seems to have good luck.
**luckily** ADVERB

**luggage**
NOUN **Luggage** is all the suitcases, bags and things that you take with you when you are travelling.

**lump** **lumps**
NOUN 1 A **lump** is a piece of something solid. *She took a lump of modelling clay.*
NOUN 2 A **lump** on someone's body is a small swelling.

**lunar**
ADJECTIVE **Lunar** is used to describe something that is to do with the moon.

**lunch** **lunches**
NOUN **Lunch** is a meal that you have in the middle of the day.

**lung** **lungs**
NOUN Your **lungs** are the two parts of your body inside your chest that fill with air when you breathe.

**luxury** **luxuries**
NOUN A **luxury** is something quite expensive to buy, which you like very much but do not need.
**luxurious** ADJECTIVE

**lying**
VERB **Lying** is the present participle of **lie**.

# Mm

**machine**  **machines**
NOUN A **machine** is a piece of equipment which does a particular kind of work. It is usually powered by an engine or by electricity.

**machinery**
NOUN **Machinery** is machines in general.

**mad**  **madder, maddest**
ADJECTIVE **1** Someone who is **mad** has an illness in their mind.
ADJECTIVE **2** If you describe someone as **mad**, you mean they are foolish or silly.
ADJECTIVE **3** INFORMAL Someone who is **mad** is angry.
ADJECTIVE **4** INFORMAL If you are **mad** about someone or something, you like them very much.

**made**
VERB **Made** is the past tense of **make**.

**magazine**  **magazines**
NOUN A **magazine** is a thin book which comes out regularly, usually once a week or once a month. It has articles, stories and pictures.

**maggot**  **maggots**
NOUN A **maggot** looks like a tiny worm. Maggots change into flies.

**magic**
NOUN **1** In stories, **magic** is the thing that makes impossible things happen.
ADJECTIVE **2** **Magic** tricks entertain and puzzle people.
**magical** ADJECTIVE

**magician**  **magicians**
NOUN **1** In stories, a **magician** is a man who has magic powers.

NOUN **2** A **magician** is also a real person who can do magic tricks.

**magnet**  **magnets**
NOUN A **magnet** is a special piece of metal. It pulls or attracts iron or steel towards it. Magnets can also push other magnets away.
**magnetic** ADJECTIVE

**magnificent**
ADJECTIVE Something that is **magnificent** is very grand.

**magnifying glass**  **magnifying glasses**
NOUN A **magnifying glass** is a piece of glass that makes objects appear to be bigger than they really are.

**magpie**  **magpies**
NOUN A **magpie** is a bird of the crow family. It has black and white markings and a long tail.

**mail**
NOUN **Mail** is things like letters and parcels that are sent through the post.

**main**
ADJECTIVE The **main** part of something is the most important part.

**maize**
NOUN **Maize** is a tall plant that produces sweet corn.

**major**
ADJECTIVE You use **major** to describe something important. *This is a major discovery.*

**make**  **makes, making, made**
VERB **1** If you **make** something new, you use your skill to shape it or put it together.

VERB **2** To **make** something happen is to cause it. *My new boots **made** a loud squeak.*

VERB **3** If you **make** a mistake, you do something wrong.

VERB **4** If you **make** someone do something, you force them to do it. *My mum **makes** me eat vegetables.*

**male** males

NOUN A **male** is a person or animal that belongs to the sex that cannot have babies.

**male** ADJECTIVE

**mammal** mammals

NOUN A **mammal** is a warm-blooded animal. Female mammals give birth to live babies. They feed their babies with milk from their own bodies.

**man** men

NOUN A **man** is an adult male human being. See **woman**.

**manage** manages, managing, managed

VERB **1** If you **manage** to do something, you succeed in doing it. *He **managed** to get a seat on the bus.*

VERB **2** Someone who **manages** an organization is in charge of it.

**mane** manes

NOUN The **mane** of an animal such as a horse or a male lion is the long thick hair that grows from its neck.

**mango** mangoes or mangos

NOUN A **mango** is a sweet yellowish fruit which grows in tropical countries. *See Fruit on page 257.*

**manner** manners

NOUN **1** The **manner** in which you do something is how you do it.

NOUN **2** Your **manner** is the way in which you behave and talk. *It is good **manners** to be polite.*

**mantelpiece** mantelpieces

NOUN A **mantelpiece** is a shelf over a fireplace.

**manufacture** manufactures, manufacturing, manufactured

VERB To **manufacture** goods is to make them in a factory.

**many**

ADJECTIVE **1** If there are **many** people or things, there are a large number of them.

ADJECTIVE **2** You also use **many** to ask how great a quantity is or to give information about it. *How **many** tickets do you want?*

**map** maps

NOUN A **map** is a drawing of a particular area as it would look from above.

**marathon** marathons

NOUN A **marathon** is a race in which people have to run 26 miles (about 42 kilometres) along roads.

**marble** marbles

NOUN **1** Marble is a very hard stone which shines when it is polished. Statues and parts of buildings are sometimes made of marble.

NOUN **2** Marbles is a children's game played with small coloured glass balls. These balls are also called marbles.

**march** marches, marching, marched

VERB When you **march**, you walk with quick regular steps like a soldier.

**March**

NOUN **March** is the third month of the year. It has 31 days.

**mare** mares

NOUN A **mare** is an adult female horse.

a b c d e f g h i j k l **Mm** n o p q r s t u v w x y z

**margarine**

NOUN **Margarine** is a food that looks like butter but is made from vegetable oil and animal fats. You can spread it on bread and use it for cooking.

**margin** **margins**

NOUN The **margin** is the blank space at each side on a written or printed page.

**mark** **marks**

NOUN **1** A **mark** is a small stain. *I can't get that **mark** off your shirt.*

NOUN **2** A **mark** is also something that has been written or drawn. *He made little **marks** on the paper with his pencil.*

NOUN **3** At school, a **mark** is a letter or number showing how well you have done in homework or in a test.

**market** **markets**

NOUN A **market** is a place with many small stalls selling different goods.

**marmalade**

NOUN **Marmalade** is a jam made from fruit like oranges or lemons. People often eat it spread on toast for breakfast.

**marriage** **marriages**

NOUN **Marriage** is the relationship between a husband and wife.

**married**

ADJECTIVE Someone who is **married** has a husband or wife.

**marry** **marries, marrying, married**

VERB A man and woman who **marry** become husband and wife.

**marsh** **marshes**

NOUN A **marsh** is an area of land which is always very wet and muddy.

**marsupial** **marsupials**

NOUN A **marsupial** is a mammal whose babies are carried in a pouch at the front of their mother's body. Kangaroos are marsupials.

**marvellous**

ADJECTIVE Something that is **marvellous** is wonderful.

**masculine**

ADJECTIVE **Masculine** refers to qualities and things that are typical of men.

**mask** **masks**

NOUN A **mask** is something you wear over your face to protect or disguise you.

**mass** **masses**

NOUN **1** A **mass** of things is a large number of them grouped together.

NOUN **2** The **mass** of something is the amount of matter it contains. Mass is measured in grams and kilograms. People often say "weight" when they mean "mass". Mass and weight are different. If you were on the Moon, you would weigh less than on Earth but your mass would not change. See **weight**.

NOUN **3** In the Roman Catholic church, a **Mass** is a religious service.

**massive**

ADJECTIVE Something **massive** is extremely large.

**mast** **masts**

NOUN A **mast** is the tall upright pole that supports the sail of a boat.

**mat** **mats**

NOUN **1** A **mat** is a small piece of carpet.

NOUN **2** A **mat** is also something used to protect a table from plates or glasses.

## match matches, matching, matched

NOUN **1** A **match** is an organized game of something like tennis or football.

NOUN **2** A **match** is also a thin stick of wood that can make a flame.

VERB **3** If you **match** things, you find a connection between them. *Match the animals with the countries they come from.*

## mate mates

NOUN **1** INFORMAL A **mate** is a friend.

NOUN **2** An animal's **mate** is its partner.

## material materials

NOUN **1** **Material** is cloth.

NOUN **2** A **material** is anything that can be used to make something else. Wood, stone, plastic and water are all materials.

## mathematics

NOUN **Mathematics** is the study of numbers, quantities and shapes.

## maths

NOUN **Maths** is an abbreviation of **mathematics**.

## matter matters, mattering, mattered

VERB **1** If something **matters** to you, you care about it and feel it is important.

NOUN **2** A **matter** is something that you have to deal with or think about. *This is a matter for the police.*

## mattress mattresses

NOUN A **mattress** is a large flat cushion which is put on a bed to make it comfortable to lie on.

## may

VERB If someone says you **may** do something, you are allowed to do it.

## May

NOUN **May** is the fifth month of the year. It has 31 days.

## maybe

ADVERB You say **maybe** when something is possible but you are not sure about it. *Maybe we could go tomorrow.*

## mayor mayors

NOUN The **mayor** of a town or city is the man or woman who has been chosen to be its head.

## maze mazes

NOUN A **maze** is a system of paths which is made like a puzzle so that it is difficult to find your way through it.

## meadow meadows

NOUN A **meadow** is a field of grass and wild flowers.

## meal meals

NOUN A **meal** is food that people eat, usually at set times during the day.

## mean means, meaning, meant; meaner, meanest

VERB **1** If you ask what something **means**, you want it explained to you.

VERB **2** If you **mean** what you say, you are serious about it.

VERB **3** If something **means** a lot to you, it is important to you.

VERB **4** If you **mean** to do something, you intend to do it. *I meant to phone you, but I didn't have time.*

ADJECTIVE **5** Someone who is **mean** does not like spending money or sharing.

## meaning meanings

NOUN The **meaning** of a word or sentence is the thing or idea that it is explaining. *Do you know the meaning of the proverb "Look before you leap"?*

## meanwhile

ADVERB **Meanwhile** means while something else is happening.

**measles**

NOUN **Measles** is an illness caught especially by children. It gives you a fever and red spots on your skin.

**measure** measures, measuring, measured

VERB **1** If you **measure** something, you find out how large or heavy it is.

NOUN **2** A **measure** is a unit in which something such as size or speed is expressed. *Kilometres are a measure of distance.*

See *Measures* on page 270.

**measurement** measurements

NOUN A **measurement** is a result that you get by measuring something.

**meat** meats

NOUN **Meat** is the flesh of animals that is cooked and eaten.

**mechanical**

ADJECTIVE A **mechanical** object has moving parts and is used to do a physical task.

**medal** medals

NOUN A **medal** is a small metal disc or cross given as an award for bravery or as a prize for sport.

**medical**

ADJECTIVE **Medical** means to do with medicine or the care of people's health.

**medicine** medicines

NOUN **Medicine** is a tablet or liquid given to people who are ill to make them better.

**medium**

ADJECTIVE **Medium** means somewhere in the middle of two extremes. *He's of medium height – neither tall nor short.*

**meet** meets, meeting, met

VERB If you **meet** someone, you go to the same place at the same time as they do.

**meeting** meetings

NOUN A **meeting** is when a group of people meet to talk about particular things.

**melon** melons

NOUN A **melon** is a large fruit that is sweet and juicy inside. It has a thick, hard green or yellow skin. See *Fruit* on page 257.

**melt** melts, melting, melted

VERB When something like ice **melts**, it changes from a solid into a liquid because it has become warmer.

**member** members

NOUN A **member** of a group is one of the people, animals or things belonging to that group.

**membership** NOUN

**memorize** memorizes, memorizing, memorized; also spelt memorise

VERB If you **memorize** something, you learn it so that you can repeat it exactly using only your memory.

**memory** memories

NOUN **1** Your **memory** is what allows you to remember things.

NOUN **2** A **memory** is something you remember from the past.

**men**

NOUN **Men** is the plural of **man**.

**mend** mends, mending, mended

VERB If you **mend** something that is broken or does not work, you put it right so that it can be used again.

**mental**

ADJECTIVE **Mental** means to do with your mind or brain. For example, mental maths is working out the answers to calculations in your head.

**mention** mentions, mentioning, mentioned

VERB If you **mention** something, you talk about it briefly.

**menu** menus

NOUN **1** A **menu** is a list of food that you can order in a restaurant.

NOUN **2** A **menu** on a computer is a list of choices.

**mercury**

NOUN **Mercury** is a silver-coloured metal. Liquid mercury is used in thermometers.

**mercy**

NOUN If you show **mercy** to someone, you do not hurt or punish them.

**mermaid** mermaids

NOUN In stories, a **mermaid** is a woman with a fish's tail.

**merry** merrier, merriest

ADJECTIVE **Merry** means happy and cheerful.

**mess** messes

NOUN If you say something is a **mess**, you mean it is very untidy.

**messy** ADJECTIVE

**message** messages

NOUN A **message** is words that you send or leave when you cannot speak directly to someone.

**messenger** messengers

NOUN A **messenger** is a person who takes a message to someone.

**met**

VERB **Met** is the past tense of **meet**.

**metal** metals

NOUN A **metal** is a hard, strong material that melts when it is heated, such as iron, gold or steel. Metals are used to make things like jewellery, tools, cars and machines.

**meter** meters

NOUN A **meter** is an instrument for measuring something, such as the amount of gas that you have used.

**method** methods

NOUN A **method** is a particular way of doing something.

**metre** metres

NOUN **1** A **metre** (m) is a measure of length. It is equal to 100 centimetres.

NOUN **2** In poetry, **metre** is the rhythmic arrangement of words and syllables.

**metric**

ADJECTIVE **Metric** relates to the system of measurement that uses metres, kilograms and litres.

**miaow**

NOUN A **miaow** is the short high-pitched sound that a cat makes.

**mice**

NOUN **Mice** is the plural of **mouse**.

**micro-**

PREFIX **Micro-** means small.

See *Prefixes* on page 264.

**microchip** microchips

NOUN A **microchip** is a small piece of silicon on which electronic circuits for a computer are printed.

**microphone** microphones

NOUN A **microphone** is a piece of equipment that is used to make sounds louder, or to record them.

**microscope** microscopes

NOUN A **microscope** is a piece of equipment which makes small objects appear much larger.

**microscopic** ADJECTIVE

a
b
c
d
e
f
g
h
i
j
k
l
**Mm**
n
o
p
q
r
s
t
u
v
w
x
y
z

**microwave** microwaves

NOUN A **microwave** is a type of oven which cooks food very quickly.

**mid-**

PREFIX **Mid-** is used to form words that refer to the middle part of a place or period of time, for example "midday". See *Prefixes* on page 264.

**midday**

NOUN **Midday** is 12 o'clock (noon) in the middle of the day.

**middle** middles

NOUN **1** The **middle** of something is the part furthest from the edges.
ADJECTIVE **2** The **middle** one in a series or a row is the one that has an equal number of people or things on each side of it.

**midnight**

NOUN **Midnight** is 12 o'clock at night.

**might**

VERB **1** If you say something **might** happen, you are not sure if it will.
VERB **2** If you say something **might** be true, you are not sure about it.

**migrate** migrates, migrating, migrated

VERB When birds, fish or animals **migrate**, they move to another place at a particular time of year so that they can find food.

**mild** milder, mildest

ADJECTIVE **1** Something that is **mild** is gentle and does no harm. *You need to use a mild shampoo.*
ADJECTIVE **2** **Mild** weather in the winter is warmer than usual.

**mile** miles

NOUN A **mile** is a unit of distance equal to about one and a half kilometres.

**military**

ADJECTIVE **Military** means to do with the armed forces of a country.

**milk**

NOUN **Milk** is the white liquid that female mammals make in their bodies to feed their young. People drink milk from cows and use it to make butter, cheese and yogurt.

**mill** mills

NOUN **1** A **mill** is a building in which grain is crushed to make flour. The photo shows a water mill. The water makes the mill wheel turn.

NOUN **2** A **mill** is also a factory used for making things such as cotton or paper.

**millennium** millennia or millenniums

NOUN A **millennium** is a period of 1000 years.

**millilitre** millilitres

NOUN A **millilitre** is a measure of volume and capacity. There are 1000 millilitres in a litre.

**millimetre** millimetres

NOUN A **millimetre** (mm) is a measure of length. There are 1000 millimetres in a metre. There are 10 millimetres in a centimetre.

**million** millions

NOUN A **million** is the number 1,000,000.

**millionaire** millionaires

NOUN A **millionaire** is a person who has more than a million pounds or dollars.

**mince**

NOUN **Mince** is meat which has been cut into very small pieces.

**mincemeat**

NOUN **Mincemeat** is a sticky mixture of dried fruit and other sweet things.

**mind** minds, minding, minded

NOUN **1** Your **mind** is your ability to think, together with your memory and all the thoughts you have.

NOUN **2** If you **change your mind**, you change a decision you have made.

VERB **3** If you **mind** about something, it worries you or makes you angry.

**mine** mines

PRONOUN **1** Mine refers to something belonging to the person who is speaking or writing. *That book is* **mine**.

NOUN **2** A **mine** is a place under the ground where people dig out things like diamonds, coal or other minerals.

NOUN **3** A **mine** can be a bomb hidden in the ground or underwater, which explodes when people or things touch it.

**mineral** minerals

NOUN **Minerals** are substances such as tin, salt or coal that are formed naturally in rocks and in the earth.

**mini-**

PREFIX **Mini-** is used to form nouns that refer to something smaller or less important than similar things, for example a minibus.

See *Prefixes* on page 264.

**minibus** minibuses

NOUN A **minibus** is a van with seats in the back that is used as a small bus.

**minister** ministers

NOUN **1** A **minister** is an important member of the government of a country.

NOUN **2** A **minister** is also a person in charge of a church.

**minor**

ADJECTIVE Something that is **minor** is not very important or serious. *She had a* **minor** *accident.*

**mint** mints

NOUN **1** Mint is a small plant. Its leaves have a strong taste and smell, and are used in cooking.

NOUN **2** A **mint** is a kind of sweet.

NOUN **3** A **mint** is also a place where coins are made.

**minus**

PREPOSITION **1** You use **minus** to show that one number is being subtracted from another. For example, ten minus six equals four (written $10 - 6 = 4$).

ADJECTIVE **2** Minus is used when talking about temperatures below 0° Celsius. *The temperature is* **minus** *two degrees.*

**minute** minutes

(*said* **min**-nit) NOUN **1** A **minute** is a unit of time equal to 60 seconds.

(*said* my-**nyoot**) ADJECTIVE **2** Something **minute** is extremely small.

**miracle** miracles

NOUN **1** A **miracle** is a wonderful event, believed to have been caused by God.

NOUN **2** A **miracle** can also be any very surprising event. *By some* **miracle** *he got to school early.*

**mirror** mirrors

NOUN A **mirror** is a piece of glass that reflects light. When you look in a mirror you can see yourself.

**mis-**

PREFIX **Mis-** is added to some words to form other words, often ones that refer to things being done wrongly, for example "misprint" or "misunderstand".

See *Prefixes* on page 264.

**misbehave** misbehaves, misbehaving, misbehaved

VERB If a child **misbehaves**, they are naughty or behave badly.

# mischief

**mischief**

NOUN **Mischief** is silly things that some children do to annoy other people.

**mischievous**

ADJECTIVE **1** A **mischievous** person likes to have fun by embarrassing people or playing tricks.
ADJECTIVE **2** A **mischievous** child is often naughty but does not do any real harm.

**miserable**

ADJECTIVE Someone who is **miserable** is unhappy.
**miserably** ADVERB

**misery**

NOUN **Misery** is great unhappiness.

**misfortune** misfortunes

NOUN **Misfortune** is bad luck.

**mislay** mislays, mislaying, mislaid

VERB If you **mislay** something, you forget where you have put it.

**mislead** misleads, misleading, misled

VERB To **mislead** someone is to give them an idea that is not true.

**misprint** misprints

NOUN A **misprint** is a mistake in something that has been printed, for example "cow" instead of "cot".

**miss** misses, missing, missed

VERB **1** If you are aiming at something and **miss**, you fail to hit it.
VERB **2** If you **miss** a bus or train, you are too late to get on it.
VERB **3** If you **miss** somebody, you are lonely without them.

**Miss**

NOUN **Miss** is used before the name of a girl or an unmarried woman.

**missile** missiles

NOUN A **missile** is a weapon that goes through the air and explodes when it reaches its target.

**missing**

ADJECTIVE If something is **missing**, it is not in its usual place and you cannot find it.

**misspell** misspells, misspelling, misspelt or misspelled

VERB If you **misspell** a word, you spell it wrongly.

**mist** mists

NOUN A **mist** is a large number of tiny drops of water in the air. When there is a mist, you cannot see very far.
**misty** ADJECTIVE

**mistake** mistakes

NOUN A **mistake** is something that is done wrong.

**misunderstand** misunderstands, misunderstanding, misunderstood

VERB If you **misunderstand** someone, you do not understand them properly.

**mix** mixes, mixing, mixed

VERB If you **mix** things, you stir them or put them together. *The children made paste by mixing flour and water.*

**mixture** mixtures

NOUN A **mixture** is several different things mixed up.

**moan** moans, moaning, moaned

VERB If you **moan**, you make a low sad sound because you are in pain or trouble.

**moat** moats

NOUN A **moat** is a wide water-filled ditch around a building such as a castle.

**mobile** mobiles

ADJECTIVE **1** If you are **mobile**, you are able to travel or move to another place.
NOUN **2** A **mobile** is a decoration that you hang up so that it moves around when a breeze blows.

**mobile phone** **mobile phones**

NOUN A **mobile phone** is a telephone you can carry about.

**model** **models**

NOUN **1** A **model** is a small copy of something. It shows what it looks like or how it works.

NOUN **2** A **model** is also someone who shows clothes to people by wearing them.

**modern**

ADJECTIVE **Modern** is to do with new ideas and equipment. *We live in a* **modern** *house.*

**modest**

ADJECTIVE People who are **modest** do not boast about themselves.

**moist** **moister, moistest**

ADJECTIVE Something that is **moist** is slightly wet.

**moisten** VERB

**moisture**

NOUN **Moisture** is tiny drops of water in the air or on a surface.

**mole** **moles**

NOUN **1** A **mole** is a small burrowing animal with tiny eyes and dark silky fur.

NOUN **2** A **mole** is also a small dark lump on someone's skin.

**moment** **moments**

NOUN **1** A **moment** is a very short time.

NOUN **2** A **moment** is also a point in time when something happens. *At that* **moment**, *the teacher came into the room.*

**Monday** **Mondays**

NOUN **Monday** is the day between Sunday and Tuesday.

**money**

NOUN **Money** is the coins or banknotes you use to buy something.

**mongrel** **mongrels**

NOUN A **mongrel** is a dog with parents of different breeds.

**monitor** **monitors**

NOUN A **monitor** is the part of a computer that contains the screen.

**monkey** **monkeys**

NOUN A **monkey** is an animal that lives in hot countries. It has a long tail and climbs trees.

**monster** **monsters**

NOUN A **monster** is an imaginary creature that is large and terrifying.

**month** **months**

NOUN A **month** is a measure of time. There are 12 months in a year.

**mood** **moods**

NOUN Your **mood** is the way you are feeling about things at a particular time, such as how cheerful or angry you are.

**moon** **moons**

NOUN The **moon** is a satellite that moves round the Earth. It shines in the sky at night. You can only see it because the moon's surface reflects sunlight.

**moonlight**

NOUN **Moonlight** is the light that comes from the moon at night.

**moor** **moors**

NOUN A **moor** is an open area of land covered mainly with grass and heather.

a
b
c
d
e
f
g
h
i
j
k
l
**Mm**
n
o
p
q
r
s
t
u
v
w
x
y
z

# moose

**moose**

NOUN A **moose** is a large North American deer. Moose have very flat, branch-shaped horns called antlers.

**mop** mops

NOUN A **mop** is a tool for washing floors. It has a long handle with sponge or pieces of string fixed to the end.

**more**

ADJECTIVE OR ADVERB **More** means a greater number or amount of something. It is the comparative of "many" or "much". *Jill thinks football is **more** fun than maths. He's got **more** chips than me.*

**morning** mornings

NOUN **Morning** is the part of the day before noon.

**mosque** mosques

NOUN A **mosque** is a building where Muslims worship.

**mosquito** mosquitoes or mosquitos

NOUN A **mosquito** is a small flying insect that lives in damp places. The female bites people and other animals to suck their blood.
*See Insects on page 259.*

**moss** mosses

NOUN **Moss** is a small green plant without roots. It grows in flat clumps on trees, rocks and damp ground.

**most**

ADJECTIVE, ADVERB OR NOUN **Most** means the greatest number or amount of something. It is the superlative of "many" or "much". *I saw the **most** fantastic film. **Most** children like sweets. The **most** I can give you is three pieces.*

**moth** moths

NOUN A **moth** is an insect like a butterfly that usually flies at night.

**mother** mothers

NOUN A **mother** is a woman who has a child or children of her own.

**motion** motions

NOUN A **motion** is a movement.

**motive** motives

NOUN A **motive** is a reason for doing something. *There was no **motive** for the attack.*

**motor** motors

NOUN A **motor** is part of a vehicle or machine. The motor uses fuel to make the vehicle or machine work.

**motorbike** motorbikes

NOUN A **motorbike** is a two-wheeled vehicle that is driven by an engine.

**motorway** motorways

NOUN A **motorway** is a wide road built for fast travel over long distances.

**mould** moulds

NOUN **1 Mould** is a soft grey or green substance that can form on old food.
NOUN **2** A **mould** is a container used to make something into a particular shape, for example a jelly mould.

**moult** moults, moulting, moulted

VERB When an animal **moults**, it loses its hair or feathers so that new ones can grow.

**mount** mounts, mounting, mounted

VERB If you **mount** a horse, you climb on its back.

**mountain** mountains

NOUN A **mountain** is a very high piece of land with steep sides.

## mouse mice

NOUN **1** A **mouse** is a small rodent with a long tail.

NOUN **2** A **mouse** is also a small object that you use to move the cursor on a computer screen.

## moustache moustaches

NOUN A man's **moustache** is hair growing on his upper lip.

## mouth mouths

NOUN **1** Your **mouth** is your lips, or the space behind them where your tongue and teeth are.

NOUN **2** The **mouth** of a cave or hole is the entrance to it.

NOUN **3** The **mouth** of a river is the place where it flows into the sea.

## move moves, moving, moved

VERB **1** To **move** means to go to a different place or position.

VERB **2** To **move** something means to change its place or position.

**movement** NOUN

## mow mows, mowing, mowed

VERB If a person **mows** an area of grass, they cut it with a lawnmower.

## Mr (said **miss**-ter)

**Mr** is used before a man's name.

## Mrs (said **miss**-iz)

**Mrs** is used before the name of a married woman.

## Ms (said **miz**)

**Ms** can be used before a woman's name. Some women choose to be called Ms because it says nothing about whether they are married or not.

## much

ADVERB **1** You use **much** to show that something is true to a great extent. *I feel **much** better now.*

ADVERB **2** If something does not happen **much**, it does not happen very often.

ADJECTIVE **3** You use **much** to ask questions or give information about the size or amount of something. *How **much** money do you need?*

## mud

NOUN **Mud** is wet sticky earth.

**muddy** ADJECTIVE

## muddle muddles

NOUN If things such as papers are in a **muddle**, they are all mixed up.

## muffled

ADJECTIVE A **muffled** sound is quiet or difficult to hear.

## mug mugs

NOUN A **mug** is a large deep cup, usually with straight sides and a handle.

## multiple multiples

NOUN The **multiples** of a number are other numbers that it will divide into exactly. For example, 6, 9 and 12 are multiples of 3.

## multiplication

NOUN **Multiplication** is when you multiply one number by another. The sign you use for multiplication is ×.

## multiply multiplies, multiplying, multiplied

VERB **1** When something **multiplies**, it increases greatly in number. *Fleas **multiply** very fast.*

VERB **2** When you **multiply** a number, you make it bigger by a number of times. For example, two multiplied by three (two plus two plus two) equals six. $2 \times 3 = 6$ or $2 + 2 + 2 = 6$

# mum

**mum** **mums**
NOUN Your **mum** is your mother.

**mumble** **mumbles, mumbling, mumbled**
VERB If you **mumble**, you speak very quietly and not clearly.

**mumps**
NOUN **Mumps** is an illness caught especially by children. Your neck swells and your throat hurts.

**munch** **munches, munching, munched**
VERB If you **munch** something, you chew it steadily and thoroughly.

**murder** **murders**
NOUN **Murder** is the deliberate killing of a person.

**murmur** **murmurs, murmuring, murmured**
VERB If you **murmur**, you say something very softly.

**muscle** **muscles**
NOUN **Muscles** are the parts inside your body that you use when you move.

**museum** **museums**
NOUN A **museum** is a building where many interesting or valuable objects are kept and displayed.

**mushroom** **mushrooms**
NOUN A **mushroom** is a small fungus with a short thick stem and a round top. You can eat some kinds of mushroom, but others are poisonous.

**music**
NOUN **1 Music** is a pattern of sounds made by people singing or playing instruments.

NOUN **2 Music** is also the written symbols that stand for musical sounds.

**musical**
ADJECTIVE **Musical** means relating to playing or studying music. *He wants to learn to play a **musical** instrument.*

**musician** **musicians**
NOUN A **musician** is a person who plays a musical instrument well.

**Muslim** **Muslims;** also spelt **Moslem**
NOUN A **Muslim** is a person who follows the religion of Islam.

**must**
VERB If something **must** happen, it is important or necessary that it happens. *You **must** be home by 5 p.m.*

**mustard**
NOUN **Mustard** is a hot spicy yellow paste made from mustard seeds.

**my**
ADJECTIVE **My** refers to something belonging or relating to the person speaking or writing. *I held **my** breath.*

**myself**
PRONOUN **Myself** is used when the person speaking does something and no one else does it. *I hung the picture **myself**.*

**mysterious**
ADJECTIVE Something that is **mysterious** is strange and puzzling.

**mystery** **mysteries**
NOUN **1** A **mystery** is something strange that cannot be explained.
NOUN **2** A **mystery** is also a story in which strange things happen.

**myth** **myths**
NOUN A **myth** is a story which was made up long ago to explain natural events and religious beliefs.

# Nn

**nail** **nails**

NOUN **1** A **nail** is a small piece of metal with a sharp point at one end, which you hammer into objects to hold them together.

NOUN **2** Your **nails** are the thin hard areas at the ends of your fingers and toes.

**naked**

ADJECTIVE Someone who is **naked** is not wearing any clothes.

**name** **names**

NOUN A **name** is what someone or something is called.

**nappy** **nappies**

NOUN A **nappy** is a thick piece of soft material wrapped round a baby's bottom to help keep it dry and clean.

**narrative** **narratives**

NOUN A **narrative** is a story or an account of events.

**narrator** **narrators**

NOUN A **narrator** is a person who tells a story or explains what is happening.

**narrow** **narrower, narrowest**

ADJECTIVE Something **narrow** is a short distance from one side to the other. *The stream was **narrow** enough to jump across.*

**nasty** **nastier, nastiest**

ADJECTIVE **1** Something that is **nasty** is very unpleasant.

ADJECTIVE **2** Someone who is **nasty** is very unkind.

**nastily** ADVERB

**nation** **nations**

NOUN A **nation** is a country with its own laws.

**national**

ADJECTIVE Something that is **national** is to do with the whole of a country. *The Observer is a **national** newspaper.*

**native**

ADJECTIVE **1** Your **native** country is the country where you were born.

ADJECTIVE **2** Your **native** language is the language that you first learned to speak.

ADJECTIVE **3** Animals or plants that are **native** to a place live there naturally. They have not been brought there by people.

**natural**

ADJECTIVE **1** **Natural** means existing or happening in nature. For example, an earthquake is a natural disaster.

ADJECTIVE **2** Something that is **natural** is normal and to be expected.

**nature** **natures**

NOUN **1** **Nature** is animals, plants and all the other things in the world not made by people.

NOUN **2** The **nature** of a person or thing is their basic character.

**naughty** **naughtier, naughtiest**

ADJECTIVE A child who is **naughty** behaves badly.

**navigate** **navigates, navigating, navigated**

VERB When someone **navigates**, they work out the direction in which a ship, plane or car should go, using maps and sometimes instruments.

a
b
c
d
e
f
g
h
i
j
k
l
m
**Nn**
o
p
q
r
s
t
u
v
w
x
y
z

**navy** navies

NOUN **1** A **navy** is the part of a country's armed forces that fights at sea.

ADJECTIVE **2** Something that is **navy** is a very dark blue.

See *Colours* on page 271.

**near** nearer, nearest

ADJECTIVE **1** Something that is **near** is not far away. *Where is the nearest garage?*

ADVERB **2** If you are **near** something or somewhere, you are not far away from it. *We must be getting nearer.*

**nearly**

ADVERB **Nearly** means almost but not quite. *I nearly caught him but he ran off.*

**neat** neater, neatest

ADJECTIVE Something that is **neat** is very tidy and clean.

**necessary**

ADJECTIVE Something that is **necessary** is needed or must be done.

**necessarily** ADVERB

**neck** necks

NOUN Your **neck** is the part of your body that joins your head to the rest of your body.

**necklace** necklaces

NOUN A **necklace** is a piece of jewellery that you wear around your neck.

**need** needs, needing, needed

VERB **1** If you **need** something, you must have it in order to live and be healthy.

VERB **2** Sometimes you **need** something to help you do a particular job. *Now I need a paintbrush.*

VERB **3** If you **need** to do something, you have to do it.

**needle** needles

NOUN **1** A **needle** is a small thin piece of metal used for sewing. It has a hole in one end and a sharp point at the other. You put thread through the hole.

NOUN **2** A **needle** is also a thin metal tube with a sharp point, that people like doctors use to give injections.

NOUN **3** **Needles** are long thin pieces of metal or plastic used for knitting.

NOUN **4** The thin leaves on pine trees are called **needles**.

**negative** negatives

ADJECTIVE **1** A **negative** sentence is one that has the word "no" or "not" in it.

ADJECTIVE **2** A **negative** number is less than zero.

NOUN **3** A **negative** is a film from a camera. You can get your photographs printed from negatives.

**neglect** neglects, neglecting, neglected

NOUN If you **neglect** something, you do not look after it.

**neighbour** neighbours

NOUN Your **neighbour** is someone who lives near you.

**neighbourhood** neighbourhoods

NOUN A **neighbourhood** is a district where people live. *This is a friendly neighbourhood.*

**nephew** nephews

NOUN Someone's **nephew** is a son of their sister or brother. See **niece**.

**nerve** nerves

NOUN **1** Your **nerves** are the long thin threads in your body that carry messages between your brain and the other parts of your body.

NOUN **2** **Nerve** is courage. *I wanted to go on the ride but I hadn't got the nerve.*

**nervous**

ADJECTIVE **1** If you are **nervous**, you are worried about doing something.

ADJECTIVE **2** A **nervous** person is easily frightened.

**nest** nests

NOUN A **nest** is a place that a bird or other animal makes for its babies.

**net** nets

NOUN **1** Net is material made from threads woven together with small spaces in between.

NOUN **2** The **net** is the same as the Internet.

NOUN **3** In maths, the **net** of a three-dimensional shape is the flat shape that you could fold to make the three-dimensional shape.

ADJECTIVE **4** The **net** weight of something is its weight without its wrapping.

**netball**

NOUN **Netball** is a game played by two teams of seven players. Each team tries to score goals by throwing a ball through a net at the top of a pole.

**nettle** nettles

NOUN A **nettle** is a wild plant covered with little hairs that sting.

**never**

ADVERB **Never** means at no time in the past or future. *You must **never** cross the road without looking carefully.*

**new** newer, newest

ADJECTIVE **1** Something that is **new** has just been made or bought. *They have built some **new** houses close to us.*

ADJECTIVE **2** New can mean different. *We've got a **new** car – it's only a year old.*

**news**

NOUN **News** is information about something that has just happened.

**newspaper** newspapers

NOUN A **newspaper** is sheets of paper that are printed and sold regularly. Newspapers contain news and articles.

**newt** newts

NOUN A **newt** is a small animal that looks like a lizard. It lives near water. See *Amphibians* on page 259.

**next**

ADJECTIVE **1** The **next** period or thing is the one that comes immediately after this one. *The **next** programme will follow after the break.*

ADJECTIVE **2** The **next** place is the one nearest to you. *She's in the **next** room.*

**nib** nibs

NOUN A **nib** is a small pointed piece of metal at the end of a pen. Ink comes out of the nib as you write.

**nibble** nibbles, nibbling, nibbled

VERB If you **nibble** something, you eat it slowly by taking small bites out of it.

**nice** nicer, nicest

ADJECTIVE **1** You say something is **nice** when you like it. *This cake is **nice**.*

ADJECTIVE **2** If you say the weather is **nice**, it is warm and pleasant.

ADJECTIVE **3** If you are **nice** to people, you are friendly and kind.

**nickname** nicknames

NOUN A **nickname** is a name that is given to a person by friends or family. *The baby's name is Sam but his **nickname** is Dribbler.*

**niece** nieces

NOUN Someone's **niece** is a daughter of their sister or brother. See **nephew**.

**night** nights

NOUN The **night** is the time between evening and morning when it is dark.

**nightfall**

NOUN **Nightfall** is the time of day when it starts to get dark.

a
b
c
d
e
f
g
h
i
j
k
l
m
**Nn**
o
p
q
r
s
t
u
v
w
x
y
z

**nightingale** **nightingales**

NOUN A **nightingale** is a small brown European bird. Nightingales sing after dark as well as during the day.

**nightmare** **nightmares**

NOUN A **nightmare** is a frightening dream.

**no**

**1** You say **no** when you do not want something or do not agree. *"More tea?" "No, thank you."*

ADJECTIVE **2** You can use **no** to mean not any. *I had no help at all.*

ADVERB **3** You can use **no** to mean not. *Competition entries must be in no later than Friday.*

**nobody**

PRONOUN **Nobody** means not a single person.

**nocturnal**

ADJECTIVE An animal that is **nocturnal** is active mostly at night.

**nod** **nods, nodding, nodded**

VERB If you **nod**, you move your head quickly down and up to answer yes to a question, or to show that you agree.

**noise** **noises**

NOUN **1** A **noise** is a sound that someone or something makes.

NOUN **2** Noise is loud or unpleasant sounds.

**noisy** ADJECTIVE

**non-**

PREFIX Putting **non-** in front of a word makes it mean the opposite. *This is a non-smoking area.*

See *Prefixes* on page 264.

**none**

PRONOUN **None** means not any, or not one. *None of us wanted to go.*

**non-fiction**

NOUN **Non-fiction** is writing that is based on fact. For example, dictionaries are non-fiction. See **fiction**.

**nonsense**

NOUN **Nonsense** is words that do not make sense.

**noon**

NOUN **Noon** is 12 o'clock in the middle of the day.

**no one** also spelt no-one

PRONOUN **No one** means not a single person.

**normal**

ADJECTIVE Something that is **normal** is what you would expect.

**north**

NOUN **North** is one of the four main points of the compass. If you face the point where the sun rises, north is on your left. See **compass point**.

**northern** ADJECTIVE

**north-east**

NOUN **North-east** is halfway between north and east.

**north-west**

NOUN **North-west** is halfway between north and west.

**nose** **noses**

NOUN Your **nose** is the part of your face that sticks out above your mouth. It is used for smelling and breathing.

**nostril** **nostrils**

NOUN Your **nostrils** are the two openings at the end of your nose. You breathe through your nostrils.

**note** notes

NOUN **1** A **note** is a short written message.

NOUN **2** You take **notes** to help you remember what has been said.

NOUN **3** A **note** is also a single sound in music.

NOUN **4** A bank **note** is a printed piece of paper that is used as money.

**nothing**

PRONOUN **Nothing** means not anything.

**notice** notices, noticing, noticed

VERB **1** If you **notice** something, you pay attention to it. *She **noticed** that it was raining.*

NOUN **2** A **notice** is a sign that tells people something. *The **notice** said, "Cameras are not allowed in the museum".*

**nought**

NOUN **Nought** is the number 0, or zero.

**noun** nouns

NOUN In grammar, a **noun** is a word which names a person, a thing or an idea. "James", "newt", and "success" are all nouns.

See *Noun* on page 262.

**nourishment**

NOUN **Nourishment** is the food that you need in order to grow and stay healthy.

nourishing ADJECTIVE

**novel** novels

NOUN A **novel** is a long written story that has been made up by the author. Novels are fiction.

**November**

NOUN **November** is the 11th month of the year. It has 30 days.

**now**

ADVERB **Now** means at the present time.

**nowhere**

ADVERB **Nowhere** means not anywhere.

**nude**

ADJECTIVE Someone who is **nude** is not wearing any clothes.

**nudge** nudges, nudging, nudged

VERB If you **nudge** somebody, you push them gently, usually with your elbow.

**nuisance** nuisances

NOUN If you say that someone or something is a **nuisance**, you mean they annoy you.

**numb**

ADJECTIVE If something is **numb**, it does not feel anything. *My foot is so cold it is **numb**.*

**number** numbers

NOUN A **number** is a word or sign that tells you how many of something there are.

See *Number bank* on page 272.

**numeracy**

NOUN **Numeracy** is the ability to understand and work with numbers.

**numerous**

ADJECTIVE If there are **numerous** things or people, there are a lot of them.

**nurse** nurses

NOUN A **nurse** is a person whose job is to care for people who are ill or injured.

**nursery** nurseries

NOUN **1** A **nursery** is a place where young children can be looked after during the day.

NOUN **2** A **nursery** can also be a place where plants are grown and sold.

**nut** nuts

NOUN **1** A **nut** is the hard fruit of certain trees such as walnuts and chestnuts.

NOUN **2** A **nut** is also a small piece of metal with a hole in it. It screws onto a bolt to fasten things together.

**nylon**

NOUN **Nylon** is a strong artificial material.

a
b
c
d
e
f
g
h
i
j
k
l
m
**Nn**
o
p
q
r
s
t
u
v
w
x
y
z

## Oo

**oak** **oaks**

NOUN An **oak** is a large tree with nuts called acorns. The wood of oak trees is often used to make furniture.

**oar** **oars**

NOUN An **oar** is a wooden pole with a wide flat end, used for rowing a boat.

**oasis** **oases**

NOUN An **oasis** is a place in a desert where water and plants are found.

**oats**

PLURAL NOUN **Oats** are the grains of a cereal. They are used especially for making porridge or for feeding animals.

**obedient**

ADJECTIVE If you are **obedient**, you do what you are told to do.

**obey** **obeys, obeying, obeyed**

VERB If you **obey** someone, you do as they say.

**object** **objects**

NOUN **1** An **object** is anything that you can touch or see, and that is not alive.
NOUN **2** In grammar, the **object** of a verb or preposition is the word or phrase which describes the person or thing affected. In the sentence "She fed the cat", "cat" is the object.

**oblong** **oblongs**

NOUN An **oblong** is a four-sided shape with two parallel short sides and two parallel long sides. See **rectangle**.
See *Colours and flat shapes* on page 271.

**observe** **observes, observing, observed**

VERB If you **observe** something or somebody, you watch them carefully.

**obstinate**

ADJECTIVE Someone who is **obstinate** is determined to do what they want and will not change their mind.

**obvious**

ADJECTIVE Something that is **obvious** is easy to see or understand.

**occasion** **occasions**

NOUN An **occasion** is an important event or celebration.

**occasional**

ADJECTIVE **Occasional** means happening sometimes, but not regularly or often.
**occasionally** ADVERB

**occupant** **occupants**

NOUN The **occupant** of a place is the person who lives or works there.

**occupy** **occupies, occupying, occupied**

VERB **1** To **occupy** a place means to live, stay or work in it.
VERB **2** If something **occupies** you, you are busy doing it or thinking about it.
ADJECTIVE **3** If something like a chair is **occupied**, someone is using it.

**occur** **occurs, occurring, occurred**

VERB **1** When something **occurs**, it happens.
VERB **2** If something **occurs** to you, you suddenly think of it or realize it.

**ocean** **oceans**

NOUN An **ocean** is one of the five large seas on the earth's surface.

**o'clock**

ADVERB You say **o'clock** after numbers when you say a time that is exactly on the hour.

**octagon** **octagons**

NOUN An **octagon** is a flat shape with eight straight sides.
**octagonal** ADJECTIVE
See *Colours and flat shapes* on page 271.

## October

NOUN **October** is the 10th month of the year. It has 31 days.

## octopus  octopuses

NOUN An **octopus** is a sea animal with eight long arms called tentacles.

## odd  odder, oddest

ADJECTIVE **1** If you say something is **odd**, you mean it is strange or unusual.

ADJECTIVE **2 Odd** numbers are those which cannot be divided exactly by two. 13, 25 and 79 are odd numbers.

ADJECTIVE **3 Odd** things are those which do not belong in a pair or a set. *You can't go out wearing **odd** socks.*

**odds and ends** PHRASE **Odds and ends** are small unimportant things. *His pockets were full of **odds and ends**.*

## odour  odours

NOUN An **odour** is a particular smell.

## off

PREPOSITION **1 Off** can show movement away from or out of a place. *They stepped **off** the plane.*

ADVERB **2 Off** can mean not switched on. *He turned the radio **off**.*

ADVERB **3 Off** can also mean time spent away from work. *He took the afternoon **off**.*

ADVERB **4** People use **off** to show a reduction. *All right, I'll take ten per cent **off**.*

ADJECTIVE **5** If food is **off**, it is going bad.

## offend  offends, offending, offended

VERB If you **offend** someone, you upset them by doing or saying something rude.

**offensive** ADJECTIVE

## offer  offers, offering, offered

VERB **1** If you **offer** something to someone, you ask them if they would like to have it.

VERB **2** If you **offer** to do something, you say you will do it without being asked.

## office  offices

NOUN An **office** is a room where people work at desks.

## officer  officers

NOUN **1** An **officer** is a member of the police, or of a government organization.

NOUN **2** An **officer** is also a person in the army, navy or air force who gives orders to other people.

## official

ADJECTIVE Something that is **official** is written or done by the government or by someone else in charge.

## often

ADVERB If something happens **often**, it happens many times.

## ogre  ogres

NOUN In fairy tales, an **ogre** is a man who is large, cruel and frightening.

## oil  oils

NOUN **1 Oil** is a smooth thick liquid that is found under the ground. It is used to keep machines running smoothly, and also for fuel.

NOUN **2 Oil** can also be made from plants or animals. This oil can sometimes be used for cooking.

## ointment  ointments

NOUN An **ointment** is an oily cream that you put on sore skin to help it get better.

## old  older, oldest

ADJECTIVE **1** Someone or something **old** has been in the world for many years.

ADJECTIVE **2** You say something is **old** if it has been used a lot, or you have had it for a long time. *These are my **old** shoes.*

ADJECTIVE **3** If you ask how **old** someone is, you want to know how long they have lived. *How **old** is your baby?*

a b c d e f g h i j k l m n **Oo** p q r s t u v w x y z

## old-fashioned

ADJECTIVE Something **old-fashioned** belongs to the past and has been replaced by something more modern.

## olive  olives

NOUN An **olive** is a small green or black fruit. Olives are eaten as a snack, or used to make oil for cooking.

## omelette  omelettes

NOUN An **omelette** is a food made by beating eggs and cooking them.

## once

ADVERB **1** If something happens **once**, it happens one time only.

ADVERB **2** Once means at some time in the past. *Once, the Romans ruled in Britain.*

at once PHRASE If you do something **at once**, you do it straight away.

## one

**1** One is the number 1.

PRONOUN **2** One refers to a particular thing or person. *I think Tim's idea is the best one.*

## onion  onions

NOUN An **onion** is a small round vegetable with a brown papery skin and a very strong taste.

## only

ADJECTIVE **1** Only means one and no more. *She was the only girl in the group.*

ADJECTIVE **2** An **only** child is someone who has no brothers or sisters.

ADVERB **3** You say **only** when you mean one person or thing and not others. *He's only interested in football.*

ADVERB **4** You can say **only** when something is not very important. *It was only a sparrow.*

ADVERB **5** Only can be used when something was less than you expected. *It only took me ten minutes.*

## onomatopoeia

NOUN **Onomatopoeia** is the use of words that sound like what they mean, for example "hiss" and "buzz".

## opaque

ADJECTIVE If something is **opaque**, it does not let light through and you cannot see through it.

## open  opens, opening, opened

VERB **1** If you **open** a door, you move it so that people can go through it.

VERB **2** If you **open** a box or a bottle, you take the lid off or unfasten it.

VERB **3** When flowers **open**, you can see their petals.

ADJECTIVE **4** When a place such as a shop or library is **open**, you can use it.

## opening  openings

NOUN An **opening** is a hole or space that things or people can go through.

## opera  operas

NOUN An **opera** is a musical play in which most of the words are sung.

## operate  operates, operating, operated

VERB **1** When someone **operates** a machine, they make it work.

VERB **2** When doctors **operate**, they cut open a patient's body to remove or repair a damaged part.

**operation** operations

NOUN An **operation** is when doctors cut open a patient's body to remove or repair a damaged part.

**opinion** opinions

NOUN An **opinion** is what someone thinks about something.

**opponent** opponents

NOUN An **opponent** is someone who is against you in an argument or a contest.

**opposite** opposites

NOUN **1** The **opposite** of something is the thing that is most different from it. *Hot is the opposite of cold.*

PREPOSITION **2** If one person or thing is **opposite** another, they are on the other side of something. *In the train I sat opposite a small boy.*

**optician** opticians

NOUN An **optician** is someone who tests people's eyes, and sells glasses and contact lenses.

**orange** oranges

NOUN **1** An **orange** is a round fruit with a thick skin. Oranges are juicy and sometimes sweet.
See *Fruit on page 257.*

ADJECTIVE **2** Something that is **orange** has a colour between red and yellow.
See *Colours on page 271.*

**orbit** orbits, orbiting, orbited

VERB If something **orbits** a planet or the Sun, it goes round and round it.

**orchard** orchards

NOUN An **orchard** is an area of land where fruit trees are grown.

**orchestra** orchestras

NOUN An **orchestra** is a large group of musicians who play different instruments together.

**order** orders, ordering, ordered

NOUN **1** An **order** is something you are told to do.

VERB **2** If you **order** something, for example in a restaurant, you ask for it to be brought to you.

NOUN **3** Order is the way a set of things is organized. A dictionary is written in alphabetical order.

**ordinary**

ADJECTIVE Something that is **ordinary** is not special in any way.

**organ** organs

NOUN **1** An **organ** is a part of your body that does a special job, for example your heart, lungs or stomach.

NOUN **2** An **organ** is also a large musical instrument like a piano. It has pipes that air is forced through to make the sounds.

**organic**

ADJECTIVE Food that is **organic** has been produced without the use of chemicals.

**organization** organizations;
also spelt organisation

NOUN An **organization** is a large group of people who work together. For example, the police force is an organization.

# organize

**organize** **organizes, organizing, organized**; also spelt organise
VERB **1** If you **organize** an event, you plan and arrange it.
VERB **2** If you **organize** things, you arrange them in a sensible order.

**origin** **origins**
NOUN **1** The **origin** of something is how and why it started.
NOUN **2** You can refer to where someone comes from as their **origin**. *She was of Swedish origin.*

**original**
ADJECTIVE **1** Something that is **original** is new and not a copy.
ADJECTIVE **2** If you say someone's ideas are **original**, you mean they are clever at thinking of new ways of doing things.

**ornament** **ornaments**
NOUN An **ornament** is an object that you put somewhere because you think it is nice to look at.

**orphan** **orphans**
NOUN An **orphan** is a child whose parents are dead.

**ostrich** **ostriches**
NOUN An **ostrich** is the largest living bird. It cannot fly, but it can run very fast. Ostriches live in sandy places in Africa. Their eggs are large, weighing more than a kilo each.

**other**
ADJECTIVE **1** When you say **other** things or other people, you can mean more of the same kind. *He found it hard to make friends with other children.*
ADJECTIVE **2** You can also use **other** to mean different. *We got lost last time. I think we'll try some other way.*
**every other** PHRASE **Every other** means one in every two. *We meet every other week.*

**otherwise**
ADVERB You say **otherwise** to explain what will happen if you do not do something. *I'd better take an umbrella, otherwise I'll get soaked.*

**otter** **otters**
NOUN An **otter** is an animal with brown fur, short legs and a long tail. Otters swim well and eat fish.

**ought**
VERB If you **ought** to do something, you should do it. *I ought to leave early.*

**our**
ADJECTIVE **Our** refers to something belonging or relating to the speaker or writer and one or more other people. *We recently sold our house.*

**ourselves**
PRONOUN **Ourselves** is used when the people speaking do something and no one else does it. *We made the beds ourselves.*

**out**
ADVERB **1** **Out** means towards the outside of a place. *Two dogs rushed out of the house.*
ADVERB **2** **Out** can also mean not at home. *She was out when I rang last night.*
ADVERB **3** **Out** can mean no longer shining or burning. *The lights went out.*

**outer**
ADJECTIVE The **outer** parts of something are the parts furthest from the centre. *The outer layer of an onion is brown and papery.*

**outing** **outings**
NOUN An **outing** is a short trip somewhere to enjoy yourself.

**outline** **outlines**

NOUN An **outline** is the shape of something, especially when you cannot see any details.

**outside**

NOUN **1** The **outside** of something is the part which surrounds the rest of it. *The outside of the box had a picture on it.*

ADVERB **2** You can use **outside** with a verb to mean out of a building. *Let's go outside.*

PREPOSITION **3** You can use **outside** before a noun to say which building you are referring to. *The bicycle was chained up outside the church.*

**oval** **ovals**

NOUN **1** An **oval** is a shape like an egg.

ADJECTIVE **2** **Oval** describes something shaped like an egg, such as an oval mirror or oval frame.

See *Colours and flat shapes* on page 271.

**oven** **ovens**

NOUN The **oven** is the part of a cooker that you use for baking or roasting food.

**over**

PREPOSITION **1** **Over** something means directly above it or covering it. *He put his hands over his eyes.*

PREPOSITION **2** A view **over** an area is a view across that area. *The front windows look out over the sea.*

PREPOSITION **3** Something that is **over** a particular amount is more than that amount.

PREPOSITION **4** If something happens **over** a period of time, it happens during that period. *I went to London over Christmas.*

ADVERB **5** If you lean **over**, you bend your body in a particular direction.

ADVERB **6** You can use **over** to show movement from one place to another. *She went over to the door.*

**over-**

PREFIX **Over-** is placed in front of an adjective or a verb to mean too much or to too great an extent, for example "overestimate".
See *Prefixes* on page 264.

**overalls**

PLURAL NOUN **Overalls** are a piece of clothing with trousers and jacket in one. You wear overalls to protect your other clothes when you are working.

**overboard**

ADVERB If someone falls **overboard**, they fall over the side of a ship into the water.

**overcoat** **overcoats**

NOUN An **overcoat** is a thick warm coat that people wear in winter.

**overdue**

ADJECTIVE If someone or something is **overdue**, they are late. *My library book is overdue.*

**overflow** **overflows, overflowing, overflowed**

VERB **1** If a liquid **overflows**, it spills over the edges of its container.

VERB **2** If a river **overflows**, it flows over its banks.

a
b
c
d
e
f
g
h
i
j
k
l
m
n
**Oo**
p
q
r
s
t
u
v
w
x
y
z

# overgrown

**overgrown**

ADJECTIVE If a place is **overgrown**, it is thickly covered with plants and weeds, usually because it has not been looked after for a long time.

**overhead**

ADVERB **Overhead** means above you. *Seagulls were flying **overhead**.*

**overhear** **overhears, overhearing, overheard**

VERB If you **overhear** someone's conversation, you hear what they are saying to someone else.

**overlap** **overlaps, overlapping, overlapped**

VERB If one thing **overlaps** another, one part of it covers part of the other thing.

**overseas**

ADVERB If you go **overseas**, you go to a country which is on the other side of a sea or ocean.

**oversleep** **oversleeps, oversleeping, overslept**

VERB If you **oversleep**, you sleep longer than you meant to, and wake up late.

**overtake** **overtakes, overtaking, overtook, overtaken**

VERB If you **overtake** someone, you pass them because you are moving faster than they are.

**owe** **owes, owing, owed**

VERB **1** If you **owe** someone money, they have lent it to you and you have not yet paid it back.

VERB **2** If you **owe** someone something, such as thanks, you need to give it to them.

**owl** **owls**

NOUN An **owl** is a bird with a flat face and large eyes. Usually owls hunt at night for small animals.

**own** **owns, owning, owned**

VERB **1** If you **own** something, it belongs to you.

VERB **2** If you **own up** to something wrong, you say that you did it.

**on your own** PHRASE If you are **on your own**, you are alone.

If you do something **on your own**, you do it without any help.

**owner** **owners**

NOUN The **owner** of something is the person it belongs to.

**ox** **oxen**

NOUN **Oxen** are cattle which are used for carrying or pulling things.

**oxygen**

NOUN **Oxygen** is a gas that forms part of the air we breathe. Other animals and plants also need oxygen to live, and things will not burn without it.

**oyster** **oysters**

NOUN An **oyster** is a large flat shellfish. Some oysters produce pearls. See **pearl**.

**ozone**

NOUN **Ozone** is a form of oxygen.

**ozone layer** PHRASE The **ozone layer** is the part of the Earth's atmosphere that protects living things from the dangerous rays of the Sun.

a b c d e f g h i j k l m n **Oo** p q r s t u v w x y z

# Pp

**pace** **paces**
NOUN **1** The **pace** of something is the speed at which it happens.
NOUN **2** A **pace** is a step that you take when you walk.

**pack** **packs, packing, packed**
VERB **1** When you **pack**, you put your clothes in a case or bag.
NOUN **2** A **pack** is a set of playing cards.
NOUN **3** A **pack** of wolves or other animals is a group that hunts together. See *Collective nouns* on page 262.

**package** **packages**
NOUN A **package** is a small parcel.

**packaging**
NOUN **Packaging** is the container that something is sold or sent in.

**packet** **packets**
NOUN A **packet** is a thin cardboard box or paper container.

**pad** **pads**
NOUN **1** A **pad** is a number of pieces of paper fixed together on one side.
NOUN **2** An animal's **pads** are the soft parts under its paws.

**paddle** **paddles, paddling, paddled**
VERB **1** If you **paddle** in the sea, you stand or walk in the shallow water.
VERB **2** If you **paddle** a small boat such as a canoe, you use a special type of oar called a paddle to move the boat along.

**padlock** **padlocks**
NOUN A **padlock** is a special kind of lock. You can use it to lock gates and bicycles.

**page** **pages**
NOUN A **page** is one side of a piece of paper in a book or newspaper.

**pagoda** **pagodas**
NOUN A **pagoda** is a tall building which is used as a temple. Pagodas can be seen in China, Japan and south-east Asia.

**paid**
VERB **Paid** is the past tense of **pay**.

**pail** **pails**
NOUN A **pail** is a bucket.

**pain** **pains**
NOUN A **pain** is an unpleasant feeling that you have in part of your body if you have been hurt or are ill.

**painful**
ADJECTIVE If you say that something is **painful**, you mean it is hurting you.
**painfully** ADVERB

**paint** **paints, painting, painted**
NOUN **1** **Paint** is a coloured liquid that you put onto a surface to make it look fresh.
VERB **2** When you **paint** a picture, you use paint to make a picture on paper or canvas.

**painting** **paintings**
NOUN A **painting** is a picture that has been painted.

**pair** **pairs**
NOUN **1** A **pair** is a set of two things that go together. *I need a new **pair** of shoes.*
NOUN **2** Some objects, such as trousers and scissors, have two main parts which are the same size and shape. This sort of object is also called a **pair**.

**palace** **palaces**
NOUN A **palace** is a large important house, especially one which is the home of a king, queen or president.

**pale** **paler, palest**
ADJECTIVE Something that is **pale** is light in colour, and not strong or bright.

# palm

**palm** **palms**

NOUN **1** The **palm** of your hand is the inside surface of it. Your fingers and thumb are not part of your palm.

NOUN **2** A **palm** is a tree which grows in hot countries. It has long pointed leaves that grow out of the top of a tall trunk.

**pan** **pans**

NOUN A **pan** is a container with a long handle that is used for cooking.

**pancake** **pancakes**

NOUN A **pancake** is a thin flat cake made of flour, eggs and milk, which is fried.

**panda** **pandas**

NOUN A **panda** is an animal like a black and white bear that lives in the bamboo forests of China.

**pane** **panes**

NOUN A **pane** is a sheet of glass in a window or door.

**panic** **panics, panicking, panicked**

VERB If you **panic**, you suddenly get so worried you cannot act sensibly.

**pant** **pants, panting, panted**

VERB If you **pant**, you breathe quickly with your mouth open. You usually pant when you have been running fast.

**panther** **panthers**

NOUN **Panther** is another name for a black leopard.

**pantomime** **pantomimes**

NOUN A **pantomime** is a funny musical play for children.

**pants**

PLURAL NOUN **Pants** are a piece of clothing that you wear under your other clothes. They have two holes for your legs and elastic round the waist.

**paper** **papers**

NOUN **1** **Paper** is the material that you write on or wrap things in.

NOUN **2** A newspaper is also called a **paper**.

**parable** **parables**

NOUN A **parable** is a short story which aims to teach you something about the way you should behave.

**parachute** **parachutes**

NOUN A **parachute** is a large piece of thin cloth. It has strings fixed to it so that a person attached to it can float down to the ground from an aircraft.

**parade** **parades**

NOUN A **parade** is a lot of people marching in the road on a special day.

**paraffin**

NOUN **Paraffin** is a liquid used as a fuel in things like heaters and lamps.

**paragraph** **paragraphs**

NOUN A **paragraph** is a section of a piece of writing. Paragraphs begin on a new line.

**parallel**

ADJECTIVE Two lines or other things that are **parallel** are the same distance apart all the way along. *The road along the sea front is **parallel** with the sea.*

**paralysed**

ADJECTIVE Someone who is **paralysed** cannot move or feel some or all of their body.

**parcel** **parcels**

NOUN A **parcel** is one or more objects wrapped in paper. This is usually done so that it can be sent by post.

**parent** **parents**

NOUN Your **parents** are your mother and father.

**park** **parks, parking, parked**

NOUN **1** A **park** is an area of land with grass and trees, usually in a town. People go there to walk or play.
VERB **2** When someone **parks** a vehicle, they put it somewhere until they need it again.

**parliament** **parliaments**

NOUN The **parliament** of a country is the people who make the country's laws.

**parrot** **parrots**

NOUN A **parrot** is a brightly-coloured bird with a curved beak.

**parsnip** **parsnips**

NOUN A **parsnip** is a long, pointed, cream-coloured root vegetable.
See *Vegetables* on page 256.

**part** **parts**

NOUN **1** A **part** of something is one of the pieces that it is made from. *We need a new part for the washing machine.*
NOUN **2** A **part** is also a particular bit of something such as an area or a body. *This part of the park is for young children only.*
NOUN **3** If you have a **part** in a play, you are one of the people in it.

**participle** **participles**

NOUN In grammar, a **participle** is a form of a verb. English has two participles – the past participle and the present participle. In the sentence "He has gone" the word "gone" is a past participle; in the sentence "She is winning" the word "winning" is a present participle.

**particular**

ADJECTIVE When you talk about a **particular** person or thing, you mean just that person or thing and not others of the same kind.

**partly**

ADVERB **Partly** means not completely. *The table was **partly** covered with a cloth.*

**partner** **partners**

NOUN Your **partner** is the person you are doing something with, for example when dancing or playing games.

**party** **parties**

NOUN A **party** is a group of people having fun together.

**pass** **passes, passing, passed**

VERB **1** If you **pass** someone, you go past them without stopping.
VERB **2** If you **pass** something to someone, you hand it to them.
VERB **3** If you **pass** a test or an exam, you are successful in it.

**passage** **passages**

NOUN **1** A **passage** is a long narrow space with walls on both sides.
NOUN **2** A **passage** is also a section in a piece of writing. *There's a wonderful **passage** in the book that describes their arrival at the castle.*

**passenger** **passengers**

NOUN A **passenger** is a person who travels in a vehicle but is not the driver.

**passive**

NOUN In grammar, the **passive** or **passive voice** is the form of the verb in which the person or thing to which an action is being done is the subject of the sentence. For example, the sentence "The ball was hit by the boy" is in the passive. See **voice**.

**passport** **passports**

NOUN A **passport** is a book with your name and photograph in it, that you need when you leave your own country.

# password

**password**  **passwords**
NOUN A **password** is a secret word or phrase that you must say to be allowed into a particular place.

**past**
NOUN **1** The **past** is the period of time before the present.
ADVERB **2** If you go **past** something, you move towards it and continue until you are on the other side.
PREPOSITION **3** You use **past** when you are telling the time. *It's ten **past** three.*
NOUN **4** In grammar, the **past tense** of a verb is the form used to show that something happened in the past.

**pasta**
NOUN **Pasta** is a type of food made from flour, eggs and water, which is formed into different shapes. Spaghetti, macaroni and noodles are types of pasta.

**paste**  **pastes**
NOUN **Paste** is a thick wet mixture that is easy to spread.

**pastime**  **pastimes**
NOUN A **pastime** is something you like to do in your free time.

**pastry**
NOUN **Pastry** is a food made of flour, fat and water, rolled flat and used for making pies.

**pasture**  **pastures**
NOUN **Pasture** is land that is used for farm animals to graze on.

**pat**  **pats, patting, patted**
VERB If you **pat** something, you hit it gently, usually with your open hand.

**patch**  **patches**
NOUN A **patch** is a piece of material you put over a hole in something to mend it.

**path**  **paths**
NOUN A **path** is a strip of ground that people walk on.

**patience**
NOUN **Patience** is being able to wait calmly for something, or to do something difficult without giving up.

**patient**  **patients**
ADJECTIVE **1** If you are **patient**, you are able to wait calmly for something, or to do something difficult without giving up.
NOUN **2** A **patient** is someone who is being treated by a doctor.

**patrol**  **patrols, patrolling, patrolled**
VERB When people like the police **patrol** a particular area, they go round it to make sure there is no trouble or danger.

**pattern**  **patterns**
NOUN A **pattern** is a regular way something is organized. For example, lines and shapes can make patterns.

**pause**  **pauses, pausing, paused**
VERB If you **pause** while you are doing something, you stop for a moment.

**pavement**  **pavements**
NOUN A **pavement** is a path with a hard surface beside a road, so that people can walk in safety.

**paw**  **paws**
NOUN A **paw** is the foot of some animals. Paws have claws at the front and soft pads underneath.

**pay**  **pays, paying, paid**
VERB When a person **pays** someone, they give them money in exchange for work or for things that they have bought.
**payment** NOUN

## PC **PCs**

NOUN **1** A **PC** is a personal computer.

NOUN **2** In Britain, a **PC** is also a police constable.

## PE

NOUN **PE** is an abbreviation of **physical education**.

## pea **peas**

NOUN **Peas** are round green seeds which are eaten as a vegetable. They grow inside a covering called a pod.
*See Vegetables on page 256.*

## peace

NOUN **1 Peace** is a feeling of quiet and calm.

NOUN **2** When a country has **peace** or is **at peace**, it is not fighting a war.

## peaceful

ADJECTIVE A **peaceful** place is quiet and calm.

## peach **peaches**

NOUN A **peach** is a round juicy fruit with a large stone in the middle. It has sweet yellow flesh and a yellow and red skin.
*See Fruit on page 257.*

## peacock **peacocks**

NOUN A **peacock** is a large male bird with bright blue and green feathers, and long tail feathers which it spreads in a fan. The female is called a peahen.

## peak **peaks**

NOUN **1** The **peak** of a mountain is the pointed top of it.

NOUN **2** The **peak** of a cap is the part that sticks out at the front.

## peanut **peanuts**

NOUN **Peanuts** are small hard seeds which grow under the ground. You can buy roasted and salted peanuts to eat.

## pear **pears**

NOUN A **pear** is a sweet juicy fruit which grows on trees. It is narrow near its stalk, and wider and rounded at the bottom.
*See Fruit on page 257.*

## pearl **pearls**

NOUN A **pearl** is a hard round object which grows inside the shell of an oyster. It is creamy-white in colour. Pearls are used to make valuable jewellery.

## pebble **pebbles**

NOUN A **pebble** is a small smooth stone found on seashores and river beds.

## peck **pecks, pecking, pecked**

VERB When a bird **pecks**, it bites at something with its beak.

## peculiar

ADJECTIVE Something that is **peculiar** is strange or unusual.

## pedal **pedals**

NOUN The **pedals** on a cycle are the two parts that you push with your feet to make it move.

## pedestrian **pedestrians**

NOUN A **pedestrian** is a person who is walking.

## peek **peeks, peeking, peeked**

VERB If you **peek** at something, you have a quick look at it.

## peel **peels, peeling, peeled**

VERB If you **peel** fruit or vegetables, you remove the skin.

## peep **peeps, peeping, peeped**

VERB If you **peep** at something, you look at it very quickly, and usually secretly.

## peg **pegs**

NOUN **1** A **peg** is a thin piece of metal or plastic that is used to hang things on.

NOUN **2** A **peg** is also a small clip that is used to hold washing on a line.

a b c d e f g h i j k l m n o **Pp** q r s t u v w x y z

# pelican

### pelican pelicans
NOUN A **pelican** is a water bird. Its large beak has a soft lower part like a pouch.

### pen pens
NOUN A **pen** is a long thin tool that you use to write in ink.

### pence
NOUN **Pence** is the plural of **penny**.

### pencil pencils
NOUN A **pencil** is a long thin piece of wood with a dark material called graphite in the middle. It is used for writing or drawing.

### pendulum pendulums
NOUN A **pendulum** is a large weight which hangs from a clock. It swings from side to side to keep the clock going at the right speed.

### penguin penguins
NOUN A **penguin** is a large black and white bird found in the Antarctic. Penguins cannot fly. They use their wings for swimming in the water.

### penis penises
NOUN Boys and men have a **penis**. It is used to get rid of waste liquid from the body. Men can also use their penis to help make babies.

### penknife penknives
NOUN A **penknife** is a small knife with blades that fold back into the handle.

### penny pennies or pence
NOUN A **penny** is a small British coin. A hundred pence are worth one pound. The abbreviation for pence is p.

### pentagon pentagons
NOUN A **pentagon** is a flat shape that has five straight sides.
pentagonal ADJECTIVE
See *Colours and flat shapes* on page 271.

### people
PLURAL NOUN **People** are men, women and children.

### pepper peppers
NOUN **1 Pepper** is a hot-tasting powder which is used to flavour food.
NOUN **2** A **pepper** is a red, green or yellow vegetable. It can be cooked or eaten raw in salads.

### per cent
PHRASE You use **per cent** to talk about amounts as a proportion of 100. For example, ten per cent (10%) means 10 out of every 100.

### perch perches
NOUN A **perch** is a short piece of wood for a bird to stand on.

### percussion
ADJECTIVE **Percussion** instruments are instruments that you play by hitting them. Drums and cymbals are percussion instruments.

### perfect
ADJECTIVE **1** Something that is **perfect** is done so well it could not be done better.
ADJECTIVE **2** If you say something is **perfect**, you mean it is wonderful.
perfectly ADVERB

### perform performs, performing, performed
VERB If someone **performs**, they do something to entertain an audience.

**performance** **performances**

NOUN A **performance** is something done in front of people, like acting or dancing.

**perfume** **perfumes**

NOUN **1** A **perfume** is a pleasant smell.

NOUN **2** Perfume is a liquid that you put on your body so that you smell nice.

**perhaps**

ADVERB **1** If you say **perhaps** something will happen, you mean it might happen but you are not sure.

ADVERB **2** You can also say **perhaps** when you are suggesting something. *He's late – **perhaps** he missed the train.*

**perimeter** **perimeters**

NOUN The **perimeter** of a shape is the distance all round it.

**period** **periods**

NOUN A **period** is a particular length of time. *Mrs Smith will be away for a **period** of six months.*

**periscope** **periscopes**

NOUN A **periscope** is a tube with mirrors. When you look in one end, you can see what would otherwise be out of sight.

**permanent**

ADJECTIVE Something that is **permanent** lasts for ever, or for a very long time.

**permission**

NOUN If you have **permission** to do something, you are allowed to do it.

**permit** **permits, permitting, permitted**

VERB If someone **permits** you to do something, they allow you to do it.

**persist** **persists, persisting, persisted**

VERB If you **persist**, you go on doing something even when it is difficult or other people have told you to stop.

**person** **people**

NOUN A **person** is a man, woman or child.

**personal**

ADJECTIVE **Personal** matters relate to your feelings, relationships and health, which you may not want to talk about with other people.

**persuade** **persuades, persuading, persuaded**

VERB If someone **persuades** you to do something you did not want to do, you agree because they gave you a good reason.

persuasion NOUN

**persuasive**

ADJECTIVE **1** Someone who is **persuasive** is good at persuading others to believe or do a particular thing.

ADJECTIVE **2** **Persuasive** text aims to persuade the reader of something.

**pest** **pests**

NOUN A **pest** is an insect, rat or other small animal that causes damage.

**pester** **pesters, pestering, pestered**

VERB If you **pester** someone, you keep bothering them.

**pet** **pets**

NOUN A **pet** is a tame animal that you keep and look after in your home.

**petal** **petals**

NOUN A **petal** is part of a flower. Petals may have bright colours or scents to attract insects.

**petrol**

NOUN **Petrol** is a liquid used as fuel in motor vehicles.

**phantom** **phantoms**

NOUN A **phantom** is a ghost.

a b c d e f g h i j k l m n o **Pp** q r s t u v w x y z

# phone

**phone** phones
NOUN **Phone** is an abbreviation of **telephone**.

**photo** photos
NOUN **Photo** is an abbreviation of **photograph**.

**photocopier** photocopiers
NOUN A **photocopier** is a machine that makes copies of documents.

**photocopy** photocopies
NOUN A **photocopy** is a copy of a document produced by a photocopier.

**photograph** photographs
NOUN A **photograph** is a picture that is made using a camera.

**phrase** phrases
NOUN A **phrase** is a short group of words used together.

**physical**
ADJECTIVE **1 Physical** means to do with things that can be touched or seen.
ADJECTIVE **2 Physical** also means to do with a person's body, rather than their mind.
**physically** ADVERB

**piano** pianos
NOUN A **piano** is a large musical instrument with black and white keys that you press with your fingers.

**pick** picks, picking, picked
VERB **1** To **pick** means to choose. *We need to **pick** three more people for our team.*
VERB **2** When you **pick** flowers or fruit, you take them off the plant.
VERB **3** If you **pick** something **up**, you lift it up from where it is.

**pickle** pickles
NOUN **Pickles** are vegetables or fruit that have been kept in vinegar or salt water.

**picnic** picnics
NOUN A **picnic** is a meal that you take with you and eat out of doors.

**pictogram** pictograms
NOUN **1** A **pictogram** is a picture or symbol used instead of a word or words.
NOUN **2** A **pictogram** is also a graph that uses pictures to show information.

**picture** pictures
NOUN A **picture** is a drawing, painting or photograph.

**pie** pies
NOUN A **pie** is fruit, vegetables, meat or fish baked in pastry.

**piece** pieces
NOUN A **piece** is a part of something.

**pier** piers
NOUN A **pier** is a long platform which sticks out over the sea. Piers often have some kind of entertainment on them.

**pierce** pierces, piercing, pierced
VERB If a sharp object **pierces** something, it goes through it and makes a hole in it.

**pig** pigs
NOUN A **pig** is a farm animal kept for its meat. It has pinkish skin and short legs.

**pigeon** pigeons
NOUN A **pigeon** is a large bird with grey feathers, often seen in towns.

**piglet** piglets
NOUN A **piglet** is a young pig.
See *Young animals* on page 260.

## pile  piles
NOUN A **pile** is a lot of things, such as books, which have been put one on top of the other.

## pill  pills
NOUN A **pill** is medicine made into a small round object that you swallow.

## pillar  pillars
NOUN A **pillar** is a tall post made of something such as stone or brick. It usually helps to hold up a building.

## pillar box  pillar boxes
NOUN A **pillar box** is an iron cylinder with a slot in it for letters.

## pillow  pillows
NOUN A **pillow** is a bag filled with soft material to rest your head on in bed.

## pilot  pilots
NOUN A **pilot** is a person who is trained to fly an aircraft.

## pimple  pimples
NOUN A **pimple** is a small red spot, especially on your face.

## pin  pins
NOUN A **pin** is a small thin piece of metal with a point at one end. Pins can be pushed through things such as pieces of paper or cloth, to hold them together.

## pincers
PLURAL NOUN **1** The **pincers** of a crab or lobster are its front claws.
PLURAL NOUN **2** Pincers are also a tool used for gripping and pulling things.

## pinch  pinches, pinching, pinched
VERB If someone **pinches** you, they squeeze part of you quickly between their thumb and first finger.

## pine  pines
NOUN A **pine** is a tall evergreen tree with sharp thin leaves called needles.

## pineapple  pineapples
NOUN A **pineapple** is a large oval fruit with yellow flesh and a thick, lumpy skin. Pineapples grow in hot countries.

## pink  pinker, pinkest
ADJECTIVE Something that is **pink** has a colour between white and red. *See Colours on page 271.*

## pint  pints
NOUN A **pint** is a measure for liquids. A pint is equal to just over half a litre.

## pipe  pipes
NOUN A **pipe** is a long hollow tube, usually made of metal or plastic. Pipes are used to carry liquid or gas.

## pirate  pirates
NOUN In the past, a **pirate** was a robber who stole from ships.

## pistol  pistols
NOUN A **pistol** is a small gun.

## pit  pits
NOUN **1** A **pit** is a large hole that has been dug in the ground.
NOUN **2** A **pit** is also a coal mine.

## pitch  pitches, pitching, pitched
NOUN **1** A **pitch** is an area of ground where a game such as hockey or football is played.
NOUN **2** The **pitch** of a sound is how high or low it is.
VERB **3** When you **pitch** a tent, you put it up so that you can use it.

## pity
NOUN **1** If you feel **pity** for someone, you feel sorry for them.
NOUN **2** If you say something is a **pity**, you mean it is disappointing. *What a pity Mark isn't coming.*

a
b
c
d
e
f
g
h
i
j
k
l
m
n
o
**Pp**
q
r
s
t
u
v
w
x
y
z

**pizza** pizzas

NOUN A **pizza** is a flat round piece of dough covered with cheese, tomato and other savoury food.

**place** places

NOUN **1** A **place** is any building or area.

NOUN **2** A **place** is also the position where something belongs. *Please put the tools back in their right place.*

**place value**

NOUN In maths, the **place value** of a digit tells you what the digit is worth in hundreds, tens or units (HTU).

**plague** plagues

NOUN A **plague** is a disease that spreads quickly and kills many people.

**plaice**

NOUN A **plaice** is a flat sea fish.

**plain** plainer, plainest; plains

ADJECTIVE **1** A **plain** object has no pattern on it. *She wore a plain skirt.*

ADJECTIVE **2** If something is **plain**, it is clear and easy to see.

NOUN **3** A **plain** is a large, flat area of land with very few trees on it.

**plait** plaits, plaiting, plaited

VERB **1** If you **plait** three lengths of hair or rope together, you twist them over each other in turn.

NOUN **2** A **plait** is a length of hair that has been plaited.

**plan** plans, planning, planned

NOUN **1** If you have a **plan**, you have thought of a way of doing something.

NOUN **2** A **plan** is a drawing that shows what something looks like from above.

VERB **3** If you **plan** what you are going to do, you decide exactly how to do it.

**plane** planes

NOUN **1** A **plane** is a flying vehicle. It has wings and one or more engines. **Plane** is an abbreviation of **aeroplane**.

NOUN **2** A **plane** is also a tool used for smoothing wood.

**planet** planets

NOUN A **planet** is a large round object in space that moves around a star. Earth is one of the nine planets that go round the Sun.

**plank** planks

NOUN A **plank** is a long flat piece of wood.

**plant** plants, planting, planted

NOUN **1** A **plant** is any living thing that is not an animal. Plants can make their own food.

VERB **2** When you **plant** things, such as seeds, flowers or trees, you put them in the ground so that they will grow.

**plaster** plasters

NOUN **1** A **plaster** is a strip of sticky material used for covering small cuts.

NOUN **2** **Plaster** is a smooth paste that dries and forms a hard layer. It is used to cover walls and ceilings inside buildings.

**plastic**

NOUN **1** **Plastic** is a light artificial material that does not break easily. It is used to make all sorts of things, such as buckets, bowls and plates.

ADJECTIVE **2** Something that is **plastic** is made of plastic.

**Plasticine**

NOUN; TRADEMARK **Plasticine** is a soft material like clay, which can be used to make models.

**plate** plates

NOUN A **plate** is a flat dish for food.

**platform** **platforms**

NOUN **1** A **platform** is the area in a station where you wait for the train.

NOUN **2** A **platform** is also a raised area for people to stand on so that they can be seen more easily.

**play** **plays, playing, played**

VERB **1** When you **play**, you spend time doing things you enjoy.

VERB **2** When one person or team **plays** another, they take part in a game and each side tries to win.

VERB **3** If you **play** a musical instrument, you make musical sounds with it.

NOUN **4** A **play** is a story which is acted on the stage, or on radio or television.

**player** NOUN

**playground** **playgrounds**

NOUN A **playground** is a piece of land for children to play on.

**playscript** **playscripts**

NOUN A **playscript** is the written version of a play.

**playtime**

NOUN **Playtime** is a break in the school day when you can play.

**pleasant**

ADJECTIVE If something is **pleasant**, you enjoy it or like it.

**please** **pleases, pleasing, pleased**

VERB If you **please** someone, you make them feel happy.

**pleasure**

NOUN **Pleasure** is a feeling of happiness or enjoyment.

**pleat** **pleats**

NOUN A **pleat** is a permanent fold in fabric.

**pleated** ADJECTIVE

**plenty**

NOUN If there is **plenty** of something, there is more than enough of it.

**pliers**

PLURAL NOUN **Pliers** are a tool used for pulling out small things like nails, or for bending or cutting wire.

**plot** **plots, plotting, plotted**

NOUN **1** A **plot** is a secret plan.

NOUN **2** The **plot** of a film, novel or play is the story and the way it develops.

NOUN **3** A **plot** of land is a small piece that has been marked out for a special purpose such as building houses or growing vegetables.

VERB **4** If people **plot** something, they plan secretly to do it.

**plough** **ploughs**

NOUN A **plough** is a farming tool that is pulled across a field to turn the soil over.

**pluck** **plucks, plucking, plucked**

VERB **1** When someone **plucks** a musical instrument, such as a guitar, they pull the strings and let them go quickly.

VERB **2** When you **pluck** a feather, flower or fruit, you pull it from where it is growing.

**plug** **plugs, plugging, plugged**

NOUN **1** A **plug** is a thick piece of rubber or plastic that fits in the drain hole of a bath or washbasin.

NOUN **2** A **plug** is also a small object that joins pieces of equipment to the electricity supply.

VERB **3** If someone **plugs** a hole, they block it with something.

**plum** **plums**

NOUN A **plum** is a small fruit with a thin, dark red or yellow skin and juicy flesh. It has a large stone in the middle.

See *Fruit* on page 257.

a b c d e f g h i j k l m n o **Pp** q r s t u v w x y z

**plumber** plumbers

NOUN A **plumber** is a person who fits and mends water pipes.

**plump** plumper, plumpest

ADJECTIVE Someone or something that is **plump** is rather fat.

**plunge** plunges, plunging, plunged

VERB If someone **plunges** into the water, they dive or throw themselves into it.

**plural** plurals

NOUN **Plural** means more than one. The **plural** of "boy" is "boys". The **plural** of "box" is "boxes". See **singular**.

**plus**

PREPOSITION **1** You use **plus** ( + ) to show that one number is being added to another. Two **plus** two equals four.
PREPOSITION **2** You can use **plus** when you mention an additional item. You get a television **plus** a free radio.

**p.m.**

ADVERB **p.m.** is the time between 12 noon and 12 midnight. See **a.m.**

**poach** poaches, poaching, poached

VERB If you **poach** an egg, you remove its shell and cook the egg gently in boiling water.

**pocket** pockets

NOUN A **pocket** is a small bag that is sewn into clothing.

**pod** pods

NOUN A **pod** is a seed cover. Peas and beans grow inside pods. See **pea**.

**poem** poems

NOUN A **poem** is a piece of writing in short lines, which sometimes rhyme. The lines usually have a particular rhythm.

**poet** poets

NOUN A **poet** is a person who writes poems.

**poetry**

NOUN **Poetry** is writing in which the lines have a rhythm and sometimes rhyme.

**point** points, pointing, pointed

NOUN **1** The **point** of something such as a pin is the sharp end of it.
NOUN **2** A **point** is a position or time. I'll call you at some **point** during the day.
NOUN **3** The **point** of doing something is the reason for doing it. The **point** of playing is to have fun.
NOUN **4** In a game or sport, a **point** is part of the score.
NOUN **5** The decimal **point** in a number is the dot separating the whole number from the fraction.
VERB **6** If you **point** at something, you show where it is by using your finger.
VERB **7** If something **points** in a particular direction, it faces that way.

**pointed**

ADJECTIVE Something that is **pointed** has a point at one end.

**poison** poisons

NOUN **Poison** is something that harms or kills people or animals if it gets into their body.
**poisonous** ADJECTIVE

**poke** pokes, poking, poked

VERB If you **poke** something, you push it hard with your finger.

**polar bear** polar bears

NOUN A **polar bear** is a large white bear that lives near the North Pole.

**pole** poles

NOUN **1** A **pole** is a long round post, used especially for holding things up.
NOUN **2** A **pole** is also one of the two points on the Earth that are the furthest from the equator. They are known as the North Pole and the South Pole.

**police**

PLURAL NOUN The **police** are an organization whose job is to protect people and their belongings, and to make sure that people obey the law.
**policeman** NOUN    **policewoman** NOUN

**police officer**    **police officers**

NOUN A **police officer** is a policeman or policewoman.

**polish**    **polishes, polishing, polished**

NOUN **1 Polish** is a substance that you put on an object to clean and shine it.
VERB **2** If you **polish** something, you put polish on it or rub it with a cloth to make it shine.

**polite**

ADJECTIVE Someone who is **polite** is well-behaved and thinks about other people's feelings.

**politician**    **politicians**

NOUN A **politician** is a person involved in the government of a country.

**politics**

NOUN **Politics** is the study of the way in which a country is governed.

**pollen**

NOUN **Pollen** is a fine, yellow powder in flowers that the wind or insects carry to other flowers to make seeds.

**pollution**

NOUN **Pollution** is making things like the air and water dirty and dangerous to live in or use.

**poly-**

PREFIX **Poly-** means many or much. For example, a polygon is a shape with many sides.
See *Prefixes* on page 264.

**polyester**

NOUN **Polyester** is an artificial fibre used especially to make clothes.

**polygon**    **polygons**

NOUN A **polygon** is a flat shape with three or more straight sides.

**polyhedron**    **polyhedrons** or **polyhedra**

NOUN A **polyhedron** is a solid shape with four or more faces.

**polythene**

NOUN **Polythene** is a thin plastic material that is often made into bags.

**pond**    **ponds**

NOUN A **pond** is a small lake.

**pony**    **ponies**

NOUN A **pony** is a kind of horse which is smaller than an ordinary horse.

**ponytail**    **ponytails**

NOUN A **ponytail** is long hair which is tied behind the head and hangs down like a tail.

**pool**    **pools**

NOUN A **pool** is a small area of still or slow-moving water.

**poor**    **poorer, poorest**

ADJECTIVE **1** Someone who is **poor** has very little money and few belongings.
ADJECTIVE **2** Something that is **poor** is not good. *If my work is **poor**, I have to do it again.*

**pop**    **pops**

NOUN **1 Pop** is modern music played and enjoyed especially by young people.
NOUN **2** A **pop** is a short sharp sound.

**popcorn**

NOUN **Popcorn** is a snack made from a type of corn that pops open when heated.

**poppy**    **poppies**

NOUN A **poppy** is a plant with a large red flower on a hairy stem.

**popular**

ADJECTIVE If someone or something is **popular**, they are liked by a lot of people.

a
b
c
d
e
f
g
h
i
j
k
l
m
n
o
**Pp**
q
r
s
t
u
v
w
x
y
z

# population

**population**

NOUN **1** The **population** of a country or area is all the people who live in it.

NOUN **2** The **population** of a place is also the number of people who live there.

**porch**  **porches**

NOUN A **porch** is a sheltered place at the entrance to a building.

**porcupine**  **porcupines**

NOUN A **porcupine** is an animal with lots of stiff hairs called quills on its back.

**pork**

NOUN **Pork** is meat from a pig.

**porpoise**  **porpoises**

NOUN A **porpoise** is a sea mammal that looks like a dolphin or a small whale.

**porridge**

NOUN **Porridge** is a thick sticky food made from oats cooked in water or milk.

**port**  **ports**

NOUN A **port** is a place where boats come to load and unload.

**portable**

ADJECTIVE Something that is **portable** is made to be easily carried, for example a portable television.

**porter**  **porters**

NOUN A **porter** is a person whose job is to look after the entrance of a building, greeting and directing visitors.

**portion**  **portions**

NOUN A **portion** of food is the amount that is given to one person at a meal.

**portrait**  **portraits**

NOUN A **portrait** is a picture of a person.

**position**  **positions**

NOUN **1** The **position** of someone or something is the place where they are.

NOUN **2** Someone's **position** can also be the way they are sitting or standing. *Try to stay in that **position** while I draw you.*

**positive**

ADJECTIVE **1** If you are **positive** about something, you are very sure about it.

ADJECTIVE **2** **Positive** numbers are those which are greater than zero.

**possess**  **possesses, possessing, possessed**

VERB If you **possess** something, you have it or own it.

**possession** NOUN

**possible**

ADJECTIVE **1** Something that is **possible** can be done.

ADJECTIVE **2** You can also use **possible** to talk about something that may happen but is not certain. *It's **possible** we might go abroad next year.*

**possibly** ADVERB

**possum**  **possums**

NOUN A **possum** is a marsupial with thick fur and a long tail.

**post**  **posts, posting, posted**

NOUN **1** **Post** is letters or parcels that are collected and delivered.

NOUN **2** A **post** is a strong piece of wood or metal fixed upright in the ground.

VERB **3** If you **post** a letter, you send it to someone by putting it in a postbox.

**postbox**  **postboxes**

NOUN A **postbox** is a metal box with a slot in it where you can post letters.

**postcard**  **postcards**

NOUN A **postcard** is a piece of thin card, often with a picture on one side, that you can use to send a message to someone.

**postcode**  **postcodes**
NOUN A **postcode** is the letters and numbers at the end of an address to help the sorting of mail.

**poster**  **posters**
NOUN A **poster** is a large notice or picture that is put on a wall or notice board.

**postman**  **postmen**
NOUN A **postman** is a man whose job is to deliver letters and parcels sent by post.

**post office**  **post offices**
NOUN A **post office** is a building where you can take things to be posted.

**postpone**  **postpones, postponing, postponed**
VERB If you **postpone** something, you put it off until later. *We had to* ***postpone*** *the picnic because the weather was so bad.*

**pot**  **pots**
NOUN A **pot** is a round container for things like paint or jam, or for growing plants in.

**potato**  **potatoes**
NOUN A **potato** is a round vegetable that grows under the ground. Potatoes can be boiled, baked or fried.
See *Vegetables* on page 256.

**pottery**
NOUN **Pottery** is objects such as dishes and ornaments that are made from clay.

**pouch**  **pouches**
NOUN **1** A **pouch** is a small bag for keeping things in.
NOUN **2** A **pouch** can also be a pocket of skin on an animal. Female kangaroos and other marsupials have a pouch on their stomach. Their babies grow in this pouch. Hamsters have pouches in their cheeks for storing food.

**pounce**  **pounces, pouncing, pounced**
VERB When an animal **pounces** on something, it leaps on it and grabs it.

**pound**  **pounds**
NOUN **1** The **pound** (£) is a unit of money in Britain and in some other countries.
NOUN **2** A **pound** is also a unit of weight equal to just under half a kilogram.

**pour**  **pours, pouring, poured**
VERB **1** If you **pour** a liquid out of a container, you make it flow out by tipping the container.
VERB **2** When it is raining heavily, you can say that it is **pouring**.

**powder**
NOUN **Powder** is something that has been ground into tiny pieces.

**power**  **powers**
NOUN **1** If someone or something has **power**, they have control over other people.
NOUN **2** The **power** of something, such as the wind or the sea, is its strength.

**powerful**
ADJECTIVE If someone or something is **powerful**, they are very strong.

**practical**
ADJECTIVE **1** **Practical** people are good at working with their hands.
ADJECTIVE **2** **Practical** ideas are ones that are likely to work.

**practice**
NOUN **Practice** is doing something many times so that you get better at it.

**practise**  **practises, practising, practised**
VERB If you **practise**, you do something again and again, in order to get better at it. *She has been* ***practising*** *this piece of music for months.*

**praise**  **praises, praising, praised**
VERB If someone **praises** you for something you have done, they say how well you have done it.

**pram** **prams**

NOUN A **pram** is a small carriage that a baby can be pushed around in.

**prawn** **prawns**

NOUN A **prawn** is a small edible shellfish with a long tail.

**pray** **prays, praying, prayed**

VERB When someone **prays**, they speak to the god they believe in, to give thanks or to ask for help.

**prayer** **prayers**

NOUN A **prayer** is the words someone says when they are praying.

**pre-**

PREFIX **Pre-** is used to form words that describe something as taking place before a particular time or event. *We shop early to miss the **pre**-Christmas rush.* See *Prefixes* on page 264.

**precious**

ADJECTIVE Something that is **precious** is worth a lot of money.

**precipice** **precipices**

NOUN A **precipice** is a steep side on a mountain or rock.

**precise**

ADJECTIVE Something that is **precise** is exact and accurate in every detail. *Take **precise** measurements of the room.*
**precisely** ADVERB

**predator** **predators**

NOUN A **predator** is an animal that kills and eats other animals.

**predict** **predicts, predicting, predicted**

VERB If someone **predicts** an event, they say that it will happen in the future.

**prefer** **prefers, preferring, preferred**

VERB If you **prefer** someone or something, you like that person or thing better than another.

**prefix** **prefixes**

NOUN A **prefix** is a letter or group of letters added to the beginning of a word to make a new word, for example "dis-", "pre-" and "un-". See *Prefixes* on page 264.

**pregnant**

ADJECTIVE A woman who is **pregnant** is expecting a baby.

**prehistoric**

ADJECTIVE Something that is **prehistoric** belongs to the time before history was written down.

**preparations**

PLURAL NOUN **Preparations** are all the things that have to be done before an event. *The children were busy with **preparations** for the school play.*

**prepare** **prepares, preparing, prepared**

VERB 1 If you **prepare** for something that is going to happen, you get ready for it.
VERB 2 If you **prepare** someone or something, you get them ready.

**preposition** **prepositions**

NOUN In grammar, a **preposition** is a word such as "by", "for" or "with", that goes in front of a noun group. In the sentence "She fell into the pond", "into" is a preposition and "the pond" is a noun group.

**present** **presents, presenting, presented**

NOUN 1 A **present** is something that you give to someone for them to keep.
ADJECTIVE 2 If someone is **present** somewhere, they are there.
NOUN 3 The **present** is the time now.
VERB 4 If someone **presents** you with something, they give it to you. *The mayor **presented** her with a certificate.*
VERB 5 The person who **presents** a show introduces each part or each guest.
NOUN 6 The **present tense** of a verb is the form used to show something is happening now.

**preserve** **preserves, preserving, preserved**
VERB **1** If you **preserve** something, you do something to keep it the way it is.
VERB **2** To **preserve** food means to stop it from going bad.

**president** **presidents**
NOUN The **president** of a country or an organization is the head of it.

**press** **presses, pressing, pressed**
VERB **1** If you **press** something against something else, you hold it there firmly.
*He **pressed** the phone against his ear.*
NOUN **2** Newspapers and the journalists who work for them are called the **press**.

**pressure**
NOUN **Pressure** is the force of one thing pressing or pushing on another.

**pretend** **pretends, pretending, pretended**
VERB If you **pretend**, you act as though something is true although it is not.
*Let's **pretend** to be working.*

**pretty** **prettier, prettiest**
ADJECTIVE Someone who is **pretty** is nice to look at.

**prevent** **prevents, preventing, prevented**
VERB If you **prevent** someone from doing something, you stop them doing it.

**prey**
NOUN The **prey** of an animal is the creatures that it hunts for food.
**bird of prey** PHRASE A **bird of prey** is a bird such as an eagle or a hawk, that kills and eats smaller birds and animals.

**price** **prices**
NOUN The **price** of something is the amount of money that you must pay to buy it.

**prick** **pricks, pricking, pricked**
VERB To **prick** something means to make a tiny hole with something sharp.

**prickle** **prickles**
NOUN **Prickles** are small sharp points or thorns on plants.

**pride**
NOUN **1** **Pride** is the good feeling you have when you have done something well.
NOUN **2** A **pride** of lions is a group of lions that live together.
See *Collective nouns* on page 262.

**prime minister** **prime ministers**
NOUN The **prime minister** of a country is the leader of that country's government.

**prince** **princes**
NOUN A **prince** is the son of a king or queen.

**princess** **princesses**
NOUN A **princess** is the daughter of a king or queen, or the wife of a prince.

**print** **prints, printing, printed**
VERB **1** When someone **prints** something such as a poster or a newspaper, they use a machine to make lots of copies of it.
VERB **2** If you **print** words, you write in letters that are not joined together.

**printer** **printers**
NOUN **1** A **printer** is a machine that is linked to a computer to print information on paper.
NOUN **2** A **printer** is also a person who prints things like books and magazines.

**print-out** **print-outs**
NOUN A **print-out** is a printed copy of information from a computer.

**prism** **prisms**
NOUN **1** A **prism** is an object made of clear glass with many flat sides. It separates light passing through it into the colours of the rainbow.
NOUN **2** A **prism** is also any three-dimensional shape that has the same size and shape of face at each end.

# prison

**prison** prisons

NOUN A **prison** is a building where people are kept when they have broken the law.

**prisoner** prisoners

NOUN **1** A **prisoner** is someone who is kept in prison as a punishment.

NOUN **2** A **prisoner** is also someone who has been captured by an enemy.

**private**

ADJECTIVE If something is **private**, it is for one person or group only. *All the rooms have a private bath.*

**in private** PHRASE If you do something **in private**, you do it without other people being there.

**prize** prizes

NOUN A **prize** is something that is given to someone as a reward.

**probable**

ADJECTIVE Something that is **probable** is likely to be true, or likely to happen.

**probably** ADVERB

**problem** problems

NOUN **1** A **problem** is something that is difficult.

NOUN **2** A **problem** is also something, like a puzzle, that you have to work out.

**process** processes

NOUN A **process** is a series of actions for doing or making something.

**procession** processions

NOUN A **procession** is a line of people walking or riding through the streets on a special occasion.

**prod** prods, prodding, prodded

VERB If you **prod** something, you push it with your finger.

**produce** produces, producing, produced

VERB **1** To **produce** something means to make it.

VERB **2** If you **produce** an object from somewhere such as a pocket, you bring it out so that it can be seen.

VERB **3** Someone who **produces** a play, film or television programme gets it ready to show to the public.

**product** products

NOUN **1** A **product** is something that is made to be sold.

NOUN **2** In maths, the **product** of two numbers is the answer you get when you multiply them together. For example, the product of four and two is eight.

**profit** profits

NOUN A **profit** is the money you gain when you sell something for more than it cost you to make or buy.

**program** programs

NOUN A **program** is a set of instructions that a computer uses in order to do particular things.

**programme** programmes

NOUN **1** A radio or television **programme** is the thing that is being broadcast.

NOUN **2** A **programme** is a plan of things that will take place.

**progress** progresses, progressing, progressed

NOUN **1** Progress is moving forward or getting better at something. *I'm making progress with my spelling.*

VERB **2** If you **progress**, you get better at something.

**project** projects

NOUN A **project** is work that you do to learn about something and then write about it.

**promise** promises, promising, promised

VERB If you **promise** to do something, you mean you really will do it.

**prong** prongs

NOUN The **prongs** of a fork are the long pointed parts.

**pronoun** pronouns

NOUN **1** In grammar, a **pronoun** is a word that is used to replace a noun.

NOUN **2 Personal pronouns** replace the subject or object of a sentence. In the sentence "She caught a fish", "she" is a personal pronoun.

NOUN **3 Possessive pronouns** replace the subject or object when you want to show who owns it. In the sentence "This book is mine", "mine" is a possessive pronoun.

See *Pronoun* on page 263.

**pronounce** pronounces, pronouncing, pronounced

VERB To **pronounce** a word means to say it in a particular way.

**pronunciation**

NOUN **Pronunciation** is the way a word is usually said.

**proof**

NOUN **Proof** of something is the facts that show that it is true or that it exists.

**prop** props, propping, propped

VERB If you **prop** an object somewhere, you support it against something.

**propeller** propellers

NOUN A **propeller** is the blades that turn to drive an aircraft or ship.

**proper**

ADJECTIVE **1 Proper** means right. *Put those things back in the **proper** place.*

ADJECTIVE **2** You can also use **proper** to mean real. *You need a **proper** screwdriver for that job.*

**properly**

ADVERB If something is done **properly**, it is done correctly.

**proper noun** proper nouns

NOUN A **proper noun** is the name of a particular person or place. It starts with a capital letter. "Ben" and "London" are both proper nouns.

See *Noun* on page 262.

**property** properties

NOUN **1** Someone's **property** is the things that belong to them.

NOUN **2** A **property** is a building and the land belonging to it.

**prophet** prophets

NOUN A **prophet** is a person who predicts what will happen in the future.

**proportion** proportions

NOUN The **proportion** of one amount to another is its size in comparison with the other amount. *There was a large **proportion** of boys in the class.*

**prose**

NOUN **Prose** is written language that is not poetry or a play.

**protect** protects, protecting, protected

VERB To **protect** someone or something is to prevent them from being harmed.

**protection** NOUN

**protein** proteins

NOUN **Protein** is a substance found in meat, eggs and milk that is needed by bodies for growth.

**protest** protests

NOUN A **protest** is something you say or do to show that you disagree with something.

**proud** prouder, proudest

ADJECTIVE If you feel **proud**, you feel glad about something you have done, or about something that belongs to you. *She was **proud** of her new bike.*

**prove** proves, proving, proved
VERB When you **prove** something, you show that it is definitely true.

**proverb** proverbs
NOUN A **proverb** is a short sentence that people say which gives advice about life. For example, the proverb "Look before you leap" means that you should think carefully before you do something.

**provide** provides, providing, provided
VERB If you **provide** something for someone, you give it to them so that they have it when they need it.

**prune** prunes, pruning, pruned
VERB 1 When someone **prunes** a tree, they cut off some of the branches so that it will grow better.
NOUN 2 A **prune** is a dried plum.

**psalm** psalms
NOUN A **psalm** is a poem or prayer from the Bible.

**pub** pubs
NOUN A **pub** is a building where people go to drink and talk with their friends.

**public**
ADJECTIVE Something that is **public** can be used by anyone. For example, anyone can pay to travel on public transport, such as trains and buses.

**publish** publishes, publishing, published
VERB When a company **publishes** a book, newspaper or magazine, they print copies of it and sell them.
**publisher** NOUN

**pudding** puddings
NOUN A **pudding** is a sweet food which is usually eaten after the main part of a meal.

**puddle** puddles
NOUN A **puddle** is a small shallow pool of liquid.

**pull** pulls, pulling, pulled
VERB 1 When you **pull** something, you hold it firmly and move it towards you.

VERB 2 When you **pull** a curtain, you move it across a window.
VERB 3 When a vehicle **pulls away**, **pulls out** or **pulls in**, it moves in that direction.

**pulley** pulleys
NOUN A **pulley** is for lifting heavy weights. The weight is attached to a rope or a chain which passes over a wheel.

**pullover** pullovers
NOUN A **pullover** is a jumper.

**pulse**
NOUN Your **pulse** is the regular beating of blood through your body. You can feel your pulse in your neck or wrist.

**pump** pumps, pumping, pumped
NOUN 1 A **pump** is a machine that is used to force gas or liquid to move the way it is wanted.
VERB 2 To **pump** is to force gas or liquid somewhere using a pump. *I must **pump** up these balloons.*

**pumpkin** pumpkins
NOUN A **pumpkin** is a very large, orange-coloured vegetable with a thick skin. It is soft inside, with a lot of seeds.

**pun** puns
NOUN A **pun** is a joke using a word which has two different meanings. For example, the sentence "My dog's a champion boxer" has a pun on the word "boxer".

**punch** punches, punching, punched
VERB If you **punch** someone, you hit them hard with your fist.

**punctual**
ADJECTIVE Someone who is **punctual** arrives somewhere or does something at exactly the right time.

**punctuation**

NOUN **Punctuation** is the marks such as full stops and commas that you use in writing.

**punctuate** VERB

See *Punctuation* on page 264.

**puncture** **punctures**

NOUN A **puncture** is a small hole in a tyre. When a tyre has a puncture, the air inside escapes and the tyre goes flat.

**punish** **punishes, punishing, punished**

VERB To **punish** someone means to make them suffer because they have done something wrong.

**punishment** NOUN

**pupil** **pupils**

NOUN **1** The **pupils** at a school are the children who go there.

NOUN **2** Your **pupils** are the small round black holes in the centre of your eyes.

**puppet** **puppets**

NOUN A **puppet** is a kind of doll that you can move. Some puppets have strings which you can pull. Others are made so that you can put your hand inside.

**puppy** **puppies**

NOUN A **puppy** is a young dog.

See *Young animals* on page 260.

**purchase** **purchases, purchasing, purchased**

VERB When you **purchase** something, you buy it.

**pure** **purer, purest**

ADJECTIVE Something that is **pure** is not mixed with anything else.

**purple**

ADJECTIVE Something that is **purple** is of a reddish-blue colour.

See *Colours* on page 271.

**purpose** **purposes**

NOUN A **purpose** is the reason for doing something.

**on purpose** PHRASE If you do something **on purpose**, you mean to do it. It does not happen by accident.

**purr** **purrs, purring, purred**

VERB When a cat **purrs**, it keeps making a low sound that shows it is happy.

**purse** **purses**

NOUN A **purse** is a small bag that people keep their money in.

**push** **pushes, pushing, pushed**

VERB When you **push** something, you press it hard.

**pushchair** **pushchairs**

NOUN A **pushchair** is a small folding chair on wheels in which a baby or toddler can be wheeled around.

**put** **puts, putting, put**

VERB **1** When you **put** something somewhere, you move it there.

VERB **2** If you **put** something **off**, you delay doing it.

VERB **3** If you **put** a light **out**, you make it stop shining.

**puzzle** **puzzles, puzzling, puzzled**

VERB **1** If something **puzzles** you, you do not understand it.

NOUN **2** A **puzzle** is a game or question that needs a lot of thought to solve it.

**pyjamas**

PLURAL NOUN **Pyjamas** are loose trousers and a top that people wear in bed.

**pyramid** **pyramids**

NOUN **1** A **pyramid** is a solid shape with a flat base and flat triangular faces that meet at the top in a point.

See *Solid shapes* on page 271.

PLURAL NOUN **2** The **Pyramids** are ancient stone structures built over the bodies of Egyptian kings and queens.

# Qq

**quack** quacks, quacking, quacked
VERB When a duck **quacks**, it makes a loud harsh sound.

**quadrilateral** quadrilaterals
NOUN A **quadrilateral** is a flat shape with four straight sides.
See *Colours and flat shapes* on page 271.

**quaint** quainter, quaintest
ADJECTIVE Something that is **quaint** is unusual and rather pretty.

**qualify** qualifies, qualifying, qualified
VERB **1** When someone **qualifies**, they pass the examination they need to do a particular job.
VERB **2** You **qualify** if you get enough points in a competition to go on to the next stage.

**quality** qualities
NOUN The **quality** of something is how good or bad it is, compared with other things of the same kind.

**quantity** quantities
NOUN A **quantity** is an amount you can measure or count. *We shall need a huge quantity of food for the weekend.*

**quarrel** quarrels
NOUN A **quarrel** is an angry argument.

**quarry** quarries
NOUN A **quarry** is a deep hole that has been dug in a piece of land. Quarries are dug to provide materials such as stone for building and other work.

**quarter** quarters
NOUN A **quarter** is one of four equal parts of something.
See *Fractions* on page 272.

**quay** quays
(*said* **kee**)
NOUN A **quay** is a place where boats are tied up to be loaded or unloaded.

**queen** queens
NOUN **1** A **queen** is a woman who rules a country. Queens are not chosen by the people. They are born into a royal family.
NOUN **2** The wife of a king is also called a **queen**.
NOUN **3** In the insect world, a **queen** is a large female bee, ant or wasp which can lay eggs.

**query** queries, querying, queried
NOUN **1** A **query** is a question.
VERB **2** If you **query** something, you ask about it because you think it might not be right.

**question** questions
NOUN A **question** is words you say or write when you want to ask something.

**question mark** question marks
NOUN A **question mark** is the punctuation mark (**?**) which you use in writing at the end of a question.
See *Punctuation* on page 264.

**questionnaire** questionnaires
NOUN A **questionnaire** is a list of questions which asks for information for a survey.

**queue** queues
NOUN A **queue** is a line of people or vehicles waiting for something.

**quiche** quiches
NOUN A **quiche** is a sort of tart with a filling of eggs, and cheese or other food.

**quick** **quicker, quickest**

ADJECTIVE **1** Someone or something that is **quick** moves very fast.

ADJECTIVE **2** Something that is **quick** lasts only a short time. *I'll have a **quick** look at it.*

**quickly**

ADVERB Things that happen **quickly** happen very fast.

**quiet** **quieter, quietest**

ADJECTIVE **1** Someone or something that is **quiet** makes only a little noise or no noise at all.

ADJECTIVE **2** **Quiet** also means peaceful. *Let's have a **quiet** evening at home.*

**quilt** **quilts**

NOUN A **quilt** is a soft cover for a bed.

**quit** **quits, quitting, quit**

VERB **1** If you **quit** something, you stop doing it. ***Quit** teasing me!*

VERB **2** If you **quit**, you leave. *My dad has just **quit** his job.*

VERB **3** If you **quit** a file on a computer, you close it.

**quite**

ADVERB **1** **Quite** means rather. *I think he's **quite** nice.*

ADVERB **2** **Quite** can also mean completely. *The work is now **quite** finished.*

**quiver** **quivers, quivering, quivered**

VERB **1** If something **quivers**, it trembles.

NOUN **2** A **quiver** is a container for carrying arrows.

**quiz** **quizzes**

NOUN A **quiz** is a game or test. Someone tries to find out how much you know by asking you questions.

**quotation** **quotations**

NOUN A **quotation** is an extract from a book or speech that you use in your own work.

**quotation marks**

PLURAL NOUN **Quotation marks** are punctuation marks ( " " ) or ( ' ' ) used in writing to show where speech begins and ends.

**quote** **quotes, quoting, quoted**

VERB **1** If you **quote** something that someone has written or said, you repeat their exact words.

NOUN **2** A **quote** is a piece out of a book or speech.

**quotient** **quotients**

NOUN In maths, a **quotient** is a whole number you get when you divide one number into another. For example, if you divide eight by two, the quotient is four.

a
b
c
d
e
f
g
h
i
j
k
l
m
n
o
p
**Qq**
r
s
t
u
v
w
x
y
z

# Rr

### rabbit  rabbits

NOUN A **rabbit** is a small furry animal with long ears.

### race  races, racing, raced

NOUN **1** A **race** is a competition to see who is the fastest.

NOUN **2** A **race** is also a large group of people who look alike in some way. For example, different races have different skin colour, or differently shaped eyes.

VERB **3** If you **race** someone, you try to beat them in a race.

### rack  racks

NOUN A **rack** is a frame that is used for holding things or for hanging things on.

### racket  rackets

NOUN **1** A **racket** is a bat with an oval frame and strings across and down it. It is used in tennis and similar games.

NOUN **2** If someone makes a **racket**, they make a loud unpleasant noise.

### radar

NOUN **Radar** is a way of showing the position and speed of ships and aircraft when they cannot be seen. Radio signals give the information on a screen.

### radiator  radiators

NOUN **1** A **radiator** is a hollow metal object that can be filled with liquid in order to heat a room.

NOUN **2** In a car, the **radiator** holds the water that is used to cool the engine.

### radio  radios

NOUN A **radio** is a piece of equipment which receives sounds through the air. You can use a radio to listen to programmes that are broadcast.

### radish  radishes

NOUN A **radish** is a small salad vegetable with a red skin and white flesh. *See Vegetables on page 256.*

### radius  radii

NOUN The **radius** of a circle is the length of a straight line drawn from its centre to any point on its edge.

### raffle  raffles

NOUN A **raffle** is a competition. You buy a numbered ticket and win a prize if your number is chosen.

### raft  rafts

NOUN A **raft** is a floating platform. Rafts are often made of large pieces of wood fixed together.

### rag  rags

NOUN **1** A **rag** is a piece of old cloth that you can use to clean or wipe things.

NOUN **2** Rags are old torn clothes.

### rage

NOUN **Rage** is great anger. *Dad's face showed his rage.*

### ragged

ADJECTIVE Clothes that are **ragged** are old and torn.

### raid  raids

NOUN A **raid** is a sudden attack against an enemy.

### rail  rails

NOUN **1** A **rail** is a horizontal bar that is firmly fixed to posts. Rails are used as fences, or for people to lean on.

NOUN **2** Rails are the heavy metal bars that trains run on.

### railing  railings

NOUN A **railing** is a kind of fence made from metal bars.

**railway**  railways

NOUN A **railway** is a route along which trains travel on metal rails.

**rain**  rains, raining, rained

NOUN **1** Rain is water that falls from the clouds in small drops.

VERB **2** When it is **raining**, rain is falling.

**rainbow**  rainbows

NOUN A **rainbow** is an arch of different colours that sometimes appears in the sky when the sun shines through rain.

**rainforest**  rainforests

NOUN A **rainforest** is a dense forest in a tropical area where there is a lot of rain.

**raise**  raises, raising, raised

VERB **1** If you **raise** something, you move it so that it is higher.

VERB **2** If you **raise** your voice, you speak more loudly.

VERB **3** To **raise** money for a cause means to get people to give money towards it.

**raisin**  raisins

NOUN A **raisin** is a dried grape.

**rake**  rakes

NOUN A **rake** is a garden tool with a row of metal teeth fixed to a long handle.

**ram**  rams, ramming, rammed

VERB **1** If one vehicle **rams** another, it crashes into it.

NOUN **2** A **ram** is an adult male sheep.

**Ramadan**

NOUN **Ramadan** is the ninth month of the Muslim year, when Muslims eat and drink nothing from sunrise to sunset.

**ramp**  ramps

NOUN A **ramp** is a sloping surface between two places at different levels.

**ran**

VERB **Ran** is the past tense of **run**.

**ranch**  ranches

NOUN In the United States, a **ranch** is a large farm for raising cattle, sheep or horses.

**rang**

VERB **Rang** is the past tense of **ring**.

**range**  ranges

NOUN **1** The **range** of something is the area or distance over which it can be used.

NOUN **2** A **range** is a row of hills or mountains.

**rank**  ranks

NOUN A **rank** is a position that a person holds in an organization. The higher the rank, the more important they are.

**rap**  raps, rapping, rapped

VERB **1** If you **rap** something, you hit it with a series of quick blows.

NOUN **2** Rap is a style of poetry spoken to music with a strong beat.

**rapid**

ADJECTIVE Something that is **rapid** is very quick.

**rare**  rarer, rarest

ADJECTIVE Something that is **rare** is not often seen, or does not happen very often.

**rash**  rashes

NOUN A **rash** is a lot of spots that appear on your skin in certain illnesses.

**raspberry**  raspberries

NOUN A **raspberry** is a small red fruit which is soft and juicy, with a lot of small seeds called pips. *See Fruit on page 257.*

**rat**  rats

NOUN A **rat** is a rodent with a long tail.

## rather

**ADVERB 1 Rather** means quite. *I'm **rather** angry about that.*

**ADVERB 2** You can say **rather** if there is something else you want to do. *I don't want to go out. I'd **rather** watch television.*

## rattle  rattles, rattling, rattled

**VERB 1** When something **rattles**, it makes short rapid knocking sounds. *Can you stop that window **rattling**?*

**NOUN 2** A baby's **rattle** is a toy that makes a noise when it is shaken.

## raw

**ADJECTIVE** Food that is **raw** is not cooked.

## ray  rays

**NOUN** A **ray** is a line of light.

## razor  razors

**NOUN** A **razor** is a tool that people use for shaving.

## re-

**PREFIX Re-** is added to words to show that something is done again. For example, to "reread" means to read again. *See Prefixes on page 264.*

## reach  reaches, reaching, reached

**VERB 1** When you **reach** a place, you arrive there.

**VERB 2** If you **reach** somewhere, you stretch out your hand. *He **reached** across the table for the salt.*

## react  reacts, reacting, reacted

**VERB** When you **react** to something, you behave in a particular way because of it. *He **reacted** badly to the news.*

reaction **NOUN**

## read  reads, reading, read

**VERB 1** When you **read**, you look at words and understand what they mean.

**VERB 2** When you **read aloud**, you say the words that are written.

## reading  readings

**NOUN Reading** is the activity of reading books or other written material.

## ready

**ADJECTIVE** If someone or something is **ready**, they are properly prepared for doing something.

## real

**ADJECTIVE 1** Something that is **real** is true. It is not imaginary. *I've seen a **real** princess.*

**ADJECTIVE 2** You also say **real** when you mean the thing itself and not a copy. *I've got a lovely toy pony. But Jenny's got a **real** one.*

## realize  realizes, realizing, realized; also spelt realise

**VERB** If you **realize** something, you work it out or notice it. *I've just **realized** you must be Tara's sister.*

## really

**ADVERB** You can use **really** to make something you are saying stronger. *I **really** don't like that boy.*

## rear

**NOUN** The **rear** of something is the part that is at the back of it.

## rearrange  rearranges, rearranging, rearranged

**VERB** To **rearrange** something means to organize or arrange it in a different way.

## reason  reasons

**NOUN** The **reason** for something is why it happens. *I'm sorry I'm late, but there is a good **reason**.*

## reasonable

**ADJECTIVE 1** People who are **reasonable** behave in a fair and sensible way.

**ADJECTIVE 2** A price that is **reasonable** seems fair and not too high.

reasonably **ADVERB**

**rebel** **rebels, rebelling, rebelled**
VERB To **rebel** means to fight against authority.
**rebellious** ADJECTIVE

**receive** **receives, receiving, received**
VERB When you **receive** something, you get it after it has been given or sent to you.

**recent**
ADJECTIVE Something that is **recent** happened only a short time ago.
**recently** ADVERB

**recipe** **recipes**
NOUN A **recipe** is a list of ingredients and instructions for cooking something.

**recite** **recites, reciting, recited**
VERB When you **recite** something like a poem, you say it aloud from memory.

**reckon** **reckons, reckoning, reckoned**
VERB If you **reckon** that something is true, you think it is true.

**recognize** **recognizes, recognizing, recognized**; also spelt **recognise**
VERB If you **recognize** someone, you realize that you know who they are.

**recommend** **recommends, recommending, recommended**
VERB If you **recommend** something to someone, you tell them it is good.

**record** **records, recording, recorded**
NOUN **1** If you keep a **record** of something, you keep a written account or store information in a computer.
NOUN **2** A **record** is also the best that has been done so far.
VERB **3** If someone **records** information, they write it down, put it onto tape or film, or into a computer.
VERB **4** To **record** sound means to put it on tape or compact disc.

**recorder** **recorders**
NOUN A **recorder** is a small musical instrument which you play by blowing into one end and putting your fingers over the holes.

**recover** **recovers, recovering, recovered**
VERB When you **recover** from something such as an illness, you become well again.

**recreation**
NOUN **Recreation** is all the things that you like doing in your spare time.
**recreational** ADJECTIVE

**rectangle** **rectangles**
NOUN A **rectangle** is a flat shape with four straight sides and four right angles.
**rectangular** ADJECTIVE
See *Colours and flat shapes* on page 271.

**recycle** **recycles, recycling, recycled**
VERB To **recycle** used products means to process them so they can be used again.

**red** **redder, reddest**
ADJECTIVE Something that is **red** is the colour of a ripe tomato.
See *Colours* on page 271.

**redraft** **redrafts, redrafting, redrafted**
VERB If you **redraft** a piece of text, you make another draft.

**reduce** **reduces, reducing, reduced**
VERB To **reduce** something means to make it smaller in size or amount.

# reed

**reed** **reeds**
NOUN A **reed** is a plant with a tall hollow stem. Reeds grow in or near water.

**reef** **reefs**
NOUN A **reef** is a long line of rocks that is just below the surface of the sea.

**reel** **reels**
NOUN A **reel** is a round object that you wrap thread, wire or film around.

**refer** **refers, referring, referred**
VERB If you **refer** to someone or something, you mention them.

**referee** **referees**
NOUN A **referee** is a person whose job is to make sure that the players in a game follow the rules properly.

**reference book** **reference books**
NOUN A **reference book** is a book that gives you information in a way that is easy to find. Dictionaries and encyclopedias are reference books.

**refill** **refills, refilling, refilled**
NOUN **1** A **refill** is a full container that replaces an empty one. *Have you got a refill for this pen?*
VERB **2** If you **refill** something, you fill it again after it has been emptied.

**reflect** **reflects, reflecting, reflected**
VERB **1** When a surface **reflects** rays of something like light or heat, the rays bounce back from the surface.
VERB **2** When a mirror **reflects** a person or thing, it shows what they look like.

**reflection** **reflections**
NOUN A **reflection** is what you see when you look in a mirror or shiny surface.

**refreshing**
ADJECTIVE Something that is **refreshing** makes you feel energetic or cool again after you have been tired or hot.

**refreshments**
PLURAL NOUN **Refreshments** are drinks and snacks.

**refrigerator** **refrigerators**
NOUN A **refrigerator** is a large cooled container in which you store food to keep it fresh. A refrigerator is often called a **fridge** for short.

**refuse** **refuses, refusing, refused**
(*said* rif-**yooz**) VERB **1** If you **refuse** to do something, you say you will not do it.
(*said* **ref**-yoos) NOUN **2** Refuse is rubbish or waste.

**region** **regions**
NOUN A **region** is a large area of land.

**register** **registers, registering, registered**
NOUN **1** A **register** is an official list or record of things.
VERB **2** When something is **registered**, it is recorded on an official list. *The car was registered in my mother's name.*

**regret** **regrets, regretting, regretted**
VERB If you **regret** something, you wish it had not happened.

**regular**
ADJECTIVE **1** Something that is **regular** does not change its pattern, for example a regular heartbeat.
ADJECTIVE **2** A **regular** polygon has all its angles and sides equal.

**rehearsal** **rehearsals**
NOUN A **rehearsal** is a practice of a play, dance or piece of music, to prepare for a public performance.

**reign** **reigns, reigning, reigned**
VERB **1** When a king or queen **reigns**, they rule a country.
NOUN **2** The **reign** of a king or queen is the period during which they reign.

**rein** reins

NOUN A **rein** is one of the leather straps that are used to control a horse.

**reindeer**

NOUN A **reindeer** is a large deer that lives in cold northern countries.

**relate** relates, relating, related

VERB If something **relates** to something else, it is connected or concerned with it.

**related**

ADJECTIVE 1 People who are **related** belong to the same family.

ADJECTIVE 2 If one thing is **related** to another, there is a connection between them. *A graph shows how two sets of numbers are related.*

**relation** relations

NOUN If someone is your **relation**, they belong to the same family as you.

**relative** relatives

NOUN If someone is your **relative**, they belong to the same family as you.

**relax** relaxes, relaxing, relaxed

VERB When you **relax**, you stop worrying and feel more calm.

**release** releases, releasing, released

VERB If someone **releases** a person or animal that has been trapped or held in some way, they set them free.

**reliable**

ADJECTIVE If something or someone is **reliable**, you can depend on them.

**relief**

NOUN **Relief** is the feeling you have if you do not need to worry about something any more.

**relieved**

ADJECTIVE If you are **relieved**, you are glad because you can stop worrying about something.

**religion** religions

NOUN A **religion** is a set of beliefs about a god, or about several gods.
**religious** ADJECTIVE

**reluctant**

ADJECTIVE If you are **reluctant** to do something, you do not want to do it.
**reluctantly** ADVERB

**rely** relies, relying, relied

VERB 1 If you **rely** on someone, you need them and depend on them.

VERB 2 If you can **rely** on someone to do something, you can trust them to do it.

**remain** remains, remaining, remained

VERB 1 If you **remain** in a place, you stay there and do not go away.

PLURAL NOUN 2 The **remains** of something are the parts that are left after most of it has been destroyed. *They found the remains of an ancient pyramid.*

**remainder**

NOUN 1 The **remainder** of something is the part that is left. *He gulped down the remainder of his coffee.*

NOUN 2 In maths, the **remainder** is the amount left over when one number cannot be exactly divided by another. For example, if nine is divided by four, the answer is two remainder one.

**remark** remarks, remarking, remarked

VERB If you **remark** on something, you mention it. *The teacher remarked on his strange haircut.*

**remarkable**

ADJECTIVE Someone or something that is **remarkable** is unusual in some way so that people notice them and feel surprised.

**remember** remembers, remembering, remembered

VERB If you can **remember** something, you can bring it back into your mind. *Can you remember that actor's name?*

a
b
c
d
e
f
g
h
i
j
k
l
m
n
o
p
q
**Rr**
s
t
u
v
w
x
y
z

# remind

**remind** **reminds, reminding, reminded**
VERB **1** If someone or something **reminds** you to do something, they make you remember it. *That **reminds** me – I must get a card for Auntie Mary.*
VERB **2** If someone **reminds** you of someone else, something about them makes you think of the other person.

**remote** **remoter, remotest**
ADJECTIVE **Remote** areas are far away from places where most people live.

**remote control**
NOUN **Remote control** is a system of controlling a machine from a distance, using radio or electronic signals.

**removal** **removals**
NOUN **1** The **removal** of something is the act of taking it away or getting rid of it.
NOUN **2** A **removal company** takes furniture from one building to another when people move house.

**remove** **removes, removing, removed**
VERB If you **remove** something from somewhere, you take it off or away.

**rent** **rents**
NOUN **Rent** is the amount of money you pay regularly for a house or flat.

**repair** **repairs, repairing, repaired**
VERB If you **repair** something that is broken or not working, you mend it.

**repeat** **repeats, repeating, repeated**
VERB If you **repeat** something, you say it or do it again.
**repetition** NOUN

**replace** **replaces, replacing, replaced**
VERB **1** If you **replace** something, you put it back where it was before.
VERB **2** If you **replace** something that is old, lost or broken, you get a new one.

**reply** **replies, replying, replied**
VERB When you **reply**, you answer someone.

**report** **reports, reporting, reported**
VERB **1** If you **report** that something has happened, you tell someone about it. *He **reported** the theft to the police.*
NOUN **2** A **report** is an account of an event or situation.

**reporter** **reporters**
NOUN A **reporter** is someone who works for a newspaper, radio or television. Their job is to find out what is happening in the world so that their report can be printed or broadcast.

**represent** **represents, representing, represented**
VERB **1** If you **represent** someone, you act for them. *The class chose Meena to **represent** them.*
VERB **2** If a sign or symbol **represents** something, it stands for it.

**reptile** **reptiles**
NOUN A **reptile** is a cold-blooded animal with a scaly skin. Female reptiles lay eggs. Snakes and crocodiles are reptiles. See *Reptiles* on page 259.

**request** **requests, requesting, requested**
VERB **1** If you **request** something, you ask for it politely.
NOUN **2** A **request** is a polite demand for something.

**require** **requires, requiring, required**
VERB If you **require** something, you need it.

**rescue** **rescues, rescuing, rescued**
VERB If you **rescue** someone, you save them from danger.

**research** researches, researching, researched
NOUN **1 Research** is studying something and trying to find out facts about it.
VERB **2** If you **research** something, you try to discover facts about it.

**resent** resents, resenting, resented
VERB If you **resent** something, you feel angry about it.

**reserve** reserves, reserving, reserved
VERB If you **reserve** something, like a book at the library, you arrange for it to be kept for you.

**reservoir** reservoirs
NOUN A **reservoir** is a lake that is used for storing drinking water for an area.

**resign** resigns, resigning, resigned
VERB If someone **resigns** from a job, they say they want to leave it.

**resist** resists, resisting, resisted
VERB If you **resist** something, you fight against it and do not give up.

**resource** resources
NOUN The **resources** of a country, organization or person are the materials, money or skills they have.

**respect** respects, respecting, respected
VERB If you **respect** someone, you look up to them and think their opinions are important.

**respectable**
ADJECTIVE Someone who is **respectable** behaves in a way that other people think is right.

**respond** responds, responding, responded
VERB When you **respond** to someone, you react to them by doing or saying something.
**response** NOUN

**responsible**
ADJECTIVE **1** If you are **responsible** for something, it is your job to deal with it, and you are to blame if it goes wrong.

ADJECTIVE **2** A **responsible** person behaves properly and sensibly.

**rest** rests, resting, rested
VERB **1** When you **rest**, you sit or lie down and keep still for a while.
NOUN **2** A **rest** is a period of time when you do not work.
NOUN **3** The **rest** is all the things in a group that are left. *I've done some of the washing-up. I'll do the **rest** tomorrow.*

**restaurant** restaurants
NOUN A **restaurant** is a place where meals are served.

**restless**
ADJECTIVE If you feel **restless**, you find it hard to relax.

**result** results
NOUN **1** A **result** is something that happens because of something else. *The milk boiled over and the **result** was a real mess.*
NOUN **2** A **result** is also the score at the end of a game.

**retire** retires, retiring, retired
VERB When someone **retires**, they stop doing their job, usually because they are getting old.

**retreat** retreats, retreating, retreated
VERB If you **retreat** from something difficult or dangerous, you move backwards away from it. *The army **retreated** from the enemy.*

**return** returns, returning, returned
VERB **1** When you **return** to a place, you go back there after you have been away.
VERB **2** If you **return** something to someone, you give it back to them.
NOUN **3** A **return** is a ticket for the journey to a place and back again.

a
b
c
d
e
f
g
h
i
j
k
l
m
n
o
p
q
**Rr**
s
t
u
v
w
x
y
z

**reveal** reveals, revealing, revealed
VERB If you **reveal** something that has been secret or hidden, you tell people about it or show it to them.

**revenge**
NOUN **Revenge** is something a person does to hurt someone who has hurt them.

**reverse** reverses, reversing, reversed
VERB **1** If a car **reverses**, it goes backwards.
VERB **2** If you **reverse** the order of things, you put them in the opposite order.

**revise** revises, revising, revised
VERB **1** If you **revise** something, you alter it or correct it.
VERB **2** When you **revise**, you read something again so that you can learn it for a test.
**revision** NOUN

**revolver** revolvers
NOUN A **revolver** is a small gun.

**reward** rewards
NOUN A **reward** is something you are given for doing well.

**rhinoceros** rhinoceroses
NOUN A **rhinoceros** is a large African or Asian animal with a thick skin and one or two horns on its nose. Rhinoceroses are often called **rhinos** for short.

**rhyme** rhymes, rhyming, rhymed
VERB If two words **rhyme**, they have a similar sound. For example, "dog" rhymes with "log".

**rhythm** rhythms
NOUN **Rhythm** is a regular pattern of sound or movement. Music and dancing have rhythm.

**rib** ribs
NOUN Your **ribs** are the curved bones that go from your backbone to your chest.

**ribbon** ribbons
NOUN A **ribbon** is a long narrow piece of fine cloth. It is used for tying things together, or as a decoration.

**rice**
NOUN **Rice** is white or pale brown grains which are boiled and eaten.

**rich** richer, richest
ADJECTIVE Someone who is **rich** has a lot of money or valuable things.

**rid**
**get rid of** PHRASE When you **get rid of** something that you do not want, you remove it or throw it away.

**riddle** riddles
NOUN A **riddle** is a kind of puzzle. You ask a question which has a funny answer.

**ride** rides, riding, rode, ridden
NOUN **1** A **ride** is a journey using a bus, car, train, horse or bicycle.
VERB **2** When a person **rides** a horse or a bicycle, they sit on it and control it.
VERB **3** When you **ride** in a vehicle such as a car, you travel in it.

**ridiculous**
ADJECTIVE If you say something is **ridiculous**, you mean it is foolish.

**right**
ADJECTIVE **1** If something is **right**, it is correct.
ADJECTIVE OR ADVERB **2** **Right** means on or towards the right side of something. Most people write with their right hand.

**right angle** right angles
NOUN A **right angle** is an angle or turn of 90 degrees.

**rigid**
ADJECTIVE Something that is **rigid** is very stiff and does not bend or stretch.

**rim** rims

NOUN **1** The **rim** of a container, such as a cup, is the edge round the top.

NOUN **2** The **rim** of a round object, such as a wheel, is the outside edge of it.

**rind** rinds

NOUN The **rind** of a fruit such as an orange or a lemon is its thick outer skin.

**ring** rings, ringing, rang, rung

NOUN **1** A **ring** is an ornament that people wear on a finger.

NOUN **2** Anything in the shape of a circle can be called a **ring**.

VERB **3** If you **ring** someone, you phone them.

VERB **4** When a bell **rings**, it makes a loud clear sound.

**rinse** rinses, rinsing, rinsed

VERB When you **rinse** something, you wash it in clean water with no soap.

**rip** rips, ripping, ripped

VERB If someone **rips** something, they tear it violently.

**ripe** riper, ripest

ADJECTIVE When fruit or grain is **ripe**, it is ready to be eaten or harvested.

**ripple** ripples

NOUN A **ripple** is a little wave on the surface of water.

**rise** rises, rising, rose, risen

VERB **1** If something **rises**, it moves upwards.

VERB **2** When the sun or the moon **rises**, it appears above the horizon.

**risk** risks

NOUN A **risk** is a danger that something bad might happen.

take a risk PHRASE If someone **takes a risk**, they do something knowing that it could be dangerous.

risky ADJECTIVE

**rival** rivals

NOUN Your **rival** is someone who is trying to win the same things as you are.

**river** rivers

NOUN A **river** is a large amount of fresh water flowing towards the sea.

**road** roads

NOUN A **road** is a long piece of hard ground, specially treated so that people and vehicles can travel along it easily.

**roam** roams, roaming, roamed

VERB If you **roam**, you wander around without any particular purpose.

**roar** roars, roaring, roared

VERB If something **roars**, it makes a very loud noise like a lion. *The car* **roared** *off down the road.*

**roast** roasts, roasting, roasted

VERB When someone **roasts** meat or other food, they cook it in an oven or over a fire.

**rob** robs, robbing, robbed

VERB If someone **robs** you, they steal something from you.

robber NOUN    robbery NOUN

**robin** robins

NOUN A **robin** is a small brown bird with a red neck and chest.

**robot** robots

NOUN A **robot** is a machine which is programmed to move and perform tasks automatically.

**rock** rocks, rocking, rocked

NOUN **1** Rock is the very hard material that is in the earth. Cliffs and mountains are made of rock.

NOUN **2** A **rock** is a large piece of rock.

VERB **3** When something **rocks**, it moves slowly backwards and forwards, or from side to side.

NOUN **4** Rock or **rock music** is music with a very strong beat.

NOUN **5** Rock is also a sweet shaped into long hard sticks.

rocky ADJECTIVE

a b c d e f g h i j k l m n o p q **Rr** s t u v w x y z

# rocket

**rocket** **rockets**
NOUN **1** A **rocket** is a space vehicle, usually shaped like a long pointed tube.
NOUN **2** **Rockets** are fireworks that explode when they are high in the air.

**rod** **rods**
NOUN A **rod** is a long thin pole or bar, usually made of wood or metal. *His uncle gave him a new fishing rod.*

**rode**
VERB **Rode** is the past tense of **ride**.

**rodent** **rodents**
NOUN A **rodent** is a small mammal with sharp front teeth for gnawing. Rats, mice, squirrels and hamsters are rodents.

**roll** **rolls, rolling, rolled**
VERB **1** When something **rolls**, or when you roll it, it moves along a surface, turning over and over.
NOUN **2** A **roll** of something like paper is a long piece of it that has been rolled into a tube.
NOUN **3** A **roll** is a small loaf of bread for one person.

**Rollerblade** **Rollerblades**
NOUN; TRADEMARK **Rollerblades** are roller skates which have the wheels set in one straight line on the bottom of the boot.

**roller skate** **roller skates**
NOUN **Roller skates** are shoes with four small wheels underneath.

**roof** **roofs**
NOUN **1** The **roof** of a building or car is the covering on top of it.
NOUN **2** The **roof** of your mouth or of a cave is the highest part.

**room** **rooms**
NOUN **1** A **room** is a section in a building, divided from other rooms by walls.
NOUN **2** If there is plenty of **room**, there is a lot of space.

**root** **roots**
NOUN **1** A **root** is the part of a plant that grows underground.
NOUN **2** The **root** of a hair, tooth or nail is the part that you cannot see because it is covered with skin.

**root word** **root words**
NOUN A **root word** is a word to which prefixes and suffixes can be added to make other words. In the word "clearly", the root word is "clear".

**rope** **ropes**
NOUN **Rope** is thick strong string.

**rose** **roses**
NOUN **1** A **rose** is a flower. Most roses grow on thorny stems.
VERB **2** **Rose** is also the past tense of **rise**.

**rot** **rots, rotting, rotted**
VERB **1** When vegetables and other foods **rot**, they go bad.
VERB **2** When wood **rots**, it goes soft and can easily be pulled to pieces.

**rotate** **rotates, rotating, rotated**
VERB When something **rotates**, it turns with a circular movement.

**rotten**
ADJECTIVE Something that is **rotten** has gone bad or soft so that it cannot be used.

**rough** **rougher, roughest**
ADJECTIVE **1** If something is **rough**, the surface is uneven and not smooth.
ADJECTIVE **2** If someone is being **rough**, they are not being gentle.
ADJECTIVE **3** A **rough** estimate is not meant to be exact.
ADJECTIVE **4** A **rough** draft is an early version of something you are writing.

a b c d e f g h i j k l m n o p q **Rr** s t u v w x y z

## roughly

ADVERB **1** If you say **roughly**, you mean approximately. *There are roughly twice as many boys as girls in this club.*

ADVERB **2** If someone speaks **roughly** to you, they sound angry and aggressive.

## round **rounder, roundest**

ADJECTIVE **1** Something **round** is shaped like a ball or a circle.

PREPOSITION **2** If something is **round** something else, it surrounds it. *There was a wall round the garden.*

PREPOSITION **3** If something moves **round** you, it keeps moving in a circle with you in the centre.

ADVERB **4** If you turn or look **round**, you turn so you are facing a different way.

**round up** or **round down** PHRASE If you **round a number**, you raise it up or lower it down to the nearest 10, 100 or 1000. *If you round 34 to the nearest ten, it would be 30. 675 rounded up to the nearest hundred is 700.*

## roundabout **roundabouts**

NOUN **1** A **roundabout** is a place where several roads meet, with a circle in the centre which vehicles have to go round.

NOUN **2** A **roundabout** is also a large machine at a fair that children can sit on and go round and round.

## rounders

NOUN **Rounders** is a game in which players run between posts after hitting the ball.

## route **routes**

NOUN A **route** is a way from one place to another. *David took his usual route to school.*

## routine **routines**

ADJECTIVE **1 Routine** things happen regularly.

NOUN **2** Your **routine** is the usual way that you do things.

## row **rows, rowing, rowed**
(*rhymes with* **snow**)

NOUN **1** A **row** of people or things is several of them arranged in a line.

VERB **2** When you **row** a boat, you use oars to make it move through the water.

(*rhymes with* **now**) NOUN **3** A **row** is a noisy argument.

## royal

ADJECTIVE **1** Someone who is **royal** belongs to the family of a king or queen.

ADJECTIVE **2** Something that is **royal** is connected with a royal family.

## rub **rubs, rubbing, rubbed**

VERB When you **rub** something, you wipe it hard.

## rubber **rubbers**

NOUN **1 Rubber** is a strong stretchy material that is made from the sap of a tree. It is used to make things like tyres.

NOUN **2** A **rubber** is a small piece of rubber used to get rid of pencil marks.

## rubbish

NOUN **1 Rubbish** is waste material, such as used paper or empty tins.

NOUN **2** If you say something is **rubbish**, you think it is of very poor quality. *This new television programme is rubbish.*

## ruby **rubies**

NOUN A **ruby** is a dark red jewel.

## rudder **rudders**

NOUN A **rudder** is a piece of wood or metal on the back of a boat or plane which is moved to make the boat or plane turn.

# rude

**rude**   **ruder, rudest**

ADJECTIVE If someone is **rude**, they behave badly and are not polite. *It's **rude** to stare at people.*

**rug**   **rugs**

NOUN A **rug** is a piece of thick material like a small carpet.

**rugby**

NOUN **Rugby** is a game played with an oval ball. Two teams try to score points by carrying the ball across a line, or by kicking the ball over a bar.

**ruin**   **ruins, ruining, ruined**

VERB **1** To **ruin** something means to spoil it completely. *Mark and Joe **ruined** my party by fighting.*

NOUN **2** The **ruins** of a building are the parts of it that are left after it has fallen down or been badly damaged.

**rule**   **rules, ruling, ruled**

VERB **1** To **rule** a country means to be in charge of the way the country works.

NOUN **2** **Rules** tell you what you are allowed to do and what you are not allowed to do. They are used in games, and in places such as schools.

**ruler**   **rulers**

NOUN **1** A **ruler** is a person who rules a country.

NOUN **2** A **ruler** is also a long flat piece of wood or plastic with straight edges, used for measuring or drawing straight lines.

**rumour**   **rumours**

NOUN A **rumour** is a story or piece of information which a lot of people are talking about, but which may not be true.

**run**   **runs, running, ran, run**

VERB **1** When you **run**, you move quickly, leaving the ground during each stride.

VERB **2** When liquid **runs**, it flows. *Don't leave the hot water **running**.*

VERB **3** Someone who **runs** something, like a school or country, is in charge of it.

VERB **4** When a vehicle such as a train or bus **runs** somewhere, it travels at set times. *The bus **runs** every 20 minutes.*

VERB **5** If you **run** out of something, you have no more of it left.

**rung**   **rungs**

NOUN **1** A **rung** is a wooden or metal step on a ladder.

VERB **2** **Rung** is the past participle of **ring**.

**running**

NOUN **1** **Running** is the activity of running, especially as a sport.

ADJECTIVE **2** **Running** water is flowing rather than standing still.

**runway**   **runways**

NOUN A **runway** is a long narrow strip of ground at an airport which planes use when they take off or land.

**rush**   **rushes, rushing, rushed**

VERB If you **rush** somewhere, you go there quickly.

**rust**   **rusts, rusting, rusted**

NOUN **1** **Rust** is a reddish-brown substance that forms on iron or steel which has been in contact with water.

VERB **2** When something **rusts**, rust forms on it.

**rusty** ADJECTIVE

**rustle**   **rustles, rustling, rustled**

VERB When something **rustles**, it makes soft sounds as it moves. *Dry leaves **rustled** underfoot.*

**rut**   **ruts**

NOUN A **rut** is a deep groove in the ground made by the wheels of a vehicle.

# Ss

**sack**  **sacks**
NOUN A **sack** is a large strong bag made of cloth or plastic.

**sad**  **sadder, saddest**
ADJECTIVE If you are **sad**, you are unhappy because something has happened that you do not like.

**saddle**  **saddles**
NOUN A **saddle** is a seat for a rider on a horse or bicycle.

**safari**  **safaris**
NOUN A **safari** is a journey to see wild animals.

**safari park**  **safari parks**
NOUN A **safari park** is a large protected area of land where wild animals live and move around freely.

**safe**  **safer, safest; safes**
ADJECTIVE **1** If you are **safe**, you are not in any danger.
ADJECTIVE **2** If something is in a **safe** place, it cannot be lost or stolen.
NOUN **3** A **safe** is a strong metal cupboard with special locks. People keep money or valuable things in a safe.
**safety** NOUN

**said**
VERB **Said** is the past tense of **say**.

**sail**  **sails, sailing, sailed**
NOUN **1** A **sail** is a large piece of material fixed to a boat. The wind blows against the sail and pushes the boat along.

NOUN **2** A **sail** is also one of the flat pieces of wood on the top of a windmill.
VERB **3** To **sail** a boat means to make it move across water using its sails.

**sailor**  **sailors**
NOUN A **sailor** is a person who works on a ship as a member of the crew.

**salad**  **salads**
NOUN A **salad** is a mixture of raw vegetables, for example lettuce, cucumber and tomatoes.

**sale**  **sales**
NOUN **1** The **sale** of anything is the selling of it for money.
NOUN **2** A **sale** is a time when a shop sells things at less than their usual price.

**saliva**
NOUN **Saliva** is the liquid in your mouth that helps you eat food.

**salmon**
NOUN A **salmon** is a large silvery fish. Salmon live in the sea, but they swim up rivers to lay their eggs.

**salt**
NOUN **Salt** is a white powder or crystal with a bitter taste. Salt is found in the earth and in sea water. It is used to flavour or preserve food.

**salute**  **salutes, saluting, saluted**
NOUN **1** A **salute** is a sign of respect used especially in the armed forces.
VERB **2** If you **salute** someone, you give them a salute.

**same**
ADJECTIVE **1** If two things are the **same**, they are exactly like each other in some way. *Look! Your dress is the **same** as mine.*
ADJECTIVE **2** **Same** means one shared thing and not two different ones. *Amy and I are in the **same** class.*

**sample**  **samples**
NOUN A **sample** of something is a small quantity of it that you can try.

a
b
c
d
e
f
g
h
i
j
k
l
m
n
o
p
q
r
**Ss**
t
u
v
w
x
y
z

# sand

**sand**
NOUN **Sand** is tiny grains of rock, shells and other material. Most deserts and beaches are made of sand.

**sandal** **sandals**
NOUN **Sandals** are light shoes for warm weather. The soles are held on by straps which go over your foot.

**sandpit** **sandpits**
NOUN A **sandpit** is a shallow box in the ground with sand in it, where small children can play.

**sandwich** **sandwiches**
NOUN A **sandwich** is two slices of bread with a layer of food in between.

**sang**
VERB **Sang** is the past tense of **sing**.

**sank**
VERB **Sank** is the past tense of **sink**.

**sap**
NOUN **Sap** is the liquid that carries food through plants and trees.

**sardine** **sardines**
NOUN A **sardine** is a small sea fish.

**sari** **saris**
NOUN A **sari** is a piece of clothing worn especially by Asian women.

**sat**
VERB **Sat** is the past tense of **sit**.

**satchel** **satchels**
NOUN A **satchel** is a leather or cloth bag with a long strap.

**satellite** **satellites**
NOUN **1** A **satellite** is a natural object in space that moves around a larger object. The moon is a satellite of the Earth.

NOUN **2** A **satellite** is also an object sent into space to send signals back to Earth.

**satellite dish** **satellite dishes**
NOUN A **satellite dish** is an aerial which receives signals from an artificial satellite.

**satellite television**
NOUN **Satellite television** is where the programmes are sent from an artificial satellite. They can be received using a satellite dish.

**satisfactory**
ADJECTIVE Something that is **satisfactory** is good enough for its purpose.

**satisfy** **satisfies, satisfying, satisfied**
VERB To **satisfy** someone means to give them enough of something to make them pleased or contented.

**Saturday** **Saturdays**
NOUN **Saturday** is the day between Friday and Sunday.

**sauce** **sauces**
NOUN A **sauce** is a thick liquid served with other food to add to the taste.

**saucepan** **saucepans**
NOUN A **saucepan** is a deep metal cooking pot, usually with a long handle. Most saucepans have lids.

**saucer** **saucers**
NOUN A **saucer** is a small plate on which you stand a cup.

**sausage** **sausages**
NOUN A **sausage** is a finely minced meat mixture put into a skin.

**savage**
ADJECTIVE A **savage** animal is wild and fierce.

**save** **saves, saving, saved**
VERB **1** If you **save** someone or something, you help them to escape from harm or danger. *He fell in the river and his father dived in to save him.*

VERB **2** If you **save** money, you gradually collect it by not spending it all.

**savings**

PLURAL NOUN Your **savings** are the money you have saved.

**saw**  saws, sawing, sawed, sawn

VERB **1** Saw is the past tense of **see**.

NOUN **2** A **saw** is a tool for cutting wood and other materials. It has a blade with sharp teeth along one edge.

VERB **3** If you **saw** something, you cut it with a saw.

**sawdust**

NOUN **Sawdust** is the dust and small bits of wood made when wood is sawn.

**say**  says, saying, said

VERB When you **say** something, you speak words.

**scald**  scalds, scalding, scalded

VERB If you **scald** yourself, you burn yourself with very hot liquid or steam.

**scale**  scales

NOUN **1** The **scale** of a map is how its size relates to the place in the real world.

NOUN **2** The **scales** of a fish or reptile are the small pieces of hard skin covering its body.

**scales**

PLURAL NOUN **Scales** are a piece of equipment you use for weighing things.

**scamper**  scampers, scampering, scampered

VERB When people or small animals **scamper**, they move quickly and lightly.

**scan**  scans, scanning, scanned

VERB **1** If you **scan** a piece of writing, you look through it quickly.

VERB **2** If a machine **scans** something, it examines it using a beam of light, X-rays or sound waves.

**scar**  scars

NOUN A **scar** is a mark that is left on the skin after a wound has healed.

**scarce**  scarcer, scarcest

ADJECTIVE Something that is **scarce** is not often found.

**scare**  scares, scaring, scared

VERB Someone or something that **scares** you makes you feel frightened.

**scarecrow**  scarecrows

NOUN A **scarecrow** is an object in the shape of a person, put in a field of crops to frighten birds away.

**scared**

ADJECTIVE If you are **scared**, you are frightened.

**scarf**  scarves

NOUN A **scarf** is a piece of cloth that you wear round your neck to keep you warm.

**scarlet**

ADJECTIVE Something **scarlet** is a bright red colour.

**scatter**  scatters, scattering, scattered

VERB **1** If you **scatter** things, you throw or drop a lot of them all over an area.

VERB **2** If people **scatter**, they suddenly move away in different directions.

**scene**  scenes

NOUN **1** The **scene** of an event is the place where it happened. *The police went to the scene of the crime.*

NOUN **2** A **scene** is part of a play or film in which things happen in one place.

**scenery**

NOUN **1** **Scenery** is what you can see when you are out in the country.

NOUN **2** **Scenery** is also all the cloths and boards that are used as a background for the stage in a theatre.

# scent

**scent** scents
NOUN A **scent** is a pleasant smell.

**scheme** schemes, scheming, schemed
NOUN **1** A **scheme** is a plan for doing something.
VERB **2** When people **scheme**, they make secret plans.

**school** schools
NOUN **1** A **school** is a place for teaching and learning.
NOUN **2** You can refer to a large group of dolphins or fish as a **school**.
See *Collective nouns* on page 262.

**science**
NOUN **Science** is the study of plants and animals, materials, and things like electricity, forces, light and sound.

**science fiction**
NOUN **Science fiction** is stories about events happening in the future or in other parts of the universe.

**scientist** scientists
NOUN A **scientist** is a person who finds out why things happen by doing tests and by careful study.

**scissors**
PLURAL NOUN **Scissors** are a cutting tool with two sharp blades.

**scoop** scoops, scooping, scooped
VERB **1** If you **scoop** something up, you pick it up using a spoon or the palm of your hand.
NOUN **2** A **scoop** is an object like a large spoon which is used for picking up food such as ice cream.

**score** scores, scoring, scored
VERB **1** If someone **scores**, they get a goal or other point in a game.
NOUN **2** The **score** in a game is the total number of points made by the two teams or players.

**scowl** scowls, scowling, scowled
VERB If you **scowl**, you look very cross.

**scramble** scrambles, scrambling, scrambled
VERB If you **scramble** over rough or difficult ground, you move over it quickly, using your hands to help you.

**scrap** scraps
NOUN A **scrap** of something is a small piece of it. *I need a scrap of paper.*

**scrapbook** scrapbooks
NOUN A **scrapbook** is a book in which you stick things such as pictures or newspaper articles.

**scrape** scrapes, scraping, scraped
VERB If you **scrape** something, you take off its surface by pulling a rough or sharp object over it.

**scratch** scratches, scratching, scratched
VERB **1** If you **scratch** your skin, you rub your fingernails against it.
VERB **2** If you **scratch** something, you damage it by making small cuts on it. *I fell into the hedge and scratched my bike.*
NOUN **3** A **scratch** is a small cut.

**scream** screams, screaming, screamed
VERB If you **scream**, you shout or cry in a loud high-pitched voice.

**screech** screeches, screeching, screeched
VERB To **screech** means to make an unpleasant high-pitched noise. *The car wheels screeched.*

**screen** screens
NOUN A **screen** is a flat surface on which pictures or words are shown, for example a television or computer screen.

**screw**   **screws, screwing, screwed**

NOUN **1** A **screw** is a small sharp piece of metal used for fixing things together.

VERB **2** If you **screw** things together, you fix them together using screws.

VERB **3** If you **screw** something onto something else, you fix it there by twisting it round and round. *He screwed the top back onto the bottle of water.*

**screwdriver**   **screwdrivers**

NOUN A **screwdriver** is a tool used for turning screws.

**scribble**   **scribbles, scribbling, scribbled**

VERB If you **scribble**, you write quickly and roughly.

**script**   **scripts**

NOUN The **script** of a play or film is the written version of it.

**scrub**   **scrubs, scrubbing, scrubbed**

VERB If you **scrub** something, you rub it hard with a stiff brush and water.

**sculptor**   **sculptors**

NOUN A **sculptor** is someone who makes sculptures.

**sculpture**   **sculptures**

NOUN **1** A **sculpture** is a statue or model made by shaping stone, clay or other materials.

NOUN **2** Sculpture is the art of making sculptures.

**sea**   **seas**

NOUN The **sea** is the salty water that covers about three-quarters of the earth.

**seagull**   **seagulls**

NOUN **Seagulls** are common white, grey and black birds that live near the sea.

**seahorse**   **seahorses**

NOUN A **seahorse** is a small fish which swims upright, with a head that looks like a horse's head.

**seal**   **seals, sealing, sealed**

NOUN **1** A **seal** is a large mammal with flippers that lives partly on land and partly in the sea.

VERB **2** If you **seal** an envelope, you stick down the flap.

**seam**   **seams**

NOUN A **seam** is the line where two pieces of material are sewn together.

**search**   **searches, searching, searched**

VERB If you **search** for something, you try to find it by looking carefully.

**seaside**

NOUN The **seaside** is a place by the sea, especially one where people go for their holidays.

**season**   **seasons**

NOUN A **season** is one of the four parts of a year: spring, summer, autumn and winter.

**seat**   **seats**

NOUN A **seat** is a place where you can sit, for example a chair or a stool.

**seat belt**   **seat belts**

NOUN A **seat belt** is a strap that you fasten across your body for safety when travelling in a car, coach or aircraft.

**seaweed**

NOUN **Seaweed** is a plant that grows in the sea.

# second

**second  seconds**

ADJECTIVE **1** The **second** item in a series is the one counted as number two.

NOUN **2** A **second** is a short period of time. There are 60 seconds in a minute.

**second person**

NOUN In grammar, the **second person** is the person who is addressed in speech or writing. It is expressed as "you".

**secret  secrets**

NOUN A **secret** is something that only a few people know and that they are not to tell other people.

**section  sections**

NOUN A **section** of something is one of the separate parts it is divided into.

**secure**

ADJECTIVE **1** If you feel **secure**, you feel safe and confident.

ADJECTIVE **2** If something is **secure**, it is fixed firmly in position.

**security** NOUN

**see  sees, seeing, saw, seen**

VERB **1** If you **see** something, you are looking at it or you notice it.

VERB **2** To **see** something also means to understand it. *I see what you mean.*

VERB **3** If you **see** someone, you visit them or meet them. *I went to see the doctor.*

**seed  seeds**

NOUN The **seeds** of a plant are the small hard parts from which new plants grow.

**seek  seeks, seeking, sought**

VERB If you **seek** someone or something, you try to find them.

**seem  seems, seeming, seemed**

VERB **1** If you say that someone **seems**, for example, to be happy or sad, you mean that is the way they look. *Tim seems to be a bit upset today.*

VERB **2** If something **seems** a certain way, that is the way it feels to you. *I only waited for ten minutes but it seemed like hours.*

**seen**

VERB **Seen** is the past participle of **see**.

**seesaw  seesaws**

NOUN A **seesaw** is a long plank. A child sits on each end and they move up and down in turn.

**segment  segments**

NOUN A **segment** of something is a small part of it.

**seize  seizes, seizing, seized**

VERB If you **seize** something, you grab it firmly.

**select  selects, selecting, selected**

VERB When you **select** someone or something, you choose them.

**selfish**

ADJECTIVE People who are **selfish** only think about themselves. They do not care about other people.

**sell  sells, selling, sold**

VERB When someone **sells** something, they give it in exchange for money.

**Sellotape**

NOUN; TRADEMARK **Sellotape** is a transparent sticky tape.

**semi-**

PREFIX Putting **semi-** in front of a word makes it mean half or partly. For example, a "semicircle" is half of a circle.

See *Prefixes* on page 264.

**semicircle  semicircles**

NOUN A **semicircle** is half of a circle.

See *Colours and flat shapes* on page 271.

**semicolon** **semicolons**

NOUN A **semicolon** is the punctuation mark (;) which is used in writing to separate different parts of a sentence or list, or to show a pause.

See *Punctuation* on page 264.

**semifinal** **semifinals**

NOUN The **semifinals** are the two matches in a competition played to decide who plays in the final.

**send** **sends, sending, sent**

VERB **1** When you **send** something to someone, you arrange for it to be delivered to them.

VERB **2** If someone **sends** someone somewhere, they tell them to go there. *She was **sent** home because she was ill.*

VERB **3** If someone **sends** for you, you get a message to go and see them.

**senior**

ADJECTIVE People who are **senior** are older or more important.

**sensation** **sensations**

NOUN A **sensation** is a physical feeling.

**sense** **senses**

NOUN **1** Your **senses** are your power to see, hear, smell, touch and taste.

NOUN **2** Sense is knowing the right thing to do. *You should have had more sense.*

NOUN **3** If something makes **sense**, you can understand it.

**sensible**

ADJECTIVE People who are **sensible** know what is the right thing to do.

**sensibly** ADVERB

**sensitive**

ADJECTIVE **1** If someone or something is **sensitive**, they are easily hurt. *He is very sensitive about his big ears.*

ADJECTIVE **2** If you are **sensitive** to other people's feelings, you understand them.

**sent**

VERB **Sent** is the past tense of **send**.

**sentence** **sentences**

NOUN A **sentence** is a group of words that mean something.

**separate** **separates, separating, separated**

ADJECTIVE **1** If two things are **separate**, they are not connected.

VERB **2** To **separate** people or things means to part them. *Separate the yolk from the white.*

**September**

NOUN **September** is the ninth month of the year. It has 30 days.

**sequel** **sequels**

NOUN A **sequel** to a book or film is another book or film which continues the story.

**sequence** **sequences**

NOUN A **sequence** of events is a number of them coming one after the other.

**series**

NOUN **1** A **series** is a number of things of the same kind that follow each other.

NOUN **2** A radio or television **series** is a set of programmes about the same thing.

**serious**

ADJECTIVE **1** People who are **serious** are often quiet and do not laugh very much.

ADJECTIVE **2** Things that are **serious** are important and need careful thought.

ADJECTIVE **3** A **serious** problem or situation is very bad and worrying.

**servant** **servants**

NOUN A **servant** is someone paid to work in another person's house.

# serve

**serve** serves, serving, served
VERB **1** If you **serve** food or drink to people, you give it to them.
VERB **2** To **serve** customers in a shop means to help them to buy what they want.

**service** services
NOUN A **service** is something useful that a person or company does for people.

**serviette** serviettes
NOUN A **serviette** is a small piece of cloth or paper that you use to wipe your hands and mouth when you are eating.

**set** sets, setting, set
NOUN **1** A **set** is a number of things of the same kind that belong together, for example a set of golf clubs or a set of tools.
VERB **2** When something such as jelly or concrete **sets**, it becomes firm or hard.
VERB **3** When the sun **sets**, it goes down behind the horizon.
VERB **4** When you **set** a clock or control, you adjust it to a particular position.

**settee** settees
NOUN A **settee** is a long, comfortable seat for two or more people.

**setting** settings
NOUN The **setting** of a story or play is where it takes place. *That old castle would make a great **setting** for a creepy story.*

**settle** settles, settling, settled
VERB **1** If you **settle**, you sit or make yourself comfortable.
VERB **2** If something such as dust or snow **settles**, it sinks slowly and becomes still.
VERB **3** If you **settle** something, you decide it.

**several**
ADJECTIVE **Several** people or things means a number of them. *He was gone for **several** hours.*

**severe**
ADJECTIVE **Severe** is used to describe something extremely bad or unpleasant. *She woke with **severe** toothache.*

**sew** sews, sewing, sewed
VERB When someone **sews**, they join pieces of cloth together by using a needle and thread.

**sewer** sewers
NOUN A **sewer** is a large underground pipe that carries rainwater and waste away from houses and other buildings.

**sex** sexes
NOUN The two **sexes** are the two groups that people and other living things are divided into. One sex is male and the other is female. Only female animals can have babies.

**shabby** shabbier, shabbiest
ADJECTIVE Something that is **shabby** looks old and nearly worn out.

**shade** shades, shading, shaded
NOUN **1** **Shade** is the darkness in a place where the sun cannot reach. *She sat in the **shade** of an apple tree.*
NOUN **2** A **shade** is something that covers a light to stop it shining in your eyes.
VERB **3** If you **shade** something, you stop the sun from shining on it.
NOUN **4** **Shade** is how dark or light a colour is. *I love this **shade** of blue.*

**shadow** shadows
NOUN A **shadow** is a dark shape. It is formed when something opaque blocks the light coming from a lamp, a torch or the sun.

**shake**  **shakes, shaking, shook, shaken**
VERB **1** If you **shake** something, or it shakes, it moves quickly from side to side or up and down.
VERB **2** If your voice **shakes**, it trembles because you are nervous or angry.

**shaky**  **shakier, shakiest**
ADJECTIVE If someone or something is **shaky**, they are weak and unsteady.
**shakily** ADVERB

**shallow**  **shallower, shallowest**
ADJECTIVE Something that is **shallow**, such as a hole, a container or water, measures only a short distance from top to bottom.

**shame**
NOUN **1** **Shame** is an unhappy feeling that people have when they have done something wrong or foolish.
NOUN **2** If you say something is a **shame**, you mean you are sorry about it. *It's a shame you can't come round.*

**shampoo**  **shampoos**
NOUN **Shampoo** is a soapy liquid that you use for washing your hair.

**shape**  **shapes**
NOUN **1** The **shape** of something is the form of its outline, for example whether it is round or square.
NOUN **2** A **shape** is something that has its outside edges joining in a particular way. Shapes can be flat (two-dimensional), like a circle or a triangle, or solid (three-dimensional), like a cube or sphere.
See *Colours and flat shapes* and *Solid shapes* on page 271.

**share**  **shares, sharing, shared**
VERB **1** If you **share** something with another person, you both use it. *She shared a bedroom with her sister.*
VERB **2** If you **share** something among a group of people, you divide it so that everyone gets some.
NOUN **3** A **share** of something is a portion of it.

**shark**  **sharks**
NOUN **Sharks** are large powerful fish with sharp teeth.

**sharp**  **sharper, sharpest**
ADJECTIVE **1** A **sharp** object has a fine edge or point that is good for cutting or piercing things.
ADJECTIVE **2** A **sharp** person is quick to notice or understand things.
ADJECTIVE **3** A **sharp** pain is sudden and hurts a lot.

**sharpen**  **sharpens, sharpening, sharpened**
VERB If you **sharpen** something, you make its edge or point sharper.

**shatter**  **shatters, shattering, shattered**
VERB If something **shatters**, it breaks into a lot of small pieces.

**shave**  **shaves, shaving, shaved**
VERB When a man **shaves**, he removes hair from his face with a razor.

**shawl**  **shawls**
NOUN A **shawl** is a large piece of woollen cloth. Shawls are worn by women over their shoulders or head. They are also used to wrap babies in.

**shear**  **shears, shearing, sheared**
VERB To **shear** a sheep means to cut the wool off it.

**shears**
PLURAL NOUN **Shears** are a tool like a large pair of scissors, used especially for cutting hedges.

**shed**  **sheds, shedding, shed**
NOUN **1** A **shed** is a small building used for storing things.
VERB **2** When a tree **sheds** its leaves, they fall off.

a
b
c
d
e
f
g
h
i
j
k
l
m
n
o
p
q
r
**Ss**
t
u
v
w
x
y
z

# sheep

**sheep**

NOUN A **sheep** is a farm animal with a thick woolly coat. Sheep are kept for meat or wool.

**sheet** sheets

NOUN **1** A **sheet** is a large piece of thin cloth which is put on a bed.

NOUN **2** A **sheet** of something, such as paper or glass, is a thin flat piece.

**shelf** shelves

NOUN A **shelf** is something flat which is fixed to a wall or inside a cupboard. It is for putting things on.

**shell** shells

NOUN **1** The **shell** of an egg or nut is the hard covering round it.

NOUN **2** The **shell** of an animal such as a tortoise is the hard covering on its back.

**shelter** shelters, sheltering, sheltered

NOUN **1** A **shelter** is a small building or covered place where people or animals can be safe from bad weather or danger.

VERB **2** If you **shelter** in a place, you stay there and are safe.

**shepherd** shepherds

NOUN A **shepherd** is a person who looks after sheep.

**sheriff** sheriffs

NOUN **1** In America, a **sheriff** is a person who keeps the law in a county.

NOUN **2** In Scotland, a **sheriff** is the senior judge of a county or district.

NOUN **3** In Australia, a **sheriff** is an officer of the Supreme Court.

**shield** shields, shielding, shielded

NOUN **1** A **shield** is a large piece of strong material like metal or plastic which soldiers or policemen carry to protect themselves.

VERB **2** To **shield** someone means to protect them from something.

**shift** shifts, shifting, shifted

VERB **1** If you **shift** something, you move it.

VERB **2** If something **shifts**, it moves.

NOUN **3** A **shift** is a set period during which people work in a factory or hospital. *My dad works the night **shift**.*

**shimmer** shimmers, shimmering, shimmered

VERB If something **shimmers**, it shines with a faint flickering light, for example as the moon does on water.

**shin** shins

NOUN Your **shin** is the front part of your leg, between your knee and your ankle.

**shine** shines, shining, shone

VERB **1** When something **shines**, it gives out a bright light.

VERB **2** If you make an object **shine**, you make it bright by polishing it.

**shiny** ADJECTIVE

**ship** ships

NOUN A **ship** is a large boat which carries passengers or cargo.

**shirt** shirts

NOUN A **shirt** is a light piece of clothing for the top part of your body, with a collar, sleeves, and buttons down the front.

**shiver** shivers, shivering, shivered

VERB When you **shiver**, your body shakes slightly, usually because you are cold or frightened.

**shoal** shoals

NOUN A **shoal** of fish is a large group of them swimming together.

See *Collective nouns* on page 262.

**shock**   **shocks, shocking, shocked**
NOUN **1** If you have a **shock**, something happens suddenly which upsets you.
VERB **2** If you **shock** someone, you give them an unpleasant surprise.
**shocking** ADJECTIVE

**shoe**   **shoes, shoeing, shod**
NOUN **1** **Shoes** are strong coverings for your feet.
VERB **2** To **shoe** a horse means to fix horseshoes onto its hooves.

**shoelace**   **shoelaces**
NOUN A **shoelace** is a long piece of material like string that is used to fasten a shoe.

**shone**
VERB **Shone** is the past tense of **shine**.

**shook**
VERB **Shook** is the past tense of **shake**.

**shoot**   **shoots, shooting, shot**
NOUN **1** A **shoot** is a new part growing from a plant or tree.
VERB **2** To **shoot** means to fire a bullet from a gun, or an arrow from a bow.
VERB **3** If someone **shoots** in a game such as football, they try to score a goal.
VERB **4** When a film is **shot**, it is filmed.

**shop**   **shops, shopping, shopped**
NOUN **1** A **shop** is a place where things are sold.
VERB **2** When you **shop**, you go to the shops to buy things.
**shopping** NOUN

**shopkeeper**   **shopkeepers**
NOUN A **shopkeeper** is a person who owns or looks after a small shop.

**shore**   **shores**
NOUN The **shore** of a sea or lake is the land along the edge of it.

**short**   **shorter, shortest**
ADJECTIVE **1** Someone who is **short** is not as tall as most other people.
ADJECTIVE **2** Something that is **short** is not very long.
PHRASE **3** If one word is **short for** another, it is a quick way of saying it. *Phone is **short for** telephone.*

**shorts**
PLURAL NOUN **Shorts** are trousers with short legs.

**shot**   **shots**
VERB **1** **Shot** is the past tense of **shoot**.
NOUN **2** A **shot** is when a gun is fired.
NOUN **3** In football and tennis, a **shot** is the act of kicking or hitting the ball.

**should**
VERB **1** You use **should** to say that something ought to happen. *You **should** write a thank-you letter.*
VERB **2** You also use **should** to say that you expect something to happen. *We **should** have heard by now.*

**shoulder**   **shoulders**
NOUN Your **shoulders** are the parts of your body between your neck and the tops of your arms.

**shout**   **shouts, shouting, shouted**
VERB If you **shout** something, you say it very loudly.

**shove**   **shoves, shoving, shoved**
VERB If you **shove** someone or something, you push them roughly.

**shovel**   **shovels, shovelling, shovelled**
NOUN **1** A **shovel** is a tool like a spade with a rounded blade.
VERB **2** If you **shovel** earth or snow, you move it with a shovel.

# show

**show** shows, showing, showed, shown
VERB **1** If you **show** someone something, you let them see it. *Show me your passport.*
VERB **2** If you **show** someone how to do something, you do it yourself so that they can watch you.
VERB **3** If something **shows**, people can see it. *Do you think that mark will show?*
VERB **4** If you **show** your feelings, you let people see them.
NOUN **5** A **show** is something that you watch at the theatre or on television.

**shower** showers
NOUN **1** A **shower** is a piece of equipment which sprays you with water so that you can wash yourself.

NOUN **2** A **shower** is also a short period of rain or snow.

**shrank**
VERB **Shrank** is the past tense of **shrink**.

**shred** shreds, shredding, shredded
NOUN **1** A **shred** of paper or material is a small narrow piece of it. *He tore the paper into shreds.*
VERB **2** If you **shred** something, you cut or tear it into small pieces.

**shriek** shrieks, shrieking, shrieked
VERB If you **shriek**, you give a sudden sharp scream.

**shrill** shriller, shrillest
ADJECTIVE A **shrill** sound is loud and high-pitched, like a whistle.

**shrimp** shrimps
NOUN A **shrimp** is a small edible shellfish with a long tail and many legs.

**shrink** shrinks, shrinking, shrank, shrunk
VERB If something **shrinks**, it becomes smaller.

**shrivel** shrivels, shrivelling, shrivelled
VERB When something **shrivels**, it becomes dry and curled up.

**shrug** shrugs, shrugging, shrugged
VERB If you **shrug** your shoulders, you raise them slightly to show that you are not interested in something.

**shrunk**
VERB **Shrunk** is the past participle of **shrink**.

**shudder** shudders, shuddering, shuddered
VERB If you **shudder**, you tremble with fear or horror.

**shuffle** shuffles, shuffling, shuffled
VERB **1** If you **shuffle**, you walk without lifting your feet properly off the ground.
VERB **2** If you **shuffle** a pack of cards, you mix them up before you begin a game.

**shut** shuts, shutting, shut
VERB **1** If you **shut** something, such as a door, you move it so that it fills a gap.
VERB **2** When a shop **shuts** you can no longer go into it.
ADJECTIVE **3** If something is **shut**, it is closed.

**shy** shier, shiest
ADJECTIVE A **shy** person is nervous with people they do not know well.

**sick** sicker, sickest
ADJECTIVE If you are **sick**, you are ill.

**side** sides
NOUN **1** The **side** of something is to the left or right of it. *He parted his hair on the left side.*
NOUN **2** The **side** of something can be the edge of it. *A triangle has three sides.*
NOUN **3** The **sides** of a river are its banks.
NOUN **4** The **sides** of a piece of paper are its front and back.
NOUN **5** The two **sides** in a game are the teams playing against each other.
ADJECTIVE **6** A **side** road is a small road leading off a larger one.

**sideways**
ADVERB **Sideways** means moving or facing towards one side. *She had to squeeze sideways through the gap.*

**sigh**   **sighs, sighing, sighed**

VERB When you **sigh**, you breathe out heavily. People usually sigh when they are tired, sad or bored.

**sight**

NOUN **Sight** is being able to see.

**sign**   **signs, signing, signed**

VERB **1** If you **sign** something, you write your name on it.

NOUN **2** A **sign** is a mark that means something, for example a plus sign (+).

NOUN **3 Signs** can be words, pictures or symbols that tell you something.

NOUN **4** You can make a **sign** with your body that means something to other people. For example, if you shake your head it is a sign that you mean "No".

**signal**   **signals, signalling, signalled**

NOUN **1** A **signal** is a message that is given by signs. For example, a flashing light is a signal that a driver is turning left or right.

VERB **2** If you **signal** to someone, you do something to give them a message.

**signature**   **signatures**

NOUN Your **signature** is the way you write your own name.

**sign language**

NOUN **Sign language** is a way of communicating using your hands. It is often used by deaf people.

**Sikh**   **Sikhs**

NOUN A **Sikh** is a person who believes in Sikhism, an Indian religion which teaches that there is only one God.

**silence**

NOUN **Silence** is when there is no noise.

**silent**

ADJECTIVE **1** If someone or something is **silent**, they are not saying anything or making any noise.

ADJECTIVE **2** A **silent** letter is one that is written but not pronounced, for example, the "g" in the word "gnat". See *Silent letters* on page 261.

**silhouette**   **silhouettes**

NOUN A **silhouette** is the outline of a dark shape against a light background.

**silk**   **silks**

NOUN **Silk** is a fine soft cloth. It is made from threads produced by a kind of caterpillar called a silkworm.

**silky** ADJECTIVE

**silly**   **sillier, silliest**

ADJECTIVE If someone says you are **silly**, they mean you are behaving in a foolish or childish way.

**silver**

NOUN **Silver** is a greyish-white metal used for making jewellery.

**similar**

ADJECTIVE If things are **similar**, they are rather alike.

**simile**   **similes**

NOUN A **simile** is an expression in which a person or thing is described as being similar to someone or something else. "She went as red as a beetroot" is a simile.

**simple**   **simpler, simplest**

ADJECTIVE Something that is **simple** is easy to do or understand.

**simply** ADVERB

**simplify**   **simplifies, simplifying, simplified**

VERB To **simplify** something means to make it easier to do or understand.

a
b
c
d
e
f
g
h
i
j
k
l
m
n
o
p
q
r
Ss
t
u
v
w
x
y
z

**since**

PREPOSITION **1 Since** means from a particular time until now. *I've been waiting since half past three.*
CONJUNCTION **2 Since** also means because. *I had a drink, since I was feeling thirsty.*

**sincere**

ADJECTIVE If you are **sincere**, you say things that you really mean.
**sincerely** ADVERB

**sing** sings, singing, sang, sung

VERB **1** If you **sing** a song, you make music with your voice.
VERB **2** When birds **sing**, they make pleasant sounds.

**single**

ADJECTIVE **1 Single** means one of something. *We can't park here. It's a single yellow line.*
ADJECTIVE **2** People who are **single** are not married.
ADJECTIVE **3** A **single** bed or bedroom is for one person.
ADJECTIVE **4** A **single** ticket only allows you to travel one way.

**singular**

NOUN **Singular** means one. *The singular of "girls" is "girl". The singular of "children" is "child".* See **plural**.

**sink** sinks, sinking, sank, sunk

NOUN **1** A **sink** is a large basin with water taps and a drain.
VERB **2** If something **sinks**, it moves slowly down until it disappears, especially below the surface of water.
VERB **3** To **sink** something sharp into an object means to make it go deeply into it. *The tiger sank its teeth into his leg.*

**sip** sips, sipping, sipped

VERB If you **sip** a drink, you drink it a little at a time.

**sir**

NOUN **Sir** is a polite way of addressing a man. *Please sir, can I leave early?*

**siren** sirens

NOUN A **siren** is something that makes a loud wailing noise as a warning. Fire engines, police cars and ambulances have sirens.

**sister** sisters

NOUN Your **sister** is a girl or woman who has the same parents as you.

**sit** sits, sitting, sat

VERB **1** When you **sit**, you put your bottom on something such as a chair or the floor.
VERB **2** When a bird **sits** on its eggs, it covers them with its body to hatch them.

**site** sites

NOUN A **site** is a piece of ground that is used for a particular purpose. *Let's stop at the next camp site.*

**situation** situations

NOUN **1** A **situation** is the place where something is. *Our hotel was in a lovely situation.*
NOUN **2** A **situation** is the things that are happening to you. *You have put me in a difficult situation.*

**size** sizes

NOUN The **size** of something is how big or small it is.

**sizzle** sizzles, sizzling, sizzled

VERB If something **sizzles**, it makes a hissing sound. *The meat sizzled in the frying pan.*

**skate** skates

NOUN **1 Skates** are ice skates or roller skates.
NOUN **2** A **skate** is an edible flat sea fish.

**skateboard** skateboards

NOUN A **skateboard** is a narrow board on wheels which you stand on and ride for fun.

**skeleton** **skeletons**

NOUN Your **skeleton** is all the bones in your body joined together. It supports your body and protects your organs.

**sketch** **sketches**

NOUN A **sketch** is a quick drawing.

**ski** **skis**

NOUN **Skis** are long pieces of wood, metal or plastic that you fasten to special boots so that you can move easily on snow.

**skid** **skids, skidding, skidded**

VERB If a vehicle **skids**, it slides out of control, for example because the road is wet or icy.

**skill** **skills**

NOUN **Skill** is the ability to do something well.

**skilful** ADJECTIVE

**skim** **skims, skimming, skimmed**

VERB 1 If you **skim** something from the surface of a liquid, you remove it.

VERB 2 If you **skim** a piece of writing, you read it to get a general idea of what it is about.

**skin** **skins**

NOUN 1 Your **skin** is the natural covering of your body.

NOUN 2 The **skin** of a fruit or vegetable is its outer covering.

**skinny** **skinnier, skinniest**

ADJECTIVE Someone **skinny** is very thin.

**skip** **skips, skipping, skipped**

VERB 1 When you **skip**, you move along almost as though you were dancing, with little jumps.

VERB 2 If you **skip** with a rope, you swing the rope over your head and under your feet while jumping.

VERB 3 If you **skip** something, you miss it out. *I'm going to skip lunch.*

NOUN 4 A **skip** is a large metal container for holding rubbish and rubble.

**skirt** **skirts**

NOUN A **skirt** is a piece of clothing worn by women and girls. It hangs from the waist.

**skull** **skulls**

NOUN Your **skull** is the bony part of your head. It protects your brain, which is inside it.

**sky** **skies**

NOUN The **sky** is the space around the earth which you can see when you stand outside and look upwards.

**skyscraper** **skyscrapers**

NOUN A **skyscraper** is a very tall building.

**slab** **slabs**

NOUN A **slab** is a thick flat piece of something such as stone or concrete.

**slack** **slacker, slackest**

ADJECTIVE Something that is **slack** is loose, and not firmly stretched.

**slam** **slams, slamming, slammed**

VERB If you **slam** a door, you shut it hard so that it makes a loud noise.

**slang**

NOUN **Slang** is words that you use in everyday talk but not when you are writing or being polite.

**slant** **slants, slanting, slanted**

VERB If something **slants**, it is not straight but lies at an angle.

# slap

**slap** slaps, slapping, slapped
VERB If you **slap** someone, you hit them with the palm of your hand.

**slate** slates
NOUN **Slate** is a dark grey rock that can be split into thin layers. It is often used for roofs.

**sledge** sledges
NOUN A **sledge** is a vehicle on runners used for travelling over snow.

**sleek** sleeker, sleekest
ADJECTIVE Hair or fur that is **sleek** is smooth and shiny.

**sleep** sleeps, sleeping, slept
VERB When you **sleep**, you close your eyes and your whole body rests.
**sleepy** ADJECTIVE

**sleet**
NOUN **Sleet** is a mixture of snow and rain.

**sleeve** sleeves
NOUN The **sleeves** of a coat or jumper are the parts that cover your arms.

**sleigh** sleighs
NOUN A **sleigh** is a sledge pulled by animals.

**slept**
VERB **Slept** is the past tense of **sleep**.

**slice** slices, slicing, sliced
NOUN **1** A **slice** is a thin piece of food that has been cut from a larger piece.
VERB **2** If you **slice** food, you cut it into thin pieces.

**slide** slides, sliding, slid
VERB **1** When something **slides**, it moves smoothly over a surface.
NOUN **2** A **slide** is a piece of playground equipment for sliding down.

**slight** slighter, slightest
ADJECTIVE Something that is **slight** is small. *She has a slight cut.*
**slightly** ADVERB

**slim** slimmer, slimmest
ADJECTIVE Someone who is **slim** has a body that is thin but not too thin.

**slime**
NOUN **Slime** is a thick slippery substance which covers a surface and which looks unpleasant. *The pond was covered in green slime.*
**slimy** ADJECTIVE

**sling** slings, slinging, slung
NOUN **1** A **sling** is a piece of cloth which you hang from your neck to support a broken or injured arm.
VERB **2** If you **sling** something somewhere, you throw it carelessly.

**slip** slips, slipping, slipped
VERB **1** If you **slip**, you accidentally slide and lose your balance.
VERB **2** If you **slip** somewhere, you go there quickly and quietly. *She slipped out of the house.*
NOUN **3** A **slip** of paper is a small piece of paper.

**slipper** slippers
NOUN **Slippers** are soft loose shoes that people wear in the house.

**slippery**
ADJECTIVE Something that is **slippery** is smooth, wet or greasy. It is difficult to keep hold of or to walk on.

**slit** slits, slitting, slit
VERB **1** If you **slit** something, you make a long narrow cut in it. *He slit open the envelope.*
NOUN **2** A **slit** is a long narrow opening in something.

**slope** slopes

NOUN A **slope** is a flat surface which has one end higher than the other.

**slot** slots

NOUN A **slot** is a narrow opening in something, usually for putting coins in.

**slow** slower, slowest

ADJECTIVE **1** Something that is **slow** moves along without much speed.
ADJECTIVE **2** If a watch or clock is **slow**, it shows a time that is earlier than the correct time.
**slowly** ADVERB

**slug** slugs

NOUN A **slug** is a small slow-moving animal with a long slimy body, like a snail but without a shell.

**sly** slyer, slyest

ADJECTIVE Someone who is **sly** is good at tricking people in a not very nice way.

**smack** smacks, smacking, smacked

VERB If a person **smacks** someone, they hit them with an open hand.

**small** smaller, smallest

ADJECTIVE Something that is **small** is not as large as other things of the same kind.

**smart** smarter, smartest

ADJECTIVE Someone who is **smart** looks neat and clean.

**smash** smashes, smashing, smashed

VERB **1** If something **smashes**, it falls and hits the ground. It makes a loud noise and breaks into lots of pieces. *The cup **smashed** when she dropped it.*
VERB **2** If someone or something **smashes** an object, they drop it or hit it so that it breaks into lots of pieces.

**smell** smells, smelling, smelled or smelt

VERB **1** When you **smell** something, you notice it with your nose.
VERB **2** If something **smells** nice or nasty, people's noses tell them about it.
NOUN **3** Your sense of **smell** is your ability to smell things.

**smile** smiles, smiling, smiled

VERB When you **smile**, the corners of your mouth move upwards and you look happy.

**smoke** smokes, smoking, smoked

NOUN **1** Smoke is a mixture of gas and small particles sent into the air when something burns.
VERB **2** If something is **smoking**, smoke is coming from it.

**smooth** smoother, smoothest

ADJECTIVE **1** Something which is **smooth** has no roughness, lumps or holes in it.
ADJECTIVE **2** A **smooth** ride is one that is comfortable because there are no bumps.

**smother** smothers, smothering, smothered

VERB **1** If someone **smothers** a fire, they cover it with something in order to put it out.
VERB **2** If a lot of things **smother** something, they cover it all over. *The grass was **smothered** in daisies.*

**smudge** smudges, smudging, smudged

NOUN **1** A **smudge** is a dirty mark left on something.
VERB **2** If you **smudge** something, you make it dirty by touching it.

**smug** smugger, smuggest

ADJECTIVE Someone who is **smug** is too pleased with how good or clever they are.

**smuggle** smuggles, smuggling, smuggled

VERB To **smuggle** things or people into or out of a place means to take them there secretly, or against the law.

**snack** snacks

NOUN A **snack** is a small amount of food that you eat quickly. *I had an apple and some crisps for a **snack**.*

a
b
c
d
e
f
g
h
i
j
k
l
m
n
o
p
q
r
**Ss**
t
u
v
w
x
y
z

**snag** snags

NOUN A **snag** is a small problem.

**snail** snails

NOUN A **snail** is a small slow-moving animal with a shell on its back.

**snake** snakes

NOUN A **snake** is a long thin reptile with scales on its skin and no legs. See *Reptiles* on page 259.

**snap** snaps, snapping, snapped

VERB **1** If something **snaps**, it breaks suddenly with a sharp cracking noise.
VERB **2** If a dog **snaps** at you, it tries to bite you.
VERB **3** If someone **snaps** at you, they speak crossly.
NOUN **4** **Snap** is a children's card game.

**snarl** snarls, snarling, snarled

VERB When an animal **snarls**, it makes a fierce sound in its throat while showing its teeth.

**snatch** snatches, snatching, snatched

VERB If you **snatch** something, you take it quickly and suddenly.

**sneak** sneaks, sneaking, sneaked

VERB If you **sneak** somewhere, you go there very quietly, being careful that other people do not see or hear you.

**sneer** sneers, sneering, sneered

VERB If a person **sneers** at something, they show that they don't like it much.

**sneeze** sneezes, sneezing, sneezed

VERB When you **sneeze**, you blow out suddenly through your nose, making a loud noise.

**sniff** sniffs, sniffing, sniffed

VERB If you **sniff**, you breathe in through your nose hard enough to make a sound.

**snooze** snoozes, snoozing, snoozed

VERB If you **snooze**, you sleep lightly for a short time, especially during the day.

**snore** snores, snoring, snored

VERB When people **snore**, they breathe very noisily while they are sleeping.

**snorkel** snorkels

NOUN A **snorkel** is a tube that you breathe through when your face is just under the surface of the sea.

**snow** snows, snowing, snowed

NOUN **1** Snow is flakes of ice crystals which fall from the sky in cold weather.
VERB **2** When it **snows**, snow falls from the sky.

**snowball** snowballs

NOUN A **snowball** is a ball of snow for throwing.

**snowflake** snowflakes

NOUN A **snowflake** is a soft piece of falling snow.

**snowman** snowmen

NOUN A **snowman** is a pile of snow that is made to look like a person.

**snug** snugger, snuggest

ADJECTIVE If you feel **snug**, you are warm and comfortable.

**snuggle** snuggles, snuggling, snuggled

VERB If you **snuggle** somewhere, you cuddle up to something or someone.

**soak** soaks, soaking, soaked

VERB **1** When liquid **soaks** something, it makes it very wet.
VERB **2** When something **soaks** up a liquid, the liquid is drawn up into it.

**soap** **soaps**

NOUN **Soap** is a substance made of natural oils and fats, used for washing yourself.

**soar** **soars, soaring, soared**

VERB If something soars into the air, it goes quickly up into it.

**sob** **sobs, sobbing, sobbed**

VERB When someone **sobs**, they cry in a noisy way, breathing in short breaths.

**soccer**

NOUN **Soccer** is another word for the game of football.

**society** **societies**

NOUN **1** Society is people in general.
NOUN **2** A **society** is an organization for people who have the same interests.

**sock** **socks**

NOUN A **sock** is a soft piece of clothing which covers your foot and ankle.

**socket** **sockets**

NOUN A **socket** is a place on a wall or on a piece of electrical equipment into which you can put a plug or bulb.

**sofa** **sofas**

NOUN A **sofa** is a long comfortable seat for more than one person. Sofas have a back, and usually arms.

**soft** **softer, softest**

ADJECTIVE **1** Something that is **soft** changes shape easily when you touch it.
ADJECTIVE **2** A **soft** sound or voice is quiet and gentle.
ADJECTIVE **3** A **soft** light or colour is not too bright.

**software**

NOUN **Software** is computer programs.

**soggy** **soggier, soggiest**

ADJECTIVE Something that is **soggy** is wet and often heavy.

**soil**

NOUN **Soil** is the top layer of earth, which plants can grow in.

**solar**

ADJECTIVE **1** Solar is used to describe something that is to do with the sun.
ADJECTIVE **2** Solar power uses the sun's energy to provide light and heat.

**sold**

VERB **Sold** is the past tense of **sell**.

**soldier** **soldiers**

NOUN A **soldier** is a person in an army.

**sole** **soles**

NOUN **1** The **sole** of your foot, shoe or sock is the underneath surface of it.

NOUN **2** A **sole** is also a flat sea fish.

**solemn**

ADJECTIVE Someone or something that is **solemn** is serious, rather than cheerful.

**solid**

ADJECTIVE **1** Something that is **solid** is firm and always keeps its shape. Metal, wood and rock are all solid.
ADJECTIVE **2** Something **solid** is not hollow.
ADJECTIVE **3** A **solid** shape is a three-dimensional shape such as a cylinder or a cone.
See *Solid shapes* on page 271.

**solution** **solutions**

NOUN **1** A **solution** is the answer to a problem.
NOUN **2** A **solution** can also be a liquid in which something, like a powder, has been dissolved.

a
b
c
d
e
f
g
h
i
j
k
l
m
n
o
p
q
r
**Ss**
t
u
v
w
x
y
z

# solve

**solve** solves, solving, solved
VERB If you **solve** a problem, you find an answer to it.

**some**
ADJECTIVE You use **some** to talk about an amount when you are not saying how much there is. *There's **some** money on the table.*

**somebody**
PRONOUN You use **somebody** to talk about a person without saying exactly who you mean.

**somehow**
ADVERB You use **somehow** to talk about a way of doing something when you do not know exactly how.

**someone**
PRONOUN You use **someone** to talk about a person without saying exactly who you mean.

**somersault** somersaults
NOUN A **somersault** is a forwards or backwards roll in which you place your head on the ground and bring your body over it.

**something**
PRONOUN You use **something** to talk about a thing without saying exactly what you mean. *We need **something** to hold the door open.*

**sometimes**
ADVERB **Sometimes** means occasionally, rather than always or never.

**somewhere**
ADVERB **1 Somewhere** is used to talk about a place without saying exactly where it is. *It must be around **somewhere**.*
ADVERB **2 Somewhere** can be used to give an approximate amount, number or time. *It was **somewhere** between 11 o'clock and midnight.*

**son** sons
NOUN A boy is the **son** of his parents.

**song** songs
NOUN A **song** is a piece of music with words.

**soon** sooner, soonest
ADVERB **Soon** means in the near future.

**soot**
NOUN **Soot** is a black powder that comes from burning coal or wood.

**sore** sorer, sorest
ADJECTIVE If part of your body is **sore**, it hurts. *Her throat was so **sore** she couldn't talk.*

**sorrow** sorrows
NOUN **Sorrow** is feeling very sad.

**sorry** sorrier, sorriest
ADJECTIVE **1** If you feel **sorry** about something, you feel disappointed or sad. *I was **sorry** to leave all my friends.*
ADJECTIVE **2** If you feel **sorry** for someone, you feel sad for them.

**sort** sorts, sorting, sorted
NOUN **1** The different **sorts** of something are the different types of it.
VERB **2** If you **sort** things, you put them into groups. *Sort your socks into pairs.*
all sorts PHRASE **All sorts** of things means lots of different things.

**sought**
VERB **Sought** is the past tense of **seek**.

**sound** sounds
NOUN A **sound** is something that you hear.

**soup** soups
NOUN **Soup** is liquid food made by boiling meat, fish or vegetables in water.

**sour** sourer, sourest
ADJECTIVE **1** Something that is **sour** tastes sharp.
ADJECTIVE **2 Sour** milk is no longer fresh.

# speak

**source** sources

NOUN **1** The **source** of something is the place that it has come from.

NOUN **2** The **source** of a river or stream is the place where it begins.

**south**

NOUN **South** is one of the four main points of the compass. If you face the point where the sun rises, south is on your right. See **compass point**.

**southern** ADJECTIVE

**south-east**

NOUN **South-east** is halfway between south and east.

**south-west**

NOUN **South-west** is halfway between south and west.

**souvenir** souvenirs

NOUN A **souvenir** is something you keep to remind you of a person or place.

**sow** sows, sowing, sowed

(*rhymes with* **no**) VERB **1** To **sow** seeds means to plant them in the ground. (*rhymes with* **now**) NOUN **2** A **sow** is an adult female pig.

**space** spaces

NOUN **1** Space is the area that is empty in a place, building or container. *There's enough space for a bigger chair in my room.*

NOUN **2** Space is also the place far above the Earth where there is no air.

**spaceship** spaceships

NOUN A **spaceship** is a vehicle that carries people through space.

**spacesuit** spacesuits

NOUN A **spacesuit** is a special suit that is worn by an astronaut, which covers the whole body.

**spade** spades

NOUN A **spade** is a tool for digging, with a flat metal blade and a long handle.

**spaghetti**

NOUN Spaghetti is long thin pieces of pasta.

**span** spans

NOUN The **span** of something is the total length of it from end to end. For example, when a bird stretches its wings, the distance from wing tip to wing tip is called its "wing span".

**spanner** spanners

NOUN A **spanner** is a tool with a specially shaped end that fits round a nut to turn it.

**spare** spares, sparing, spared

ADJECTIVE **1** Something that is **spare** is extra to what is needed. *Do you have a spare pencil you can lend me?*

VERB **2** If you **spare** something, you make it available. *Can you spare me some time?*

**spark** sparks

NOUN A **spark** is a tiny piece of fire. It can fly up from something burning, or it can be caused by electricity.

**sparkle** sparkles, sparkling, sparkled

VERB If something **sparkles**, it shines with a lot of small bright points of light.

**sparrow** sparrows

NOUN A **sparrow** is a small bird with brown and grey feathers.

**spawn**

NOUN Spawn is a jelly-like substance containing the eggs of fish or amphibians.

**speak** speaks, speaking, spoke, spoken

VERB **1** When you **speak**, you use your voice to say words.

VERB **2** If you **speak** a foreign language, you know it and can use it.

a b c d e f g h i j k l m n o p q r **Ss** t u v w x y z

# spear

**spear** **spears, spearing, speared**
NOUN **1** A **spear** is a weapon consisting of a long pole with a sharp point.
VERB **2** To **spear** something means to push or throw a pointed object into it. *He **speared** a potato with his fork.*

**special**
ADJECTIVE **1** Something that is **special** is more important or better than other things of its kind.
ADJECTIVE **2** Special can also mean that something is for a particular use. *You need a **special** tool for this job.*

**speck** **specks**
NOUN A **speck** is a tiny piece of something. *There wasn't a **speck** of dust anywhere.*

**spectator** **spectators**
NOUN A **spectator** is a person who is watching something.

**speech** **speeches**
NOUN **1** Speech is the ability to speak or the act of speaking.
NOUN **2** A **speech** is a formal talk given to an audience.
NOUN **3** In a play, a **speech** is a group of lines spoken by one of the characters.

**speech bubble** **speech bubbles**
NOUN A **speech bubble** is drawn to show what someone is saying in a picture. There is a line round the words, with a little tail near the mouth of the speaker.

This is a speech bubble!

**speechless**
ADJECTIVE If you are **speechless**, you cannot speak for a short time, usually because something has amazed you.

**speech marks**
PLURAL NOUN **Speech marks** are punctuation marks (" ") or (' ') used in writing to show where speech begins and ends.
*See Punctuation on page 264.*

**speed** **speeds, speeding, sped or speeded**
NOUN **1** The **speed** of something is how fast it moves.
VERB **2** Someone who is **speeding** is moving very fast, or too fast.

**spell** **spells, spelling, spelt or spelled**
VERB **1** When you **spell** a word, you name or write its letters in order.
NOUN **2** A **spell** is a short time. *We're in for a **spell** of bad weather.*
NOUN **3** A **spell** is also the words used to perform magic.

**spelling**
NOUN The **spelling** of a word is the correct order of letters in it.

**spend** **spends, spending, spent**
VERB **1** When you **spend** money, you buy things with it.
VERB **2** To **spend** time or energy means to use it.

**sphere**
NOUN A **sphere** is an object or shape that is like a ball.
**spherical** ADJECTIVE
*See Solid shapes on page 271.*

**spice** **spices**
NOUN A **spice** is the powder or seeds from a particular plant which people put in food to give it flavour.
**spicy** ADJECTIVE

**spider** **spiders**
NOUN A **spider** is a small animal with eight legs. Some spiders make webs that they use to catch insects for food.

**spike** **spikes**
NOUN A **spike** is a long piece of metal with a sharp point at one end.

**spill** spills, spilling, spilled or spilt
VERB If you **spill** a liquid, you let it flow out of a container by mistake.

**spin** spins, spinning, spun
VERB **1** If something **spins**, it turns round and round quickly.
VERB **2** When someone **spins**, they make thread by twisting together pieces of fibre using a machine.
VERB **3** When spiders **spin**, they give out a sticky thread and make it into a web.

**spinach**
NOUN **Spinach** is a vegetable with large green leaves.
See *Vegetables* on page 256.

**spine** spines
NOUN **1** Your **spine** is your backbone.
NOUN **2** **Spines** are long sharp points on an animal's body or on a plant.

**spiral** spirals
NOUN A **spiral** is a continuous curve which winds round and round, with each curve above or outside the previous one.

**spire** spires
NOUN The **spire** of a church is the tall cone-shaped structure on top.

**spite** spites, spiting, spited
VERB If you do something to **spite** someone, you do it deliberately to hurt or annoy them.
in spite of PHRASE When you say that you are doing something **in spite of** something else, you mean that you are not going to let it stop you. *In spite of the rain, I'm still going out.*

**spiteful**
ADJECTIVE A **spiteful** person does or says nasty things to people to hurt them.
spitefully ADVERB

**splash** splashes, splashing, splashed
VERB **1** If you **splash** around in water, you disturb the water in a noisy way.

VERB **2** If liquid **splashes** something, it scatters over it in a lot of small drops.
NOUN **3** A **splash** is the sound made when something hits or falls into water.

**splendid**
ADJECTIVE **Splendid** means extremely good.

**splinter** splinters, splintering, splintered
NOUN **1** A **splinter** is a thin sharp piece of wood or glass which has broken off a larger piece.
VERB **2** If something **splinters**, it breaks into thin sharp pieces.

**split** splits, splitting, split
VERB **1** If something is **split**, it divides into two or more. *The village was split in two by the new road.*
VERB **2** If people **split** something between them, they share it.

**spoil** spoils, spoiling, spoiled or spoilt
VERB **1** If you **spoil** something, you damage it, or make it less good than it was.
VERB **2** To **spoil** children means to give them everything they want, so that they become selfish.

**spoke** spokes
VERB **1** **Spoke** is the past tense of **speak**.
NOUN **2** The **spokes** of a wheel are the bars which connect the hub to the rim.

**spoken**
VERB **Spoken** is the past participle of **speak**.

**sponge** sponges
NOUN **1** A **sponge** is a soft thing with holes in it. It soaks up water and you use it for washing things.

NOUN **2** A **sponge** or **sponge cake** is a very light cake.

a b c d e f g h i j k l m n o p q r **Ss** t u v w x y z

**spoon** spoons

NOUN A **spoon** is a tool like a small shallow bowl with a long handle. It is used for eating, mixing or serving food.

**sport** sports

NOUN **Sports** are games that you play which exercise your body.

**spot** spots, spotting, spotted

NOUN **1 Spots** are small round marks on a surface. Some fabrics have a pattern of spots.

NOUN **2** A **spot** can be a particular place. *This would be a nice **spot** for a picnic.*

NOUN **3** A **spot** can also be a small raised mark on a person's skin.

VERB **4** If you **spot** something, you notice it.

**spotless**

ADJECTIVE Something that is **spotless** is perfectly clean.

**spout** spouts

NOUN A **spout** is a tube with an end like a lip, for pouring liquid. *Teapots have a spout.*

**sprang**

VERB **Sprang** is the past tense of **spring**.

**sprawl** sprawls, sprawling, sprawled

VERB If you **sprawl**, you sit or lie with your legs and arms spread out.

**spray** sprays, spraying, sprayed

NOUN **1 Spray** is lots of small drops of liquid splashed or forced into the air.

VERB **2** To **spray** a liquid over something means to cover it with small drops of the liquid.

**spread** spreads, spreading, spread

VERB **1** If you **spread** something, you arrange it over a surface. *They **spread** their wet clothes out to dry.*

VERB **2** If you **spread** something, such as butter, you put a thin layer of it onto something.

VERB **3** If you **spread** parts of your body, such as your arms, you stretch them out until they are far apart.

**spring** springs, springing, sprang, sprung

NOUN **1 Spring** is the season between winter and summer.

NOUN **2** A **spring** is a coil of wire which returns to its shape after being pressed or pulled.

NOUN **3** A **spring** is also a place where water comes up through the ground.

VERB **4** To **spring** means to jump. *The leopard **sprang** on its prey.*

**springbok** springboks

NOUN A **springbok** is a small South African antelope which moves in leaps.

**sprinkle** sprinkles, sprinkling, sprinkled

VERB If you **sprinkle** a liquid or powder over something, you scatter it over it.

**sprint** sprints, sprinting, sprinted

VERB To **sprint** means to run fast over a short distance.

**sprout** sprouts, sprouting, sprouted

VERB **1** When something **sprouts**, it starts to grow.

NOUN **2 Sprouts** are small round green vegetables.

See *Vegetables* on page 256.

**sprung**

VERB **Sprung** is the past participle of **spring**.

**spun**

VERB **Spun** is the past tense of **spin**.

**spurt** spurts, spurting, spurted

VERB When a liquid or flame **spurts** out, it comes out quickly in a powerful stream. *Blood **spurted** from his arm.*

**spy** spies, spying, spied

NOUN **1** A **spy** is a person sent to find out secret information about a country or organization.

VERB **2** If you **spy** on someone, you watch them secretly.

**square** squares

NOUN **1** A **square** is a shape with four equal sides and four right angles. *See Colours and flat shapes on page 271.*

NOUN **2** The **square** of a number is the number multiplied by itself. For example, the square of 3, written $3^2$, is $3 \times 3$.

ADJECTIVE **3 Square** is used before units of length when talking about the area of something. *The room measures 25 square metres.*

**squash** squashes, squashing, squashed

VERB **1** If you **squash** something, you press it so that it loses its shape.

NOUN **2** If there is a **squash** in a place, there are a lot of people pressed against each other.

NOUN **3 Squash** is a drink made from fruit juice, sugar, and water.

**squat** squats, squatting, squatted

VERB If you **squat**, you crouch down, balancing on your feet with your legs bent.

**squawk** squawks, squawking, squawked

VERB When a bird **squawks**, it makes a loud harsh noise.

**squeak** squeaks, squeaking, squeaked

VERB If something **squeaks**, it makes a short high-pitched sound.

**squeal** squeals, squealing, squealed

VERB When things or people **squeal**, they make a long high-pitched sound.

**squeeze** squeezes, squeezing, squeezed

VERB **1** When you **squeeze** something, you press it firmly from two sides.

VERB **2** When you **squeeze** something into a small amount of time or space, you manage to fit it in.

**squirrel** squirrels

NOUN A **squirrel** is a small furry animal with a long bushy tail.

**squirt** squirts, squirting, squirted

VERB If a liquid **squirts**, it comes out of a narrow opening in a thin fast stream.

**stable** stables

NOUN A **stable** is a building in which horses are kept.

**stack** stacks, stacking, stacked

NOUN **1** A **stack** of things is a pile of them, one on top of the other.

VERB **2** If you **stack** things, you arrange them one on top of the other in a pile.

**stadium** stadiums

NOUN A **stadium** is a large place where you go to watch games.

**staff**

NOUN The **staff** of an organization are the people who work for it.

**stag** stags

NOUN A **stag** is an adult male deer.

**stage** stages

NOUN **1** A **stage** is a part of a process that lasts for a period of time. *The final stage is really difficult.*

NOUN **2** In a theatre, the **stage** is a raised platform where the actors perform.

**stagger** staggers, staggering, staggered

VERB **1** If someone **staggers**, they walk unsteadily.

VERB **2** If something **staggers** you, it amazes you.

a
b
c
d
e
f
g
h
i
j
k
l
m
n
o
p
q
r
**Ss**
t
u
v
w
x
y
z

**stain** stains

NOUN A **stain** is a mark on something that is difficult to remove.

**stair** stairs

NOUN A **stair** is one of a set of steps in a building going from one floor to another.

**staircase** staircases

NOUN A **staircase** is a set of stairs.

**stake** stakes

NOUN A **stake** is a pointed wooden post that can be hammered into the ground and used as a support.

**stale** staler, stalest

ADJECTIVE **Stale** food or air is not fresh.

**stalk** stalks, stalking, stalked

NOUN **1** A **stalk** is the main stem of a plant.

VERB **2** To **stalk** a person or animal means to follow them slowly and quietly.

**stall** stalls

NOUN **1** A **stall** is a large table on which there are goods for sale.

PLURAL NOUN **2** In a theatre, the **stalls** are the seats at the lowest level, in front of the stage.

**stallion** stallions

NOUN A **stallion** is an adult male horse.

**stammer** stammers, stammering, stammered

VERB When someone **stammers**, they hesitate and repeat some sounds when they speak.

**stamp** stamps, stamping, stamped

NOUN **1** A **stamp** is a small piece of gummed paper which you stick on a letter or parcel before posting it.

VERB **2** If you **stamp**, you lift your foot and put it down hard on the ground.

**stand** stands, standing, stood

VERB **1** When you **stand**, your body is upright and you are on your feet.

VERB **2** If a letter **stands for** a particular word, it is an abbreviation of that word. *So you're J Smith. What does J stand for?*

VERB **3** If you cannot **stand** something, you cannot bear it. *I can't stand that boy.*

**standard** standards

NOUN **1** A **standard** is how good something is. *This is not up to your usual standard.*

ADJECTIVE **2** Something which is **standard** is usual, and not special or extra. *Power steering is now a standard feature on this car.*

**stank**

VERB **Stank** is the past tense of **stink**.

**star** stars, starring, starred

NOUN **1** A **star** is a large ball of burning gas in space that appears as a point of light in the sky at night.

NOUN **2** A **star** is also a shape with four, five or more points sticking out in a regular pattern.

*See Colours and flat shapes on page 271.*

NOUN **3** A **star** is also a famous person in entertainment or sport.

VERB **4** If an actor or actress **stars** in a film, they have one of the most important parts in it.

**starch**

NOUN **Starch** is a substance that gives you energy. It is found in foods such as bread and potatoes.

**stare** stares, staring, stared

VERB If you **stare** at something, you look at it for a long time.

**starfish** starfishes or starfish

NOUN A **starfish** is a flat, star-shaped sea animal with five limbs.

**starling** starlings

NOUN A **starling** is a common European bird with shiny dark feathers.

**start** starts, starting, started

VERB **1** To **start** means to begin.

VERB **2** If someone **starts** a machine or car, they use the controls to make it work.

**startle** startles, startling, startled

VERB If something **startles** you, it frightens you by making a sudden movement or noise.

**starve** starves, starving, starved

VERB When people or animals **starve**, they suffer a great deal from lack of food and sometimes die.

**state** states, stating, stated

NOUN **1** The **state** of someone or something is how they are. *Have you seen the **state** of the garden?*

NOUN **2** A **state** is a country, or a part of a country making some of its own laws.

VERB **3** If you **state** something, you say it clearly and formally.

in a state PHRASE If you are **in a state**, you are nervous or upset.

**statement** statements

NOUN A **statement** is something you say or write when you give facts or information in a formal way.

**station** stations

NOUN **1** A **station** is a building where trains or buses stop for passengers.

NOUN **2** A **station** is also a building for people such as the police or fire brigade.

**stationary**

ADJECTIVE If something like a vehicle is **stationary**, it is not moving.

**stationery**

NOUN **Stationery** is paper, pens, envelopes and other equipment used for writing.

**statue** statues

NOUN A **statue** is a large sculpture of a person or animal.

**stay** stays, staying, stayed

VERB **1** If you **stay** in a place, you do not move away from it.

VERB **2** If you **stay** with someone, you live in their house for a while.

**steady** steadier, steadiest

ADJECTIVE **1** If something such as a ladder is **steady**, it is firm and does not shake or move about.

ADJECTIVE **2** A **steady** look or voice is calm and controlled.

**steadily** ADVERB

**steak** steaks

NOUN A **steak** is a thick slice of meat or fish.

**steal** steals, stealing, stole, stolen

VERB To **steal** means to take something which does not belong to you, and keep it.

**steam**

NOUN **Steam** is the hot vapour formed when water boils.

**steel**

NOUN **Steel** is a strong metal made mostly from iron.

**steep** steeper, steepest

ADJECTIVE Something such as a road or hill that is **steep** slopes sharply.

**steeple** steeples

NOUN A **steeple** is a church tower with a high pointed top.

**steer** steers, steering, steered

VERB When someone **steers** something like a car or cycle, they make it go in the direction they want.

a b c d e f g h i j k l m n o p q r Ss t u v w x y z

# stem

**stem** stems

NOUN The **stem** of a plant is the long thin centre part.

**stencil** stencils

NOUN A **stencil** is a thin sheet with a cut-out pattern. Ink or paint passes through the stencil to form a pattern on the surface below.

**step** steps

NOUN **1** A **step** is the movement you make when you lift your foot and put it down in a different place.

NOUN **2** A **step** is also a raised flat surface which you use to move from one level to another.

**stereo** stereos

NOUN A **stereo** is a machine that plays sound from tapes or CDs, with the sound coming through two speakers.

**stern** sterner, sternest

ADJECTIVE Someone who is **stern** is serious and expects to be obeyed.

**stew** stews

NOUN A **stew** is a meal which you make by cooking meat, fish or vegetables slowly for a long time.

**stick** sticks, sticking, stuck

NOUN **1** A **stick** is a long thin piece of wood.

VERB **2** If you **stick** a pointed object, such as a drawing pin, into something, you push it in.

VERB **3** If you **stick** two things together, you fix them with something like glue.

VERB **4** If something like a drawer **sticks**, it cannot be moved.

**sticker** stickers

NOUN A **sticker** is a small piece of paper that you can stick on to a surface. It has writing or a picture on one side.

**sticky** stickier, stickiest

ADJECTIVE Something that is **sticky**, like jam or glue, can stick to other things.

**stiff** stiffer, stiffest

ADJECTIVE **1** Something that is **stiff** is quite hard or firm. *Use a **stiff** broom to sweep up the leaves.*

ADJECTIVE **2** If a person is **stiff**, their muscles or joints hurt when they move.

**stile** stiles

NOUN A **stile** is a kind of fixed gate with a step on each side. It is made so that people can get into a field without letting animals out.

**still** stiller, stillest

ADVERB **1** You say **still** when something is the same as it was before. *I've **still** got a headache.*

ADVERB OR ADJECTIVE **2 Still** means staying in the same position without moving. *He wouldn't sit **still**.*

**stilt** stilts

NOUN **Stilts** are two long pieces of wood or metal on which people walk.

**sting** stings, stinging, stung

VERB If a creature or plant **stings** you, it pricks your skin and hurts you.

**stink** stinks, stinking, stank, stunk

VERB Something that **stinks** smells bad.

**stir** stirs, stirring, stirred

VERB If you **stir** a liquid, you move it around with a spoon or a stick.

**stitch** stitches, stitching, stitched

VERB If you **stitch** fabric, you push a needle and thread in and out through it.

**stocking** stockings

NOUN **Stockings** are long pieces of thin clothing that cover a woman's legs and feet.

**stole**

VERB **Stole** is the past tense of **steal**.

**stolen**

VERB **1 Stolen** is the past participle of **steal**.

ADJECTIVE **2** If something is **stolen**, it has been taken away from its owner. *The police found the stolen bike.*

**stomach**   **stomachs**

NOUN Your **stomach** is the part of your body that holds food when you have eaten it.

**stone**   **stones**

NOUN **1 Stone** is a hard dry material that is dug out of the ground. It is often used for building houses and walls.

NOUN **2** A **stone** is a small piece of rock.

NOUN **3** The **stone** in a fruit such as a plum is the large seed in the centre.

NOUN **4** A **stone** is a unit of weight equal to just over six kilograms.

**stony**   **stonier, stoniest**

ADJECTIVE **Stony** ground is rough and contains a lot of stones.

**stood**

VERB **Stood** is the past tense of **stand**.

**stool**   **stools**

NOUN A **stool** is a seat with legs but no back.

**stoop**   **stoops, stooping, stooped**

VERB If you **stoop**, you bend your body down from the waist, usually so that you can pick something up.

**stop**   **stops, stopping, stopped**

VERB **1** If you **stop** what you are doing, you no longer do it.

VERB **2** If you **stop** somewhere, you stay there for a short while.

**store**   **stores, storing, stored**

VERB **1** When you **store** things, you put them away and keep them until they are wanted.

NOUN **2** A **store** is a large shop.

**storey**   **storeys**

NOUN A **storey** is all the rooms on one floor of a building.

**stork**   **storks**

NOUN A **stork** is a large bird with a long beak and long legs.

**storm**   **storms**

NOUN A **storm** is bad weather with heavy rain and strong winds. Often there is thunder and lightning.

**stormy** ADJECTIVE

**story**   **stories**

NOUN A **story** tells you about things that have happened. It can be about something real or something made up.

**stout**   **stouter, stoutest**

ADJECTIVE **1** Someone **stout** is rather fat.

ADJECTIVE **2** Things such as branches that are **stout** are thick and strong.

**stove**   **stoves**

NOUN A **stove** is a piece of equipment for heating a room or for cooking.

**straight**   **straighter, straightest**

ADJECTIVE **1** Something which is **straight** does not bend or curve. You use a ruler to draw a straight line.

ADVERB **2 Straight** can mean immediately and directly. *We promised to go straight to school.*

**straighten**   **straightens, straightening, straightened**

VERB If you **straighten** something, you make it straight, or neat and tidy.

**strain**   **strains, straining, strained**

VERB **1** If you **strain** to do something, you try too hard.

VERB **2** To **strain** food means to pour away the liquid from it.

VERB **3** If you **strain** a muscle, you injure it by moving awkwardly.

a b c d e f g h i j k l m n o p q r **Ss** t u v w x y z

# strange

**strange** **stranger, strangest**
ADJECTIVE **1** Something that is **strange** is odd or unexpected.
ADJECTIVE **2** A **strange** place is one you have never been to before.

**stranger** **strangers**
NOUN A **stranger** is a person you do not know.

**strap** **straps**
NOUN A **strap** is a strip of something like leather which is used to carry something around, or to fasten things together.

**straw** **straws**
NOUN **1** Straw is dried stalks of cereal such as wheat.
NOUN **2** A **straw** is a thin tube of paper or plastic, which you drink through.

**strawberry** **strawberries**
NOUN A **strawberry** is a small red fruit. It is soft and juicy and has tiny yellow seeds on its skin.
See *Fruit* on page 257.

**stray** **strays, straying, strayed**
VERB **1** If people or animals **stray**, they wander away from where they are supposed to be.
ADJECTIVE **2** A **stray** dog or cat is one that has wandered away from home.

**stream** **streams**
NOUN **1** A **stream** is a small river.
NOUN **2** A **stream** is also a steady flow of something like liquid or traffic.

**street** **streets**
NOUN A **street** is a road in a town or village, usually with buildings along it.

**strength**
NOUN **Strength** is how strong something is.

**stretch** **stretches, stretching, stretched**
VERB **1** If you **stretch**, you hold out part of your body as far as you can.
VERB **2** If you **stretch** something, you pull it so that it becomes longer or wider.
NOUN **3** A **stretch** of land or water is an area of it.

**strict** **stricter, strictest**
ADJECTIVE **1** Someone who is **strict** makes you behave well.
ADJECTIVE **2** A **strict** rule or law is one that must be obeyed.

**stride** **strides, striding, strode**
VERB **1** To **stride** along means to walk quickly with long steps.
NOUN **2** A **stride** is a long step.

**strike** **strikes, striking, struck**
VERB **1** To **strike** someone or something means to hit them.
VERB **2** When a clock **strikes**, it rings a bell to show what the time is.
VERB **3** If someone **strikes** a match, they make a flame or sparks with it.
NOUN **4** A **strike** is when workers refuse to go on working.

**string** **strings**
NOUN **1** String is thin rope.
NOUN **2** On a musical instrument like a guitar, the **strings** are the parts that you touch to make the sounds.

**strip** **strips, stripping, stripped**
NOUN **1** A **strip** of paper, cloth or other material is a long narrow piece of it.
VERB **2** If you **strip**, you take off all your clothes.

**stripe** **stripes**
NOUN A **stripe** is a coloured line on something.

**strode**
VERB **Strode** is the past tense of **stride**.

**stroke** **strokes, stroking, stroked**
VERB If you **stroke** something, you move your hand gently over it.

**stroll** **strolls, strolling, strolled**
VERB To **stroll** means to walk along slowly in a relaxed way.

**strong** stronger, strongest

ADJECTIVE **1** If you are **strong**, you can work hard and carry heavy things.

ADJECTIVE **2** Objects or materials that are **strong** will not break easily.

ADJECTIVE **3** Wind or water currents that are **strong** move very fast.

ADJECTIVE **4** Smells and flavours that are **strong** are easily noticed.

**struck**

VERB **Struck** is the past tense of **strike**.

**structure** structures

NOUN A **structure** is something that has been built.

**struggle** struggles, struggling, struggled

VERB **1** If you **struggle** to do something, you try hard to do it but find it difficult.

VERB **2** If you **struggle** when you are being held by something or someone, you twist and kick to try and get free.

**stubborn**

ADJECTIVE Someone who is **stubborn** is determined to do what they want.

**stuck**

VERB **1** **Stuck** is the past tense of **stick**.

ADJECTIVE **2** If you are **stuck**, you cannot carry on because it is too difficult.

**student** students

NOUN A **student** is a person who is studying at a university or college.

**studio** studios

NOUN **1** A **studio** is a room where a photographer or artist works.

NOUN **2** A **studio** is also a place where films, television programmes or other recordings are made.

**study** studies, studying, studied

VERB **1** If you **study** a subject, you spend time learning about it.

VERB **2** If you **study** something, you look at it carefully.

NOUN **3** A **study** is a room for writing and studying.

**stuff** stuffs, stuffing, stuffed

NOUN **1** You can talk about a substance or group of things as **stuff**.

VERB **2** If you **stuff** something with objects, you fill it with them.

**stuffy** stuffier, stuffiest

ADJECTIVE If it is **stuffy** in a room, there is not enough fresh air in it.

**stumble** stumbles, stumbling, stumbled

VERB If you **stumble** when you are walking, you trip and almost fall.

**stump** stumps

NOUN A **stump** is the small part of something, such as a tree, that remains when most of it has been removed.

**stun** stuns, stunning, stunned

VERB **1** If you are **stunned** by something, you are very surprised by it.

VERB **2** To **stun** a person or animal means to knock them unconscious by hitting them on the head.

**stung**

VERB **Stung** is the past tense of **sting**.

**stunk**

VERB **Stunk** is the past participle of **stink**.

**stupid** stupider, stupidest

ADJECTIVE Someone who is **stupid** does things that are not at all sensible.

**stupidly** ADVERB

**sturdy** sturdier, sturdiest

ADJECTIVE Someone or something that is **sturdy** is strong and firm.

a
b
c
d
e
f
g
h
i
j
k
l
m
n
o
p
q
r
**Ss**
t
u
v
w
x
y
z

a
b
c
d
e
f
g
h
i
j
k
l
m
n
o
p
q
r

t
u
v
w
x
y
z

**stutter** stutters

NOUN Someone who has a **stutter** finds it difficult to speak smoothly and often repeats sounds.

**sty** sties

NOUN A **sty** is a hut with a yard where pigs are kept.

**style** styles

NOUN The **style** of something is its design. *I'd like shoes in a different **style**.*

**sub-**

PREFIX **Sub-** is used at the beginning of words that have "under" as part of their meaning, for example "submarine" (meaning underwater).
See *Prefixes* on page 264.

**subheading** subheadings

NOUN A **subheading** is a heading which is less important than the main heading. *We'll have "animals" as a main heading, and "mammals" as a **subheading**.*

**subject** subjects

NOUN **1** A **subject** is a particular thing that people study at school or college, for example science or drawing.
NOUN **2** The **subject** of a piece of writing or a conversation is the thing or person being talked about.
NOUN **3** In grammar, the **subject** is the word or words representing a person or thing doing the action. For example, in the sentence "My cat caught a bird", "my cat" is the subject.

**submarine** submarines

NOUN A **submarine** is a ship that can travel under water.

**substance** substances

NOUN Any solid, powder, liquid or paste can be called a **substance**.

**subtract** subtracts, subtracting, subtracted

VERB If you **subtract** one number from another, you take away the first number from the second. The symbol you use for subtract is –.

**subtraction**

NOUN **Subtraction** is taking one number away from another.

**suburb** suburbs

NOUN A **suburb** is an area of a town or city that is away from its centre.

**subway** subways

NOUN A **subway** is a footpath that goes underneath a road.

**succeed** succeeds, succeeding, succeeded

VERB If you **succeed**, you manage to do what you set out to do.

**success**

NOUN **Success** is managing to do something that you set out to do.

**successful**

ADJECTIVE If you are **successful**, you achieve what you wanted to achieve.

**such**

ADVERB You can use **such** to emphasize something. *She's **such** a nice girl.*
**such as** PHRASE You can use **such as** to introduce examples of something. *I like team games **such as** football and rounders.*

**suck** sucks, sucking, sucked

VERB If you **suck** something, you hold it in your mouth and pull at it with your cheeks and tongue, usually to get liquid out of it.

**sudden**

ADJECTIVE Something that is **sudden** happens quickly and unexpectedly.

**suddenly** ADVERB

**suffer** suffers, suffering, suffered

VERB If someone is **suffering**, they feel pain or sadness.

**suffix** suffixes

NOUN A **suffix** is a group of letters which is added to the end of a word to form a new word, for example "-able" or "-ful". See *Suffixes on page 265*.

**sugar**

NOUN **Sugar** is a sweet substance used to sweeten food and drinks.

**suggest** suggests, suggesting, suggested

VERB If you **suggest** something to someone, you give a plan or an idea for them to think about.

**suggestion** NOUN

**suit** suits, suiting, suited

NOUN **1** A **suit** is a matching jacket and trousers or skirt.

VERB **2** If something **suits** you, it is right for you.

**suitable**

ADJECTIVE Something that is **suitable** for a particular purpose is right for it. *Are these shoes suitable for running?*

**suitcase** suitcases

NOUN A **suitcase** is a case that you carry clothes in when you are travelling.

**sulk** sulks, sulking, sulked

VERB If you **sulk**, you are silent and bad-tempered for a while because you are annoyed about something.

**sultana** sultanas

NOUN A **sultana** is a dried white grape.

**sum** sums

NOUN **1** A **sum** is an amount of money.

NOUN **2** In maths, the **sum** is the answer or total that you get when you add numbers. *The sum of 2 and 3 is 5.*

**summarize** summarizes, summarizing, summarized;

also spelt summarise

VERB To **summarize** something means to give a short account of its main points.

**summary** summaries

NOUN If you give a **summary** of something, you give the main points.

**summer** summers

NOUN **Summer** is the season between spring and autumn.

**summit** summits

NOUN The **summit** of a mountain is its top.

**sun** suns

NOUN The **sun** is the star that gives us heat and light.

**sunburn**

NOUN **Sunburn** is sore skin on someone's body when they have been in the sun for too long.

**Sunday** Sundays

NOUN **Sunday** is the day between Saturday and Monday.

**sundial** sundials

NOUN A **sundial** is an object that uses the sun to tell the time. It has a pointer that casts a shadow on a flat base marked with the hours.

# sunflower

**sunflower  sunflowers**
NOUN A **sunflower** is a tall plant with large yellow flowers.

**sung**
VERB **Sung** is the past participle of **sing**.

**sunglasses**
PLURAL NOUN **Sunglasses** are glasses with dark lenses that you wear to protect your eyes from the sun.

**sunk**
VERB **Sunk** is the past participle of **sink**.

**sunlight**
NOUN **Sunlight** is the bright light produced when the sun is shining.
**sunlit** ADJECTIVE

**sunny  sunnier, sunniest**
ADJECTIVE When the weather is **sunny**, the sun is shining brightly.

**sunrise  sunrises**
NOUN **Sunrise** is the time in the morning when the sun comes up.

**sunset  sunsets**
NOUN **Sunset** is the time in the evening when the sun goes down.

**sunshine**
NOUN **Sunshine** is the bright light produced when the sun is shining.

**super**
ADJECTIVE **Super** means very nice or very good. *We've just seen a **super** film.*

**super-**
PREFIX **Super-** is added to words to describe something that is larger or better, for example "supermarket". See Prefixes on page 264.

**superlative  superlatives**
NOUN In grammar, the **superlative** is the form of an adjective which has "the most" of that adjective. For example, "fattest" is the superlative of "fat". See Adjective on page 263.

**supermarket  supermarkets**
NOUN A **supermarket** is a large shop which sells all kinds of food and things for the house.

**supersonic**
ADJECTIVE A **supersonic** aircraft can travel faster than the speed of sound.

**superstitious**
ADJECTIVE People who are **superstitious** believe in things like magic and powers that bring good or bad luck.

**supper  suppers**
NOUN **Supper** is a meal or snack eaten in the evening.

**supply  supplies, supplying, supplied**
VERB **1** If someone **supplies** you with something, they provide you with it.
NOUN **2** A **supply** of something is the amount of it which someone has. *The water **supply** is getting very low.*

**support  supports, supporting, supported**
VERB **1** If you **support** someone, you want them to do well.
VERB **2** If something **supports** an object, it holds it up firmly.

**suppose  supposes, supposing, supposed**
VERB **1** If you **suppose** that something is true, you think that it is likely to be true.
CONJUNCTION **2** You can use **suppose** or **supposing** when you are thinking about doing something. ***Supposing** we just left without saying anything, what do you think would happen?*
**I suppose** PHRASE You can say **I suppose** when you are not certain about something. *Yes, **I suppose** he could come.*

## sure

ADJECTIVE **1** If you are **sure** something is true, you believe it is true.

ADJECTIVE **2** If something is **sure** to happen, it will definitely happen.

ADJECTIVE **3** If you are **sure** of yourself, you are very confident.

**make sure** PHRASE If you **make sure** of something, you check it. *Can you make sure we locked up properly?*

## surf  surfs, surfing, surfed

NOUN **1 Surf** is the white foam that forms on the top of waves when they break.

VERB **2** When you **surf**, you ride towards the shore on top of a large wave while standing on a special board.

VERB **3** When you **surf** the Internet, you go from website to website.

## surface  surfaces

NOUN The **surface** of something is the top or outside area of it.

## surgeon  surgeons

NOUN A **surgeon** is a doctor who performs operations.

## surgery  surgeries

NOUN **1 Surgery** is medical treatment in which part of the patient's body is cut open.

NOUN **2** A **surgery** is a room or building where a doctor or dentist works.

## surname  surnames

NOUN Your **surname** is the name you share with other members of your family.

## surprise  surprises

NOUN A **surprise** is something unexpected.

## surrender  surrenders, surrendering, surrendered

VERB If someone **surrenders**, they stop fighting and agree that they have lost.

## surround  surrounds, surrounding, surrounded

VERB If something **surrounds** something else, it is all round it.

## surroundings

PLURAL NOUN Your **surroundings** are the area around you.

## survey  surveys

NOUN **1** A **survey** of something is a detailed examination of it, often in the form of a report.

VERB **2** A **survey** is also a set of questions to find out what people think about things.

## survive  survives, surviving, survived

VERB If someone **survives**, they continue to live after being close to death.

## suspect  suspects, suspecting, suspected

VERB If you **suspect** someone of doing something wrong, you think they have done it.

## suspense

NOUN **Suspense** is excitement or worry caused by having to wait for something.

## suspicious

ADJECTIVE **1** If you are **suspicious** of someone, you do not trust them.

ADJECTIVE **2** If something is **suspicious**, it makes you feel something is wrong.

## swallow  swallows, swallowing, swallowed

VERB **1** When you **swallow** food or drink, it goes down your throat.

NOUN **2** A **swallow** is a small bird with pointed wings and a long forked tail.

a
b
c
d
e
f
g
h
i
j
k
l
m
n
o
p
q
r
Ss
t
u
v
w
x
y
z

**swam**

VERB **Swam** is the past tense of **swim**.

**swamp** swamps

NOUN A **swamp** is an area of extremely wet land.

**swan** swans

NOUN A **swan** is a large white bird with a long neck that lives on rivers and lakes.

**swap** swaps, swapping, swapped

VERB If you **swap** something, you give it to someone and receive something else from them in exchange.

**swarm** swarms

NOUN A **swarm** is a large group of bees or other insects flying together.
See *Collective nouns* on page 262.

**sway** sways, swaying, swayed

VERB When people or things **sway**, they lean or swing slowly from side to side.

**sweat**

NOUN **Sweat** is the salty liquid which comes from your skin when you are hot.

**sweater** sweaters

NOUN A **sweater** is a knitted piece of clothing covering your upper body and arms.

**sweatshirt** sweatshirts

NOUN A **sweatshirt** is a piece of clothing made of thick cotton. It covers your upper body and arms.

**sweep** sweeps, sweeping, swept

VERB If you **sweep** a floor or a path, you clean it by pushing a broom over it.

**sweet** sweeter, sweetest; sweets

ADJECTIVE **1** Food or drink that is **sweet** has a taste of sugar.

PLURAL NOUN **2 Sweets** are things such as chocolates and toffees.

NOUN **3** A **sweet** can be something that is eaten after the main part of a meal.

**sweet corn**

NOUN **Sweet corn** is a long stalk covered with juicy yellow seeds that can be eaten as a vegetable.
See *Vegetables* on page 256.

**swell** swells, swelling, swelled or swollen

VERB If something **swells**, it becomes larger and rounder than usual.

**swept**

VERB **Swept** is the past tense of **sweep**.

**swerve** swerves, swerving, swerved

VERB If something that is moving **swerves**, it suddenly changes direction.

**swift** swifter, swiftest

ADJECTIVE Something that is **swift** can move very quickly.

**swim** swims, swimming, swam, swum

VERB When you **swim**, you use your arms and legs to move through water.

**swimming**

NOUN **Swimming** is the activity of moving yourself through water.

**swimming costume** swimming costumes

NOUN A **swimming costume** is the clothing worn by a woman or girl when she goes swimming.

**swimming pool** swimming pools

NOUN A **swimming pool** is a place made for people to swim in.

## swimming trunks

PLURAL NOUN **Swimming trunks** are shorts worn by a man or boy when they go swimming.

## swing  **swings, swinging, swung**

VERB **1** If something **swings**, it keeps moving backwards and forwards, or from side to side, while it is hanging.

NOUN **2** A **swing** is a seat that hangs from a frame and moves backwards and forwards when you sit on it.

## switch  **switches, switching, switched**

NOUN **1** A **switch** is a small control for a piece of equipment such as a light or radio.

VERB **2** To **switch** is to change one thing for another. *I switched to another school when I moved house.*

## swollen

ADJECTIVE Something that is **swollen** has swelled up.

## swoop  **swoops, swooping, swooped**

VERB When a bird **swoops**, it suddenly flies downwards in a smooth curve.

## swop

**Swop** is another spelling of **swap**.

## sword  **swords**

NOUN A **sword** is a weapon with a long blade and a short handle.

## swum

VERB **Swum** is the past participle of **swim**.

## swung

VERB **Swung** is the past tense of **swing**.

## sycamore  **sycamores**

NOUN A **sycamore** is a tree that has large five-pointed leaves.

## syllable  **syllables**

NOUN Each beat in a word is a **syllable**. For example, "cat" has one syllable, and "cattle" has two.

## symbol  **symbols**

NOUN A **symbol** is a sign or mark that stands for something else. For example, the symbol + stands for "plus".

## symmetrical

ADJECTIVE If something is **symmetrical**, it has two halves that are exactly the same, except that one half is like a reflection of the other half.

## symmetry

NOUN **1** **Symmetry** is when one half of something is exactly like a mirror image of the other half.

NOUN **2** The **line of symmetry** is the dividing line between two symmetrical halves.

## sympathy

NOUN If you feel **sympathy** for someone who is unhappy, you are sorry for them.

## synagogue  **synagogues**

NOUN A **synagogue** is a building where Jewish people pray.

## synonym  **synonyms**

NOUN **Synonyms** are words that have the same or similar meaning. The words "nice" and "pleasant" are synonyms. *See Synonyms on page 266.*

## syrup

NOUN **Syrup** is a thick sweet liquid made by boiling sugar with water.

## system  **systems**

NOUN **1** A **system** is a way of doing something. *I've got a new system for organizing my toys.*

NOUN **2** You can refer to a set of equipment as a **system**, for example a central heating system.

# Tt

### table  tables

NOUN **1** A **table** is a piece of furniture with a flat top for putting things on.

NOUN **2** A **table** is also a set of facts or figures arranged in rows or columns.

### tablet  tablets

NOUN A **tablet** is a small round pill made of powdered medicine.

### table tennis

NOUN **Table tennis** is a game for two or four people. You use bats to hit a small hollow ball over a low net across a table.

### tackle  tackles, tackling, tackled

VERB **1** If you **tackle** a difficult task, you deal with it in a determined way.

VERB **2** If you **tackle** someone in a game such as football, you try to get the ball away from them.

### tactful

ADJECTIVE A **tactful** person is careful not to hurt someone else's feelings.

**tactfully** ADVERB

### tadpole  tadpoles

NOUN **Tadpoles** are small water animals that grow into frogs or toads. They have long tails and round black heads.

### tail  tails

NOUN **1** A **tail** is the part of an animal, bird or fish that grows out of the end of its body.

NOUN **2** The back part of a plane is called the **tail**.

### take  takes, taking, took, taken

VERB **1** If you **take** something, you put your hand round it and carry it. *Let me take your coat.*

VERB **2** If someone **takes** you somewhere, you go there with them.

VERB **3** If a person **takes** something that does not belong to them, they steal it.

VERB **4** If you **take away** one number or amount from another, you find out how much is left.

### talcum powder

NOUN **Talcum powder**, or **talc**, is a soft powder which you put on your skin to help dry it and make it smell nice.

### tale  tales

NOUN A **tale** is a story.

### talent  talents

NOUN **Talent** is the natural ability a person has to do something well.

### talk  talks, talking, talked

VERB When you **talk**, you say things to someone.

### talkative

ADJECTIVE Someone who is **talkative** talks a lot.

### tall  taller, tallest

ADJECTIVE **1** Someone who is **tall** is higher than a lot of other people.

ADJECTIVE **2** You use **tall** to say how high somebody or something is. *My little brother is only one metre tall.*

### tally  tallies

NOUN A **tally** is a record of amounts which you add to as you go along.

### tame  tamer, tamest

ADJECTIVE A **tame** animal is not afraid of humans and will not hurt them.

**tan**
NOUN If someone has a **tan**, their skin has become darker than it usually is because they have been in the sun.

**tangle**   **tangles, tangling, tangled**
NOUN **1** A **tangle** is a mass of things such as hairs or fibres that are knotted or coiled together and are hard to separate.
VERB **2** If something is **tangled**, it is twisted in knots.

**tank**   **tanks**
NOUN **1** A **tank** is a large container for liquid or gas.
NOUN **2** A **tank** is also a vehicle for soldiers which moves on tracks. Tanks are covered with strong metal armour, and have guns or rockets.

**tanker**   **tankers**
NOUN A **tanker** is a ship, truck or railway vehicle for carrying gas or liquid.

**tap**   **taps, tapping, tapped**
NOUN **1** A **tap** is a handle which controls the flow of gas or liquid from a pipe.
VERB **2** If you **tap** something, you hit it lightly.

**tape**   **tapes**
NOUN **1** Tape is a strip of sticky material which you use to stick things together.
NOUN **2** A **tape** is a long thin magnetic strip that you can record sounds or pictures on.

**tape measure**   **tape measures**
NOUN A **tape measure** is a strip of plastic or metal that is marked in centimetres or inches. It is used to measure things.

**tape recorder**   **tape recorders**
NOUN A **tape recorder** is a machine that records and plays sound on tape.

**tar**
NOUN **Tar** is a thick black substance that is used for making roads.

**target**   **targets**
NOUN A **target** is something that people aim at and try to hit.

**tart**   **tarts**
NOUN A **tart** is a piece of pastry filled with jam or fruit.

**task**   **tasks**
NOUN A **task** is a piece of work which has to be done.

**tassel**   **tassels**
NOUN A **tassel** is a tuft of loose threads tied by a knot and used for decoration.

**taste**   **tastes, tasting, tasted**
NOUN **1** Your sense of **taste** is your ability to recognize the flavour of things in your mouth.
VERB **2** When you **taste** food, you take a little bit to see what it is like.

**tasty**   **tastier, tastiest**
ADJECTIVE Something that is **tasty** has a pleasant flavour.

**taught**
VERB **Taught** is the past tense of **teach**.

**tax**   **taxes**
NOUN **Tax** is money that people have to pay to the government.

**taxi**   **taxis**
NOUN A **taxi** is a car that people pay to be driven somewhere in.

**tea**   **teas**
NOUN **1** Tea is a drink made by pouring boiling water onto the dried leaves of the tea plant.
NOUN **2** Tea is also an afternoon meal.

**tea bag**   **tea bags**
NOUN A **tea bag** is a small paper bag with tea leaves in it which is put in boiling water to make tea.

**teach**   **teaches, teaching, taught**
VERB If someone **teaches** you something, they tell or show you how to do it.

**teacher**   **teachers**
NOUN A **teacher** is a person whose job is to help people learn.

a
b
c
d
e
f
g
h
i
j
k
l
m
n
o
p
q
r
s
**Tt**
u
v
w
x
y
z

# team

**team** teams
NOUN A **team** is a number of people working or playing together.

**teapot** teapots
NOUN A **teapot** is a container for making tea. It has a lid, a handle and a spout.

**tear** tears, tearing, tore, torn
(*rhymes with* **fear**) NOUN **1** Tears are the drops of liquid that come out of your eyes when you cry.
(*rhymes with* **fair**) VERB **2** If you **tear** something, such as paper or fabric, you pull it apart.

**tease** teases, teasing, teased
VERB If someone **teases** you, they make fun of you.

**teaspoon** teaspoons
NOUN A **teaspoon** is a small spoon used for stirring drinks.

**technology**
NOUN **Technology** is the practical use of science in areas such as industry, farming or medicine.

**teddy bear** teddy bears
NOUN A **teddy bear** is a child's soft toy which looks like a friendly bear.

**teenager** teenagers
NOUN A **teenager** is someone from 13 to 19 years of age.

**teeth**
NOUN **Teeth** is the plural of **tooth**.

**telephone** telephones
NOUN A **telephone**, or **phone**, is an instrument for talking to someone else who is in another place.

**telescope** telescopes
NOUN A **telescope** is an instrument for making objects that are far away look nearer and larger.

**television** televisions
NOUN A **television** is a machine that receives signals through the air or on cable and changes them into pictures and sounds.

**tell** tells, telling, told
VERB **1** If you **tell** someone something, you let them know about it.
VERB **2** If someone **tells** you to do something, they say you must do it.
VERB **3** If you **tell** the time, you find out what the time is by looking at a clock.

**temper**
NOUN **1** Someone's **temper** is how cheerful or how angry they are feeling.
NOUN **2** If you lose your **temper**, you become angry.

**temperature** temperatures
NOUN The **temperature** of something is how hot or cold it is.

**temple** temples
NOUN A **temple** is a building used for the worship of a god in various religions.

**temporary**
ADJECTIVE Something that is **temporary** only lasts for a short time.

**tempt** tempts, tempting, tempted
VERB If something **tempts** you, you want to do it but you think it might be wrong.
**tempting** ADJECTIVE

**tender**
ADJECTIVE **1** Someone who is **tender** shows gentle and caring feelings.
ADJECTIVE **2** Meat or other food which is **tender** is very easy to cut or chew.

**tennis**
NOUN **Tennis** is a game for two or four players in which a ball is hit over a net.

**tense** tenser, tensest; tenses
ADJECTIVE **1** If you are **tense**, you are nervous and cannot relax.
NOUN **2** The **tense** of a verb is the form which shows whether you are talking about the past, present or future.

**tent** **tents**

NOUN A **tent** is a shelter made of canvas or nylon, held up by poles and ropes.

**tentacle** **tentacles**

NOUN The **tentacles** of an animal, such as an octopus, are its long thin arms.

**term** **terms**

NOUN A **term** is one of the periods that each year is divided into at school.

**terrace** **terraces**

NOUN A **terrace** is a row of houses joined together.

**terrible**

ADJECTIVE Something **terrible** is serious and unpleasant.

**terribly** ADVERB

**terrify** **terrifies, terrifying, terrified**

VERB If something **terrifies** you, it makes you feel extremely frightened.

**territory** **territories**

NOUN **1** The **territory** of a country is the land that it controls.

NOUN **2** An animal's **territory** is an area that it considers its own and defends when other animals try to enter it.

**terror**

NOUN **Terror** is great fear or panic.

**test** **tests, testing, tested**

VERB **1** If someone **tests** something, they try to find out whether it works properly.

NOUN **2** A **test** is something you have to do to show how much you know.

**tetrahedron** **tetrahedrons** or **tetrahedra**

NOUN A **tetrahedron** is a solid shape with four triangular faces.
See *Solid shapes* on page 271.

**text** **texts**

NOUN **Text** is any written material.

**textbook** **textbooks**

NOUN A **textbook** is a book about a particular subject for students to use.

**than**

PREPOSITION OR CONJUNCTION You use **than** to link two things that you are comparing. *She's older **than** me.*

**thank** **thanks, thanking, thanked**

VERB You **thank** people when you are grateful for something they have done.

**that** **those**

ADJECTIVE **1** You use **that** or **those** to describe something which is not the nearest one. *Give me **that** book, please.*

PRONOUN **2** You can use **that** or **those** to refer to people or things which have already been mentioned. *What about going by bus? Is **that** a good idea?*

**thatched**

ADJECTIVE A **thatched** roof is one made of straw or reeds.

**thaw** **thaws, thawing, thawed**

VERB When something that is frozen **thaws**, it melts.

**theatre** **theatres**

NOUN A **theatre** is a building where you go to see a play or show.

**their**

ADJECTIVE **Their** refers to something belonging or relating to people or things that have already been mentioned. *Leave it to Sam and Joe. It's **their** problem.*

**them**

PRONOUN **Them** refers to people or things which have already been mentioned. *I don't want any sprouts. I don't like **them**.*

**theme** **themes**

NOUN A **theme** is the main idea in a piece of writing, painting, film or music.

a
b
c
d
e
f
g
h
i
j
k
l
m
n
o
p
q
r
s
**Tt**
u
v
w
x
y
z

# themselves

**themselves**

PRONOUN If people do something **themselves**, no one else does it. *My parents had to educate **themselves**.*

**then**

ADVERB **Then** refers to a particular time in the past or future. *I left the room **then**.*

**there**

ADVERB **1 There** means in, at, or to that place. *He's sitting over **there**.*
PRONOUN **2 There** is used to say that something exists or does not exist. *Are **there** any more crisps?*

**therefore**

ADVERB **Therefore** means as a result. *It was raining, **therefore** we stayed indoors.*

**thermometer** **thermometers**

NOUN A **thermometer** is an instrument that measures temperature.

**thesaurus** **thesauruses**

NOUN A **thesaurus** is a book in which words with similar meanings are grouped together.

**these**

ADJECTIVE OR PRONOUN **These** is the plural of **this**.

**thick** **thicker, thickest**

ADJECTIVE **1** An object that is **thick** is deeper through than other things of the same kind. *I'll have a **thick** slice, please.*
ADJECTIVE **2** Something that is **thick** is made up of a lot of things growing closely together. *She has long **thick** hair.*
ADJECTIVE **3 Thick** liquids do not flow easily.

**thief** **thieves**

NOUN A **thief** is a person who steals something.

**thigh** **thighs**

NOUN Your **thighs** are the top parts of your legs above your knees.

**thin** **thinner, thinnest**

ADJECTIVE **1** Something that is **thin** is much narrower than it is long. *The witch's nose was long and **thin**.*
ADJECTIVE **2** A **thin** person weighs less than most people of the same height.
ADJECTIVE **3** Something such as paper or cloth that is **thin** has only a small distance between front and back.
ADJECTIVE **4 Thin** liquids are watery.

**thing** **things**

NOUN **1** A **thing** is an object, rather than an animal or human being.
PLURAL NOUN **2** Your **things** are your clothes or possessions.

**think** **thinks, thinking, thought**

VERB **1** When you **think**, you use your mind to consider ideas or problems.
VERB **2** If you say you **think** something is true, you mean you believe it is true but you are not sure.

**third person**

NOUN In grammar, the **third person** refers to a person, thing or group. It is expressed as "he", "she", "it", or "they".

**thirsty**

ADJECTIVE If you are **thirsty**, you feel that you need to drink something.
**thirstily** ADVERB

**this** **these**

ADJECTIVE **1 This** is used to refer to someone or something that is nearby. *Would you like to borrow **this** book?*
PRONOUN **2** You can use **this** to introduce someone. ***This** is Ranjit.*

**thistle** **thistles**

NOUN A **thistle** is a wild plant with prickly leaves and purple flowers.

**thorn** **thorns**

NOUN A **thorn** is one of the sharp points on the stem of a plant such as a rose.

## thorough

ADJECTIVE **1** Someone who is **thorough** is always careful in their work.

ADJECTIVE **2** A **thorough** action is one that is done carefully and completely. *The doctor gave him a **thorough** examination.*

**thoroughly** ADVERB

## those

ADJECTIVE OR PRONOUN **Those** is the plural of **that**.

## though

CONJUNCTION **1** You say **though** before something that makes another part of the sentence rather surprising. *She didn't take a coat, **though** it was raining.*

CONJUNCTION **2** You can use **though** to mean if. *It looks as **though** you were right.*

## thought  **thoughts**

VERB **1** **Thought** is the past tense of **think**.

NOUN **2** A **thought** is an idea that you have in your mind.

NOUN **3** **Thought** is the action of thinking carefully about something.

## thoughtful

ADJECTIVE **1** If someone is **thoughtful**, they are thinking a lot.

ADJECTIVE **2** A **thoughtful** person remembers what other people want or need, and tries to be kind to them.

**thoughtfully** ADVERB

## thoughtless

ADJECTIVE If you are **thoughtless**, you do not think about what other people feel.

## thousand

A **thousand** is the number 1000.

## thread  **threads, threading, threaded**

NOUN **1** A **thread** is a long fine piece of cotton, silk, nylon or wool.

VERB **2** When you **thread** a needle, you put thread through the hole in the top.

## threat  **threats**

NOUN A **threat** is a warning that something unpleasant may happen.

## threaten  **threatens, threatening, threatened**

VERB If someone **threatens** you, they say that something unpleasant may happen if you do not do what they want.

## three-dimensional

ADJECTIVE A **three-dimensional** or **3D** object or shape is not flat. It has height or depth as well as length and width.

See *Solid shapes* on page 271.

## threw

VERB **Threw** is the past tense of **throw**.

## thrill  **thrills**

NOUN A **thrill** is a sudden feeling of great excitement or pleasure.

**thrilling** ADJECTIVE

## throat  **throats**

NOUN **1** Your **throat** is the back of your mouth and the top part of the passages inside your neck.

NOUN **2** The front part of your neck is also called your **throat**.

## throb  **throbs, throbbing, throbbed**

VERB **1** If a part of your body **throbs**, you feel a series of strong beats or dull pains.

VERB **2** If something **throbs**, it vibrates and makes a loud rhythmic noise.

## throne  **thrones**

NOUN A **throne** is a special chair used by kings and queens on important occasions.

## through

PREPOSITION **Through** means moving from one side of something to the other. *We found a path **through** the woods.*

225

# throw

**throw** throws, throwing, threw, thrown
VERB If you **throw** an object that you are holding, you send it through the air.

**thrush** thrushes
NOUN A **thrush** is a songbird with a brown back and a pale spotted chest.

**thrust** thrusts, thrusting, thrust
VERB If you **thrust** something somewhere, you push or move it there quickly with a lot of force.

**thud** thuds
NOUN A **thud** is a dull sound, such as a heavy object makes when it falls onto a carpet.

**thumb** thumbs
NOUN Your **thumb** is the short thick finger on the side of your hand.

**thump** thumps, thumping, thumped
VERB If you **thump** something, you hit it hard, usually with your fist. *He shouted and **thumped** the table.*

**thunder**
NOUN **Thunder** is the loud noise that you hear after a flash of lightning in a storm.

**thunderstorm** thunderstorms
NOUN A **thunderstorm** is a storm with thunder, lightning and heavy rain.

**Thursday** Thursdays
NOUN **Thursday** is the day between Wednesday and Friday.

**tick** ticks
NOUN A **tick** is a sign to show that something is correct. *2+2=4* ✓

**ticket** tickets
NOUN A **ticket** is a small piece of card or paper that shows that you have paid for something such as a train ride.

**tickle** tickles, tickling, tickled
VERB When you **tickle** someone, you move your fingers lightly over their body to make them laugh.

**tide** tides
NOUN The **tide** is the regular change in the level of the sea on the shore.

**tidy** tidier, tidiest; tidies, tidying, tidied
ADJECTIVE **1** Something that is **tidy** is neat and well arranged.
VERB **2** When you **tidy** a room, you put things away in their proper place.
**tidily** ADVERB

**tie** ties, tying, tied
NOUN **1** A **tie** is a long narrow piece of cloth that is worn round the neck.
NOUN **2** A **tie** in a race or competition is when two people have the same result.
VERB **3** If you **tie** an object to something, you fasten it with something such as string.

**tiger** tigers
NOUN A **tiger** is a large wild cat that lives in Asia. Its fur is usually orange with black stripes.

**tight** tighter, tightest
ADJECTIVE **1** Clothes that are **tight** fit too closely to your body.
ADJECTIVE **2** Something that is **tight** is firmly fastened and difficult to move.

**tights**
PLURAL NOUN **Tights** are a piece of clothing made of thin material that fit closely over your hips, legs and feet.

**tile** tiles
NOUN A **tile** is a small thin piece of something such as slate or carpet, that is used to cover surfaces.

**till** tills
PREPOSITION OR CONJUNCTION **1 Till** means the same as until. *Wait **till** morning... Wait **till** I get back.*
NOUN **2** A **till** is a drawer or box in a shop or bank where money is kept.

**tilt** tilts, tilting, tilted
VERB If you **tilt** something, you make it slope.

**timber**
NOUN **Timber** is wood used for building, and making furniture.

**time**
NOUN 1 **Time** is what is measured in seconds, minutes, hours, days and years. *See Time on page 268.*
NOUN 2 If it is **time** to do something, that thing ought to be done now.

**times**
NOUN 1 **Times** is used after numbers to say how often something happens.
NOUN 2 In maths, **times** is used to link numbers that are multiplied together. *Four times three is twelve.*

**timetable** timetables
NOUN A **timetable** is a list of the times when things happen, or when trains and buses go.

**timid**
ADJECTIVE A **timid** person is not brave.

**tin** tins
NOUN 1 **Tin** is a soft silvery-white metal.
NOUN 2 A **tin** is a metal container with a lid, for storing food.

**tingle** tingles, tingling, tingled
VERB When part of your body **tingles**, you feel a slight prickling or stinging.

**tinkle** tinkles, tinkling, tinkled
VERB If something **tinkles**, it makes a sound like a small bell ringing.

**tinned**
ADJECTIVE **Tinned** food has been preserved by being sealed in a tin.

**tin opener** tin openers
NOUN A **tin opener** is something you use for opening tins of food.

**tiny** tinier, tiniest
ADJECTIVE Something that is **tiny** is very small.

**tip** tips, tipping, tipped
VERB 1 If you **tip** an object, you move it so that it is no longer straight. *She **tipped** her chair back and almost fell over.*
NOUN 2 The **tip** of something long and narrow is the end of it.

**tiptoe** tiptoes, tiptoeing, tiptoed
VERB If you **tiptoe** somewhere, you walk there very quietly on your toes.

**tired**
ADJECTIVE If you are **tired**, you feel that you want to rest or sleep.

**tissue** tissues
NOUN A **tissue** is a piece of soft paper that you can use as a handkerchief.

**title** titles
NOUN 1 A **title** is the name of something such as a book or film.
NOUN 2 Someone's **title** is a name such as Mr, Mrs or Sir, that goes in front of their own name.

**toad** toads
NOUN A **toad** is an amphibian. It looks like a frog but it has a drier skin and lives mostly on land. *See Amphibians on page 259.*

**toadstool** toadstools
NOUN A **toadstool** is a type of poisonous fungus.

**toast**
NOUN **Toast** is a slice of bread made brown and crisp by heating.

**toboggan** toboggans
NOUN A **toboggan** is a vehicle for travelling on snow. It has a flat seat, with two metal or wooden runners.

a b c d e f g h i j k l m n o p q r s **Tt** u v w x y z

**today**

ADVERB **Today** is the day that is happening now.

**toddler  toddlers**

NOUN A **toddler** is a small child who has only just learned to walk.

**toe  toes**

NOUN Your **toes** are the five parts at the end of your foot which you can move.

**toffee  toffees**

NOUN A **toffee** is a sticky, chewy sweet made from butter and sugar.

**together**

ADVERB **1** If two people do something **together**, they both do it.

ADVERB **2** If two things happen **together**, they happen at the same time.

**toilet  toilets**

NOUN **1** A **toilet** is a bowl connected to a drain and fitted with a seat. You use it to get rid of waste matter from your body.

NOUN **2** A **toilet** is also a small room containing a toilet.

**told**

VERB **Told** is the past tense of **tell**.

**tomato  tomatoes**

NOUN A **tomato** is a soft, small red fruit. It can be cooked or eaten raw in salads. See *Fruit* on page 257.

**tomorrow**

ADVERB **Tomorrow** is the day after today.

**ton  tons**

NOUN A **ton** is a unit of weight equal to about 1000 kilograms.

**tongue  tongues**

NOUN Your **tongue** is the soft, moving part inside your mouth. You use your tongue for tasting, eating and speaking.

**tongue twister  tongue twisters**

NOUN A **tongue twister** is a sentence or expression which is difficult to say properly. For example, "She sells seashells on the seashore" is a tongue twister.

**tonight**

ADVERB **Tonight** is the evening of today or the night that follows today.

**tonne  tonnes**

NOUN A **tonne** is a metric measure of weight. It is equal to 1000 kilograms.

**too**

ADVERB **1 Too** means also, or as well. *I was there **too**.*

ADVERB **2 Too** also means more than is needed. *I've had **too** much to eat.*

**took**

VERB **Took** is the past tense of **take**.

**tool  tools**

NOUN A **tool** is anything that you use to help you do something, such as a hammer.

**tooth  teeth**

NOUN **1** A **tooth** is one of the hard white objects in your mouth. You use your teeth for biting and chewing food.

NOUN **2** The **teeth** of a comb, saw or zip are the parts that stick out in a row.

**toothbrush  toothbrushes**

NOUN A **toothbrush** is a small brush that you use for cleaning your teeth.

**toothpaste**

NOUN **Toothpaste** is a substance which you use to clean your teeth.

**top  tops**

NOUN **1** The **top** of something is its highest point, part or surface.

NOUN **2** The **top** of a bottle, jar or tube is its cap or lid.

**topic  topics**

NOUN A **topic** is a particular subject that you write or talk about.

**torch** torches

NOUN A **torch** is a small electric lamp which you can carry in your hand.

**tore**

VERB **Tore** is the past tense of **tear**.

**torn**

VERB **Torn** is the past participle of **tear**.

**tornado** tornadoes or tornados

NOUN A **tornado** is a very strong wind that moves round in a circle and can cause a lot of damage.

**tortoise** tortoises

NOUN A **tortoise** is a slow-moving reptile with a hard thick shell.
See *Reptiles* on page 259.

**toss** tosses, tossing, tossed

VERB **1** If you **toss** something, you throw it lightly and carelessly.
VERB **2** If something **tosses**, it keeps moving from side to side.

**total** totals

NOUN **1** A **total** is the number you get when you add several numbers together.
ADJECTIVE **2** Total means complete.
*The party was a total success.*

**touch** touches, touching, touched

VERB **1** If you **touch** something, you feel it with your hand.
VERB **2** If two things are **touching**, there is no space between them.

**tough** tougher, toughest

ADJECTIVE Something that is **tough** is strong and difficult to cut, tear or break.

**tour** tours

NOUN A **tour** is a journey to visit interesting places.

**tourist** tourists

NOUN A **tourist** is a person who visits places for pleasure and interest.

**tournament** tournaments

NOUN A **tournament** is a competition in which lots of matches are played, until just one person or team is left.

**tow** tows, towing, towed

VERB If a vehicle **tows** another vehicle, it pulls it along behind.

**towards**

PREPOSITION **1** If you move **towards** something, you go in that direction.
PREPOSITION **2** If you give money **towards** something, you help pay for it.

**towel** towels

NOUN A **towel** is a piece of soft thick cloth that you use to dry yourself with.

**tower** towers

NOUN A **tower** is a tall narrow building or a tall part of a building.

**town** towns

NOUN A **town** is a place with a lot of streets and buildings where people live and work.

**toy** toys

NOUN A **toy** is something you play with, such as a doll or a model car.

**trace** traces, tracing, traced

VERB **1** If you **trace** something such as a map, you copy it by covering it with a piece of thin paper and drawing over the lines underneath.
VERB **2** If you **trace** something, you find it after looking for it.

**track** tracks

NOUN **1** A **track** is a rough narrow road or path.
NOUN **2** A **track** is also a special road or path that is used for racing.
NOUN **3** A railway **track** is a strip of ground with rails that trains travel on.

**tracksuit** tracksuits

NOUN A **tracksuit** is a loose warm suit of trousers and a top, worn for outdoor sports.

a
b
c
d
e
f
g
h
i
j
k
l
m
n
o
p
q
r
s
**Tt**
u
v
w
x
y
z

# tractor

**tractor** tractors

NOUN A **tractor** is a vehicle with large rear wheels. Tractors are used on farms for pulling or lifting things.

**trade** trades

NOUN **Trade** is the buying and selling of goods or services. Trade can be between people, companies or countries.

**trademark** trademarks

NOUN A **trademark** is a name or symbol that a manufacturer always uses on its products. It is usually protected by law so that nobody else can use it.

**tradition** traditions

NOUN A **tradition** is something that people have done or believed in for a long time.
**traditional** ADJECTIVE
**traditionally** ADVERB

**traffic**

NOUN **Traffic** is the movement of vehicles on the road, in the air or on water.

**traffic light** traffic lights

NOUN **Traffic lights** are special signals to control the flow of traffic. Red lights mean stop and green lights mean go.

**traffic warden** traffic wardens

NOUN A **traffic warden** is a person who makes sure that cars are parked correctly.

**tragedy** tragedies

NOUN **1** A **tragedy** is an event or situation that is very sad.
NOUN **2** A **tragedy** is also a serious play, that usually ends with the death of the main character.
**tragic** ADJECTIVE

**trail** trails, trailing, trailed

NOUN **1** A **trail** is a rough path across open country or through forests.
NOUN **2** A **trail** is also the scent, footprints and other signs that people and animals leave behind them.
VERB **3** If you **trail** something or it **trails**, it drags along behind you.

**trailer** trailers

NOUN **1** A **trailer** is a vehicle pulled by a car, used for carrying things.
NOUN **2** A **trailer** can also be a series of short pieces from a film or television programme in order to advertise it.

**train** trains, training, trained

NOUN **1** A **train** is a number of carriages or trucks which are joined together and pulled by an engine along a railway.
VERB **2** If someone **trains** you to do a job, they teach you the skills you need.
VERB **3** If you **train** a dog, you teach it to behave properly.

**trainer** trainers

NOUN **1** A **trainer** is a person who coaches people in sports such as boxing.
NOUN **2** **Trainers** are special shoes people wear for running or jogging.

**tram** trams

NOUN A **tram** is a vehicle which runs on rails along the street.

**trampoline** trampolines

NOUN A **trampoline** is something that is used for jumping on. It is made of strong cloth held into a frame by springs.

**transfer** transfers, transferring, transferred

VERB If you **transfer** something, you move it to a different place or position.

**translate** translates, translating, translated
VERB If you **translate** something, you put the words into a different language.
**translation** NOUN

**translucent**
ADJECTIVE If something is **translucent**, light passes through it so that it glows.

**transparent**
ADJECTIVE If something is **transparent**, it lets light through and you can see through it.

**transplant** transplants
NOUN A **transplant** is an operation to put part of one person's body into another person.

**transport**
NOUN **Transport** is using vehicles to move people and things from one place to another.

**trap** traps, trapping, trapped
NOUN **1** A **trap** is something that is specially made to catch animals.
VERB **2** If a person is **trapped**, they cannot escape.

**trap door** trap doors
NOUN A **trap door** is a small door in a floor or ceiling.

**trapeze** trapezes
NOUN A **trapeze** is a bar hung from a high place by ropes. People swing from trapezes in circuses.

**travel** travels, travelling, travelled
VERB If you **travel**, you go from one place to another.
**traveller** NOUN

**tray** trays
NOUN A **tray** is a flat object with raised edges, used for carrying food or drinks.

**treacherous**
ADJECTIVE **1** A person who is **treacherous** cannot be trusted.
ADJECTIVE **2** If something like the sea is **treacherous**, it is dangerous.

**treacle**
NOUN **Treacle** is a thick sweet sticky liquid made from sugar.

**tread** treads, treading, trod, trodden
VERB If you **tread** on something, you walk on it or step on it.

**treasure** treasures
NOUN **Treasure** is valuable things such as jewels or paintings.

**treat** treats, treating, treated
VERB **1** If you **treat** someone in a certain way, you behave that way towards them. *My uncle **treats** me as if I'm five.*
VERB **2** If someone **treats** a person who is ill, they help them get well again.
NOUN **3** A **treat** is something enjoyable.

**tree** trees
NOUN A **tree** is a large plant with a hard woody trunk, branches and leaves.

**tremble** trembles, trembling, trembled
VERB If you **tremble**, you shake slightly, because you are frightened or cold.

**trespass** trespasses, trespassing, trespassed
VERB To **trespass** means to go on someone else's land without asking.

**trial** trials
NOUN **1** A **trial** is when you try something out to see if it works.
NOUN **2** In law, a **trial** is a time in court. People decide whether a person is guilty of a crime.

**triangle** triangles
NOUN A **triangle** is a flat shape with three straight sides and three angles.
**triangular** ADJECTIVE
See *Colours and flat shapes* on page 271.

a
b
c
d
e
f
g
h
i
j
k
l
m
n
o
p
q
r
s
**Tt**
u
v
w
x
y
z

# tribe

**tribe** tribes

NOUN A **tribe** is a group of people of the same race, customs and language, who are ruled by one chief.

**trick** tricks, tricking, tricked

NOUN **1** A **trick** is a clever or skilful act that someone does to entertain people.
VERB **2** If a person **tricks** someone, they deceive them.

**trickle** trickles, trickling, trickled

VERB When a liquid **trickles**, it flows slowly in small amounts.

**tricycle** tricycles

NOUN A **tricycle** is a vehicle similar to a bicycle, but with three wheels.

**tried**

VERB **Tried** is the past tense of **try**.

**tries**

VERB **Tries** is a present tense form of **try**.

**trifle** trifles

NOUN **Trifle** is a cold pudding made of layers of sponge, fruit, jelly and custard.

**trigger** triggers

NOUN A **trigger** is a small lever on a gun, which is pulled to fire the gun.

**trim** trims, trimming, trimmed

VERB If a person **trims** something, such as a hedge or your hair, they cut off small amounts of it to make it neat.

**trip** trips, tripping, tripped

NOUN **1** A **trip** is a journey to a place and back again.
VERB **2** If you **trip**, you catch your foot on something and fall over.

**triumph** triumphs

NOUN A **triumph** is a great success.

**triumphant**

ADJECTIVE Someone who is **triumphant** feels extremely happy because they have been very successful.

**trod**

VERB **Trod** is the past tense of **tread**.

**trolley** trolleys

NOUN A **trolley** is a small cart on wheels used for carrying heavy objects.

**troops**

PLURAL NOUN **Troops** are soldiers.

**trophy** trophies

NOUN A **trophy** is a cup or shield given to the winner of a competition.

**tropical**

ADJECTIVE **Tropical** means to do with the tropics, which are the hottest part of the world, near the equator.

**trot** trots, trotting, trotted

VERB When a horse **trots**, it moves at a speed a little faster than a walk.

**trouble** troubles

NOUN **Trouble** is something that worries or bothers you.

**trough** troughs

NOUN A **trough** is a long narrow container which holds food or drink for farm animals.

**trousers**

PLURAL NOUN **Trousers** are a piece of clothing for the body from the waist down, with a separate part for each leg.

**trout**

NOUN A **trout** is a fish that lives in lakes and rivers.

**trowel** trowels

NOUN A **trowel** is a small garden tool with a curved and pointed blade used for planting or weeding.

**truant** truants

NOUN A **truant** is a child who stays away from school without permission.

**truce** truces

NOUN A **truce** is an agreement between two people or groups to stop fighting or quarrelling for a time.

**truck** trucks

NOUN **1** A **truck** is a large motor vehicle which is open at the back. Trucks are used for carrying heavy loads.

NOUN **2** A **truck** is also an open vehicle used for carrying things on a railway.

**trudge** trudges, trudging, trudged

VERB If you **trudge**, you walk with slow heavy steps.

**true** truer, truest

ADJECTIVE **1** A **true** story or statement is based on facts and is not made up.

ADJECTIVE **2** **True** feelings are sincere.

**truly** ADVERB

**trumpet** trumpets

NOUN A **trumpet** is a brass musical instrument that you blow into.

**trunk** trunks

NOUN **1** The **trunk** of a tree is its main stem, from which the branches grow.

NOUN **2** An elephant's **trunk** is its long flexible nose.

NOUN **3** A **trunk** is also a large box with a lid used for storing things.

**trust** trusts, trusting, trusted

VERB If you **trust** someone, you believe that they are honest and will not do anything to hurt you.

**truth**

NOUN The **truth** is the facts about something or someone, rather than things that are imagined or made up.

**truthful**

ADJECTIVE A **truthful** person is honest and tells the truth.

**truthfully** ADVERB

**try** tries, trying, tried

VERB **1** If you **try** to do something, you do your best to do it.

VERB **2** If you **try** something, you test it to see what it is like.

**T-shirt** T-shirts

NOUN A **T-shirt** is a simple short-sleeved cotton shirt with no collar.

**tub** tubs

NOUN A **tub** is a round container for food.

**tube** tubes

NOUN **1** A **tube** is a round hollow pipe.

NOUN **2** A **tube** is also a container with a cap at one end that you squeeze to get the contents out.

**tuck** tucks, tucking, tucked

VERB If you **tuck** something, you put the end of it under or into something else. *He **tucked** his shirt into his trousers.*

**Tuesday** Tuesdays

NOUN **Tuesday** is the day after Monday and before Wednesday.

**tuft** tufts

NOUN A **tuft** of something, such as hair, is a bunch of it growing closely together.

**tug** tugs, tugging, tugged

VERB If you **tug** something, you give it a quick strong pull.

**tug-of-war**

NOUN A **tug-of-war** is a sport in which two teams pull against each other on opposite ends of a rope.

**tulip** tulips

NOUN A **tulip** is a spring flower shaped like an upside-down bell.

**tumble** tumbles, tumbling, tumbled

VERB If you **tumble**, you fall over and over.

**tuna**

NOUN **Tuna** are large edible fish that live in warm seas.

**tune** tunes

NOUN A **tune** is a series of musical notes that are nice to listen to.

a b c d e f g h i j k l m n o p q r s **Tt** u v w x y z

# tunnel

**tunnel** tunnels

NOUN A **tunnel** is a long passage under the ground or through a hill.

**turkey** turkeys

NOUN A **turkey** is a large bird that is kept on a farm for its meat.

**turn** turns, turning, turned

VERB **1** When you **turn**, you move so that you are facing a different way.

VERB **2** When you **turn** something, you move it round.

VERB **3** When something **turns into** something else, it becomes that thing. *When water freezes, it **turns into** ice.*

NOUN **4** If people take **turns** to do something, they do it one after the other.

**turnip** turnips

NOUN A **turnip** is a round root vegetable with a white or yellow skin. *See Vegetables on page 256.*

**turquoise**

ADJECTIVE Something **turquoise** is a blue-green colour. *See Colours on page 271.*

**turtle** turtles

NOUN A **turtle** is a large reptile with a thick shell. It lives mostly in the sea. *See Reptiles on page 259.*

**tusk** tusks

NOUN **Tusks** are long pointed teeth that some animals have. For example, elephants and walruses have tusks.

**TV** TVs

NOUN **TV** is an abbreviation of **television**.

**twice**

ADVERB **Twice** means two times.

**twig** twigs

NOUN A **twig** is a small thin branch of a tree or bush.

**twilight**

NOUN **Twilight** is the time after sunset when it is just getting dark.

**twin** twins

NOUN If two people are **twins**, they have the same mother and were born on the same day.

**twinkle** twinkles, twinkling, twinkled

VERB If something **twinkles**, it shines with little flashes.

**twirl** twirls, twirling, twirled

VERB If something **twirls**, or if you twirl it, it spins round and round.

**twist** twists, twisting, twisted

VERB **1** When you **twist** something, you turn one end in the opposite direction to the other.

VERB **2** When something **twists**, it moves or bends into a strange shape.

**two-dimensional**

ADJECTIVE Something that is **two-dimensional**, or **2D**, is a flat shape. For example, a circle is two-dimensional. *See Colours and flat shapes on page 271.*

**tying**

VERB **Tying** is a present tense form of **tie**.

**type** types, typing, typed

NOUN **1** **Type** means kind or sort. *What type of plant is it?*

VERB **2** If you **type** words, you use a computer or typewriter.

**typhoon** typhoons

NOUN A **typhoon** is a storm with extremely strong winds.

**typical**

ADJECTIVE Something that is **typical** is what you would expect.

**tyre** tyres

NOUN A **tyre** is a thick ring of rubber fitted round each wheel of a vehicle.

a b c d e f g h i j k l m n o p q r s **Tt** u v w x y z

# Uu

### ugly   uglier, ugliest

ADJECTIVE Someone or something that is **ugly** is not pleasant to look at.

### umbrella   umbrellas

NOUN An **umbrella** is a shelter from the rain. It consists of a folding frame covered in thin cloth, attached to a long stick.

### un-

PREFIX **Un-** is added to the beginning of a word to make it mean the opposite, for example "happy" → "unhappy". *See Prefixes on page 264.*

### unable

ADJECTIVE If you are **unable** to do something, you cannot do it.

### unaware

ADJECTIVE If you are **unaware** of something, you do not know about it.

### unbearable

ADJECTIVE Something **unbearable** is so unpleasant, painful or upsetting you feel you cannot stand it.

### unbelievable

ADJECTIVE **1** Something **unbelievable** is extremely great or surprising. *She showed* **unbelievable** *courage.*

ADJECTIVE **2 Unbelievable** can also be used to describe something that is so unlikely you cannot believe it.

### unbreakable

ADJECTIVE Something that is **unbreakable** cannot be broken.

### uncertain

ADJECTIVE If you are **uncertain**, you are not sure what to do.

### uncle   uncles

NOUN Your **uncle** is the brother of one of your parents, or your aunt's husband.

### uncomfortable

ADJECTIVE If you are **uncomfortable**, you do not feel easy.

### uncommon

ADJECTIVE Something **uncommon** does not often happen, or is not often seen.

### unconscious

ADJECTIVE Someone who is **unconscious** is unable to see, hear or feel anything that is going on. This is usually because they have fainted or have been badly injured.

### under

PREPOSITION **1 Under** means below or beneath.

PREPOSITION **2 Under** can also mean less than. *Children* **under** *five can go in free.*

### under-

PREFIX **1 Under-** is added to the beginning of a word to form a new word meaning under the thing mentioned, for example "ground" → "underground".

PREFIX **2 Under-** can also be used as a prefix to mean not enough. *The hungry rabbit was* **underfed**.

*See Prefixes on page 264.*

a
b
c
d
e
f
g
h
i
j
k
l
m
n
o
p
q
r
s
t
**Uu**
v
w
x
y
z

## underground

ADJECTIVE **1** Something **underground** is below the surface of the ground.

NOUN **2** The **underground** is a railway that runs in tunnels under some cities.

## undergrowth

NOUN **Undergrowth** is bushes or plants growing together under the trees in a forest or jungle.

## underline  underlines, underlining, underlined

VERB If you **underline** a word or sentence, you draw a line under it.

## underneath

PREPOSITION OR ADVERB **Underneath** means below or beneath. *They found the missing card* **underneath** *the table... They couldn't move the car because their cat was* **underneath***.*

## understand  understands, understanding, understood

VERB If you **understand** something, you know what it means.

## underwear

NOUN Your **underwear** is the clothing that you wear next to your skin under your other clothes.

## undo  undoes, undoing, undid, undone

VERB If you **undo** something that is tied up, you untie it.

## undress  undresses, undressing, undressed

VERB When you **undress**, you take off your clothes.

## uneasy

ADJECTIVE If you are **uneasy**, you are worried that something is wrong.

## unemployed

ADJECTIVE Someone who is **unemployed** does not have a job.

## uneven

ADJECTIVE Something that is **uneven** does not have a flat, smooth surface.

## unexpected

ADJECTIVE Something that is **unexpected** surprises you.
**unexpectedly** ADVERB

## unfair

ADJECTIVE If you think that something is **unfair**, it does not seem right or reasonable to you.
**unfairly** ADVERB

## unfortunate

ADJECTIVE **1** Someone who is **unfortunate** is unlucky.
ADJECTIVE **2** If you say something is **unfortunate**, you mean you wish it had not happened.
**unfortunately** ADVERB

## unfriendly

ADJECTIVE Someone who is **unfriendly** is not kind to you.

## ungrateful

ADJECTIVE If someone is **ungrateful**, they are not thankful for something that has been given to them or done for them.

## unhappy  unhappier, unhappiest

ADJECTIVE Someone who is **unhappy** is sad or miserable.
**unhappily** ADVERB

## unhealthy  unhealthier, unhealthiest

ADJECTIVE **1** Someone who is **unhealthy** is often ill.
ADJECTIVE **2** Something that is **unhealthy** is likely to cause illness.

## unicorn  unicorns

NOUN A **unicorn** is an imaginary animal like a white horse with a horn in the middle of its forehead.

**uniform**  **uniforms**

NOUN A **uniform** is a special set of clothes that is worn by people to show that they belong to the same group.

**unique**

ADJECTIVE If something is **unique**, it is the only one of its kind.

**unit**  **units**

NOUN **1** A **unit** is an amount that is used for measuring things. For example, a second is a unit of time.

NOUN **2** In maths, the number of ones is the number of **units**. *The number 37 has 3 tens and 7 **units**.*

**unite**  **unites, uniting, united**

VERB If people **unite**, they work as a group.

**united** ADJECTIVE

**universe**

NOUN The **universe** is the whole of space including all the stars and planets.

**university**  **universities**

NOUN A **university** is a place where people can carry on their education when they have left school.

**unkind**

ADJECTIVE Someone who is **unkind** is rather cruel and unpleasant.

**unleaded**

ADJECTIVE **Unleaded** petrol has a smaller amount of lead in it, in order to reduce the pollution from vehicles.

**unless**

CONJUNCTION You use **unless** to introduce a condition which is necessary for something else to happen. *I won't come **unless** you invite me.*

**unlike**

PREPOSITION If one thing is **unlike** another, the two things are different.

**unlikely**

ADJECTIVE If something is **unlikely**, it is probably not true or probably will not happen.

**unload**  **unloads, unloading, unloaded**

VERB If people **unload** something, such as a lorry, they take the load off it.

**unlock**  **unlocks, unlocking, unlocked**

VERB If you **unlock** something, such as a door, you open it with a key.

**unlucky**

ADJECTIVE Someone who is **unlucky** has bad luck.

**unluckily** ADVERB

**unnatural**

ADJECTIVE Something **unnatural** is strange because it is not usual. *There was an **unnatural** stillness.*

**unnaturally** ADVERB

**unnecessary**

ADJECTIVE Something that is **unnecessary** is not needed.

**unpack**  **unpacks, unpacking, unpacked**

VERB When you **unpack**, you take everything out of a suitcase, bag or box.

**unpleasant**

ADJECTIVE Something that is **unpleasant** is rather nasty and not enjoyable.

**unpopular**

ADJECTIVE Someone or something that is **unpopular** is disliked by most people.

**unsafe**

ADJECTIVE If something like a building or a machine is **unsafe**, it is dangerous.

**unselfish**

ADJECTIVE People who are **unselfish** care more about other people than they do about themselves.

a
b
c
d
e
f
g
h
i
j
k
l
m
n
o
p
q
r
s
t
**Uu**
v
w
x
y
z

# untidy

**untidy** untidier, untidiest
ADJECTIVE **1** Someone who is **untidy** does not care whether things are neat and well arranged.
ADJECTIVE **2** An **untidy** place is not neat or well arranged.

**untie** unties, untying, untied
VERB If you **untie** something, you undo the knots in the string around it.

**until**
PREPOSITION OR CONJUNCTION **Until** means up to a certain time. *The shop was open **until** midnight... He waited **until** the dog was asleep.*

**untrue**
ADJECTIVE Something that is **untrue** is false and not based on facts.

**unusual**
ADJECTIVE Someone or something that is **unusual** is different from the ordinary.

**up**
PREPOSITION OR ADVERB **1** Up means towards or in a higher place. *She ran **up** the stairs... It was high **up** in the mountains.*
ADVERB **2** If an amount of something goes **up**, it increases. *The price of butter has gone **up**.*

**upper-case**
ADJECTIVE **Upper-case** letters are capital letters. See **lower-case**.

**upright**
ADJECTIVE If you are **upright**, you are standing up straight.

**uproar** uproars
NOUN An **uproar** is a lot of noise and shouting.

**upset** upsets, upsetting, upset
VERB **1** If someone **upsets** something, they turn it over by accident. *He **upset** a tin of paint on the carpet.*
ADJECTIVE **2** If you are **upset**, you are unhappy or disappointed.

**upside down**
ADJECTIVE Something that is **upside down** has been turned so that the part that should be at the top is at the bottom.

**upstairs**
ADVERB **1** If you go **upstairs** in a building, you go up to a higher floor.
ADVERB **2** Someone or something that is **upstairs** is on a higher floor than you.

**up-to-date**
ADJECTIVE Something that is **up-to-date** is new or modern.

**urgent**
ADJECTIVE Something that is **urgent** needs to be done at once.

**use** uses, using, used
VERB If you **use** something, you do something with it that helps you.

**used**
VERB Something that **used** to be done was done in the past.
**used to** PHRASE If you are **used to** something, you are familiar with it and have often experienced it.

**useful**
ADJECTIVE If something is **useful**, it helps you in some way.

**useless**
ADJECTIVE If something is **useless**, you cannot use it.

**usual**
ADJECTIVE Something that is **usual** happens, or is done or used, most often.

**usually**
ADVERB If something **usually** happens, it happens most often.

# Vv

**vacant**

ADJECTIVE Somewhere that is **vacant** has nobody in it.

**vaccination**  **vaccinations**

NOUN A **vaccination** is an injection that stops you getting an illness.

**vacuum cleaner**  **vacuum cleaners**

NOUN A **vacuum cleaner** is an electric machine which cleans by sucking up dirt.

**vagina**  **vaginas**

NOUN The **vagina** is an opening in a woman's body through which babies pass when they are being born.

**vague**  **vaguer, vaguest**

ADJECTIVE Things that are **vague** are not definite or clear. *He had a vague feeling he should be doing something.*

**vain**

ADJECTIVE A **vain** person is too proud of how they look or what they can do.

**valley**  **valleys**

NOUN A **valley** is a low piece of land between hills. Valleys often have rivers flowing through them.

**valuable**

ADJECTIVE **1** Things that are **valuable** are worth a lot of money.

ADJECTIVE **2** Help or advice that is **valuable** is very useful.

**value**

NOUN **1** The **value** of something is its importance or usefulness.

NOUN **2** The **value** of something such as jewellery is the amount of money that it is worth.

**vampire**  **vampires**

NOUN In horror stories, **vampires** are creatures that suck the blood of living people.

**van**  **vans**

NOUN A **van** is a vehicle larger than a car but smaller than a lorry. Vans are used for carrying goods.

**vandal**  **vandals**

NOUN A **vandal** is someone who damages something useful or beautiful on purpose and for no good reason.

**vanilla**

NOUN **Vanilla** is a flavouring for food. It comes from the pods of a tropical plant.

**vanish**  **vanishes, vanishing, vanished**

VERB If something **vanishes**, it disappears suddenly.

**vapour**  **vapours**

NOUN **Vapour** is a mass of tiny drops of water or other liquids in the air, which appear as clouds, mist or fumes.

**variety**  **variety**

NOUN A **variety** of things is lots of different types.

**various**

ADJECTIVE You say **various** to mean several different things of one kind. *There were various questions she wanted to ask.*

**vase**  **vases**

NOUN A **vase** is a kind of jar used as an ornament, or to hold cut flowers.

**vast**

ADJECTIVE Something that is **vast** is extremely large.

a b c d e f g h i j k l m n o p q r s t u **Vv** w x y z

239

**vegetable** **vegetables**

NOUN **Vegetables** are plants, or parts of plants such as leaves, that can be eaten.

See *Vegetables* on page 256.

**vegetarian** **vegetarians**

NOUN A **vegetarian** is a person who does not eat meat or fish.

**vehicle** **vehicles**

NOUN A **vehicle** is a machine such as a car or bus that carries people or things from place to place.

**veil** **veils**

NOUN A **veil** is a piece of thin soft cloth that some women wear over their face or head.

**vein** **veins**

NOUN A **vein** is a tube inside the body which carries blood to the heart.

**velvet**

NOUN **Velvet** is a material which has soft short threads on one side.

**verb** **verbs**

NOUN In grammar, a **verb** is a word that expresses actions and states, for example "take" and "run".

See *Verb* on page 263.

**verdict** **verdicts**

NOUN In a law court, a **verdict** is whether a prisoner is guilty or not guilty.

**verse** **verses**

NOUN 1 **Verse** is another word for poetry.

NOUN 2 A **verse** is one of the parts that a poem or song is divided into.

**version** **versions**

NOUN A **version** of something is a form of it in which some details are different from earlier or later forms. *This is a different **version** of my story.*

**vertex** **vertexes** or **vertices**

NOUN 1 The **vertex** of something is its highest point.

NOUN 2 The **vertex** can also be the corner point of a polygon or polyhedron. For example, a triangle has three vertices and a cuboid has eight.

**vertical**

ADJECTIVE Something that is **vertical** stands straight up from a flat surface. See **horizontal**.

**very**

ADVERB **Very** is used before words to make them stronger. *He had **very** bad dreams.*

**vessel** **vessels**

NOUN A **vessel** is a ship or boat.

**vest** **vests**

NOUN A **vest** is a piece of underwear for the top half of the body.

**vet** **vets**

NOUN A **vet** is a person whose job is to look after sick and injured animals. Vet is an abbreviation of **veterinary surgeon**.

**via**

PREPOSITION If you go **via** a particular place, you go through it to get to somewhere else. *We go to Cambridge **via** the Dartford Tunnel.*

**viaduct** **viaducts**

NOUN A **viaduct** is a long high bridge that carries a road or railway across a valley.

**vibrate** **vibrates, vibrating, vibrated**

VERB If something **vibrates**, it shakes with a very slight, very quick movement.

**vicious**

ADJECTIVE Someone or something that is **vicious** is cruel and violent.

**victim** victims

NOUN A **victim** is someone who has been harmed or injured by someone or something.

**victory** victories

NOUN A **victory** is a success in a battle or competition.

**video** videos, videoing, videoed

NOUN **1** A **video** is a machine that records television programmes so that you can watch them later.

NOUN **2** A **video** is also a tape that you use to record television programmes.

NOUN **3** A **video** is also a taped recording of a film that you can watch on your television set.

VERB **4** If you **video** something, you record it on tape so that you can watch it later.

**view** views

NOUN The **view** from a window or a high place is everything that can be seen from there.

**village** villages

NOUN A **village** is a small group of houses and other buildings in a country area.

**vine** vines

NOUN A **vine** is a climbing plant that produces grapes.

**vinegar**

NOUN **Vinegar** is a sharp-tasting liquid that is used to add taste to some foods, and is also used for pickling.

**violence**

NOUN **Violence** is behaviour that is meant to hurt or kill people.

**violent**

ADJECTIVE **1** Someone who is **violent** uses force to hurt or kill people.

ADJECTIVE **2** Something that is **violent** happens suddenly and with great force. *A **violent** earthquake shook the city.*

**violently** ADVERB

**violet** violets

NOUN A **violet** is a small plant with purple or white flowers.

**violin** violins

NOUN A **violin** is a musical instrument with four strings. It is held under the chin and played with a bow.

**virtual**

ADJECTIVE **Virtual** means something that is very like a real thing but is not actually the same. *What he said was a **virtual** lie.*

**virtual reality**

NOUN **Virtual reality** is an image created by a computer that looks real to the person using it.

**virus** viruses

NOUN **1** A **virus** is a tiny germ which you cannot see without a microscope. Viruses can cause diseases.

NOUN **2** A disease caused by a virus can also be called a **virus**.

**visible**

ADJECTIVE Something that is **visible** can be seen.

**visibly** ADVERB

**vision** visions

NOUN **1** Vision is the ability to see clearly. *Your **vision** will be better if you wear glasses.*

NOUN **2** A **vision** is a picture in your mind.

**visit** visits, visiting, visited

VERB If you **visit** a person or a place, you go to see them.

**visitor** visitors

NOUN A **visitor** is someone who is visiting a person or place.

a
b
c
d
e
f
g
h
i
j
k
l
m
n
o
p
q
r
s
t
u
**Vv**
w
x
y
z

**vital**

ADJECTIVE If something is **vital** when you are doing something, you will not succeed without it. *It is **vital** to get the measurements exactly right.*

**vitamin** **vitamins**

NOUN A **vitamin** is one of the substances which you need to stay healthy. There are vitamins in many kinds of food.

**vivid**

ADJECTIVE **1** A **vivid** colour is very bright.
ADJECTIVE **2** Memories or descriptions that are **vivid** are clear and remain firmly fixed in your mind.
**vividly** ADVERB

**vixen** **vixens**

NOUN A **vixen** is a female fox.

**vocabulary**

NOUN Someone's **vocabulary** is the total number of words in a language that they know.

**voice** **voices**

NOUN **1** Someone's **voice** is the sound they make when they speak or sing.
NOUN **2** In grammar, the active **voice** and the passive voice refer to the relation between a verb and its subject. For example, the sentence "Tom hit the ball" is in the active voice, and "The ball was hit by Tom" is in the passive voice. See **active** and **passive**.

**volcano** **volcanoes**

NOUN A **volcano** is a mountain with a hole called a crater in the top. Sometimes hot melted rock, gas, steam and ash burst from the crater.

**volume** **volumes**

NOUN **1** A **volume** is a book.
NOUN **2** The **volume** of something is the amount of space that it takes up.

NOUN **3** The **volume** of something, such as a radio or television, is how loud or quiet its sound is. *He played his radio at full **volume**.*

**voluntary**

ADJECTIVE **1** **Voluntary** actions are ones that you offer to do, rather than being asked to or made to.
ADJECTIVE **2** **Voluntary** work is done by people who are not paid for what they do.
**voluntarily** ADVERB

**volunteer** **volunteers, volunteering, volunteered**

VERB **1** If you **volunteer** to do something, you offer to do it without expecting any reward.
NOUN **2** A **volunteer** is someone who does work for which they are not paid.

**vote** **votes, voting, voted**

VERB **1** If you **vote**, you make a choice, usually by raising your hand or writing on a piece of paper. *We **voted** for Tim as group leader.*
VERB **2** If you **vote** that a particular thing should happen, that is what you suggest. *I **vote** we all go swimming.*

**voucher** **vouchers**

NOUN A **voucher** is a ticket or piece of paper that can be used instead of money.

**vowel** **vowels**

NOUN In the English language, the letters a, e, i, o and u are **vowels**. See **consonant**.

**voyage** **voyages**

NOUN A **voyage** is a long journey on a ship or in a spacecraft.

**vulture** **vultures**

NOUN A **vulture** is a large bird which feeds on dead animals. Vultures live in hot countries.

### wade  wades, wading, waded
VERB To **wade** means to walk through fairly shallow water.

### wafer  wafers
NOUN A **wafer** is a thin crisp biscuit.

### wag  wags, wagging, wagged
VERB When a dog **wags** its tail, it waves it from side to side because it is happy.

### wagon  wagons
NOUN **1** A **wagon** is a strong cart for carrying heavy loads. Wagons are usually pulled by a horse or tractor.
VERB **2** A **wagon** is also a railway truck.

### wail  wails, wailing, wailed
VERB If someone **wails**, they make a long crying noise.

### waist  waists
NOUN Your **waist** is the narrow middle part of your body, just below your chest.

### wait  waits, waiting, waited
VERB If you **wait**, you spend time before something happens.

### wake  wakes, waking, woke, woken
VERB When you **wake**, you stop sleeping.

### walk  walks, walking, walked
VERB When you **walk**, you move along by putting one foot in front of the other.

### wall  walls
NOUN **1** A **wall** is one of the vertical sides of a building or a room.
NOUN **2** A **wall** can also be used to divide or go round an area of land.

### wallet  wallets
NOUN A **wallet** is a small flat case that fits in a pocket. It is used to hold things such as paper money and credit cards.

### wallpaper  wallpapers
NOUN **Wallpaper** is thick coloured or patterned paper that is used for covering and decorating the walls of a room.

### walnut  walnuts
NOUN A **walnut** is a nut with a wrinkled shape and a light brown shell.

### walrus  walruses
NOUN A **walrus** is a mammal that lives in the sea and looks like a large seal. It has coarse whiskers and two long tusks.

### wand  wands
NOUN A **wand** is a long thin rod that magicians wave when they are performing tricks and magic.

### wander  wanders, wandering, wandered
VERB If you **wander**, you walk around without going in any particular direction.

### want  wants, wanting, wanted
VERB If you **want** something, you wish for it or need it.

### war  wars
NOUN A **war** is a period of fighting between countries.

### wardrobe  wardrobes
NOUN A **wardrobe** is a tall cupboard where you can hang your clothes.

### warehouse  warehouses
NOUN A **warehouse** is a large building which is used to store things.

### warm  warmer, warmest
ADJECTIVE **1** Something that is **warm** has some heat but not enough to be hot.
ADJECTIVE **2** Clothes and blankets that are **warm** are made of a material that stops you feeling cold.

a b c d e f g h i j k l m n o p q r s t u v **Ww** x y z

# warmth

**warmth**
NOUN **Warmth** is a comfortable amount of heat.

**warn** **warns, warning, warned**
VERB If you **warn** someone, you tell them about a danger or problem that they might meet.

**warning** **warnings**
NOUN A **warning** is something that tells you about a possible problem or danger.

**warren** **warrens**
NOUN A **warren** is a group of holes in the ground which rabbits live in. The holes are connected by tunnels.

**wary** **warier, wariest**
ADJECTIVE If you are **wary** about something, you are careful because you are not sure about it.
**warily** ADVERB

**wash** **washes, washing, washed**
VERB If you **wash** something, you clean it with soap and water.

**washable**
ADJECTIVE Clothes or materials that are **washable** can be washed in water without being damaged.

**washing**
NOUN **Washing** is clothes, towels and bedding that need to be washed.

**washing machine** **washing machines**
NOUN A **washing machine** is a machine for washing clothes in.

**washing-up**
NOUN If you do the **washing-up**, you wash things such as plates, pans and knives after a meal.

**wasp** **wasps**
NOUN A **wasp** is a flying insect with yellow and black stripes across its body. Wasps can sting.

**waste** **wastes, wasting, wasted**
VERB **1** If you **waste** something, such as time or money, you use too much of it on something that is not important.
NOUN **2** Waste is material that is no longer wanted. This is often because the useful part of it has been taken out.

**watch** **watches, watching, watched**
NOUN **1** A **watch** is a small clock that you can wear on your wrist.
VERB **2** If you **watch** something, you look at it carefully to see what happens.

**water** **waters, watering, watered**
NOUN **1** Water is a clear liquid that all living things need in order to live.
VERB **2** If you **water** a plant or animal, you give it water to drink.

**waterfall** **waterfalls**
NOUN A **waterfall** is water that flows over the edge of a cliff to the ground below.

**waterlogged**
ADJECTIVE Land that is **waterlogged** is so wet the soil cannot contain any more water.

**waterproof**
ADJECTIVE A material that is **waterproof** does not let water pass through it.

**watertight**
ADJECTIVE Something that is **watertight** is closed so tightly that it does not allow water to pass through.

**wave** waves, waving, waved

VERB **1** If you **wave**, you move your hand in the air, to say hello or goodbye.

VERB **2** If something **waves**, it moves gently up and down or from side to side. *The flags waved in the wind.*

NOUN **3** A **wave** is a raised line of water on the surface of the sea caused by wind or tides.

NOUN **4** A **wave** is also a gentle curving shape in someone's hair.

**wax**

NOUN **Wax** is a solid, slightly shiny substance, made of fat or oil. It is used to make candles and polish.

**way** ways

NOUN **1** A **way** of doing something is how it can be done.

NOUN **2** The **way** to a particular place is the direction you have to go to get there.

**weak** weaker, weakest

ADJECTIVE **1** People or animals that are **weak** do not have much strength or energy.

ADJECTIVE **2** If an object or part of an object is **weak**, it could break easily.

ADJECTIVE **3** Drinks, such as tea or coffee, that are **weak** do not have a strong taste.

**wealthy** wealthier, wealthiest

ADJECTIVE Someone who is **wealthy** has a lot of money.

**weapon** weapons

NOUN A **weapon** is an object such as a gun or missile which is used to hurt or kill people in a fight or war.

**wear** wears, wearing, wore, worn

VERB **1** When you **wear** things, such as clothes, you have them on your body.

VERB **2** When something **wears out**, it has been used so much that it cannot be used any more.

**weary** wearier, weariest

ADJECTIVE If you are **weary**, you are tired.

**wearily** ADVERB

**weather**

NOUN The **weather** is what it is like outside, for example raining, sunny or windy.

*See Weather words on page 269.*

**weave** weaves, weaving, wove, woven

VERB When someone **weaves** cloth, they make it by crossing threads over and under each other, using a machine called a loom.

**web** webs

NOUN **1** A **web** is a fine net made by a spider to catch flies.

NOUN **2** The **web** is short for the World Wide Web, which is where information can be stored on the Internet.

**webbed**

ADJECTIVE **Webbed** feet have the toes connected by a piece of skin.

**website** websites

NOUN A **website** is a group of pages on the Internet which contain information about a particular subject.

**wedding** weddings

NOUN A **wedding** is when a man and woman become husband and wife.

**Wednesday** Wednesdays

NOUN **Wednesday** is the day between Tuesday and Thursday.

**weed** weeds

NOUN A **weed** is any wild plant that grows where it is not wanted. Weeds grow strongly and stop other plants growing properly.

**week** weeks

NOUN A **week** is a period of seven days.

a
b
c
d
e
f
g
h
i
j
k
l
m
n
o
p
q
r
s
t
u
v
**Ww**
x
y
z

# weekend

**weekend** **weekends**
NOUN A **weekend** is Saturday and Sunday.

**weep** **weeps, weeping, wept**
VERB If someone **weeps**, they cry.

**weigh** **weighs, weighing, weighed**
VERB **1** If something **weighs** a particular amount, that is how heavy it is.
VERB **2** If you **weigh** something, you use scales to measure how heavy it is.

**weight**
NOUN The **weight** of something is its heaviness. Weight and mass are connected. Weight is usually measured in grams and kilograms. See **mass**.

**weird** **weirder, weirdest**
ADJECTIVE Something that is **weird** seems strange and peculiar.

**welcome** **welcomes, welcoming, welcomed**
VERB If you **welcome** someone, you speak to them in a friendly way when they arrive.

**well** **better, best; wells**
ADJECTIVE **1** If you are **well**, you are healthy.
ADVERB **2** If you do something **well**, you do it to a high standard.
NOUN **3** A **well** is a deep hole in the ground that has been dug to reach water or oil.

**wellington** **wellingtons**
NOUN **Wellingtons** are long waterproof rubber boots.

**went**
VERB **Went** is the past tense of **go**.

**wept**
VERB **Wept** is the past tense of **weep**.

**west**
NOUN The **west** is one of the four main points of the compass. It is the direction in which you look to see the sun set. See **compass point**.
**western** ADJECTIVE

**wet** **wetter, wettest**
ADJECTIVE **1** If something is **wet**, it is covered in water or some other liquid.
ADJECTIVE **2** If the weather is **wet**, it is raining.
ADJECTIVE **3** If something such as ink or cement is **wet**, it has not yet dried.

**whale** **whales**
NOUN A **whale** is a huge mammal that lives in the sea. Whales breathe through an opening in the top of their head.

**what**
ADJECTIVE OR PRONOUN **1** What is used in questions. *What time is it? What is your name?*
PRONOUN **2** You can use **what** to refer to information about something. *I don't know **what** you mean.*
**what about** PHRASE You say **what about** at the beginning of a question when you are making a suggestion or offer. *What about a sandwich?*

**wheat**
NOUN **Wheat** is a cereal plant grown for its grain, which is used to make flour.

**wheel** **wheels**
NOUN A **wheel** is a circular object which turns round on a rod fixed to its centre. Wheels are fitted under things such as cars, bicycles and prams so that they can move along.

**wheelbarrow** **wheelbarrows**
NOUN A **wheelbarrow** is a small cart with a single wheel at the front.

**wheelchair** **wheelchairs**
NOUN A **wheelchair** is a chair with large wheels for use by people who find walking difficult or impossible.

**when**

ADVERB **1** You use **when** to ask what time something happened or will happen. *When are you leaving?*

CONJUNCTION **2** You use **when** to refer to a certain time. *I met him when we were at school together.*

**where**

ADVERB **1** You use **where** to ask questions about place. *Where is my book?*

CONJUNCTION **2** You use **where** to talk about the place in which something is situated or happening. *I don't know where we are.*

**whether**

CONJUNCTION You can use **whether** instead of **if**. *I don't know whether I can go.*

**which**

ADJECTIVE **1** You use **which** to ask for information about something when there are two or more possibilities. *Which room are you in?*

PRONOUN **2** You also use **which** when you are going to say more about something you have already mentioned. *We have a car which is dropping to bits.*

**while**

CONJUNCTION **1** If something happens **while** something else is happening, the two things happen at the same time.

NOUN **2** A **while** is a period of time. *She had to wait a little while.*

**whimper** **whimpers, whimpering, whimpered**

VERB When children or animals **whimper**, they make soft unhappy sounds, as if they are about to cry.

**whine** **whines, whining, whined**

VERB To **whine** is to make a long high-pitched noise because you are unhappy about something.

**whip** **whips, whipping, whipped**

VERB If you **whip** cream or eggs, you beat them until they are thick and frothy or stiff.

**whirl** **whirls, whirling, whirled**

VERB When something **whirls**, it turns round very fast.

**whirlpool** **whirlpools**

NOUN A **whirlpool** is a small place in a river or the sea where the water is moving quickly round and round, so that anything floating near it is pulled into its centre.

**whirlwind** **whirlwinds**

NOUN A **whirlwind** is a tall column of air which spins round and round very quickly.

**whirr** **whirrs, whirring, whirred**

VERB When something like a machine **whirrs**, it makes a series of low sounds so fast that it seems like one sound.

**whisk** **whisks, whisking, whisked**

VERB If you **whisk** something like cream, you stir it very fast.

**whisker** **whiskers**

NOUN The **whiskers** of an animal such as a cat or mouse are the long stiff hairs near its mouth.

**whisper** **whispers, whispering, whispered**

VERB When you **whisper**, you talk very quietly, using your breath and not your voice.

**whistle** **whistles, whistling, whistled**

NOUN **1** A **whistle** is a small metal tube which makes a loud sound when you blow it.

VERB **2** When you **whistle**, you make a loud high noise by using a whistle or by forcing your breath out between your lips.

a b c d e f g h i j k l m n o p q r s t u v **Ww** x y z

# white

**white** whiter, whitest; whites

ADJECTIVE **1** Something that is **white** is the colour of milk.
See *Colours* on page 271.
ADJECTIVE **2** If someone goes **white**, their face becomes very pale because they are afraid, shocked or ill.
NOUN **3** The **white** of an egg is the transparent liquid surrounding the yolk.

**who**

PRONOUN **1** You use **who** when you are asking about someone. *Who told you?*
PRONOUN **2** You use **who** at the beginning of a clause when you want to say more about someone you have just mentioned. *I've got a brother **who** wants to be a vet.*

**whole** wholes

NOUN **1** The **whole** of something is all of it. *It was the only pair in the **whole** of Brighton.*
ADJECTIVE **2** You use **whole** to describe all of something. *Take the **whole** cake.*
ADJECTIVE **3** **Whole** means in one piece.

**whose**

PRONOUN **1** You use **whose** to ask who something belongs to. *Whose book is this?*
PRONOUN **2** You use **whose** in front of information relating to a person or thing you have just mentioned. *That's the girl **whose** mother is a lawyer.*

**why**

ADVERB **1** You use **why** in questions when you ask about the reason for something. *Why did you do that?*
ADVERB **2** You also use **why** to talk about the reasons for something. *She wondered **why** he was there.*

**wicked**

ADJECTIVE Someone or something **wicked** is very bad.

**wide** wider, widest

ADJECTIVE **1** Something that is **wide** measures a lot from one side to the other.
ADVERB **2** If you open something **wide**, you open it a long way.

**widow** widows

NOUN A **widow** is a woman whose husband has died. See **widower**.

**widower** widowers

NOUN A **widower** is a man whose wife has died. See **widow**.

**width** widths

NOUN The **width** of something is the distance from one side to the other.

**wife** wives

NOUN A man's **wife** is the woman he is married to.

**wig** wigs

NOUN A **wig** is a false head of hair. People wear wigs because they are bald, or to cover their own hair.

**wigwam** wigwams

NOUN A **wigwam** is a kind of tent used by some North American Indians.

**wild** wilder, wildest

ADJECTIVE **1** **Wild** animals, birds and plants live in natural surroundings and are not looked after by people.
ADJECTIVE **2** **Wild** behaviour is excited and not controlled.

**wildlife**

NOUN **Wildlife** means wild animals and plants.

**will**

VERB **1** You use **will** to form the future tense. *Robin **will** be quite annoyed.*
VERB **2** You use **will** when asking or telling someone to do something. *Will you do me a favour?*

**willing**

ADJECTIVE **1** If you are **willing** to do something, you are ready and happy to do it if someone wants you to.

a b c d e f g h i j k l m n o p q r s t u v **Ww** x y z

ADJECTIVE **2** A **willing** person is someone who does things cheerfully.

**willow** **willows**

NOUN A **willow** is a tree with long thin branches and narrow leaves that likes to grow near water.

**win** **wins, winning, won**

VERB **1** If you **win** a race or game, you do better than the others taking part.

VERB **2** If you **win** a prize, you get it as a reward for doing something well.

**wind** **winds, winding, wound**

(*rhymes with* **tinned**) NOUN **1** A **wind** is a current of air that moves across the earth's surface.

(*rhymes with* **mind**) VERB **2** If a road or river **winds**, it has lots of bends in it.

(*rhymes with* **mind**) VERB **3** When you **wind** something round something else, you wrap it round several times.

**windmill** **windmills**

NOUN A **windmill** is a building with large sails on the outside, which turn as the wind blows. This works a machine that grinds corn to make flour.

**window** **windows**

NOUN A **window** is a space in a wall or vehicle. It has glass in it so that light can come in and you can see through.

**windscreen** **windscreens**

NOUN The **windscreen** of a vehicle is the glass window at the front.

**windy** **windier, windiest**

ADJECTIVE If it is **windy**, the wind is blowing hard.

**wine** **wines**

NOUN **Wine** is a strong drink usually made from the juice of grapes.

**wing** **wings**

NOUN **1** The **wings** of a bird or insect are the two limbs on its body that it uses for flying.

NOUN **2** The **wings** of an aeroplane are the long flat parts sticking out of its sides, which support it in the air.

**wink** **winks, winking, winked**

VERB When you **wink**, you close one eye for a moment. *She winked to show that she was joking.*

**winner** **winners**

NOUN If someone or something wins a prize, race or competition, they are the **winner**.

**winter** **winters**

NOUN **Winter** is the season between autumn and spring.

**wipe** **wipes, wiping, wiped**

VERB If you **wipe** something, you rub its surface lightly to remove dirt or liquid.

**wire** **wires**

NOUN **Wire** is a long, thin, flexible piece of metal which can be used to make or fasten things or to carry an electric current.

**wise** **wiser, wisest**

ADJECTIVE Someone who is **wise** can use their experience and knowledge to make sensible decisions.

**wisdom** NOUN

**wish** **wishes, wishing, wished**

VERB **1** If you **wish** that something would happen, you would like it to happen.

NOUN **2** A **wish** is the act of wishing for something you would like to happen.

**witch** **witches**

NOUN In fairy stories, a witch is a woman who has magic powers. See **wizard**.

a
b
c
d
e
f
g
h
i
j
k
l
m
n
o
p
q
r
s
t
u
v
Ww
x
y
z

**with**

PREPOSITION **1** If you are **with** someone, you are in their company. *I was there **with** Mum and Dad.*

PREPOSITION **2 With** can mean using or having. *She worked **with** a big brush.*

**wither** **withers, withering, withered**

VERB If a plant **withers**, it shrivels up and dies.

**within**

PREPOSITION **1 Within** means not going outside certain limits. *Stay **within** the school grounds.*

PREPOSITION **2 Within** can also mean before a period of time has passed. *You must write back **within** ten days.*

**without**

PREPOSITION **1 Without** means not having or using. *You can't get in **without** a key.*

PREPOSITION **2 Without** can mean not in someone's company. *He went **without** me.*

PREPOSITION **3 Without** can also mean that something does not happen. *She rang three times **without** an answer.*

**witness** **witnesses, witnessing, witnessed**

NOUN **1** A **witness** is someone who has seen an event such as an accident and can describe what happened.

VERB **2** If you **witness** an event, you see it happen.

**wizard** **wizards**

NOUN In fairy stories, a **wizard** is a man who has magic powers. See **witch**.

**wobble** **wobbles, wobbling, wobbled**

VERB If something **wobbles**, it makes small movements from side to side.

**woke**

VERB **Woke** is the past tense of **wake**.

**woken**

VERB **Woken** is the past participle of **wake**.

**wolf** **wolves**

NOUN A **wolf** is a wild animal that looks like a large dog. Wolves live in a group called a pack.

**woman** **women**

NOUN A **woman** is an adult female human being. See **man**.

**won**

VERB **Won** is the past tense of **win**.

**wonder** **wonders, wondering, wondered**

VERB **1** If you **wonder** about something, you wish you knew more about it.

VERB **2** If you **wonder** what to do about something, you are not sure what to do about it.

NOUN **3 Wonder** is a feeling of great and pleasant surprise.

**wonderful**

ADJECTIVE If something is **wonderful**, it makes you feel very happy.

**won't**

VERB **Won't** is a contraction of **will not**.

**wood** **woods**

NOUN **1 Wood** is the substance which forms the trunks and branches of trees.

NOUN **2** A **wood** is a large area of trees growing near each other.

**wooden**

ADJECTIVE Something that is **wooden** is made of wood.

**woodpecker** **woodpeckers**

NOUN A **woodpecker** is a bird with a long sharp beak. It drills holes in trees to find insects.

## woodwork

NOUN **1** The **woodwork** in a house is all the parts that are made of wood, such as the doors and window frames.

NOUN **2 Woodwork** is making things out of wood.

## woof woofs

NOUN **Woof** is the noise that a dog makes when it barks.

## wool

NOUN **1 Wool** is the hair that grows on sheep and on some other animals.

NOUN **2 Wool** is also the yarn spun from the wool of animals which is used to knit, weave, and make things like clothes, blankets and carpets.

## woollen

ADJECTIVE Something that is **woollen** is made from wool.

## woolly woollier, woolliest

ADJECTIVE Something that is **woolly** is made of wool, or looks like wool.

## word words

NOUN A **word** is a set of sounds or letters that has a meaning. A word can be written or spoken. When it is written, there are no spaces between the letters.

## word processor word processors

NOUN A **word processor** is a computer which is used to store and print words that are typed into it.

## wore

VERB **Wore** is the past tense of **wear**.

## work works, working, worked

VERB **1** When you **work**, you spend time and energy doing something useful.

VERB **2** People who **work** have a job that they are paid to do.

VERB **3** If something **works**, it does what it is supposed to do.

## work out works out, working out, worked out

VERB **1** If you **work out** the answer to a problem, you find the answer.

VERB **2** If you **work out**, you do exercises to make your body fit and strong.

## world worlds

NOUN The **world** is the planet we live on.

## worm worms

NOUN A **worm** is a small animal with a long thin body. Worms have no bones and no legs. They live in the soil.

## worn

VERB **1 Worn** is the past participle of **wear**.

ADJECTIVE **2** Something that is **worn** is damaged or thin because it is old and has been used a lot.

## worry worries, worrying, worried

VERB If you **worry**, you keep thinking about problems or about unpleasant things that might happen.

## worse

ADJECTIVE **1 Worse** is the comparative form of **bad**.

ADJECTIVE **2** If someone who is ill gets **worse**, they are more ill than before.

## worship worships, worshipping, worshipped

VERB If you **worship** a god, you show your respect by praying and singing hymns.

## worst

ADJECTIVE **Worst** is the superlative form of **bad**.

## worth

ADJECTIVE **1** If something is **worth** a particular amount of money, it could be sold for that amount.

ADJECTIVE **2** If something is **worth** doing, it is enjoyable or useful. *That film is worth seeing.*

## would

VERB **1** You use **would** to say what someone thought was going to happen. *We were sure it would rain.*

VERB **2** You also use **would** to say you want something to happen. *I would like to know how they do that.*

# wound

**wound** **wounds**

(*rhymes with* **round**) VERB **1** Wound is the past tense of **wind**.

(*said* **woond**) NOUN **2** A **wound** is an injury to your body, especially a cut in your skin.

**wove**

VERB Wove is the past tense of **weave**.

**woven**

VERB Woven is the past participle of **weave**.

**wrap** **wraps, wrapping, wrapped**

VERB When you **wrap** something, you cover it tightly with something like paper.

**wrapping** **wrappings**

NOUN **Wrapping** is the material used to cover and protect something.

**wreath** **wreaths**

NOUN A **wreath** is an arrangement of flowers and leaves, often in the shape of a circle.

**wreck** **wrecks, wrecking, wrecked**

VERB **1** If someone or something **wrecks** something, they destroy it completely.

VERB **2** If a ship is **wrecked**, it is so badly damaged that it can no longer sail.

NOUN **3** A **wreck** is a vehicle that has been badly damaged in an accident.

**wren** **wrens**

NOUN A **wren** is a tiny brown bird.

**wrestle** **wrestles, wrestling, wrestled**

VERB If you **wrestle** with someone, you fight them by holding or throwing them, but not hitting them.

**wriggle** **wriggles, wriggling, wriggled**

VERB When you **wriggle**, you twist and turn your body with quick movements.

**wring** **wrings, wringing, wrung**

VERB If you **wring** a wet piece of cloth, you squeeze the water out of it by twisting it.

**wrinkle** **wrinkles**

NOUN **1** A **wrinkle** is a line in someone's skin, especially on their face, that forms as they grow old.

NOUN **2** A **wrinkle** is also a raised fold in something like cloth or thin paper.

**wrinkled**

ADJECTIVE If something is **wrinkled**, it has folds or lines in it.

**wrist** **wrists**

NOUN Your **wrist** is the part of your body between your hand and your arm, which bends when you move your hand.

**write** **writes, writing, wrote, written**

VERB **1** When you **write**, you use a pen or pencil to make words, letters or numbers.

VERB **2** If you **write** something such as a poem or a story, you create it.

VERB **3** When you **write** to someone, you tell them about something in a letter.

**writing**

NOUN **1** **Writing** is something that has been written or printed.

NOUN **2** Your **writing** is the way you write with a pen or pencil.

**written**

VERB Written is the past participle of **write**.

**wrong**

ADJECTIVE **1** Something that is **wrong** is not correct.

ADJECTIVE **2** If there is something **wrong** with a machine, vehicle, or piece of equipment, it is not working properly.

ADJECTIVE **3** If a person does something **wrong**, they do something bad.

**wrote**

VERB Wrote is the past tense of **write**.

**wrung**

VERB Wrung is the past tense of **wring**.

### X-ray  X-rays

NOUN An **X-ray** is a ray that can pass through some solid materials. X-rays are used by doctors to examine bones or organs inside people's bodies.

### xylophone  xylophones

NOUN A **xylophone** is a musical instrument made of wooden bars of different lengths which are arranged in a row. You play a xylophone by hitting the bars with special hammers.

### yacht  yachts

NOUN A **yacht** is a large boat with sails or a motor. Yachts are used for racing or for pleasure trips.

### yam  yams

NOUN A **yam** is a root vegetable which grows in tropical regions.

### yard  yards

NOUN **1** A **yard** is a unit of length equal to just under one metre.

NOUN **2** A **yard** is also an enclosed area that is usually next to a building.

### yarn  yarns

NOUN **Yarn** is thread made from something such as wool or cotton. It is used for knitting or making cloth.

### yawn  yawns, yawning, yawned

VERB When you **yawn**, you open your mouth wide and take in more air than usual. You often yawn when you are tired or bored.

a
b
c
d
e
f
g
h
i
j
k
l
m
n
o
p
q
r
s
t
u
v
w
**X x**
**Y y**
z

# year

**year** **years**

NOUN A **year** is a period of time. It is equal to 12 months, or 52 weeks, or 365 days.

**yeast**

NOUN **Yeast** is a kind of fungus that is used to make bread rise. It is also used in making drinks such as beer.

**yell** **yells, yelling, yelled**

VERB If you **yell**, you shout loudly. People sometimes yell if they are excited, angry, or in pain.

**yellow**

ADJECTIVE Something that is **yellow** is the colour of lemons or egg yolks.
See *Colours* on page 271.

**yelp** **yelps, yelping, yelped**

VERB If people or animals **yelp**, they give a sudden short cry. This is often because they are frightened or in pain.

**yes**

You say **yes** to agree with someone, to say that something is true, or to accept something.

**yesterday**

ADVERB **Yesterday** is the day before today.

**yet**

ADVERB **1** You say **yet** when you mean up till now. *She hasn't come yet.*
ADVERB **2** If something should not be done **yet**, it should be done later. *Don't switch it off yet.*
CONJUNCTION **3** You can use **yet** to introduce something which is rather surprising. *He doesn't like maths, yet he always does well.*

**yew** **yews**

NOUN A **yew** is an evergreen tree with thin, dark green leaves. Some yew trees have red berries.

**yogurt** **yogurts**; also spelt **yoghurt**

NOUN **Yogurt** is a slightly sour, thick liquid food made from milk.

**yolk** **yolks**

NOUN A **yolk** is the yellow part in the middle of an egg.

**young** **younger, youngest**

ADJECTIVE **1** A **young** person, animal or plant has not been alive for very long.
NOUN **2** The **young** of an animal are its babies.

**your**

ADJECTIVE **Your** means belonging or relating to the person or group of people that someone is speaking to. *Your teacher seems nice.*

**yourself** **yourselves**

PRONOUN If you do something **yourself**, no one else does it. *If you do that, you'll hurt yourself.*
**by yourself** PHRASE If you are **by yourself**, you are on your own. *What are you doing here all by yourself?*

**youth** **youths**

NOUN **1** A **youth** is a boy or young man.
NOUN **2** Your **youth** is the time in your life when you are young.

**yo-yo** **yo-yos**

NOUN A **yo-yo** is a round wooden or plastic toy attached to a piece of string. You play by making the yo-yo rise and fall on the string.

# Zz

## zap  zaps, zapping, zapped
VERB **1** If you **zap** something or somebody in a computer game, you get rid of them.

VERB **2** To **zap** also means to keep changing channels on the television.

## zebra  zebras
NOUN A **zebra** is a type of African wild horse with black and white stripes over its body.

## zebra crossing  zebra crossings
NOUN A **zebra crossing** is a place where you can cross the road safely. The road is marked with black and white stripes.

## zero  zeros
**1** Zero is the number 0.

NOUN **2** Zero is also the freezing point of water, 0°C.

## zigzag  zigzags
NOUN A **zigzag** is a line which keeps changing direction sharply.

## zinc
NOUN **Zinc** is a bluish-white metal which is used to make other metals, or to cover other metals such as iron to stop them rusting.

## zip  zips
NOUN A **zip** is a long narrow fastener with two rows of teeth that are closed or opened by a small clip pulled between them.

## zone  zones
NOUN A **zone** is an area of land or sea that is considered to be different from the areas around it. *My dad wants to turn the garden into a cat-free zone.*

## zoo  zoos
NOUN A **zoo** is a park where wild animals are kept so that people can look at them or study them.

## zoom  zooms, zooming, zoomed
VERB **1** To **zoom** somewhere means to go there very quickly.

VERB **2** If a camera **zooms** in on a person or thing being photographed, it gives a close-up picture of them.

a b c d e f g h i j k l m n o p q r s t u v w x y

**Zz**

# Vegetables

celery

garlic

broccoli

aubergine

cabbage

radish

cauliflower

cucumber

lettuce

onion

courgette

asparagus

beetroot

pea

mangetout

potato

pepper

turnip

bean

parsnip

sprout

spinach

sweet potato

sweet corn

carrot

leek

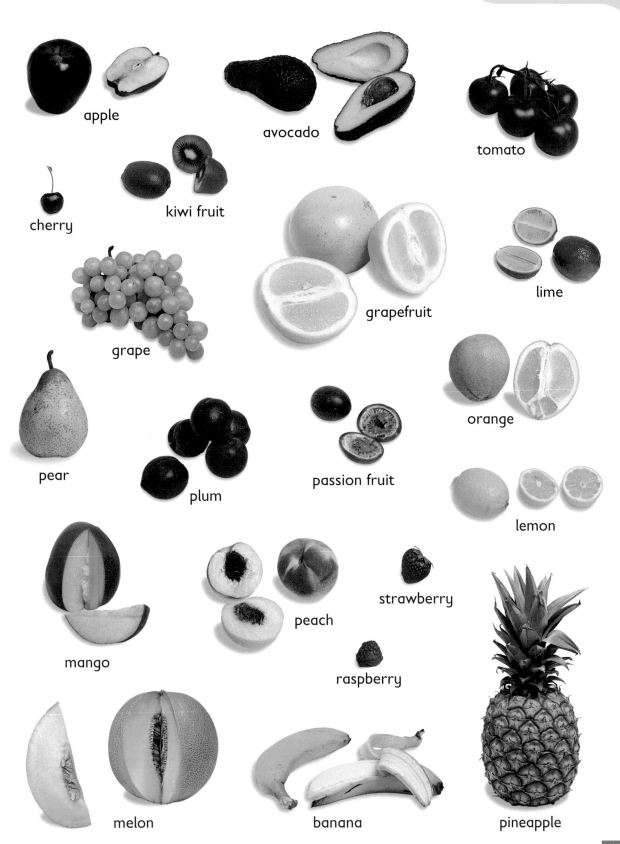

apple

avocado

tomato

kiwi fruit

cherry

grapefruit

lime

grape

orange

pear

plum

passion fruit

lemon

strawberry

peach

mango

raspberry

melon

banana

pineapple

# Your body ☆☆☆

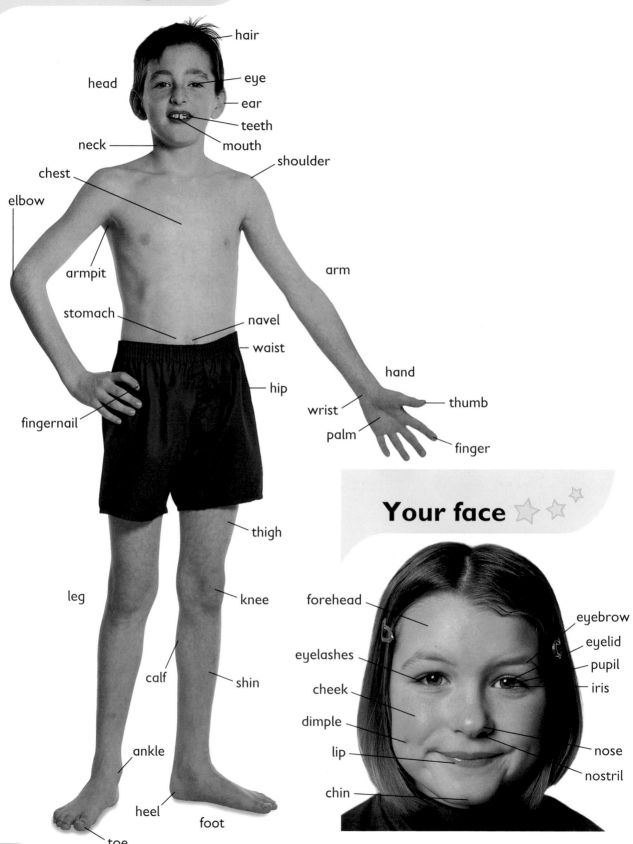

hair

head

eye

ear

teeth

mouth

neck

shoulder

chest

elbow

armpit

arm

stomach

navel

waist

hip

hand

fingernail

wrist

thumb

palm

finger

thigh

## Your face ☆☆☆

leg

knee

forehead

eyebrow

eyelid

eyelashes

pupil

calf

shin

cheek

iris

dimple

ankle

lip

nose

nostril

heel

chin

foot

toe

# Insects

ant

bee

beetle

fly

butterfly

grasshopper

ladybird

mosquito

dragonfly

# Amphibians

frog

newt

toad

# Reptiles

alligator

crocodile

lizard

snake

tortoise

turtle

# Young animals

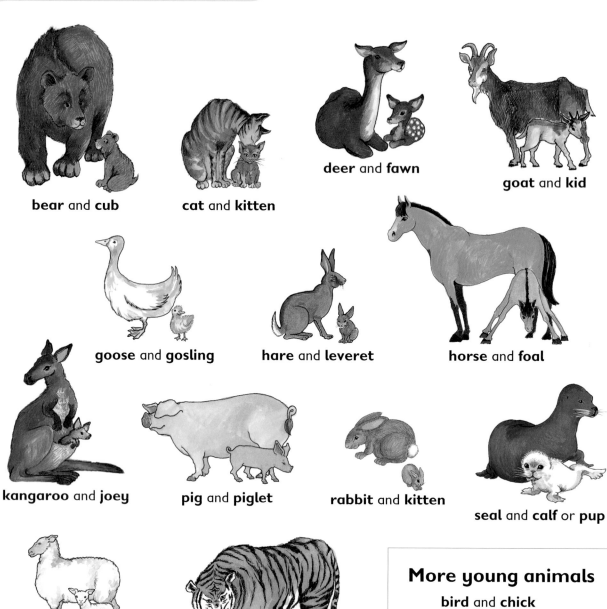

**bear** and **cub**

**cat** and **kitten**

**deer** and **fawn**

**goat** and **kid**

**goose** and **gosling**

**hare** and **leveret**

**horse** and **foal**

**kangaroo** and **joey**

**pig** and **piglet**

**rabbit** and **kitten**

**seal** and **calf** or **pup**

**sheep** and **lamb**

**tiger** and **cub**

## More young animals

**bird** and **chick**

**chicken** and **chick**

**cow** and **calf**

**dog** and **puppy**

**duck** and **duckling**

**elephant** and **calf**

**fox** and **cub**

**lion** and **cub**

**wolf** and **cub**

**swan** and **cygnet**

**whale** and **calf**

# Words we use a lot

| | | | | | | | |
|---|---|---|---|---|---|---|---|
| a | began | for | home | must | said | this | when |
| about | being | from | how | my | saw | three | where |
| after | but | get | I | name | say | to | which |
| again | by | go | if | next | seen | too | who |
| all | came | goes | in | no | she | took | why |
| along | can | going | is | not | should | two | will |
| am | can't | got | it | now | so | up | with |
| an | come | had | its | of | some | upon | woman |
| and | coming | hadn't | it's | off | suddenly | us | would |
| another | could | has | just | okay | take | very | wouldn't |
| are | couldn't | hasn't | last | on | than | want | yes |
| aren't | did | have | made | once | that | was | you |
| as | didn't | haven't | make | one | the | wasn't | your |
| at | do | he | man | or | their | way | |
| away | does | heard | many | our | them | we | |
| back | doesn't | her | may | out | then | went | |
| be | don't | here | me | over | there | were | |
| because | every | him | more | people | these | weren't | |
| been | first | his | much | put | they | what | |

## Silent letters

Each of these words has a silent letter. Can you think of any other words like these?

| | |
|---|---|
| clim**b** | **k**nit |
| colum**n** | **k**nock |
| com**b** | **k**not |
| dou**b**t | **k**now |
| **g**host | lam**b** |
| **g**nat | s**c**issors |
| **g**naw | s**w**ord |
| **g**nome | **w**rap |
| **h**our | **w**riggle |
| **k**nee | **w**rite |
| **k**nife | |

## Confusable words

These words have different meanings but are easy to mix up.

**its** (belongs to it) — *The dog wagged <u>its</u> tail.*
**it's** (it is) — *<u>It's</u> not funny.*

**loose** — *My tooth's <u>loose</u>.*
**lose** — *Don't <u>lose</u> your pen.*

**passed** — *I <u>passed</u> my test.*
**past** — *It's ten <u>past</u> three.*

**their** (belongs to them) — *The girls counted <u>their</u> money.*
**they're** (they are) — *<u>They're</u> going to the shop.*
**there** — *<u>There</u> are 26 chairs in this room.*
*Put your bag down <u>there</u>.*

**than** — *I am shorter <u>than</u> you.*
**then** (at that time) — *<u>Then</u> I heard footsteps.*

**too** — *Can I come <u>too</u>? This is <u>too</u> hard.*
**two** — *I'd like <u>two</u> cakes.*
**to** — *I want <u>to</u> swim. Let's go <u>to</u> the beach.*

**whose** (belongs to whom) — *<u>Whose</u> bag is this?*
**who's** (who is or who has) — *<u>Who's</u> that?*
*I know <u>who's</u> been sending you notes.*

# Parts of speech

## Noun

A **noun** is a person, place, thing or idea. There are different types of noun.

**cat**

**cats**

A noun can be **singular**, which means one ...

... or **plural**, which means more than one.

**Common nouns** name people, places, things, or ideas in general. For example, "boy", "dog", "school", "computer" and "happiness" are common nouns.

**Proper nouns** are the names of particular people, places or things. They start with a capital letter. For example, "Ben", "France" and "Buckingham Palace" are proper nouns.

## Collective nouns

A **collective noun** names a group of things.

a **bunch** of grapes

a **clutch** of eggs

a **flock** of sheep

a **pack** of wolves

a **litter** of puppies

a **herd** of cows

a **pride** of lions

a **school** of dolphins

a **shoal** of fish

a **swarm** of bees

# Pronoun

A **pronoun** is used to replace a noun.

| | | | | |
|---|---|---|---|---|
| I | me | my | mine | myself |
| you | you | your | yours | yourself, yourselves |
| he, she, it | him, her, it | his, her, its | his, hers, its | himself, herself, itself |
| we | us | our | ours | ourselves |
| they | them | their | theirs | themselves |

**Personal pronouns** are used for a person or thing that has already been named, for example "me", "her", "you", "it". *John jumped for the ball. He caught it!*

**Possessive pronouns** show that a noun belongs to a person or thing that has already been named, for example, "my", "their", "his", "our". *The bird flapped its wings.*

# Adjective

An **adjective** describes a noun. For example, "tall", "happy" and "lucky" are all adjectives.

Some adjectives have a **comparative** and a **superlative** form. In most cases, these forms are made by adding "-er" or "-est" to the adjective.

| adjective | comparative (more) | superlative (most) |
|---|---|---|
| tall | taller | tallest |
| hot | hotter | hottest |
| good | better | best |
| lucky | luckier | luckiest |

# Verb

A **verb** is an action word. It tells you what people and things do. For example, "sleep", "think" and "play" are all verbs.

Verbs have different forms called **tenses**. A tense shows whether you are talking about the past, present or future.

| past | present | future |
|---|---|---|
| I *played* | I *play* | I *will play* |
| | I *am playing* | |

# Adverb

An **adverb** tells you more about a verb. For example, "shyly", "brightly" and "happily" are all adverbs. Many adverbs end in the suffix "-ly".

How did Mary and Brian talk?
   *They talked **loudly**.*

Other adverbs tell you "where", "when", or "how often" something happens.

**where**: outside, inside, here, there
**when**: today, soon, immediately
**how often**: never, frequently, often, always

# Punctuation

| | | |
|---|---|---|
| A B C | A **capital letter** is used at the beginning of a sentence and for proper nouns. | *My brother Jim lives in New Zealand.* |
| . | You put a **full stop** at the end of a sentence. | *This is a sentence.* |
| ? | You put a **question mark** at the end of a question. | *Can you come to my party?* |
| , | You use a **comma** to separate parts of a sentence or items on a list. | *She brought sandwiches, crisps, apples and juice to the picnic.* |
| ! | You use an **exclamation mark** at the end of a sentence to show a strong feeling. | *Wow!* |
| ' | An **apostrophe** is used in contractions and to show belonging. | *I didn't mean to break my brother's toy.* |
| " " ' ' | **Speech marks** show where speech begins and ends. | *"I like your hair," she said.* |
| - | You use a **hyphen** to join together words or parts of words. | *I'm left-handed.* |
| ( ) | **Brackets** are used to show that something is not part of the main text. | *My cousin (the one from America) is coming to stay.* |
| — | A **dash** can be used instead of brackets, or to show a change of subject. | *My best friend – besides you – is George.* |
| : | You can use a **colon** for several things, for example in front of a list. | *You will need the following: strong walking boots, a map and a compass.* |
| ; | A **semicolon** is used to separate different parts of a sentence or list, or to show a pause. | *The pizza choices are: cheese; onions, peppers and mushrooms; ham and pineapple; pepperoni; or sausage.* |

# Prefixes

A **prefix** is a group of letters added to the beginning of a word to make a new word.

| prefix | meaning | example | prefix | meaning | example |
|---|---|---|---|---|---|
| anti- | opposite of, against | anticlockwise | over- | too much | oversleep |
| | | | poly- | many | polygon |
| co- | together | copilot | pre- | before | prehistoric |
| de- | take away | decode | re- | again | rearrange |
| dis- | opposite of | disappear | semi- | half | semicircle |
| ex- | former | ex-husband | sub- | under, part of | subheading |
| micro- | very small | microscope | super- | larger, more than | supersonic |
| mid- | middle | midnight | | | |
| mini- | smaller | minibus | un- | not | unlucky |
| mis- | wrong | misspell | under- | under or not enough | underground |
| non- | not | non-fiction | | | |

A **suffix** is a letter or group of letters added to the end of a word to make a new word.

Some suffixes can change nouns into other nouns:

| | |
|---|---|
| **-hood** | child → child**hood** |
| **-ist** | art → art**ist**    science → scient**ist** |
| **-ship** | friend → friend**ship** |

Some suffixes can make nouns feminine:

| | |
|---|---|
| **-ess** | lion → lion**ess**    prince → princ**ess** |

Some suffixes can form a diminutive (a small word):

| | |
|---|---|
| **-ette** | disk → disk**ette** |

Some suffixes can change nouns or verbs into adjectives:

| | |
|---|---|
| **-able** | comfort → comfort**able**    enjoy → enjoy**able** |
| **-al** | music → music**al** |
| **-ary** | imagine → imagin**ary** |
| **-ful** | help → help**ful** |
| **-ible** | sense → sens**ible** |
| **-ic** | angel → angel**ic**    drama → dramat**ic** |
| **-ish** | child → child**ish** |
| **-ive** | act → act**ive**    persuade → persuas**ive** |
| **-less** | care → care**less** |
| **-like** | life → life**like** |
| **-ous** | poison → poison**ous** |
| **-worthy** | trust → trust**worthy** |
| **-y** | thirst → thirst**y** |

Some suffixes can change adjectives into adverbs:

| | |
|---|---|
| **-ally** | automatic → automatic**ally** |
| **-ly** | slow → slow**ly**    happy → happi**ly** |

Some suffixes can change verbs or adjectives into nouns:

| | |
|---|---|
| **-ment** | advertise → advertise**ment**    enjoy → enjoy**ment** |
| **-ness** | ill → ill**ness**    happy → happi**ness** |
| **-sion** | divide → divi**sion** |
| **-tion** | add → addi**tion**    invite → invita**tion** |

Some suffixes can change nouns into verbs:

| | |
|---|---|
| **-ate** | illustration → illustr**ate** |

# Synonyms ☆☆☆

**Synonyms** are words that have the same, or almost the same, meaning.
Here are some useful synonyms for everyday words.

**angry**
furious, mad, annoyed, outraged, indignant

**bad**
a bad person – wicked, nasty
a bad child – naughty, spiteful, defiant
bad food – rotten, decayed
a bad pain – severe
bad news – distressing, grave, terrible

**big**
huge, large, enormous, gigantic, vast, colossal

**good**
a good dog – well-behaved
a good painting – fine
a good film – enjoyable
a good worker – able, clever

**happy**
cheerful, content, delighted, glad, pleased, thrilled

**kind**
kind of person or thing – type, class, group

**level**
grade, position, stage

**lots** or **a lot**
plenty, a great deal, heaps, loads, many,
a large amount, masses, piles

**lovely**
a lovely day – pleasant, glorious, sunny, splendid
a lovely meal – tasty, scrumptious, delicious
a lovely person – warm, kind, helpful, friendly
a lovely time – enjoyable, great, fantastic, wonderful, fabulous

**nasty**
a nasty person – unkind, rude, unpleasant
a nasty taste – horrible, foul, disgusting, awful

**nice**
nice food – delicious
a nice person – kind, helpful, pleasant
a nice view – lovely

**rough**
a rough road – bumpy, stony
a rough sea – choppy, stormy

**small**
a small problem – unimportant, trivial
a small child – little, tiny, young
a small room – cramped, cosy, modest

## What else can you say?

The word "said" is useful, but here are some more interesting words that you can use to describe speech.

**answer**
reply, respond, retort, admit, agree

**ask**
enquire, demand, beg, query, wonder

**said**
announced, whispered, shouted, stammered, mumbled, yelled, shrieked, screamed, cried, murmured, remarked, declared, groaned, snarled, whimpered, admitted

**Antonyms** are words that have the opposite meaning.

for    against

exact    approximate

on    off

left                    right

old    young

wide    narrow

up    down

before    after

old    new

digital    analogue

right    wrong

formal    informal

exciting    boring

to    from

gentle    rough

above    below

empty    full

under    over

deep    shallow

fiction    non-fiction

rough    smooth

with    without

in    out

sink    float

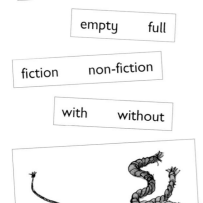

thin    thick

thin    fat

concave    convex

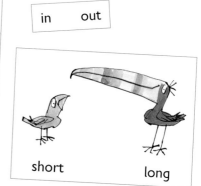

short    long

closed    open

short    tall

beginning    end

happy    sad

ascend    descend

hollow    solid

# Time ⭐⭐⭐

9:50 a.m.

10 minutes to 10

7:25 p.m.

25 minutes past 7

## Telling time

a.m.

p.m.

o'clock

half past

quarter past

quarter to

analogue

digital

clock

watch

timer

## More time words

| | | | |
|---|---|---|---|
| yesterday | second | dawn | bedtime |
| today | minute | morning | daytime |
| tomorrow | hour | midday | dinnertime |
| | day | noon | playtime |
| | week | afternoon | |
| | fortnight | dusk | |
| calendar | month | evening | |
| date | year | night | |
| weekend | leap year | midnight | |
| holiday | decade | | |
| birthday | century | | |
| | millennium | | |

**Months**
January
February

### How often?
never
once
twice
sometimes
often
usually
always

### Days
Monday
Tuesday
Wednesday
Thursday
Friday
Saturday
Sunday

March
April
May
June
July
August
September
October
November
December

### Seasons
spring
summer
autumn
winter

bright     sunny     dry     breeze     clear     hot

freezing  cold  icy  snow  frost

dry     hot     drought     sun

cloudy  chilly  foggy  drizzle  misty

rain    windy    wet    sleet    cool

hail  lightning  gale  storm  thunder

showers  rainbow  sunshine  warm  breeze

# Measures

### Length
millimetre (mm)
centimetre (cm)
metre (m)
kilometre (km)
mile

### Mass or weight
gram (g)
half-kilogram
kilogram (kg)

### Capacity
millilitre (ml)
half-litre
litre (l)
pint (pt)

# Abbreviations

| | |
|---|---|
| a.m. | in the morning |
| °C | degrees Celsius |
| CD | compact disc (such as a music CD) |
| CD-ROM | a CD that is played on a computer (an abbreviation of "compact disc read-only memory") |
| cm | centimetre |
| cm² | square centimetre |
| DIY | do-it-yourself |
| Dr | Doctor |
| DVD | digital video disc or digital versatile disc |
| etc. | "et cetera", which means "and so on" in Latin |
| EU | European Union |
| g | gram |
| GP | general practitioner (a doctor) |
| ICT | information and communications technology |
| IT | information technology |
| kg | kilogram |
| km | kilometre |
| l | litre |
| m | metre |
| ml | millilitre |
| MP | Member of Parliament |

| | |
|---|---|
| Mr | a title used before a man's name |
| Mrs | a title used before the name of a married woman |
| Ms | a title used before a woman's name |
| OAP | old age pensioner |
| p | pence |
| p. | page |
| PC | personal computer or police constable |
| PE | physical education |
| p.m. | in the afternoon or evening |
| pp. | pages |
| PS | PS is written at the end of a letter, before an extra message (an abbreviation of "postscript") |
| PTO | please turn over |
| RSVP | please reply (an abbreviation of the French phrase "répondez s'il vous plaît") |
| SOS | a Morse code signal for help, especially used by ships or planes (sometimes said to be an abbreviation of "save our souls") |
| TV | television |
| UFO | unidentified flying object |
| VIP | very important person |
| www | World Wide Web |

# Colours and flat shapes (2D)

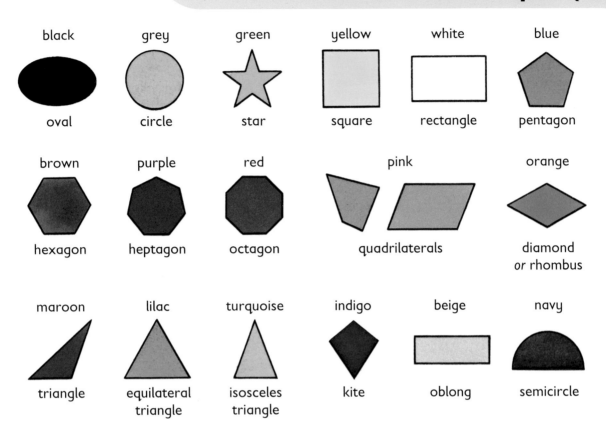

black — oval

grey — circle

green — star

yellow — square

white — rectangle

blue — pentagon

brown — hexagon

purple — heptagon

red — octagon

pink — quadrilaterals

orange — diamond *or* rhombus

maroon — triangle

lilac — equilateral triangle

turquoise — isosceles triangle

indigo — kite

beige — oblong

navy — semicircle

# Solid shapes (3D)

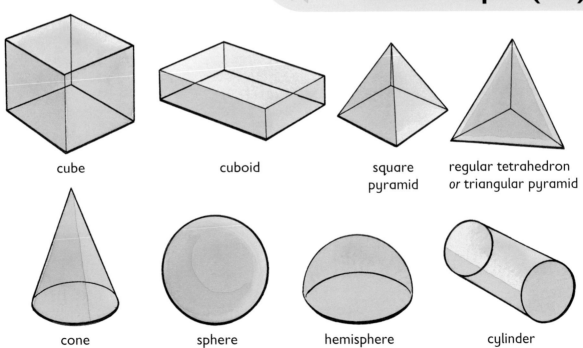

cube

cuboid

square pyramid

regular tetrahedron *or* triangular pyramid

cone

sphere

hemisphere

cylinder

# Number bank ⭐⭐

| | | | | | | |
|---|---|---|---|---|---|---|
| 0 | zero | 30 | thirty | 1st | first |
| 1 | one | 31 | thirty-one | 2nd | second |
| 2 | two | 40 | forty | 3rd | third |
| 3 | three | 41 | forty-one | 4th | fourth |
| 4 | four | 50 | fifty | 5th | fifth |
| 5 | five | 51 | fifty-one | 6th | sixth |
| 6 | six | 60 | sixty | 7th | seventh |
| 7 | seven | 61 | sixty-one | 8th | eighth |
| 8 | eight | 70 | seventy | 9th | ninth |
| 9 | nine | 71 | seventy-one | 10th | tenth |
| 10 | ten | 80 | eighty | 11th | eleventh |
| 11 | eleven | 81 | eighty-one | 12th | twelfth |
| 12 | twelve | 90 | ninety | 13th | thirteenth |
| 13 | thirteen | 91 | ninety-one | 14th | fourteenth |
| 14 | fourteen | 100 | one hundred | 15th | fifteenth |
| 15 | fifteen | 101 | one hundred and one | 16th | sixteenth |
| 16 | sixteen | 150 | one hundred and fifty | 17th | seventeenth |
| 17 | seventeen | 200 | two hundred | 18th | eighteenth |
| 18 | eighteen | 1000 | one thousand | 19th | nineteenth |
| 19 | nineteen | 10 000 | ten thousand | 20th | twentieth |
| 20 | twenty | 100 000 | one hundred thousand | 21st | twenty-first |
| 21 | twenty-one | 1 000 000 | one million | | |

# Fractions ⭐⭐

$\frac{1}{2}$ half

$\frac{1}{4}$ quarter

$\frac{1}{8}$ eighth

$\frac{1}{3}$ third

$\frac{1}{6}$ sixth

$\frac{1}{5}$ fifth

$\frac{1}{10}$ tenth

# Where words come from

## Days of the week

Most of the days of the week were named by the Saxons. The Saxons came from Denmark and Germany to live in Britain over 1500 years ago.

**Sunday** is named after the sun.

**Monday** is named after the moon.

**Tuesday** is named after Tiu, the Saxon god of war and of the sky.

**Wednesday** is named after Woden, leader of the Viking gods.

**Thursday** is named after Thor, the Saxon god of thunder and lightning.

**Friday** was named after Frigga. She was goddess of love, and sat on a throne beside her husband, Woden.

**Saturday** is named after Saturn, the Roman god of farmers and farming.

## Months of the year

The months of the year were given their names by the Romans.

**January** is named after **Janus**, the Roman god of doorways and beginnings.

**February** is named after **Februa**, a Roman festival when people were purified.

**March** is named after **Mars**, the Roman god of war.

**April**'s name comes from the Latin word **aperire**, meaning "to open". Spring is when the year "opens".

**May** is named after **Maiesta**, Roman goddess of honour and reverence.

**June** is named after the Roman goddess **Juno**, queen of heaven.

**July** was named after **Julius Caesar**, army general and ruler of Ancient Rome.

**August** was named after the Roman emperor **Augustus**.

**September** comes from the Latin word **septem**, meaning "seven". The Roman year used to begin in March, so September was their seventh month.

**October** comes from the Latin word **octo**, meaning "eight". October was once the eighth month.

**November** comes from the Latin word **novem**, meaning "nine". November was once the ninth month.

**December** comes from the Latin word **decem**, meaning "ten". December was once the tenth month.

# Where words come from

## Words from the world

Lots of the words we use in the English language today come from other parts of the world. Here are some examples.

### alphabet
This word comes from Greece. **Alpha** was the first letter of the Greek alphabet, and **beta** was the second. The two words together give us alphabet.

### amphibian
This is another word from Greece. It comes from the Greek word **amphibious**, which means "living a double life". Amphibians are animals that can live on land or in water – so they live a double life!

### bungalow
This word, which means a low house, comes from India. The Hindi word for house is **bangla**.

### bus
This word comes from Italy. It is short for **omnibus**, the Latin word for "everybody". Buses carry lots of people.

### dandelion
This word comes from the French words **dent de lion**, meaning a lion's tooth. This is because people thought the petals of the dandelion looked like a lion's teeth!

### fete
This is another French word. It means "feast" in French. In English it means an outdoor event with competitions and stalls which sell things.

### jungle
Jungle is a word from India. The Hindi word for jungle is **jangal**.

### muscle
This word comes from the Latin word **musculus**, meaning "little mouse", because people thought muscles looked like mice beneath the skin!

### porcupine
This comes from the Old French words **porc-espin**, meaning "pig with spines".

### pyjamas
This word comes from Iran (which used to be called Persia). In Persia, **pay jama** meant "leg clothes".

We write letters for all sorts of reasons, such as asking for information and exchanging news. Each kind of letter has its own style. Here are some examples.

## Asking for information

your address —— Sundown Primary
School
Sundown Lane
Hilltown
AN14 8DB

17 September 2007 —— date

The Manager ____ address of person
Black Sheep Wool Company you are writing to
Ramside Mills
Eweton
EN7 1WL

Dear Sir or Madam
greeting when you don't
know the name of the
person you are writing to

My class is doing a project on sheep. I am
writing to ask you for any information you may
have on how wool is made from sheep's fleeces.

Thank you in anticipation of your help.

Yours faithfully —— sign off when you don't
know the name of the
person you are writing to

Jack Uphill
your signature

## An invitation

your address —— 32 Forge Street
Hilltown
AN12 9TC

30 November 2007 —— date

Jack Uphill
16 Smith Road—— address of person
Hilltown you are writing to
AN13 8TZ

greeting when you know the
person you are writing to
Dear Jack

I am having a birthday party at my house on
Saturday 5 December at 3 o'clock. I should be
very pleased if you could come.

Best wishes —— sign off when you know the
person you are writing to

Jill
your signature

## Saying thank you

your address —— Sundown Primary School
Sundown Lane
Hilltown
AN14 8DB

21 October 2007—— date

Mr. H. Dumpty
Yolk Street —— address of person
Walltown you are writing to
EG1 3XX

greeting when you know
the name of the person
you are writing to
Dear Mr. Dumpty

Thank you very much for sending me the
information on how eggs are packed and sent to
shops. It will be very useful for my class project.

Yours sincerely —— sign off when you know
the name of the person
you are writing to

Jill Pailwater— your
signature

P.S. I was sorry to hear of your recent fall from
a wall. I hope you are soon put together again.

post script: when you want to add to a letter

## A reply

your address —— 16 Smith Road
Hilltown
AN13 8TZ

1 December 2007 —— date

Jill Pailwater
32 Forge Street—— address of person
Hilltown you are writing to
AN12 9TC

greeting when you know the
person you are writing to
Dear Jill

Thank you very much for inviting me to your
party on Saturday 5 December at 3 o'clock. I
shall be very pleased to come.

Best wishes —— sign off when you know the
person you are writing to

Jack— your signature

# Word families

A **word family** is a set of words containing the same groups of letters.

These words are members of the **oa** word family.

toad        goat        coast

**?** Using the dictionary, find some more **oa** words beginning with these letters.

**t**    a heated slice of bread.

**b**    to talk too proudly about something.

**r**    to wander around.

These words are members of the **ar** word family.

dart        market        star

**?** Using the dictionary, find some more **ar** words beginning with these letters.

**p**    the person you are doing something with.

**s**    a small sea fish

**b**    something which is sold at a low price.

These words are members of the **oi** family.

oil        soil        point

**?** Using the dictionary, find some more **oi** words beginning with these letters.

**m**    slightly wet.

**n**    a sound that someone or something makes.

**c**    a series of loops into which something has been wound.

These words are members of the **air** word family.

stairs        fairy        aircraft

**?** Using the dictionary, find some more **air** words beginning with these letters.

**f**    quite or rather.

**p**    a set of two things that go together.

**d**    a shop or company that sells milk and food made from milk.

# Top tips for tricky words

Sometimes thinking of a silly phrase or sentence can help you remember how to spell tricky words. Here are some examples.

**beautiful**

Big elephants are useful.

**qu words (q is always followed by u)**

The Queen always carries an umbrella.

See how many of these you can remember. Then see if you can think up some of your own!

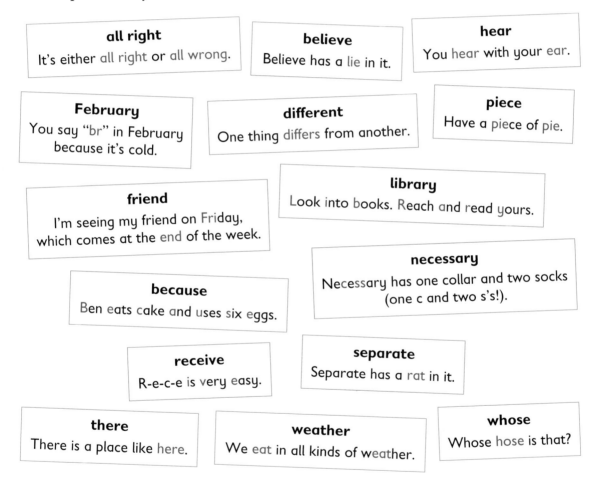

**all right**

It's either all right or all wrong.

**believe**

Believe has a lie in it.

**hear**

You hear with your ear.

**February**

You say "br" in February because it's cold.

**different**

One thing differs from another.

**piece**

Have a piece of pie.

**friend**

I'm seeing my friend on Friday, which comes at the end of the week.

**library**

Look into books. Reach and read yours.

**necessary**

Necessary has one collar and two socks (one c and two s's!).

**because**

Ben eats cake and uses six eggs.

**receive**

R-e-c-e is very easy.

**separate**

Separate has a rat in it.

**there**

There is a place like here.

**weather**

We eat in all kinds of weather.

**whose**

Whose hose is that?

## Sound it out!

Another good way to remember the spelling of some words is to sound out their different parts. Try these!

| answer | cupboard | Wednesday | together |
|--------|----------|-----------|----------|
| ans-wer | cup-board | Wed-nes-day | to-get-her |

# Top tips for tricky words

## Top tips for learning to spell a tricky word

- **Look** at the word in the dictionary and point to it.
- **Say** the word out loud, then spell it out.
- **Cover** the word up, remembering what it looks like.
- **Write** the word down on a piece of paper and say it out loud again.
- **Check** your spelling against the dictionary.
- If you got it wrong, cover the page again and **try again**!

## Tricky words to learn

The words on this list are tricky, so learn all of them to be a top speller!

| | | |
|---|---|---|
| address | definite | remember |
| among | does | rhyme |
| autumn | everybody | scissors |
| awful | exciting | sentence |
| beginning | exercise | straight |
| breakfast | guess | through |
| build | interest | trouble |
| careful | necessary | until |
| certain | people | usually |
| course | really | whole |

# Plurals

A plural word is what we use when there is more than one of something. It is often made by adding **s** to a word, like this.

singular **day**
plural **days**

Sometimes plurals are made by taking away the **y** at the end of the word and adding **ies**, like this.

singular **pony**
plural **ponies**

**?** Now use the dictionary to find the plural of these words. See how many ways you can find to make a word plural.

1. **horse**
2. **thief**
3. **party**
4. **class**
5. **torch**
6. **volcano**
7. **child**
8. **fly**
9. **monkey**
10. **woman**

# Word jumble

❓ Here are some words with their meanings. The letters in the words are all jumbled up. Can you put them in the right order? (Clue! They all begin with **d**.) Use the dictionary to help you.

1. **streed** — A very dry land with very little plant life.

2. **ogunned** — A dark underground prison in a castle.

3. **caddee** — A period of ten years.

4. **mode** — A round roof.

5. **loadinned** — A wild plant with bright yellow flowers.

6. **rotcod** — A person who treats people when they are ill.

7. **cilisudoe** — Food that tastes or smells very nice.

8. **reapsapid** — What happens when someone goes out of sight.

9. **zoed** — A light sleep.

10. **flagondry** — A brightly coloured insect, usually found near water.

# Getting the most from guide words

The guide words in this dictionary are at the top of the page. They can help you find the word you want quickly.

ve **forward** or
ove the way you are

ASE If you **look**
ing, you want it to

| | frequent |
|---|---|
| **fracture** **fractures** | a |
| NOUN A **fracture** is a crack or break in something, especially a bone. | b |
| **fragile** | c |
| ADJECTIVE Something that is **fragile** is easily broken or damaged. | d |

## ❓ True or false?

Use the guide words in the dictionary to work out if these statements are true or false.

1. **pointed** comes between **plumber** and **popular**

2. **steep** comes between **stem** and **strain**

3. **colour** comes between **closed** and **college**

4. **fungus** comes between **fresh** and **future**

5. **awful** comes between **assembly** and **axis**

6. **somebody** comes between **solve** and **speak**

## ❓ Where is the word?

Which of these words would you find between **pizza** and **plum**?

| | |
|---|---|
| pasta | plastic |
| pram | play |
| plug | poor |
| pitch | plump |

## Surfing the net!

### Can a dictionary really teach me to surf?

Well, it can tell you a bit about surfing – but don't worry. The only kind of board you'll need is a computer keyboard, plus access to the Internet.

### What is the Internet?

Good question! The Internet is a collection of computer networks that are all linked together. The Internet can let you look at lots of different sites in just a few seconds to help you find what you're looking for.

### Do I look at all of the sites myself?

No, you don't need to. The Internet does all the work for you! All you have to do is type a word or phrase into something called a search engine and click on "go". The search engine looks like a little box on the screen. Fill in the subject you want to find out about and you're all set to go "surfing" on the Internet.

### What sort of things can I find out about?

You can find out about all kinds of things! Are you potty about pyramids? Dotty about dinosaurs? Batty about ballet? Serious about sport? You can look for information on whatever you want. You can even find out more about your favourite books or authors. Just enter the word you want into the search engine.

### But where do I start?

There are thousands and thousands of sites out there. The search engine will take you to all of them that contain the word or words you have typed into it. It helps if you make your key word (the word or words that you type into the search engine) as clear as possible. For example, you might want to find out about parrots. Parrots are birds. If you type in "birds", you'll be taken to all websites containing that word. If you type in "parrots", you'll only be shown sites about parrots. This can save a lot of time!

### Is there anything else I need to know before I start?

Just as you need to take care when you're playing out of doors, you need to take care when you're playing or working on the Internet. There are a few things you need to remember:

Never go to meet someone you have met online without a parent or carer accompanying you.

Never give out your personal details online.

If you find something online that makes you feel uncomfortable or you aren't sure about, tell a parent, carer or teacher.

Safe surfing!